DATE DUE

A FINE WILL BE CHARGED
FOR EACH OVERDUE BOOK

Caribbean Literature

A Bibliography

Marian Goslinga

Area Bibliographies, No. 15

The Scarecrow Press, Inc.
Lanham, Md., & London
1998

SCARECROW PRESS, INC.

Published in the United States of America
by Scarecrow Press, Inc.
4720 Boston Way
Lanham, Maryland 20706

4 Pleydell Gardens, Folkestone
Kent CT20 2DN, England

British Library Cataloguing in Publication Information Available

Library of Congress Cataloging-in-Publication Data

Goslinga, Marian.
    Caribbean literature : a bibliography / Marian Goslinga.
        p.   cm. — (Scarecrow area bibliographies ; no. 15)
    ISBN 0-8108-3452-9 (alk. paper)
     1. Caribbean Area—Bibliography. I. Title. II. Series: Scarecrow
  area bibliographies ; 15.
  Z1595.G69   1998
  [F2161]
  016.9729—dc21
                                  97-32289
                                     CIP

♾ ™ The paper used in this publication meets the minimum requirements of
American National Standard for Information Sciences—Permanence of Paper
for Printed Library Materials, ANSI Z39.48-1984.
Manufactured in the United States of America.

CONTENTS

EDITOR'S FOREWORD

Judged by the size and population of its countries, the Caribbean is a rather small region. Yet its cultural horizons are incredibly vast, particularly with regard to its literature. It draws on the resources of four European linguistic and literary traditions and is further sustained by a multitude of indigenous dialects, varieties of creole specific to each country or island. These are not always exclusive, with many writers expressing themselves in both creole and a European language, permitting further permutations. But it is not just the variety that matters. It is the beauty and boldness of what they write that makes Caribbean authors so fruitful and fascinating. And this book is a unique key to that literature.

The book can be used in several ways. It can open the door, through its four basic sections, to the Spanish-speaking, English-speaking, French-speaking, and Dutch-speaking Caribbean. It can also provide access more narrowly to the literature of the specific countries or islands, each under its own heading and arranged by subject or form. Finally, it can lead the reader to specific writers, both works by and about them. It is easy to use because, in addition to the various sections mentioned above, it has an author index and a title index. This bibliography makes a worthwhile contribution to facilitating the search for relevant material on the major traditions, like the Spanish- and English-language literatures, or familiar authors such as Aimé Césaire, Saint-John Perse, or V.S. Naipaul. It is far more helpful in introducing lesser known traditions, especially the literature in Dutch, and less familiar authors, whether from earlier periods or the rising generation.

The author, Marian Goslinga, is uniquely placed to write this bibliography. She knows the Caribbean region well, having lived in Curaçao and in Venezuela and visited elsewhere. She is familiar with the many literary strands, Spanish, English, French, Dutch, and Creole. And she has read many of the books included in this volume. Finally, as a librarian at Florida International University, she has served an interested public and also compiled several relevant bibliographies, including *A Bibliography of the Caribbean,* published in 1996 in this series of Area Bibliographies. This rare combination of experiences and abilities was instrumental in producing this important contribution to the knowledge of Caribbean literature.

Jon Woronoff
Series Editor

vii

INTRODUCTION

In this bibliography, the Caribbean will be defined as the area extending from Bermuda in the north to Trinidad in the south encompassing all islands as well as the mainland countries of Belize, Guyana, Guyane, and Suriname. This widespread but historically related area boasts four European-based literatures linked together by a common African/creole element, which gives each of them a distinct flavor and sets them apart from their Old World counterparts.

The Spanish-speaking Caribbean has a rich literary heritage rooted in this combination of European and Afro-Caribbean legacies finding its supreme culmination in the genius of Cuba's Nicolás Guillén.

The English-speaking Caribbean counts Jamaica's Louise Bennett and Barbados' George Lamming among the best representatives of this cultural fusion. Written either in creole or in English, Bennett's Anancy stories provide a direct link to Suriname's Ismene Krishnmadath and Curaçao's Elis Juliana, from the Dutch Caribbean, whose Nanzi tales are strikingly similar. In addition, there is a distinct Indo-Caribbean element that is particularly noticeable in the English- and Dutch-language literatures.

Also sharing this dual legacy are the French-speaking islands as evident in the works of the unparalleled Aimé Césaire, writing both in French as well as in his native Martiniquan dialect, and St.-John Kauss, Haiti's foremost creole poet.

To do justice to this diverse and fragmented, yet at the same time unified, area of research has been a source of enjoyment and intrigue. In many ways, due to the limitations set on the project, only the surface has been scratched and much remains to be done. One particularly neglected area, for the English-speaking audience, has been the Dutch Caribbean, about which little is written and less known. Of the 3,500 entries in this bibliography, for instance, a mere 100 specifically refer to the Netherlands Antilles and Suriname.

Suriname's most famous author, Albert Helman, remains virtually unknown outside the Netherlands and the Dutch Caribbean. Yet this remarkable man, whose death in 1996 put an end to many years of voluntary exile in the Netherlands for refusing to live under the Bouterse dictatorship, deserves to be studied further. Were it not for the unfortunate incidence of having written in a little-known language (and an even lesser known creole dialect) and never having been translated, Helman's works would undoubtedly have reached a much larger audience as well as universal critical acclaim.

At times, there were unexpected surprises. Nobel-prizewinning poet Saint-John Perse, from Guadeloupe, turned out to be one of the most written-about authors in the area, eclipsing such literary giants as V.S. Naipaul, Jacques Roumain, and Nicolás Guillén in the number of critical citations to his credit.

Last but not least, this bibliography attempts to list as many women writers as possible. Although many of these have reached international status—Jean Rhys, Rosario Ferré, Merle Hodge, and Maryse Condé come to mind immediately—many others have for too long been neglected. This time, they have been given their full due. At the same time, current writers have been introduced—those who are just now beginning to be heard of and read.

Included in this survey are published monographs in the four main languages spoken in the Caribbean—Spanish, English, French, and Dutch—with an occasional entry in German or creole. Works of less than fifty pages have, with some exceptions, been omitted;[1] 1996 was established as the cutoff date for this work. Additional criteria for inclusion follow those of the Area Bibliography Series.

ORGANIZATION

The 3,500 entries in this bibliography have been organized geographically and topically. Part I lists books dealing with the Caribbean area in general, that is, comparative surveys, etc. Parts II–V lists books in the four major languages (Spanish, English, French, and Dutch). Within these groupings, the materials have been listed by subject and/or form (i.e., dictionaries and encyclopedias, bibliographies and bio-bibliographies, anthologies, history and criticism, poetry, fiction, and drama). Whenever warranted by the amount of output, they have been further subdivided chronologically. A summary of the organization is listed below:

1. Bibliographies and Bio-bibliographies
2. Dictionaries and Encyclopedias
3. Anthologies (divided by time period when warranted)
   a. General
   b. Poetry
   c. Fiction
   d. Drama
4. History and Criticism (divided by time period when warranted)
   a. General
   b. Poetry

c. Fiction
d. Drama
5. Individual Authors
  a. Sixteenth to nineteenth centuries
  b. Twentieth century

The last section in each category (except in the General chapter) will list individual authors and their works. Inclusion in this category was determined by several factors, the most important being the author's place of birth and the Library of Congress classification number as they appeared in the OCLC authority record.[2] With one or two exceptions, this section will include only those authors born in the Caribbean.[3]

Also listed here are critical works about the authors as well as interviews, biographies, and bibliographies of their published output. Both author and title entries appear in the indexes with the corresponding item number. In order to differentiate the author entries, those listed in the individual authors sections will be in bold.

ARRANGEMENT

All entries are listed by author and will provide the following information: author(s) or editor(s), title, edition statement, place of publication, publisher, date, pagination, and a brief annotation (if required). The title will be given in the original language, with translations, provided only for the Dutch, in square brackets immediately following. The latest edition will be given with—in the case of a reprint—the original publication date added in a note. Whenever possible, a U.S. publisher has been provided.

The arrangement for the individual authors differs slightly. Authors will be listed, followed by their dates of birth and death (if known) and their genre—novelist, poet, etc., in alphabetical sequence. Their works are listed next—alphabetically with accompanying publication date(s). In those works having gone through various editions or reprints, only the first and last dates have been provided. For brevity's sake, it was decided not to include full bibliographical records in this section, except for the critical works. In the case of translations, preference has been given to the English translation listing the book by that title with the original imprint given immediately following in square brackets. The translator (or editor) has also been provided whenever known. For example, in the case of Jacques Roumain, a sample entry will appear as:

3263. Roumain, Jacques, 1907–1944 (novelist, poet, short story writer)
    Masters of the Dew, 1947–1988 (Translation of Gouverneurs de la rosée [1944–1992]; Langston Hughes, Mercer Cook, trs.)

Two indexes at the end will provide further access to all the entries in the bibliography. The author index lists all main entries (i.e., authors and/or editors, conferences, corporate bodies) cited in the bibliography; the title index is a complete record of all titles mentioned, including original titles of translations, former titles, alternative titles, etc., except those given for the works mentioned under the individual authors.

SEARCH AND SELECTION PROCEDURES

For this bibliography, as for the previous *A Bibliography of the Caribbean* (1996), the most important sources consulted were the holdings of the University of Florida Libraries accessed through LUIS,[4] supplemented by information provided by the OCLC database. Standard printed sources were also helpful—although all information acquired in this manner was always confirmed on OCLC. Only in the case of the authors and materials from the Dutch-speaking territories did OCLC prove to be less than comprehensive and local resources were needed to fill in the gaps. I am most grateful to my father, for instance, for spending considerable time in the Koninklijke Bibliotheek in The Hague in order to get a complete record of Albert Helman's considerable literary ouput. The data acquired in this fashion were incorporated with the information already on file.

ACKNOWLEDGMENTS

Grateful acknowledgment is made to the Florida International University libraries, their director Dr. Laurence Miller, and the FIU Libraries Systems staff. My thanks especially go to Ms. Judith Rassoletti, Ms. Tricia Tsang, Mrs. Maria Quintero, and Mr. George Fray. I am also indebted to Ms. Sharon Ennis, Pro-Cite representative, who was most helpful in solving technical problems associated with the program used—i.e., Pro-Cite 2.2. My thanks also to Ms. Kimberlee Mark and Mr. Pedro D. Botta (FIU's Latin American and Caribbean Center) for having contributed the map.

Similarly, I would like to extend my thanks to the many others, too numerous to mention individually, who had faith in the project by providing me with their unflinching support throughout. However, the responsibility for any errors or omissions remains mine alone.

It is hoped that, with this initial foray into the field of Caribbean literary research, enough interest will have been generated to stimulate further inquiries. Until that time, however, this bibliography lays claim to being the most comprehensive published to date.

Last, but not least, to use the idiom of my favorite island: Mi ke dediká e boeki na tur hendenan di mi dushi Korsow.

ENDNOTES

1. In the case of the Dutch Caribbean this general rule has not been applied; neither does this limit apply to the listings under the individual authors.
2. Online Computer Library Center, Dublin, OH. The OCLC authority file is generally regarded as the ultimate source for verification.
3. It was decided to include Gertrudis Gómez de Avellaneda, even though she was born in Spain, in this bibliography. However, it can be argued that, at the time she wrote, national boundaries, as we know them today, did not exist as yet. Besides, Cuba claims her as one of her own.
4. Library Users Information System.

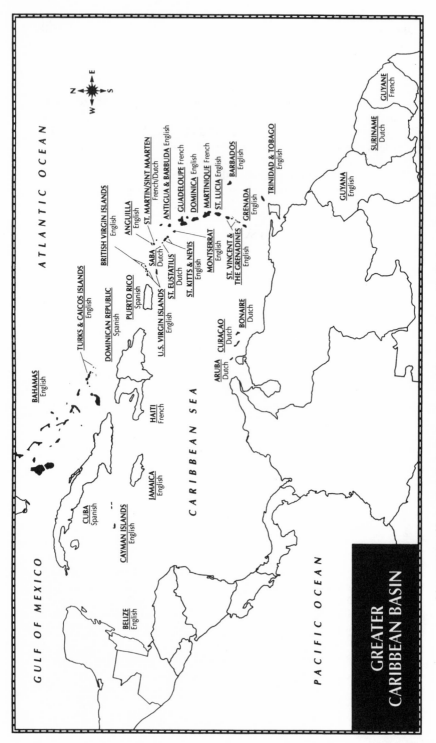

GREATER
CARIBBEAN BASIN

Map courtesy of Pedro D. Botta, Latin American and Caribbean Center, Florida International University.

I
GENERAL

A. BIBLIOGRAPHIES AND BIO-BIBLIOGRAPHIES

1. Berrian, Brenda F. *Bibliography of Women Writers from the Caribbean, 1831–1986*. Washington, DC: Three Continents Press, 1989. 360 pp.

2. Engber, Marjorie. *Caribbean Fiction and Poetry: A Bibliography*. New York: Center for Inter-American Relations, 1970. 86 pp.

3. Fenwick, M. J. *Writers of the Caribbean and Central America: A Bibliography*. New York: Garland, 1992. 2 vols.

4. Herdeck, Donald E., and Margaret Laniak-Herdeck. *Caribbean Writers: A Bio-Bibliographical-Critical Encyclopedia*. Washington, DC: Three Continents Press, 1979. 943 pp.

5. Page, James Allen, and Jae Min Roh. *Selected Black American, African and Caribbean Authors: A Bio-Bibliography*. Littleton, CO: Libraries Unlimited, 1985. 388 pp. Updates *Selected Black American Authors* (1977).

6. Paravisini-Gebert, Lizabeth, and Olga Torres-Seda, eds. *Caribbean Women Novelists: An Annotated Critical Bibliography*. Westport, CT: Greenwood Press, 1993. 427 pp.

7. UNESCO. *Selected List of Representative Works of Latin American and Caribbean Literature/Lista selectiva de obras representativas de la literatura latinoamericana y del Caribe/Liste sélective des oeuvres représentatives de la littérature latino-américaine et des Caraïbes*. Paris: Unesco, 1989. 79 pp.

B. ANTHOLOGIES

8. Breton, Marcela, ed. *Rhythm and Revolt: Tales of the Antilles*. New York: Plume, 1995. 278 pp.

9. Coulthard, George Robert, ed. *Caribbean Literature: An Anthology*. London: University of London Press, 1966. 127 pp.

10. Esteves, Carmen C., and Lizabeth Paravisini-Gebert, eds. *Green Cane and Juicy Flotsam: Short Stories by Caribbean Women.* New Brunswick, NJ: Rutgers University Press, 1991. 273 pp.

11. Hill, Errol, ed. *A Time . . . and a Season: Eight Caribbean Plays.* Port of Spain: University of the West Indies, 1976. 420 pp. Includes four plays translated from the Spanish.

12. Howes, Barbara, ed. *From the Green Antilles: Writings of the Caribbean.* London: Panther, 1980. 397 pp. Reprint of the 1966 ed.

13. Martinez, Pierre, ed. *La mer est belle, naviguez!: les poètes de la Caraïbe parlent de la mer.* Fort-de-France: Centre régional de documentation pédagogique, 1982. 74 pp.

14. Mordecai, Pamela, and Betty Wilson, eds. *Her True-True Name: An Anthology of Women's Writing from the Caribbean.* Portsmouth, NH: Heinemann, 1989. 202 pp.

15. Seymour, Arthur J., ed. *New Writing in the Caribbean.* Georgetown: Guyana Lithographic, 1972. 324 pp.

16. Smorkaloff, Pamela Maria, ed. *If I Could Write This in Fire: An Anthology of Literature From the Caribbean.* New York: New Press, 1994. 374 pp.

17. Toczec, Nick, Philip Nanton and Yann Lovelock, eds. *Melanthika: An Anthology of Pan-Caribbean Writing.* Birmingham, AL: L.W.M. Publications, 1977. 191 pp.

C. HISTORY AND CRITICISM

18. Arnold, Albert James, Julio Rodríguez-Luis and J. Michael Dash, eds. *A History of Literature in the Caribbean.* Philadelphia, PA: J. Benjamins, 1994– [vol. 1–3–]. Vol. 1. Hispanic and Francophone regions. Vol. 2. English- and Dutch-speaking countries. Vol. 3. Cross-cultural studies.

19. Bangou, Henri, René Dépestre and George Lamming. *Influencia del Africa en las literaturas antillanas.* Montevideo: [s.n.], 1972. 55 pp. Articles previously published in *Casa de las Américas.*

20. Conference on Spanish Caribbean Literature (Eighth, 1985, Kingston); Joe R. Pereira, ed. *Caribbean Literature in Compari-*

son. Mona, Jamaica: Institute of Caribbean Studies, University of the West Indies, 1990. 143 pp.

21. Coulthard, George Robert. *Race and Colour in Caribbean Literature.* New York: Oxford University Press, 1962. 152 pp. Translation of *Raza y color en la literatura antillana* (1958).

22. Cudjoe, Selwyn Reginald. *Resistance and Caribbean Literature.* Athens, OH: Ohio University Press, 1980. 319 pp.

23. Dathorne, Oscar Ronald. *Dark Ancestor: The Literature of the Black Man in the Caribbean.* Baton Rouge: Louisiana State University Press, 1981. 288 pp.

24. Davies, Carole Boyce, and Elaine Savory, eds. *Out of the Kumbla: Caribbean Women and Literature.* Trenton, NJ: Africa World Press, 1990. 399 pp.

25. Dieke, Ikenna. *The Primordial Image: African, Afro-American, and Caribbean Mythopoetic Text.* New York: P. Lang, 1993. 434 pp.

26. Glaser, Marlies, and Marion Pausch, eds. *Caribbean Writers: Between Orality and Writing.* Atlanta, GA: Rodopi, 1994. 232 pp.

27. Guinness, Gerald. *Here and Elsewhere: Essays on Caribbean Literature.* Río Piedras, P.R.: Editorial de la Universidad de Puerto Rico, 1993. 204 pp.

28. Irele, Abiola, ed. *Caribbean Literature.* Bloomington: Indiana University Press, 1994. 212 pp.

29. Loncke, Joycelynne. *In the Shadow of El Dorado: A Collection of Essays on Caribbean Themes in Literature.* Port of Spain: Fascina Edition, 1994. 83 pp.

30. Luis, William, ed. *Voices from Under: Black Narrative in Latin America and the Caribbean.* Westport, CT: Greenwood Press, 1984. 263 pp.

31. Rutgers, Wim. *Bon dia! met wie schrijf ik?: over Caraïbische jeugdliteratuur* [Good Morning! To Whom Am I Writing?: About Caribbean Juvenile Literature]. Oranjestad, Aruba: Plaza Bookshop, 1988. 271 pp.

32. Saakana, Amon Saba. *The Colonial Legacy in Caribbean Litera-ture*. Trenton, NJ: Africa World Press, 1987– [vol. 1–].

Twentieth Century

33. Ascencio, Michaelle. *Lecturas antillanas*. Caracas: Academia Nacional de la Historia, 1990. 184 pp.

34. Benítez Rojo, Antonio. *The Repeating Island: The Caribbean and the Postmodern Perspective*. James Maraniss, tr. Durham, NC: Duke University Press, 1992. 302 pp. Translation of *La isla que se repite* (1989).

35. Broek, Aart G. *Het zilt van de passaten: Caribische letteren van verzet*. [The Trade Winds' Brine: Caribbean Literature of Protest]. Haarlem: In de Knipscheer, 1988. 186 pp.

36. Cobb, Martha K. *Harlem, Haiti and Havana: A Comparative Critical Study of Langston Hughes, Jacques Roumain, and Nicolás Guillén*. Washington, DC: Three Continents Press, 1978. 250 pp.

37. King, Lloyd. *Towards a Caribbean Literary Tradition*. St. Augustine, Trinidad: [s.n.], 1990. 92 pp.

38. Laroche, Maximilien, H. Nigel Thomas and Euridice Figueiredo. *Juan Bobo, Jan Sòt, Ti Jan et Bad John: figures littéraires de la Caraïbe*. Sainte-Foy, Que.: GRELCA, 1991. 92 pp.

39. Seminar on the Acquisition of Latin American Library Materials (Thirty-ninth, 1994, Brigham Young University); Nelly S. Gonzalez, ed. *Modernity and Tradition: The New Latin American and Caribbean Literature, 1956–1994—Papers*. Austin, TX: SALALM Secretariat, Benson Latin American Collection, General Libraries, University of Texas at Austin, 1996. 433 pp.

Poetry

40. Bajeux, Jean Claude. *Antilia retrouvée: Claude McKay, Luis Palés Matos, Aimé Césaire—poètes noirs antillais*. Paris: Editions caribéennes, 1983. 427 pp.

Fiction

41. Cudjoe, Selwyn Reginald. *The Role of Resistance in the Caribbean Novel*. Ithaca, NY: Cornell University Press, 1976. 295 pp.

42. Gikandi, Simon. *Writing in Limbo: Modernism and Caribbean Literature*. Ithaca, NY: Cornell University Press, 1992. 260 pp.

43. Mateo Palmer, Margarita. *Narrativa caribeña: reflexiones y pronósticos*. Havana: Editorial Pueblo y Educación, 1990. 109 pp.

44. Pageaux, Daniel-Henri, ed. *Images et mythes d'Haïti: "El reino de este mundo" [d']Alejo Carpentier, "La tragédie du roi Christophe" [d']Aimé Césaire, "Iles de tempête" [de] Bernard Dadié*. Paris: Editiones L'Harmattan, 1984. 237 pp.

45. Webb, Barbara J. *Myth and History in Caribbean Fiction: Alejo Carpentier, Wilson Harris, and Edouard Glissant*. Amherst, MA: University of Massachusetts Press, 1992. 185 pp.

II
The Spanish-Speaking Caribbean

GENERAL

A. BIBLIOGRAPHIES AND BIO-BIBLIOGRAPHIES

46. Perrier, Joseph Louis. *Bibliografía dramática cubana: incluye a Puerto Rico y Santo Domingo*. New York: Phos, 1926. 115 pp.

B. ANTHOLOGIES

47. Ballesteros Gaibrois, Manuel, ed. *Escritores de Indias*. 5a ed. Zaragoza: Editorial Ebro, 1970– [vol. 1–].

48. Colón Zayas, Eliseo, ed. *Literatura del Caribe: antología, siglos XIX y XX—Puerto Rico, Cuba, República Dominicana*. Madrid: Playor, 1990. 418 pp. Reprint of the 1984 ed.

49. Miller, Ingrid Watson. *Afro-Hispanic Literature: An Anthology of Hispanic Writers of African Ancestry*. Miami: Ediciones Universal, 1991. 143 pp.

50. Birmingham-Pokorny, Elba D. *An English Anthology of Afro-Hispanic Writers of the Twentieth Century*. Miami: Ediciones Universal, 1995. 126 pp.

Poetry

Poetry: General

51. Boni Villegas, Arturo, ed. *Lira antillana: las mejores poesías de los mejores poetas del Parnaso antillano—Cuba, Puerto Rico, Santo Domingo*. Barcelona: Publicaciones Mundial, 1940. 251 pp.

52. Morales, Jorge Luis, ed. *Poesía afroantillana y negrista: Puerto Rico, República Dominicana, Cuba*. Nueva ed., rev. y aum. Río Piedras, P.R.: Editorial Universitaria, Universidad de Puerto Rico, 1981. 456 pp.

11

53. Ruiz del Vizo, Hortensia, ed. *Poesía negra del Caribe y otras áreas*. Miami: Ediciones Universal, 1972. 168 pp.

Poetry: Sixteenth to Nineteenth Centuries

54. Amy, Francisco Javier, ed. *Musa bilingüe: Being a Collection of Translations, Principally From the Standard Anglo-American Poets into Spanish, and Spanish, Cuban and Porto Rican Poets into English*. San Juan: Boletín Comercial, 1903. 329 pp.

55. Bazil, Osvaldo, ed. *Parnaso antillano: compilación completa de los mejores poetas de Cuba, Puerto Rico y Santo Domingo*. Barcelona: Maucci, 1918. 384 pp.

Poetry: Twentieth Century

56. Gil, Alma Rosa, ed. *Antología poética familiar*. Miami: Interamérica, 1994. 265 pp. Includes 77 Cuban poets, 12 Puerto Rican poets, and 7 others.

Fiction

57. Fernández Marcané, Leonardo, ed. *Cuentos del Caribe*. Madrid: Playor, 1978. 280 pp.

58. Fernández Olmos, Margarite, and Lizabeth Paravisini-Gebert, eds. *Remaking a Lost Harmony: Stories from the Hispanic Caribbean*. Fredonia, NY: White Pine Pres, 1995. 249 pp.

C. HISTORY AND CRITICISM

General

59. Conference of Hispanists (Fifth, 1982, University of the West Indies). *Myth and Superstition in Spanish-Caribbean Literature*. Mona, Jamaica: Dept. of Spanish, University of the West Indies, 1982. 305 pp.

60. Conference of Hispanists (Sixth, 1983, University of the West Indies). *La mujer en la literatura caribeña*. St. Augustine, Trinidad/Tobago: Dept. of Spanish, University of the West Indies, 1983. 196 pp.

61. Conference of Hispanists (Seventh, 1984, University of the West Indies). *Humour in Spanish Caribbean Literature.* Cave Hill, Barbados: Dept. of French and Spanish, University of the West Indies, 1986. 117 pp.

62. Olivera, Otto. *Breve historia de la literatura antillana.* Mexico City: Ediciones de Andrea, 1957. 222 pp.

63. Peñate Rivero, E. Julio, ed. *Literaturas del Caribe y Cono Sur, siglos XIX y XX.* Neuchâtel: Institut d'Espagnol, Université de Neuchâtel-Suisse, 1992. 122 pp.

64. Pereira, Teresinka. *La literatura antillana.* San José, C.R.: Editorial Universitaria Centroamericana, 1985. 139 pp.

65. Piñeiro de Rivera, Flor, and Isabel Freire de Matos. *Literatura infantil caribeña: Puerto Rico, República Dominicana y Cuba.* Hato Rey, P.R.: Boriken Libros, 1983. 123 pp.

66. Rodríguez, Antonio Orlando. *Panorama histórico de la literatura infantil en América Latina y el Caribe.* Bogotá: CERLALC, 1994. 200 pp.

67. Rodríguez, Emilio Jorge. *Literatura caribeña: bojeo y cuaderno de bitacora.* Havana: Editorial Letras Cubanas, 1989. 147 pp.

68. Rodriguez, Ileana, and Marc Zimmerman, eds. *Process of Unity in Caribbean Society: Ideologies and Literature.* Minneapolis, MN: Institute for the Study of Ideologies and Literature, 1983. 213 pp.

69. Yacou, Alain. *Culture et faits d'écriture dans les Antilles hispaniques.* Paris: Editions caribéennes, 1993. 108 pp.

General: Twentieth Century

70. Conference on Hispano-American Literature (Fifth, 1992, Montclair State College); Rose S. Minc, ed. *Literatures in Transition: The Many Voices of the Caribbean Area—A Symposium.* Gaithersburg, MD: Hispamérica, 1982. 197 pp.

71. Conference on Spanish Caribbean Literature (Eleventh, 1988, University of the West Indies); Claudette Williams, ed. *History and Time in Caribbean Literature.* Mona, Jamaica: Institute of Caribbean Studies, University of the West Indies, 1992. 80 pp.

72. Irish, J. A. George. *Visions of Liberation in the Caribbean*. New York: Caribbean Research Center, City University of New York, 1992. 92 pp.

73. Kozak Rovero, Gisela. *Rebelión en el Caribe hispánico: urbes e historias más allá del boom y la postmodernidad*. Caracas: Ediciones La Casa de Bello, 1993. 132 pp.

74. Rodriguez, Ileana. *House/Garden/Nation: Space, Gender, and Ethnicity in Post-Colonial Latin American Literatures by Women*. Durham, NC: Duke University Press, 1994. 223 pp.

Poetry

Poetry: General

75. Habibe, Frederick Hendrik. *El compromiso en la poética afroantillana de Cuba y Puerto Rico*. [Willemstad]: Ministerio de Educación de las Antillas Neerlandesas, 1985. 142 pp.

76. Hernández Franco, Tomás Rafael. *Apuntes sobre poesía popular y poesía negra en las Antillas*. Santo Domingo: Sociedad Dominicana de Bibliófilos, 1978. 71 pp. Reprint of the 1942 ed.

77. Wilson, Leslie N. *La poesía afroantillana*. Miami: Ediciones Universal, 1981. 182 pp.

Poetry: Twentieth Century

78. Conference of Latin Americanists (Third, 1980, University of the West Indies). *Poetry of the Spanish-Speaking Caribbean*. Mona, Jamaica: Dept. of Spanish, University of the West Indies, 1984. 166 pp. Reprint of the 1980 ed.

Fiction

Fiction: General

79. Hernández Norman, Isabel. *La novela romántica en las Antillas*. New York: Plus Ultra, 1977. 251 pp. Reprint of the 1969 ed.

Fiction: Twentieth Century

80. Capeles, Mervin Román. *El cuento fantástico en Puerto Rico y Cuba: estudio teórico y su aplicación a varios cuentos contemporáneos.* Atlanta, GA: Clark Atlanta University, 1995. 138 pp.

81. Conference of Hispanists (First, 1977, University of the West Indies), and Conference of Hispanists (Fourth, 1981, University of the West Indies) *Spanish Caribbean Narrative.* Mona, Jamaica: Dept. of Spanish, University of the West Indies, 1983. 258 pp.

82. Fernández Valledor, Roberto. *Identidad nacional y sociedad en la ensayística cubana y puertorriqueña, 1920–1940.* Santo Domingo: Centro de Estudios Avanzados de Puerto Rico y el Caribe, 1993. 264 pp.

83. Sánchez, Yvette. *Religiosidad cotidiana en la narrativa reciente hispanocaribeña.* Lausanne: Sociedad Suiza de Estudios Hispánicos, 1992. 202 pp.

84. Santiago Soto, Angel T. *Las novelas de las compañías: textos polisémicos de la cuenca del Caribe.* New York: P. Lang, 1993. 244 pp.

85. Zielina, María Carmen. *La africanía en el cuento cubano y puertorriqueño: Gerardo del Valle, Lydia Cabrera, José Luis González, Antonio Benítez Rojo, Carmelo Rodríguez Torres, Ana Lydia Vega.* Miami: Ediciones Universal, 1992. 198 pp.

Drama

86. Conference on Spanish Caribbean Literature (Second, 1979, University of the West Indies); Jesse Noel and Ena V. Thomas, eds. *Spanish Caribbean Theatre.* St. Augustine, Trinidad/Tobago: Dept. of French and Spanish, University of the West Indies, 1985. 216 pp.

CUBA

A. BIBLIOGRAPHIES AND BIO-BIBLIOGRAPHIES

87. Biblioteca Nacional José Martí. *Bibliografía de la poesía cubana en el siglo XIX*. Havana: La Biblioteca, 1965. 89 pp.

88. Fernández, José B., and Roberto G. Fernández, eds. *Bibliographical Index of Cuban Authors (Diaspora, 1959–1979): Literature/Indice bibliográfico de autores cubanos (diáspora, 1959–1979): literatura*. Miami: Ediciones Universal, 1983. 106 pp.

89. Figueras, Myriam, ed. *Catálogo de la colección de la literatura cubana en la Biblioteca Colón*. Washington, DC: Columbus Memorial Library, 1984. 114 pp.

90. Ford, Jeremiah Denis Matthias, and Raphael Isaac Maxwell. *A Bibliography of Cuban Belles-Lettres*. New York: Russell and Russell, 1970. 204 pp. Reprint of the 1933 ed.

91. Foster, David William. *Cuban Literature: A Research Guide*. New York: Garland, 1985. 522 pp.

92. Iraizoz, Antonio. *Libros y autores cubanos*. Santa María del Rosario, Cuba: Editorial Rosareña, 1956. 178 pp. Reprint of the 1942 ed.

93. Montes Huidobro, Matías, and Yara González. *Bibliografía crítica de la poesía cubana: exilio 1959–1971*. New York: Plaza Mayor, 1972. 136 pp.

94. Muriedas, Mercedes. *Bibliografía de la literatura infantil cubana, siglo XIX*. Havana: Depto. Juvenil, Biblioteca Nacional José Martí, 1969– [vol. 1–].

95. Rivero Múñiz, José. *Bibliografía del teatro cubano*. Havana: Biblioteca Nacional José Martí, 1957. 120 pp.

Poetry

Poetry: General

117. Baeza Flores, Alberto, ed. *Las mejores poesías cubanas: desde José María Heredia hasta los poetas de 1955*. 2a ed. Barcelona: Editorial Bruguera, 1958. 128 pp.

118. ———. *Las mejores poesías de amor cubanas*. Barcelona: Editorial Bruguera, 1954. 124 pp.

119. Chacón y Calvo, José María, ed. *Las cien mejores poesías cubanas*. Madrid: Ediciones Cultura Hispánica, 1958. 310 pp. Reprint of the 1922 ed.

120. Esténger, Rafael, ed. *Cien de las mejores poesías cubanas*. Miami: Mnemosyne Publishing, 1969. 363 pp. Reprint of the 1948 (2d, rev.) ed.

121. Feijóo, Samuel, ed. *Cuarteta y décima: selección*. 2a ed. aum. Havana: Editorial Letras Cubanas, 1980. 330 pp.

122. ———. *La décima culta en Cuba: muestrario*. Santa Clara, Cuba: Universidad Central de las Villas, 1963. 426 pp.

123. ———. *Sonetos en Cuba: selección*. Santa Clara, Cuba: Universidad Central de las Villas, 1964. 394 pp.

124. ———. *Los trovadores del pueblo*. Santa Clara, Cuba: Universidad Central de Las Villas, 1960– [vol. 1–].

125. Fuente, Pilar, ed. *Poesía de amor*. Havana: Editorial Arte y Literatura, 1977. 182 pp.

126. Gutiérrez Rodríguez, Antonio, ed. *Selección de poesía tunera, siglos XIX–XX*. Las Tunas, Cuba: Sanlope, 1992. 89 pp.

127. Jahn, Janheinz, ed. *Rumba macumba: Afrocubanische Lyrik*. Munich: C. Hanser, 1957. 79 pp.

128. Lezama Lima, José, ed. *Antología de la poesía cubana*. Havana: Consejo Nacional de la Cultura, 1965. 3 vols.

129. Ligaluppi, Oscar Abel, ed. *Cuba, la cercana lejanía: los poetas del éxodo.* Buenos Aires: Editor Interamericano, 1995. 281 pp.

130. Lizaso, Félix, and José Antonio Fernández de Castro, eds. *La poesía moderna en Cuba, 1882–1925: antología crítica.* Madrid: Hernando, 1926. 406 pp.

131. Orta Ruiz, Jesús, ed. *Poesía criollista y siboneísta: antología.* Havana: Editorial Arte y Literatura, 1976. 400 pp.

132. Oviedo, José Miguel, ed. *Antología de la poesía cubana.* Lima: Ediciones Paradiso, 1968. 197 pp.

133. Ripoll, Carlos, and Alfredo E. Figueredo, eds. *Naturaleza y alma de Cuba: dos siglos de poesía cubana, 1760–1960.* New York: Las Américas, 1974. 242 pp.

134. Rocasolano, Alberto, ed. *Poetisas cubanas.* Havana: Editorial Letras Cubanas, 1985. 355 pp.

135. Vitier, Cintio, ed. *Las mejores poesías cubanas: antología.* Lima: Organización Continental de los Festivales del Libro, 1959. 192 pp.

136. ———. *Los poetas románticos cubanos: antología.* Havana: Consejo Nacional de Cultura, 1962. 284 pp.

Poetry: Sixteenth to Nineteenth Centuries

137. Baeza Flores, Alberto, ed. *Poesías de la patria.* Havana: Ministerio de Educación, 1951. 149 pp.

138. Boti y Barreiro, Regino Eladio, ed. *La lira cubana: compilación de cantos populares cubanos de autores antiguos y contemporáneos.* Guantánamo, Cuba: Impr. "La Imperial," 1913. 277 pp.

139. Carbonell, José Manuel. *Los poetas de "El laúd del desterrado,": Quintero, Teurbe Tolón, Santacilia, Turla, Castellón, Zenea.* Havana: Imp. "Avisador Comercial," 1930. 193 pp.

140. Feijóo, Samuel, ed. *Cantos a la naturaleza cubana del siglo XIX: selección.* Santa Clara, Cuba: Universidad Central de Las Villas, 1964. 239 pp.

141. ———. *Romances cubanos del siglo XIX.* Havana: Editorial Arte y Literatura, 1977. 464 pp.

142. González Curquejo, Antonio, ed. *Florilegio de escritoras cubanas*. Havana: La Moderna Poesía, 1910. 356 pp.

143. Hills, Elijah Clarence, ed. *Bardos cubanos: antología de las mejores poesías líricas de Heredia, Plácido, Avellaneda, Milanés, Mendive, Luaces, y Zenea*. Boston: Heath, 1901. 162 pp.

144. León, José Socorro de, ed. *Cuba poética: colección escogida de las composiciones en verso de los poetas cubanos desde Zequeira hasta nuestros días*. Havana: Impr. de la Viuda de Barcina, 1858. 214 pp.

145. López Prieto, Antonio, ed. *Parnaso cubano: colección de poesías selectas de autores cubanos, desde Zequiera a nuestros días*. Havana: M. de Villa, 1881. 370 pp.

146. Martí, José, ed. *Los poetas de la guerra: antología*. Havana: Universidad de La Habana, 1968. 162 pp. Reprint of the 1893 ed.

147. Montes Huidobro, Matías, ed. *El laúd del desterrado: antología*. Houston, TX: Arte Público Press, 1995. 181 pp.

148. Riva Abréu, Valentín, ed. *Parnaso cubano: selectas composiciones poéticas*. Barcelona: Maucci, 1926. 350 pp.

149. Rocasolano, Alberto, ed. *Invitados de la luz: poemas para niños y jóvenes—siglo XIX*. Havana: Editorial Gente Nueva, 1990. 237 pp.

150. Sellén, Francisco et al. *Arpas amigas: colección de poesías originales*. Havana: M. de Villa, 1879. 112 pp.

151. Valle, Adrián del, ed. *Parnaso cubano: selectas composiciones poéticas*. Nueva ed. aum. Barcelona: Maucci, 1920. 287 pp.

152. Vitier, Cintio, and Fina García Marruz, eds. *Flor oculta de poesía cubana, siglos XVIII y XIX*. Havana: Editorial Arte y Literatura, 1978. 350 pp.

Poetry: Twentieth Century

153. Academia Poética de Miami, ed. *Guitarras del exilio cubano*. Miami: La Academia, 1995. 204 pp.

154. ———. *Poetisas cubanas contemporáneas*. Miami: La Academia, 1990. 335 pp.

155. ———. *Sonetario cubano*. Miami: La Academia, 1992. 194 pp.

156. Aguilera Díaz, Gaspar, ed. *Un grupo avanza silencioso: antología de poetas cubanos nacidos entre 1958 y 1972*. Mexico City: Coordinación de Difusión Cultural, Dirección de Literatura, Universidad Nacional Autónoma de México, 1990. 2 vols.

157. Alfonso Barroso, Carlos Augusto, ed. *Retrato de grupo*. Havana: Editorial Letras Cubanas, 1989. 174 pp. Selections from 26 contemporary Cuban poets.

158. Alvarez Baragaño, José. *Para el 26 [i.e. veintiseis] de julio: colección de poesía revolucionaria*. Havana: Unión de Escritores y Artistas de Cuba, 1962. 223 pp.

159. Anhalt, Nedda G. de, Víctor Manuel Mendiola and Manuel Ulacia, eds. *La fiesta innombrable: trece poetas cubanos*. Mexico City: Ediciones El Tucán de Virginia, 1992. 215 pp. Gastón Baquero, Angel Gaztelu, Eugenio Florit, Justo Rodríguez Santos, Lydia Cabrera, Guillermo Cabrera Infante, Herberto Padilla, Severo Sarduy, Belkis Cuza Malé, Reinaldo Arenas, José Kozer, Orlando González Esteva, and María Elena Cruz Varela.

160. Antología Poética Hispanoamericana (Organization), ed. *Antología de poetas cubanos*. Miami: Antología Poética Hispanoamericana, 1989. 280 pp.

161. Aparicio Laurencio, Angel, ed. *Cinco poetisas cubanas, 1935–1969*. Miami: Ediciones Universal, 1970. 134 pp. Mercedes García Tuduri, Pura del Prado, Teresa María Rojas, Rita Geada, and Ana Rosa Núñez.

162. Aray, Edmundo, ed. *Poesía de Cuba: antología viva*. Valencia, Venezuela: Dirección de Cultura, Universidad de Carabobo, 1976. 355 pp.

163. Augier, Angel I., ed. *Poemas a la Revolución Cubana*. Havana: Unión de Escritores y Artistas de Cuba, 1980. 266 pp.

164. Baeza Flores, Alberto, ed. *Cuatro poetas cubanos: Cabrisas, Acosta, Sánchez-Galarraga, Buesa*. Barcelona: Editorial Bruguera, 1956. 125 pp.

165. Cardenal, Ernesto, ed. *Poesía cubana de la Revolución*. Mexico City: Extemporáneos, 1976. 334 pp.

166. Cazorla, Roberto et al. *Poesía compartida: ocho poetas cubanos*. Miami: Ultra Graphics Corp., 1980. 99 pp. Roberto Cazorla, Amalia del Castillo, Rita Geada, Lucas Lamadrid, Pablo LeRiverend, Matías Montes Huidobro, Isel Rivero, and Orlando Rossardi.

167. Chacón, Alfredo, ed. *Poesía y poética del grupo Orígenes*. Caracas: Biblioteca Ayacucho, 1994. 326 pp.

168. Chacón Zaldívar, Carlos, and Antonio Gutiérrez Rodríguez, eds. *Poetas del mediodía: décimas cubanas*. Las Tunas, Cuba: Sanlope, 1995. 115 pp.

169. Codina, Norberto, ed. *Los ríos de la mañana: poesía cubana de los 80*. Havana: Unión de Escritores y Artistas de Cuba, 1995. 269 pp.

170. Dávila, Eliana, ed. *Jugando a juegos prohibidos: antología*. Havana: Editorial Letras Cubanas, 1992. 177 pp. On cover *Jóvenes poetas cubanos*.

171. Dopico Echevarría, Raúl, ed. *Tras la huella de lo imposible: antología de nuevos poetas cubanos—según la tendencia de la agresividad*. Guadalajara, Mex.: Secretaría de Cultura de Jalisco, 1994. 143 pp.

172. Espina Pérez, Darío, ed. *Ciento y siete poetas cubanos del exilio*. Miami: Antología Poética Hispanoamericana, 1988. 496 pp.

173. Fajardo Ledea, Nidia, ed. *De transparencia en transparencia: antología poética*. Havana: Editorial Letras Cubanas, 1993. 197 pp.

174. Fernández Retamar, Roberto, and Fayad Jamís, eds. *Poesía joven de Cuba*. Havana: Librería "La Tertulia," 1965. 127 pp. Reprint of the 1959 ed.

175. Franquiz, Roberto, ed. *Doce poetas en las puertas de la ciudad*. Havana: Ediciones Extramuros, 1992. 61 pp.

176. García Elío, Diego, ed. *Una antología de poesía cubana*. Mexico City: Editorial Oasis, 1984. 235 pp.

177. González, Daniuska, ed. *Poetas cubanos actuales*. Miranda, Venezuela: Ateneo de Los Teques, 1995. 136 pp.

178. González Herrero, Lourdes, ed. *Poetas de la isla: selección de poetas cubanos*. Holguín, Cuba: Ediciones Holguín, 1995. 115 pp.

179. ———. *Provincia del universo: selección de poetas holguineros*. Holguín, Cuba: Ediciones Holguín, 1993. 2 vols.

180. González López, Waldo, ed. *Rebelde en mar y sueño: selección de poemas y aviso*. Havana: Editorial Política, 1988. 88 pp. Thirty poems that pay homage to the city of Santiago de Cuba compiled to commemorate the thirty-fifth anniversary of the attack on the Moncada Barracks (July 26, 1953).

181. Goytisolo, José Agustín, ed. *Nueva poesía cubana: antología poética*. Barcelona: Península, 1973. 236 pp. Reprint of the 1969 ed.

182. Güirao, Ramón, ed. *Orbita de la poesía afrocubana, 1928–37: antología*. Millwood, NY: Kraus Reprint, 1970. 267 pp. Reprint of the 1938 ed.

183. Hernández Menéndez, Mayra, ed. *Nuevos poetas cubanos*. Havana: Editorial Letras Cubanas, 1994. 2 vols.

184. Herrera Ysla, Nelson, ed. *Páginas abiertas: antología poética*. Havana: Editorial Letras Cubanas, 1979. 82 pp.

185. Herrera Ysla, Nelson, and Virgilio López Lemus, eds. *Poesía por la victoria: antología*. Havana: Editorial Letras Cubanas, 1981. 112 pp.

186. Hoz, León de la, ed. *La poesía de las dos orillas: Cuba, 1959–1993—antología*. Madrid: Libertarias/Prodhufi, 1994. 428 pp.

187. Jay, Marino Wilson, ed. *Ecos para su memoria: poemas*. Havana: Unión de Escritores y Artistas de Cuba, 1989. 138 pp. Dedicated to José Lezama Lima.

188. Lázaro, Felipe, ed. *Cuban Women Poets in New York/Poetas cubanas en Nueva York*. Madrid: Editorial Betania, 1991. 121 pp.

189. ———. *Poetas cubanos en España*. Madrid: Editorial Betania, 1989. 170 pp.

190. Lázaro, Felipe, and Bladimir Zamora, eds. *Poesía cubana: la isla entera—antología*. Madrid: Editorial Betania, 1995. 382 pp.

191. Llarena Rosales, Alicia, ed. *Poesía cubana de los años 80.* Madrid: Ediciones La Palma, 1994. 241 pp.

192. López Lemus, Virgilio, and Gaetano Longo, eds. *Poetas de la isla: panorama de la poesía cubana contemporánea.* Seville: Portada Editorial, 1995. 222 pp.

193. López Montenegro, Omar, ed. *El desierto que canta: poesía "underground" cubana.* Washington, DC: Endowment for Cuban American Studies, 1993. 82 pp.

194. Luis, Raúl, ed. *Libro de buen humor.* Havana: Editorial Letras Cubanas, 1995. 169 pp.

195. Luis, Raúl, and José Prats Sariol, eds. *Tertulia poética: antología.* Havana: Editorial Letras Cubanas, 1988. 170 pp.

196. Merino, Antonio, ed. *Nueva poesía cubana: antología 1966–1986.* Madrid: Editorial Orígenes, 1987. 271 pp.

197. Nogueras, Luis Rogelio, ed. *Poesía cubana de amor: siglo XX.* Havana: Editorial Letras Cubanas, 1993. 219 pp. Reprint of the 1983 ed.

198. Núñez, Ana Rosa, ed. *Poesía en éxodo: el exilio cubano en su poesía, 1959–1969.* Miami: Ediciones Universal, 1970. 399 pp.

199. Orovio, Helio, ed. *Trescientos boleros de oro: antología.* Havana: Unión de Escritores y Artistas de Cuba, 1991. 283 pp.

200. Orta Ruiz, Jesús, ed. *Musa popular revolucionaria: decimario criollo.* Havana: Ediciones del Gobierno Provincial Revolucionario, 1960. 240 pp.

201. Pereira, Joe R., ed. and tr. *Poems from Cuba: An Anthology of Recent Cuban Poetry.* Mona, Jamaica: Research and Publication Committee, University of the West Indies, 1977. 150 pp.

202. Pino-Santos Navarro, Carina, ed. *El libro de enero: antología de poemas.* Havana: Editora Política, 1989. 135 pp.

203. Ramos Mederos, Omelio, ed. *Trabajadores poetas.* Havana: Editorial Arte y Literatura, Instituto Cubano del Libro, 1974. 227 pp.

204. Randall, Margaret, ed. and tr. *Breaking the Silence: An Anthology of 20th-Century Poetry by Cuban Women*. Vancouver: Pulp Press, 1982. 293 pp.

205. Regalado, Pedro N. *Antología de poetas güineros en el exilio*. Miami: San Lázaro Graphics, 1992. 160 pp.

206. Ríos, Soleida, ed. *Poesía infiel: selección de jóvenes poetisas cubanas*. Havana: Editora Abril, 1989. 182 pp.

207. Rodríguez, Reina María, Víctor Rodríguez Núñez and Osvaldo Sánchez, eds. *Cuba: en su lugar la poesía—antología diferente*. Mexico City: Universidad Autónoma Metropolitana-Azcapotzalco, 1982. 175 pp.

208. Rodríguez Núñez, Víctor, ed. *Usted es la culpable: antología poética*. Havana: Editora Abril, 1985. 190 pp.

209. Rodríguez-Sardiñas, Orlando, ed. *La última poesía cubana: antología reunida, 1959–1973*. Madrid: Hispanova, 1973. 575 pp.

210. Sáinz, Enrique, ed. *La poesía cubana entre 1928 y 1958*. Havana: Editorial Gente Nueva, 1980. 218 pp.

211. Sánchez Mejías, Rolando, ed. *Mapa imaginario: dossier—veintiseis nuevos poetas cubanos*. Havana: Instituto Cubano del Libro, 1995. 297 pp.

212. Sancristobal, Arsenio Cicero, ed. *Poemas transitorios: antología de nuevos poetas cubanos*. Mérida, Venezuela: Ediciones Mucuglifo, 1992. 137 pp. Ramón Fernández-Larrea, Marilyn Bobes, José Pérez Olivares, Reina María Rodríguez, and Alex Fleites Rodríguez.

213. Suardíaz, Luis, ed. *No me dan pena, los burgueses vencidos: poemas*. Havana: Editora Política, 1991. 229 pp.

214. Suardíaz, Luis, and David Chericián, eds. *La generación de los años cincuenta: antología poética*. Havana: Editorial Letras Cubanas, 1984. 586 pp.

215. Tarn, Nathaniel, ed. *Con Cuba: An Anthology of Cuban Poetry of the Last Sixty Years*. Elinor Randall [et al.], tr. London: Cape Goliard, 1969. 142 pp. Spanish and English.

216. Valdés, Manuel G., ed. *Poesía de amor: Cuba*. Hialeah, FL: Editorial Valmart, 1983. 163 pp.

217. Vázquez Espinosa, Ignacio et al. *Antología de poetas*. Santiago, Cuba: Editorial Oriente, 1981. 88 pp. Ignacio Vázquez, Raul Doblado del Rosario, Alberto de Jesús Serret, Renael González Batista, Mercedes Santos Moray, Efraín Nadereau, Carlos Padrón, and Marino Wilson Jay.

218. Vitier, Cintio, ed. *Cincuenta años de poesía cubana, 1902–1952*. Havana: Dirección de Cultura, Ministerio de Educación, 1952. 420 pp.

219. ———. *Diez poetas cubanos, 1937–1947*. Havana: Ediciones Orígenes, 1948. 298 pp. José Lezama Lima, Angel Gaztelu, Virgilio Piñera, Justo Rodríguez Santos, Gastón Baquero, Eliseo Diego, Cintio Vitier, Octavio Smith, Fina García Marruz, Lorenzo García Vega.

Fiction

Fiction: General

220. Alvarez García, Imeldo, ed. *Cuentos de amor*. Havana: Editorial Letras Cubanas, 1981. 403 pp. Reprint of the 1979 ed.

221. Bueno, Salvador, ed. *Los mejores cuentos cubanos*. Lima: Organización Continental de los Festivales del Libro, 1959. 2 vols.

222. Fernández Marcané, Leonardo, ed. *Veinte cuentistas cubanos*. Miami: Ediciones Universal, 1978. 126 pp.

223. García Vega, Lorenzo, ed. *Antología de la novela cubana*. Havana: Ministerio de Educación, Dirección General de Cultura, 1960. 508 pp.

224. Llopis, Rogelio, ed. *Cuentos cubanos de lo fantástico y lo extraordinario*. San Sebastián, Cuba: Equipo Editorial, 1968. 302 pp.

225. Ortiz Domínguez, Pedro, ed. *El valle de las delicias: selección de cuentos holguineros*. Holguín, Cuba: Ediciones Holguín, 1994. 2 vols.

226. Oviedo, José Miguel, ed. *Antología del cuento cubano*. Lima: Ediciones Paradiso, 1968. 213 pp.

227. Pérez, Emma, ed. *Cuentos cubanos: antología*. Havana: Cultural, 1945. 161 pp.

228. Travieso, Julio, ed. *Cuentos sobre el clandinestaje*. Havana: Editorial Letras Cubanas, 1983. 246 pp.

Fiction: Sixteenth to Nineteenth Centuries

229. Bueno, Salvador, ed. *Costumbristas cubanos del siglo XIX*. Caracas: Biblioteca Ayacucho, 1983. 524 pp.

230. ———. *Cuentos cubanos del siglo XIX: antología*. Havana: Editorial Arte y Literatura, 1975. 463 pp.

231. Rodríguez, Iraida, ed. *Artículos de costumbres cubanos del siglo XIX: antología*. Havana: Editorial Arte y Literatura, 1974. 255 pp.

Fiction: Twentieth Century

232. Alvarez García, Imeldo, ed. *Noveletas cubanas*. Havana: Editorial Arte y Literatura, 1977. 524 pp.

233. Arango, Arturo, ed. *Panorama del cuento cubano contemporáneo*. Montevideo: Lectores de Banda Oriental, 1986. 74 pp.

234. Arrufat, Antón, and Fausto Masó, eds. *Nuevos cuentistas cubanos*. Havana: Casa de las Américas, 1961. 253 pp.

235. Batista Reyes, Alberto, ed. *Cuentos sobre bandidos y combatientes*. Havana: Editorial Letras Cubanas, 1983. 382 pp.

236. Bueno, Salvador, ed. *Antología del cuento en Cuba, 1902–1952*. Havana: Dirección de Cultura, Ministerio de Educacion, 1953. 399 pp.

237. ———. *Cuentos cubanos del siglo XX: antología*. Havana: Editorial Arte y Literatura, 1975. 490 pp.

238. Caballero Bonald, José Manuel, ed. *Narrativa cubana de la Revolución*. Madrid: Alianza Editorial, 1971. 258 pp. Reprint of the 1968 ed.

239. Cámara, Madeline, ed. *Cuentos cubanos contemporáneos, 1966–1990*. Xalapa, Mex.: Universidad Veracruzana, 1989. 258 pp.

240. Eguren, Gustavo, ed. *Cuentos del mar.* Havana: Editorial Letras Cubanas, 1981. 364 pp.

241. ———. *Cuentos sobre la violencia.* Havana: Editorial Letras Cubanas, 1983. 281 pp.

242. Feijóo, Samuel, ed. *Cuentos cubanos de humor.* Havana: Editorial Letras Cubanas, 1979. 513 pp.

243. Ferreiro, Pilar A., ed. *Cuentos rurales cubanos del siglo XX.* Havana: Editorial Letras Cubanas, 1984. 382 pp.

244. Fleites, Alex, ed. *Hacer el amor: siete jóvenes cuentistas cubanos.* Havana: Editora Abril, 1986. 96 pp.

245. Fornet, Ambrosio, ed. *Antología del cuento cubano contemporáneo.* Mexico City: Ediciones Era, 1979. 241 pp. Reprint of the 1967 ed.

246. ———. *Cuentos de la Revolución cubana.* Santiago, Chile: Editorial Universitaria, 1971. 198 pp.

247. Garcés Larras, Cristóbal, ed. *Narradores cubanos contemporáneos.* Guayaquil: Ariel, 1973. 186 pp.

248. Heras León, Eduardo, et al. *Cuentos policíacos cubanos.* Montevideo: Signos y Amauta, 1989. 90 pp.

249. Heras León, Eduardo, ed. *Nuevos cuentistas cubanos.* Havana: Editorial Letras Cubanas, 1996. 2 vols.

250. Hernández Fuentes, Plácido, Arturo Chinea Medina and Emelicio Vázquez Tamayo. *Relatos de amor y odio.* Havana: Editorial Arte y Literatura, 1978. 189 pp.

251. Hernández Novo, Corina, ed. *Cuentos cubanos del siglo XX.* Havana: Editorial Pueblo y Educación, 1990. 107 pp.

252. Hernández-Miyares, Julio E., ed. *Narradores cubanos de hoy.* Miami: Ediciones Universal, 1975. 179 pp.

253. Hurtado, Oscar, ed. *Introducción a la ciencia ficción.* Madrid: M. Castellote, 1971. 143 pp. Includes short stories by Carlos Cabada, Juan Luis Herrero, and Agenor Martí.

254. Ibarzábal, Federico de, ed. *Cuentos contemporáneos.* Havana: Editorial Trópico, 1937. 222 pp.

255. Izquierdo-Tejido, Pedro. *El cuento cubano: panorámica y antología.* San José, C.R.: Impr. LIL, 1983. 345 pp.

256. Leyva Guerra, Juan, ed. *Cuentos de la vida y la muerte.* Santiago, Cuba: Editorial Oriente, 1987. 339 pp.

257. Lorenzo, José, and Francisco Baeza Pérez, eds. *Los cuentistas cubanos y la reforma agraria.* Havana: Editorial Tierra Nueva, 1960. 138 pp.

258. Martí, Agenor, ed. *Aventuras insólitas: cuentos.* Havana: Editorial Letras Cubanas, 1988. 296 pp.

259. ———. *Misterios para vencer: cuentos policíacos.* Havana: Editorial Letras Cubanas, 1988. 531 pp.

260. Martínez Matos, José, ed. *Cuentos fantásticos cubanos.* Havana: Editorial Letras Cubanas, 1979. 346 pp.

261. Mauri Sierra, Omar Felipe, ed. *Cuentos desde La Habana.* Alicante, Spain: Aguaclara, 1996. 190 pp.

262. Miranda, Julio E., ed. *Antología del nuevo cuento cubano.* Caracas: Editorial D. Fuentes, 1969. 298 pp.

263. Padura, Leonardo, ed. *El submarino amarillo: cuento cubano, 1966–1991—breve antología.* Mexico City: Ediciones Coyoacán, 1993. 347 pp.

264. Portuondo, José Antonio, ed. *Cuentos cubanos contemporáneos.* Mexico City: Editorial Leyenda, 1947. 237 pp.

265. Reloba, Juan Carlos, ed. *Cuentos cubanos de ciencia ficción.* Havana: Editorial Gente Nueva, 1981. 166 pp.

266. ———. *Veinte relatos cubanos.* Havana: Editorial Gente Nueva, 1980. 266 pp.

267. Rivero García, José, and Omar González, eds. *Cuentistas jóvenes.* Havana: Editorial Arte y Literatura, 1978. 277 pp.

268. Rodríguez Feo, José, ed. *Aquí once cubanos cuentan*. Montevideo: Arca, 1967. 169 pp. El caramelo (V. Piñera), El caballo de coral (O. J. Cardoso), El regreso (C. Casey), El del trece (J. L. Fuentes), El día inicial (C. Leante), Nueve viñetas (G. Cabrera Infante), Aquí me pongo (E. Desnoes), Yo no ví nada . . . (A. Fornet), En el Ford azul (L. Otero), El caballero Charles (H. Arenal), Diosito (J. Díaz).

269. Rodríguez, Luis Felipe et al. *Veinte cuentos cortos cubanos*. Havana: Instituto del Libro, 1969. 162 pp.

270. Soler Puig, José et al. *El decoro de muchos: cuentos*. Santiago, Cuba: Ediciones Uvero, 1983. 54 pp.

271. Sorel, Andrés, ed. *Cuentos de Cuba socialista*. Madrid: ZYX, 1976. 190 pp.

272. Subercaseaux, Bernardo, ed. *Narrativa de la joven Cuba: antología*. Santiago, Chile: Editorial Nascimento, 1971. 128 pp.

273. Unión de Escritores y Artistas Cuba. *El cuento en la Revolución: antología*. Havana: La Unión , 1975. 379 pp.

274. ————. *Nuevos cuentos cubanos*. Havana: La Unión, 1964. 323 pp.

275. Zamora, Bladimir, ed. *Cuentos de la remota novedad*. Havana: Editorial Gente Nueva, 1983. 173 pp.

Drama

Drama: General

276. Artiles, Freddy, ed. *Aventuras en el teatro*. Havana: Editorial Letras Cubanas, 1988. 381 pp.

277. Garzón Céspedes, Francisco, ed. *Monólogos teatrales cubanos*. Havana: Editorial Letras Cubanas, 1989. 524 pp.

278. Leal, Rine, ed. *Teatro cubano en un acto: antología*. Havana: Ediciones R[evolución], 1963. 354 pp.

279. *Teatro bufo: siete obras*. Santa Clara, Cuba: Universidad Central de Las Villas, Dirección de Publicaciones, 1961– [vol. 1–]. Half title: *Bufo cubano*. Vol. 1. Los cheverones (J. Barreiro), Don Centén (X.),

La herencia de Canuto (B. Sánchez Maldonado), Los efectos del billete/A la celaduría (O. Díaz González), El hombre de la gallina (Srs. Chacón y Nuza), Los detallistas (O. Díaz González), Los hijos de Thalía/Bufos de fin de siglo (B. Sánchez Maldonado).

280. UNESCO. *Panorama del teatro cubano*. Havana: Comisión Nacional Cubana de la Unesco, 1965. 175 pp.

Drama: Sixteenth to Nineteenth Centuries

281. González Freire, Natividad, ed. *Teatro cubano del siglo XIX: antología*. Havana: Editorial Arte y Literatura, 1975– [vol. 1–].

282. Leal, Rine, ed. *Comedias cubanas siglo XIX*. Havana: Editorial Letras Cubanas, 1979. 2 vols.

283. ———. *Teatro bufo, siglo XIX: antología*. Havana: Editora Arte y Literatura, 1975. 2 vols.

284. Milanés, José Jacinto, ed. *Teatro del siglo XIX*. Havana: Editorial Letras Cubanas, 1986. 701 pp.

Drama: Twentieth Century

285. Boudet, Rosa Ileana. *Teatro nuevo: una respuesta*. Havana: Editorial Letras Cubanas, 1983. 304 pp.

286. Chao Carbonero, Caridad, ed. *Antología de teatro cubano*. Havana: Editorial Pueblo y Educación, 1990– [vol. 1–5–].

287. Cuba, Dirección de Artistas Aficionados. *Repertorio de teatro para el movimiento de aficionados*. Santiago, Cuba: Editorial Oriente, 1986. 131 pp.

288. Editorial Letras Cubanas (Havana). *Teatro y revolución*. Havana: La Editorial, 1980. 390 pp. Llévame a la pelota (I. Gutiérrrez), El robo del cochino (A. Estorino), Santa Camila de la Habana Vieja (J. R. Brene), La emboscada (R. Orihuela Aldama), Mambrú se fué a la guerra (H. Quintero), La vitrina (A. Paz).

289. Espinosa Domínguez, Carlos, ed. *Comedias musicales*. Havana: Editorial Letras Cubanas, 1985. 327 pp. El apartamento (J. Gre-

gorio), Un día en el solar (L. Otero), Las vacas gordas (A. Estorino), Las yaguas (M. Vera, G. Piloto).

290. ———. *Teatro cubano contemporáneo: antología.* Madrid: Sociedad Estatal Quinto Centenario, 1992. 1,508 pp.

291. Leal, Rine, ed. *Seis obras de teatro cubano.* Havana: Editorial Letras Cubanas, 1989. 418 pp. Morir del cuento (A. Estorino), Molinos de viento (R. González), La familia de Benjamín García (G. Fernández), Aprendiendo a mirar las grúas (M. Coll), Kunene (I. Gutiérrez), Odebí el cazador (E. Hernández).

292. ———. *Teatro: cinco autores cubanos.* Jackson Heights, NY: Ollantay Press, 1995. 277 pp. Fefu y sus amigas (M. I. Fornés), Las monjas (E. Manet), Nadie se va del todo (P. R. Monge Rafuls), Balada de un verano en La Habana (H. Santiago), La fiesta (J. Triana).

293. ———. *Teatro Escambray.* 2a ed., rev. Havana: Editoral Letras Cubanas, 1990. 395 pp.

294. ———. *Teatro mambí.* Havana: Editorial Letras Cubanas, 1978. 538 pp.

295. Martí de Cid, Dolores, ed. *Teatro cubano contemporáneo.* 2a ed. aum. Madrid: Aguilar, 1962. 452 pp. Tragedia indiana (L. A. Baralt), Hombres de dos mundos (J. Cid Pérez), El travieso Jimmy (C. Felipe), Imagínate infinita (R. Potts), Tembladera (J. A. Ramos), Alma Guajira (M. Salinas).

296. Montes Huidobro, Matías, Ingrid González and Enrique G. Capablanca. *Tres obras dramáticas de Cuba revolucionaria.* Havana: Instituto de Cultura de Mariano, 1961. 48 pp. El tiro por la culata (M. Montes Huidobro), Gloria (I. González), La botija y la felicidad (E. G. Capablanca).

297. Pino, Amado del, ed. *Repertorio teatral.* Havana: Editorial Letras Cubanas, 1990. 421 pp.

298. Robreño, Eduardo, ed. *Teatro Alhambra: antología.* Havana: Editorial Letras Cubanas, 1979. 706 pp.

299. Suárez Durán, Esther. *Un colectivo trás el telón.* Havana: Editorial de Ciencias Sociales, 1988. 51 pp.

D. HISTORY AND CRITICISM

General

300. Alvarez Alvarez, Luis. *Conversar con el otro*. Havana: Unión de Escritores y Artistas de Cuba, 1990. 214 pp. Essays on Félix Varela, José Martí, Nicolás Guillén, Onelio Jorge Cardoso, and José Soler Puig.

301. Alvarez Bravo, Armando. *Al curioso lector: ensayos sobre arte y literatura*. Miami: Ediciones Universal, 1996. 90 pp.

302. Ares, Mercedes et al. *Características nacionales de la literatura cubana*. Miami: Patronato Ramón Guiteras Intercultural Center, 1986. 92 pp.

303. Arias, Salvador. *Búsqueda y análisis: ensayos críticos sobre literatura cubana*. Havana: Unión de Escritores y Artitas de Cuba, 1974. 129 pp.

304. Baeza Flores, Alberto. *Cuba, el laurel y la palma: ensayos literarios—José Fornaris, José Martí, Jorge Mañach, Eugenio Florit, Angel Cuadra, Carlos Alberto Montaner*. Miami: Ediciones Universal, 1977. 293 pp.

305. Bueno, Salvador. *De Merlin a Carpentier: nuevos temas y personajes de la literatura cubana*. Havana: Unión de Escritores y Artistas de Cuba, 1977. 239 pp.

306. ———. *Historia de la literatura cubana*. 3a ed. Havana: Ministero de Educación, 1963. 459 pp.

307. ———. *Temas y personajes de la literatura cubana*. Havana: Unión de Escritores y Artistas de Cuba, 1964. 299 pp.

308. Carbonell, José Manuel. *Evolución de la cultura cubana, 1608–1927*. Havana: "El Siglo XX", 1928. 18 vols. Vols. 1–5. *La poesía lírica en Cuba*. Vol. 6. *La poesía revolucionaria en Cuba*. Vols. 7–11. *La oratoria en Cuba*. Vols. 12–16. *La prosa en Cuba*. Vol. 17. *La ciencia en Cuba*. Vol. 18. *Las bellas artes en Cuba*.

309. Chaple, Sergio. *Estudios de literatura cubana*. Havana: Editorial Letras Cubanas, 1980. 214 pp.

310. García Alzola, Ernesto. *La literatura como arma*. Havana: Unión de Escritores y Artistas de Cuba, 1986. 152 pp.

311. Henríquez Ureña, Max. *Panorama histórico de la literatura cubana*. Havana: Editorial Arte y Literatura, 1978–1979. 2 vols. Reprint of the 1963 ed.

312. Lazo, Raimundo. *Historia de la literatura cubana*. 2a ed. Mexico City: Universidad Nacional Autónoma de México, 1974. 313 pp.

313. ———. *La literatura cubana: esquema histórico desde sus orígenes hasta 1964*. Mexico City: Universidad Nacional Autónoma de México, 1965. 254 pp.

314. Lezama Lima, José. *La cantidad hechizada*. Nueva ed. Madrid: Júcar, 1974. 299 pp. Paralelos, Don Ventura Pascual Ferrer y El Regañón, Prólogo a la poesía cubana, Juan Clemente Zenea, Ramón Meza: tersitismo y claro enigma, Arístides Fernández, and Homenaje a René Portocarrero.

315. Morejón, Nancy. *Fundación de la imagen*. Havana: Editorial Letras Cubanas, 1988. 294 pp.

316. Mota, Francisco M. *Efemérides literarias cubanas*. Havana: Editorial Gente Nueva, 1979. 151 pp.

317. Obaya, Alicia, Gloria Barredo and Yolanda Ricardo. *Valoraciones sobre temas y problemas de la literatura cubana*. Havana: Editorial Pueblo y Educación, 1978. 167 pp.

318. Piedra-Bueno, Andrés de. *Literatura cubana: síntesis histórica*. Havana: Editorial América, 1945. 132 pp.

319. ———. *La Virgen María en la literatura cubana*. New York: [s.n.], 1985. 58 pp. Reprint of the 1955 ed.

320. Poncet y de Cárdenas, Carolina, and Mirta Aguirre, ed. *Investigaciones y apuntes literarios*. Havana: Editorial Letras Cubanas, 1985. 668 pp.

321. Portuondo, José Antonio. *Capítulos de literatura cubana*. Havana: Editorial Letras Cubanas, 1981. 584 pp.

322. ———. *El contenido social de la literatura cubana*. Mexico City: Centro de Estudios Sociales, El Colegio de México, 1944. 936 pp.

323. Remos y Rubio, Juan Nepomuceno José. *Historia de la literatura cubana*. Miami: Mnemosyne, 1969. 3 vols. Reprint of the 1945 ed.

324. ———. *Resumen de historia de la literatura cubana*. Havana: Molina, 1930. 415 pp.

325. Torrás, Norma, and Magaly Silva, eds. *Lecciones de literatura cubana*. Havana: Editorial Pueblo y Educación, 1977– [vol. 1–3–].

326. Vitier, Cintio. *Crítica cubana*. Havana: Editorial Letras Cubanas, 1988. 570 pp.

General: Sixteenth to Nineteenth Centuries

327. Bueno, Salvador. *La crítica cubana del siglo XIX*. Havana: Editorial Letras Cubanas, 1979. 181 pp.

328. Chacón y Calvo, José María. *Ensayos de literatura cubana*. Madrid: Editorial "Saturnino Calleja," 1922. 277 pp.

329. Fernández de Castro, José Antonio. *Tema negro en las letras de Cuba, 1608–1935*. Havana: Ediciones Mirador, 1943. 95 pp.

330. González del Valle, José Zacarías. *La vida literaria en Cuba, 1836–1840*. Havana: Dirección de Cultura, Secretaría de Educación, 1938. 176 pp.

331. Instituto de Literatura y Lingüística (Academia de Ciencias de Cuba). *Pérfil histórico de las letras cubanas: desde los orígenes hasta 1898*. Havana: Editorial Letras Cubanas, 1983. 501 pp.

332. Iraizoz, Antonio. *La crítica en la literatura cubana*. Havana: Impr. "Avisador Comercial," 1930. 71 pp.

333. Mitjans, Aurelio. *Historia de la literatura cubana: Del Monte, Heredia, Milanés, Saco, Gertrúdis Gómez de Avellaneda, Zenea, etc.*. 2a ed. Madrid: Editorial América, 1918. 389 pp. First ed. (1890) has title *Estudio sobre el movimiento científico y literario de Cuba*.

334. Roig de Leuchsenring, Emilio. *La literatura costumbrista cubana de los siglos XVIII y XIX*. Havana: Oficina del Historiador de la Ciudad de la Habana, 1962– [vol. 1–].

335. Sáinz, Enrique. *La literatura cubana de 1700 a 1790*. Havana: Editorial Letras Cubanas, 1983. 305 pp.

336. Salazar y Roig, Salvador. *Historia de la literatura cubana*. Havana: Impr. Avisador Comercial, 1929. 221 pp.

337. Vitier, Cintio, ed. *La crítica literaria y estética en el siglo XIX cubano*. Havana: Biblioteca Nacional José Martí, Depto. Selección Cubana, 1974. 430 pp.

General: Twentieth Century

338. Arango, Arturo. *Reincidencias*. Havana: Editora Abril, 1990. 137 pp. Critical essays on the revolutionary literary generation.

339. Arcos, Jorge Luis. *Orígenes: la pobreza irradiante*. Havana: Editorial Letras Cubanas, 1994. 195 pp. Discusses the literary movement Grupo Orígenes.

340. Augier, Angel I. *De la sangre en la letra*. Havana: Unión de Escritores y Artistas de Cuba, 1977. 554 pp.

341. Bejel, Emilio. *Escribir en Cuba: entrevistas con escritores cubanos, 1979–1989*. Río Piedras, P.R.: Editorial de la Universidad de Puerto Rico, 1991. 387 pp.

342. Bertot, Lillian. *The Literary Imagination of the Mariel Generation*. Miami: Endowment for Cuban American Studies, Cuban American National Foundation, 1995. 105 pp.

343. Bueno, Salvador. *Medio siglo de literatura cubana, 1902–1952*. Havana: Comisión Nacional Cubana de la UNESCO, 1953. 234 pp.

344. Burness, Donald. *On the Shoulder of Martí: Cuban Literature of the Angolan War*. Colorado Springs, CO: Three Continents Press, 1995. 203 pp.

345. Cámara, Madeline. *Diálogos al pie de la letra*. Havana: Editorial Letras Cubanas, 1988. 137 pp. Interviews with contemporary Cuban authors.

346. ———, ed. *Por una nueva crítica: reflexiones sobre la crítica artístico-literaria en la Revolución*. Havana: Editorial P. de la Torriente, 1988. 98 pp.

347. Cuadra, Angel. *Escritores en Cuba socialista: experiencia y testimonio*. Washington, DC: Cuban American National Foundation, 1986. 49 pp.

348. Entralgo, Elías José. *Perfiles: apuntes críticos sobre literatura cubana contemporánea*. Havana: Editorial "Hermes," 1923. 162 pp.

349. González-Pérez, Armando. *Acercamiento a la literatura afrocubana: ensayos de interpretación*. Miami: Ediciones Universal, 1994. 212 pp.

350. Kutzinski, Vera M. *Sugar's Secrets: Race and the Erotics of Cuban Nationalism*. Charlottesville, VA: University Press of Virginia, 1993. 287 pp.

351. Marinello, Juan. *Contemporáneos: noticia y memoria*. Santa Clara, Cuba: Universidad Central de las Villas, 1964–1976. 2 vols. Vol. 2 published by Unión de Escritores y Artistas de Cuba.

352. Martí, Agenor. *Hablar con ellos*. Santiago, Cuba: Editorial Oriente, 1985. 141 pp. Interviews with contemporary Cuban authors.

353. Miranda, Julio E. *Nueva literatura cubana*. Madrid: Taurus, 1971. 141 pp.

354. Monge Rafuls, Pedro R., ed. *Lo que no se ha dicho*. Jackson Heights, NY: Ollantay Center for the Arts, 1994. 340 pp. Presentations made at two meetings on Cuban writers in exile held in New York in 1989 and 1992.

355. Otero, Lisandro. *Disidencias y coincidencias en Cuba*. Havana: Editorial José Martí, 1984. 132 pp.

356. Pérez Firmat, Gustavo. *The Cuban Condition: Translation and Identity in Modern Cuban Literature*. New York: Cambridge University Press, 1989. 185 pp.

357. Ripoll, Carlos. *La generación del veintitres en Cuba: y otros apuntes sobre el vanguardismo*. New York: Las Américas, 1968. 182 pp.

358. Rousseau, Isel, ed. *Panorama de la literatura cubana, 1959–1984*. Havana: Editorial Letras Cubanas, 1985. 52 pp.

359. Sánchez-Boudy, José. *Historia de la literatura cubana en el exilio*. Miami: Ediciones Universal, 1975– [vol. 1–].

360. Ubieta Gómez, Enrique. *Ensayos de identidad*. Havana: Editorial Letras Cubanas, 1993. 201 pp.

361. Zabala Jaramillo, Luz Elena, and Manuel Cofiño López. *La literatura cubana: brasa que quema al fuego*. Medellín, Colombia: Editorial Ediciones Gráficas, 1985. 224 pp.

362. Zurbano, Roberto. *Los estados nacientes: literatura cubana y postmodernidad*. Havana: Editorial Letras Cubanas, 1996. 74 pp.

Poetry

Poetry: General

363. Augier, Angel I. *Prosa varia*. Havana: Editorial Letras Cubanas, 1982. 499 pp. Critical essays on Cuban poets.

364. Feijóo, Samuel. *Contactos poéticos: plagio, mimetismo, originalidad*. Havana: Unión de Escritores y Artistas de Cuba, 1980. 139 pp.

365. ————. *El son cubano: poesía general*. Havana: Editorial Letras Cubanas, 1986. 310 pp.

366. Fernández de la Vega, Oscar, and Alberto N. Pamies, eds. *Iniciación a la poesía afro-americana*. Miami: Ediciones Universal, 1973. 213 pp.

367. García Garófalo y Mesa, Manuel. *Los poetas villaclareños*. Havana: Arroyo, 1927. 234 pp.

368. Menéndez Alberdi, Adolfo. *La décima escrita*. Havana: Unión de Escritores y Artistas de Cuba, 1986. 482 pp.

369. Morales Gómez, Julio. *Presencia y ausencia de María en la poesía cubana*. Miami: Saeta Ediciones, 1989. 50 pp.

370. Olivera, Otto. *Cuba en su poesía*. Mexico City: Ediciones De Andrea, 1965. 217 pp.

371. Prats Sariol, José. *Por la poesía cubana*. Havana: Unión de Escritores y Artistas de Cuba, 1988. 295 pp.

372. Vitier, Cintio. *Lo cubano en la poesía*. 2a ed. aum. Havana: Instituto del Libro, 1970. 584 pp.

Poetry: Sixteenth to Nineteenth Centuries

373. Arias, Salvador. Tres poetas en la mirilla: Plácido, Milanés, la
     Avellaneda. Havana: Editorial Letras Cubanas, 1981. 146 pp.

374. Calcagno, Francisco. Poetas de color: Plácido, Manzano, Rod-
     ríguez, Echemendía, Silveira, Medina. 4a ed. Havana: Impr. de S.
     S. Spencer, 1887. 110 pp.

375. Chacón y Calvo, José María. Los orígenes de la poesía en Cuba.
     Havana: [s.n.], 1913. 84 pp.

376. Feijóo, Samuel. Sobre los movimientos por una poesía cubana
     hasta 1856. 2a. ed. Santa Clara, Cuba: Universidad Central de Las
     Villas, 1961. 193 pp.

377. García Marruz, Fina. Hablar de la poesía: ensayo. Havana: Edito-
     rial Letras Cubanas, 1986. 441 pp.

378. González del Valle y Carvajal, Emilio Martín, marqués de la Vega
     de Anzó. La poesía lírica en Cuba: apuntes para un libro de bio-
     grafía y de crítica. Barcelona: L. Tasco, 1900. 349 pp.

379. Soler Mirabent, Antonia. Cuatro poetas. Havana: Editorial Acad-
     emia, 1990. 50 pp. M. J. Gutiérrez, A. Hurtado del Valle, U. Cés-
     pedes de Escanaverino, and M. Albaladejo.

380. Valdés Bernal, Sergio. Los indoamericanismos en la poesía
     cubana de los siglos XVII, XVIII y XIX. Havana: Editorial de
     Ciencias Sociales, 1984. 143 pp. 381.

381. Vitier, Cintio. Poetas cubanos del siglo XIX: semblanzas. Havana:
     Unión de Escritores y Artistas de Cuba, 1969. 57 pp.

Poetry: Twentieth Century

382. Bianchi Ross, Ciro. *Las palabras de otro*. Havana: Unión de Es-
     critores y Artistas de Cuba, 1982. 128 pp. Interviews with con-
     temporary Cuban poets.

383. Cuadra, Angel. *Ensayo histórico-literario: la poesía cubana
     frente al comunismo*. Miami: Unidad Nacional Revolucionaria,
     1969. 63 pp.

384. Fernández Retamar, Roberto. *La poesía contemporánea en Cuba, 1927–1953.* Havana: Editorial Orígenes, 1954. 130 pp.

385. Jiménez, José Olivio. *Estudios sobre poesía cubana contemporánea: Regino Boti, Agustín Acosta, Eugenio Florit, Angel Gaztelu, Roberto Fernández Retamar.* New York: Las Américas Pub. Co., 1967. 112 pp.

386. Linares Pérez, Marta. *La poesía pura en Cuba y su evolución.* Madrid: Playor, 1975. 240 pp.

387. López Lemus, Virgilio. *Palabras del trasfondo: estudio sobre el coloquialismo cubano.* Havana: Editorial Letras Cubanas, 1988. 414 pp.

388. López Morales, Eduardo. *Crítica de la razón poética.* Havana: Editorial Letras Cubanas, 1989. 531 pp.

389. Marinello, Juan. *Poética: ensayos en entusiasmo.* Madrid: Espasa-Calpe, 1933. 143 pp.

390. Muñoz, Elías Miguel. *Desde esta orilla: poesía cubana del exilio.* Madrid: Betania, 1988. 76 pp.

391. Orta Ruiz, Jesús. *Décima y folclor: estudio de la poesía y el cantar de los campos de Cuba.* Havana: Unión de Escritores y Artistas de Cuba, 1980. 241 pp.

392. Pereda Valdés, Ildefonso. *Lo negro y lo mulato en la poesía cubana.* Montevideo: Ediciones Ciudadela, 1970. 166 pp.

393. Prats Sariol, José. *Estudios sobre poesía cubana.* Havana: Unión de Escritores y Artistas de Cuba, 1980. 112 pp.

394. Pujalá, Grisel. *Cuatro ensayos sobre poesía cubana.* Coral Gables, FL: La Torre de Papel, 1993. 55 pp.

395. Sánchez Aguilera, Osmar. *Otros pensamientos en La Habana.* Havana: Editorial Letras Cubanas, 1994. 69 pp.

Fiction

Fiction: General

396. Barreda, Pedro. *The Black Protagonist in the Cuban Novel.* Page Bancroft, tr. Amherst, MA: University of Massachusetts Press,

1979. 179 pp. Translation of *La caracterizacion del protagonista negro en la novela cubana.*

397. Bortolussi, Marissa. *El cuento infantil cubano: un estudio crítico.* Madrid: Editorial Pliegos, 1990. 153 pp.

398. Espinosa, Ciro. *Indagación y crítica: novelistas cubanos.* Havana: Cultural, 1940. 175 pp.

399. Garrandés, Alberto. *Tres cuentistas cubanos.* Havana: Editorial Letras Cubanas, 1993. 27 pp. E. Borrero Echeverría, J. Castellanos, and A. Hernández Catá.

400. Loynaz, Dulce María. *Ensayos literarios.* Salamanca: Ediciones de la Universidad de Salamanca, 1993. 201 pp.

401. Luis, William. *Literary Bondage: Slavery in Cuban Narrative.* Austin, TX: University of Texas Press, 1990. 312 pp.

402. Souza, Raymond D. *Major Cuban Novelists: Innovation and Tradition.* Columbia, MO: University of Missouri Press, 1976. 120 pp.

403. Williams, Lorna Valerie. *The Representation of Slavery in Cuban Fiction.* Columbia, MO: University of Missouri Press, 1994. 220 pp.

Fiction: Sixteenth to Nineteenth Centuries

404. Guicharnaud-Tollis, Michèle. *L'émergence du Noir dans le roman cubain du XIXe siècle.* Paris: L'Harmattan, 1991. 594 pp.

405. Rivas, Mercedes. *Literatura y esclavitud en la novela cubana del siglo XIX.* Seville: Escuela de Estudios Hispano-Americanos, 1990. 317 pp.

406. Sosa, Enrique. *La economía en la novela cubana del siglo XIX.* Havana: Editorial Letras Cubanas, 1978. 313 pp.

Fiction: Twentieth Century

407. Alvarez García, Imeldo. *La novela cubana en el siglo XX.* Havana: Editorial Letras Cubanas, 1980. 161 pp.

408. Bernard, Jorge L., and Juan A. Pola, eds. *Quiénes escriben en Cuba: responden los narradores.* Havana: Editorial Letras Cubanas, 1985. 591 pp. Interviews with 46 writers.

409. Cairo Ballester, Ana, ed. *La Revolución del 30 en la narrativa y el testimonio cubanos*. Havana: Editorial Letras Cubanas, 1993. 431 pp.

410. Cuervo Hewitt, Julia. *Aché, presencia africana: tradiciones yoruba-lucumí en la narrativa cubana*. New York: P. Lang, 1988. 302 pp.

411. Fernández Vázquez, Antonio A. *Novelística cubana de la Revolución: testimonio y evocación en las novelas cubanas escritas fuera de Cuba, 1959–1975*. Miami: Ediciones Universal, 1980. 157 pp.

412. Huertas, Begoña. *Ensayo de un cambio: la narrativa cubana de los años '80*. Havana: Casa de las Américas, 1993. 130 pp.

413. Lolo, Eduardo. *Las trampas del tiempo y sus memorias*. Coral Gables, FL: North-South Center, University of Miami, 1991. 116 pp. Critical analysis of José Triana's *Noche de los asesinos*, Heberto Padilla's *Fuera del juego*, and Reinaldo Arenas' *El mundo alucinante*.

414. López Sacha, Francisco. *La nueva cuentística cubana*. Havana: Unión de Escritores y Artistas de Cuba, 1995. 79 pp.

415. Méndez y Soto, E. *Panorama de la novela cubana de la Revolución, 1959–1970*. Miami: Ediciones Universal, 1977. 262 pp.

416. Menton, Seymour. *Prose Fiction of the Cuban Revolution*. Ann Arbor, MI: University Microfilms, 1991. 344 pp. Reprint of the 1975 ed.

417. Montero, Susana A. *La narrativa femenina cubana, 1923–1958*. Havana: Editorial Académica, 1989. 88 pp.

418. Ortega, Julio. *Relato de la utopía: notas sobre narrativa de la Revolución*. Barcelona: La Gaya Ciencia, 1973. 232 pp.

419. Ortiz Domínguez, Pedro. *Temas orientales: ensayo*. Holguín, Cuba: Centro Provincial del Libro y la Literatura, 1990. 89 pp.

420. Phaf, Ineke. *Novelando La Habana: ubicación histórica y perspectiva urbana en la novela cubana de 1959 a 1980*. Madrid: Editorial Orígenes, 1990. 320 pp. Translation of *Havana als Fiktion* (1986).

421. Rodríguez Coronel, Rogelio. *La novela de la Revolución Cubana, 1959–1979*. Havana: Editorial Letras Cubanas, 1986. 312 pp.

422. Toledo Sande, Luis. *Tres narradores agonizantes: tanteos acerca de la obra de Miguel de Carrión, Jesús Castellanos y Carlos Loveira.* Havana: Editorial Letras Cubanas, 1980. 229 pp.

423. Valdés, Bernardo. *Panorama del cuento cubano.* Miami: Ediciones Universal, 1976. 125 pp.

Drama

Drama: General

424. Arrom, José Juan. *Historia de la literatura dramática cubana.* New York: AMS Press, 1973. 132 pp. Reprint of the 1944 ed.

425. Leal, Rine. *Breve historia del teatro cubano.* Havana: Editorial Letras Cubanas, 1980. 188 pp.

426. ———. *La selva oscura.* Havana: Editorial Arte y Literatura, 1975– [vol. 1–]. Vol. 1. *Historia del teatro cubano desde sus orígenes hasta 1868.*

427. Robreño, Eduardo. *Historia del teatro popular cubano.* Havana: Oficina del Historiador de la Ciudad de La Habana, 1961. 93 pp.

428. Tolón, Edwin Teurbe. *Teatro lírico popular de Cuba.* Miami: Ediciones Universal, 1973. 56 pp.

Drama: Twentieth Century

429. Garzón Céspedes, Francisco, ed. *El teatro de participación popular y el teatro de la comunidad: un teatro de sus protagonistas.* Havana: Unión de Escritores y Artistas de Cuba, 1977. 146 pp.

430. González Freire, Natividad. *Teatro cubano, 1927–1961.* Havana: Ministerio de Relaciones Exteriores, 1961. 181 pp.

431. Montes Huidobro, Matías. *Persona, vida y máscara en el teatro cubano.* Miami: Ediciones Universal, 1973. 469 pp.

432. Muguercia, Magaly. *El teatro cubano en vísperas de la Revolución.* Havana: Editorial Letras Cubanas, 1988. 257 pp.

433. ———. *Teatro, en busca de una expresión socialista.* Havana: Editorial Letras Cubanas, 1981. 148 pp.

434. Rodríguez Alemán, Mario, and Rine Leal, ed. *Mural del teatro en Cuba: crítica y crónica.* Havana: Unión de Escritores y Artistas de Cuba, 1990. 312 pp.

E. INDIVIDUAL AUTHORS

Sixteenth to Nineteenth Centuries

435. *Armas y Céspedes, José de,* 1834–1900 (novelist, poet). Un desafío, 1865; Frasquito, 1894–1976.

436. *Balboa, Silvestre de* (poet). Espejo de paciencia, 1608–1988 (Lázaro Santana, ed. 1988 ed.).

437. Sáinz, Enrique. *Silvestre de Balboa y la literatura cubana.* Havana: Editorial Letras Cubanas, 1982. 151 pp.

438. *Balmaseda, Francisco Javier,* 1833–1907 (novelist, playwright, poet). Los ebrios/La familia de Juan Candaya, 1903; Fábulas morales, 1858–1901; El misceláneo, 1894; Los montes de oro, 1866–1874; Obras de Francisco Javier Balmaseda, 1874; Poesías de Don Francisco Javier Balmaseda, 1887; Rimas cubanas, 1846.

439. *Betancourt, José Victoriano,* 1813–1875 (playwright, poet). Las apariencias engañan, 1847.

440. *Betancourt, Luis Victoriano,* 1843–1885 (poet). Artículos de costumbres y poesías, 1867–1929.

441. *Blanchet y Bilton, Emilio,* 1829–1915 (playwright, poet). El anillo de Isabel Tudor, 1866; La conjura de Pisón, 1906; Historia y fantasía, 1912; Ilusiones y realidades, 1885; El libro de las expiaciones, 1885 (La fruta del cercado ajeno [1868], Sabina popea, El conde de Rostopchin, El barón de Montigny, El mulato Ogé, La duquesa de Pompadour, Una aventura de Alfiri); La verdadera culpable, 1906; Vislumbres de poesía, 1912.

442. *Bobadilla, Emilio,* 1862–1921 (novelist, poet). A fuego lento, 1903–1982; Al través de mis nervios, 1903; Baturrillo, 1895; Bulevar arriba, bulevar abajo, 1912; Capirotazos, 1890; Con la capucha vuelta, 1909; En la noche dormida, 1900–1920; En pos de la paz, 1917; Escaramuzas, 1888; Fiebres, 1889; Mostaza, 1885; Muecas, 1908; Novelas en germen, 1900–1906 (La fuga, Dos crepúsculos,

Las larvas, La negra, Quico el sapo, Fiebre de análisis); Obras de
Emilio Bobadillo, 1962 (Vol. 1. Selección de poemas. Vol. 2.
Crítisátira. Vol. 3. A fuego lento); Reflejos de fray Candil, 1886;
Relámpagos, 1884; Rojeces de Marte, 1921; Selección de poemas,
1962; Sintiéndome vivir, 1906; Solfeo, 1893; Triquitraques, 1892;
Vórtice, 1902.

443. Entralgo, Elías José. *Fray Candil*. Havana: Editorial Letras
Cubanas, 1989. 169 pp.

444. *Borrero Echeverría, Esteban,* 1849–1906 (poet, short story
writer). Narraciones, 1979 (Calófilo, Aventura de las hormigas,
Lectura de Pascuas [1899], El ciervo encantado [1905]; Manuel
Cofiño López, ed.); Poesías, 1878.

See also #399.

445. *Borrero, Juana,* 1878–1896 (poet). Poesías, 1966; Poesías y cartas, 1978 (Fina García Marruz, Cintio Vitier, eds.).

446. Borrero, Juana. *Epistolario*. Havana: Academia de Ciencias
de Cuba, Instituto de Literatura y Lingüística, 1966– [vol.
1–]. Most of the letters are addressed to Carlos Pío Uhrbach.

447. Cuza Malé, Belkis E. *El clavel y la rosa: biografía de Juana
Borrero*. Madrid: Ediciones Cultura Hispánica, 1984. 238
pp.

448. *Byrne, Bonifacio,* 1861–1936 (playwright, poet, short story
writer). Efigies, 1897; En medio del camino, 1914; Excéntricas,
1893; Poemas, 1903 (El mendigo, El aldamio, La granja, El reli-
cario, De buena raza, Reina); Poesía y prosa, 1988 (Arturo
Arango, ed.); Selección poética, 1942 (Andrés Piedra-Bueno, ed.).

449. Piedra-Bueno, Andrés de. *Evocación de Byrne y Martí amer-
icanista*. Havana: Instituto Inclán, 1942. 74 pp.

450. *Calcagno, Francisco,* 1827–1903 (novelist, playwright, poet,
short story writer). Aponte, 1901; El aprendiz del zapatero, 1891;
Un casamiento misterioso, 1897–1911; Los crímenes de Concha,
1887; Don Enriquito, 1895; El emisario, 1896; En busca del eslabón, 1888–1983; Historia de un muerto, 1898; Mina/Las Lazo,
1893–1980; Recuerdos de antes de ayer, 1893; Romualdo,
1881–1891; S.I., 1895–1916.

451. *Casal, Julián del,* 1863–1893 (poet). Bustos y rimas, 1893–1993; Crónicas habaneras, 1963 (Angel Augier, ed.); Julián del Casal: sus mejores poemas, 1916; Nieve, 1893; Obra poética, 1982 (Alberto Rocasolano, ed.); Poesías, 1963; Poesías completas, 1945 (Mario Cabrera Saqui, ed.); Poesías completas y pequeños poemas en prosa (en orden cronológico), 1993 (Esperanza Figueroa, ed.); Prosa, 1979 (Emilio de Armas, ed.); Prosas, 1963–1964; Selección de poesías, 1931 (Juan J. Geada y Fernández, ed.); Selected Prose of Julián del Casal, 1949 (Marshall Elbert Nunn, Leonel Antonio de la Cuesta, eds.).

452. Armas, Emilio de. *Casal.* Havana: Editorial Letras Cubanas, 1981. 256 pp.

453. Cabrera, Rosa M., ed. *Vida y obra poética de Julián del Casal.* New York: Las Américas Pub. Co., 1970. 188 pp.

454. Chacón y Calvo, José María. *En torno a un epistolario de Julián del Casal.* Havana: Academia Cubana de la Lengua, 1958. 1 vol. (unpaged).

455. Clay Méndez, Luis Felipe. *Julián del Casal: estudio comparativo de prosa y poesía.* Miami: Ediciones Universal, 1979. 186 pp.

456. Figueroa, Esperanza et al. *Julián del Casal: estudios críticos sobre su obra.* Miami: Ediciones Universal, 1974. 150 pp.

457. Geada y Fernández, Juan J. *Julián del Casal: estudio crítico.* Havana: Editorial Cultural, 1931. 187 pp.

458. Glickman, Robert Jay, ed. *The Poetry of Julián del Casal: A Critical Edition.* Gainesville, FL: University Presses of Florida, 1976– [vol. 1–].

459. Meza y Suárez Inclán, Ramón. *Julián del Casal: estudio biográfico.* Havana: Impr. Avisador Comercial, 1910. 42 pp.

460. Monner Sans, José María. *Julián del Casal y el modernismo hispanoamericano.* Mexico City: Colegio de México, 1952. 273 pp.

461. Montero, Oscar. *Erotismo y representación en Julián del Casal.* Atlanta, GA: Rodopi, 1993. 197 pp.

462. Portuondo, José Antonio. *Angustia y evasión de Julián del Casal.* Havana: Molina, 1937. 37 pp.

463. Sos, Ciriaco. *Julián del Casal; o, Un falsario de la rima.* Havana: Impr. "La Prensa," 1893. 33 pp.

464. Vitier, Cintio and Fina García Marruz. *Estudios críticos.* Havana: Biblioteca Nacional José Martí, 1964. 100 pp.

See also #637.

465. *Castillo de González, Aurelia,* 1842–1920 (poet, short story writer). Escritos, 1913–1918; Fábulas, 1879–1910; Trozos guerreros y apoteosis, 1903; La voluntad de Dios, 1867–1957.

466. *Céspedes de Escanaverino, Ursula,* 1832–1874 (poet). Cantos postreros, 1875; Ecos de la selva, 1861; Poesías, 1948 (Juan J. Remos, ed.).

See also #379.

467. *Del Monte, Domingo,* 1804–1853 (poet, short story writer). Escritos de Domingo del Monte, 1929 (José Antonio Fernández de Castro, ed.); Humanismo y humanitarismo, 1936–1960.

468. Bueno, Salvador. *Domingo del Monte.* Havana: Unión de Escritores y Artistas de Cuba, 1986. 66 pp.

469. Del Monte, Domingo, Alexander Hill Everett and Sophie Andioc Torres, ed. *La correspondance entre Domingo del Monte et Alexander Hill Everett.* Paris: L'Harmattan, 1994. 155 pp. Prefatory material in French; correspondence in Spanish.

470. Del Monte, Domingo, and Domingo Figarola-Caneda, ed. *Centón epistolario de Domingo del Monte.* Havana: Impr. "El Siglo XX," 1923–1957. 7 vols.

471. García, Enildo A. *Indice de los documentos y manuscritos delmontinos en la Biblioteca Otto G. Richter de la Universidad de Miami, Coral Gables, Florida, USA.* Miami: Ediciones Universal, 1979. 62 pp.

472. Mesa Rodríguez, Manuel Isaías. *Apostillas en torno a una gran vida: Domingo del Monte.* Havana: Impr. "El Siglo XX," 1954. 83 pp.

473. *Estrada y Zenea, Ildefonso,* 1826–1912 (playwright). Luisa Sigea, 1878–1906.

474. *Fornaris, José,* 1827–1890 (playwright, poet). Amor y sacrificio, 1866; El arpa del hogar, 1878; Poesías, 1888 (Cantos patrióticos, Cantos sociales, Poetas europeos, Elegías, Cantos tropicales, Odas, Himnos, Romances, Cantos cubanos, Lira íntima, and Cantos del Siboney).

475. *Gómez de Avellaneda y Arteaga, Gertrudis,* 1814–1873 (novelist, playwright, poet). Antología, 1945 (Rosalía de Castro, ed); Antología: poesía y cartas amorosas, 1945–1948 (Ramón Gómez de la Serna, ed.); Antología de la poesía religiosa de la Avellaneda, 1975 (Florinda Alzaga, Ana Rosa Nuñez, eds.); Antología poética, 1983 (Mary Cruz, ed.); El aura blanca, 1863–1959; Autobiography, 1993 (translation of Autobiografía [1914]; Nina M. Scott, tr.); Baltasar, 1908 (translation of Baltasar [1858–1985]; Carlos Bransby, ed. and tr.); Catalina, 1867; Cuauhtemoc, the Last Aztec Emperor, 1898 (translation of Guatimozín, último emperador de Méjico [1846–1946]; Mrs. Wilson W. Blake, tr.); Devocionario nuevo y completísimo en prosa y verso, 1867; Diario de amor, 1928–1993 (Bernardo Callejas, ed.); Diario íntimo, 1945 (Lorenzo Cruz de Fuentes, ed.); El donativo del diablo, 1858; Dos mujeres, 1842; Errores del corazón y otras comedias, 1977 (Errores del corazón [1852], La aventurera [1853], La hija del Rey René [1855], Simpatía y antipatía [1855], Oráculos de Talía [1855]); Mary Cruz, ed.); Espatolino, 1844–1984; Flavio Recaredo, 1851; La hija de las flores, 1852–1859; Leoncia, 1917; Leyendas, novelas y artículos literarios, 1877 (Vol. 1. El artista barquero [1861] Espatolino [1844], Dolores [1860]. Vol. 2. La velada del helecho [1852], La bella toda, La montaña maldita, La flor del angel, La ondina del lago azul [1859], La dama de Amboto, Una anécdota de la vida de Cortés, El aura blanca [1863], La baronesa de Tours, El cacique de Tormequié, and La mujer); El millonario y la maleta, 1870–1981; Obra selecta, 1990 (Mary Cruz, ed.); Obras de doña Gertrudis Gómez de Avellaneda, 1974 (José María Castro y Calvo, ed.); Obras de la Avellaneda, 1914 (Mariano Aramburo y Machado, ed.); Obras literarias, 1869; Poesías, 1841–1852; Poesías escogidas, 1925; Poesías líricas, 1877; Poesías selectas, 1968 (Benito Varela Jácome, ed.); Sab, 1993 (Translation of Sab [1841–1993]: Nina M. Scott, tr.); Serenata de Cuba, 1980; Sus mejores poesías, 1953 (María Rosa Tarralba, ed.); Tradiciones, 1984 (Mary Cruz, ed.); Tragedias, 1985 (Alfonso Munio [1844], El príncipe de Viana [1844], Egilona [1845], Saúl [1849], Baltasar [1858]; Mary Cruz, ed.); Los tres amores [1858]; La verdad vence apariencias, 1852.

476. Alzaga, Florinda. *Las ansias de infinito en la Avellaneda.* Miami: Ediciones Universal, 1979. 127 pp.

477. Alzaga, Florinda and Ana Rosa Núñez. *Ensayo de diccionario del pensamiento vivo de la Avellaneda*. Miami: Ediciones Universal, 1975. 88 pp.

478. Aramburo y Machado, Mariano, ed. *Personalidad literaria de doña Gertrudis Gómez de Avellaneda*. Madrid: Impr. Teresiana, 1898. 285 pp.

479. Ballesteros, Mercedes. *Vida de la Avellaneda*. Madrid: [s.n.], 1949. 134 pp.

480. Bravo-Villasante, Carmen. *Una vida romántica: la Avellaneda*. Barcelona: Editora Distribuidora Hispano Americana, 1967. 251 pp.

481. Bravo-Villasante, Carmen, Gastón Baquero and José A. Escarpanter. *Gertrudis Gómez de Avellaneda: conferencias*. Madrid: Fundación Universitaria Española, 1974. 80 pp.

482. Cabrera, Rosa M., and Gladys Zaldívar, eds. *Homenaje a Gertrudis Gómez de Avellaneda: memorias del simposio en el centenario de su muerte*. Miami: Ediciones Universal, 1981. 353 pp.

483. Carbonell, José Manuel. *La más fermosa: historia de un soneto*. Havana: Siglo XX, 1917. 383 pp.

484. Cotarelo y Mori, Emilio. *La Avellaneda y sus obras: ensayo biográfico y crítico*. Madrid: Tip. de Archivos, 1930. 450 pp.

485. ———. *Una tragedia real de la Avellaneda*. Madrid: Impr. Municipal, 1926. 27 pp.

486. Figarola-Caneda, Domingo and Emilia Boxhorn, ed. *Gertrudis Gómez de Avellaneda: biografía, bibliografía e iconografía*. Madrid: Sociedad General Española de Librería, 1929. 292 pp.

487. Harter, Hugh A. *Gertrudis Gómez de Avellaneda*. Boston, MA: Twayne, 1981. 182 pp.

488. Lazo, Raimundo. *Gertrudis Gómez de Avellaneda: la mujer y la poetisa lírica*. Mexico City: Porrúa, 1978. 106 pp. Reprint of the 1972 ed.

489. Marquina, Rafael. *Gertrudis Gómez de Avellaneda: la peregrina*. Havana: Editorial Trópico, 1939. 241 pp.

490. Martínez Bello, Antonio M. *Dos musas cubanas: Gertrudis Gómez de Avellaneda, Luisa Pérez de Zambrana*. Havana: P. Fernández, 1954. 55 pp.

491. Valbuena, Segundo. *Un centenario, injusticia patriótica y desastre poético: crítica de actualidad*. Havana: J. Montero, 1914. 89 pp.

See also #143, #373.

492. *Guerrero y Pallarés, Teodoro,* 1820–1905 (novelist, playwright, poet). Al calor del hogar, 1886; Antomía del corazón, 1867; La cabeza y el corazón, 1871; Entre dos amores, 1900; El escabel de la fortuna, 1876; La escala del poder, 1855; Fábulas en acción, 1877; Fea y pobre, 1857; La Habana por fuera, 1866; Una historia de lágrimas, 1868; Impresiones y cantares, 1892; El libro de la familia, 1879; Las llaves, 1877; Madrid por dentro, 1872; La nube negra, 1874; Una perla en el fango, 1873; Tales padres, tales hijos, 1854; Las trece noches de Carmen, 1877; El vellocino de oro, 1872.

493. *Heredia, José Maria,* 1803–1839 (novelist, playwright, poet). Antología Herediana, 1939 (Emilio Valdés y de Latorre, ed.); Cantos patrióticos, 1916; En el destierro, 1937; Florilegio poético, 1942; Niágara y otros textos, 1990 (Angel I. Augier, ed.); No sabemos vivir, 1953; Obras poéticas, 1875 (Vol. 1. Poesías.—vol. 2. Teatro); Pequeña antología, 1939 (José María Chacón y Calvo, ed.); Poesías, 1825–1990; Poesías completas, 1940–1985 (Angel Aparicio Laurencio, ed.); Poesías de Heredia traducidas a otros idiomas, 1940 (Francisco González del Valle, ed.); Poesías, discursos y cartas, 1939 (María Lacoste de Arufe [et al.], eds.; Poesías líricas, 1832–1920; Prédicas de libertad, 1936; Prosas, 1980 (Romualdo Santos, ed.); Revisiones literarias, 1947 (José María Chacón y Calvo, ed.); Selected Poems in English Translation, 1970 (Angel Aparicio Laurencio, ed.); Selections from the Poems of Don José María Heredia, 1844 (James Kennedy, ed. and tr.); Sila, 1825; Sonnets from the Trophies, 1906 (Translated from Los trofeos; Edward Robeson Taylor, ed. and tr.); Tiberio, 1827; Trabajos desconocidos y olvidados de José María Heredia, 1972 (Angel Aparicio Laurencio, ed.); The Trophies With Other Sonnets, 1929–1978 (John Myers O'Hara, John Hervey, Frank Sewall, tr.); Versos, 1960.

494. Aparicio Laurencio, Angel. *¿Es Heredia el primer escritor romántico en lengua española?* Miami: Ediciones Universal, 1988. 46 pp.

495. Augier, Angel I. *Reencuentro y afirmación del poeta Heredia*. Havana: Molina, 1940. 31 pp.

496. Chacón y Calvo, José María. *El horacianismo en la poesía de Heredia*. Havana: Molina, 1939. 63 pp.

497. Chacón y Calvo, José María and Salvador Arias, ed. *Estudios heredianos*. Havana: Editoral Letras Cubanas, 1980. 185 pp.

498. Díaz, Lomberto. *Heredia: primer romántico hispanoamericano*. Montevideo: Ediciones Geminis, 1973. 188 pp.

499. Esténger, Rafael. *Heredia: la incomprensión de sí mismo*. Havana: Editorial Trópico, 1938. 229 pp.

500. Garcerán de Vall, Julio. *Heredia y la libertad*. Miami: Ediciones Universal, 1978. 345 pp.

501. González, Manuel Pedro. *José María Heredia: primogénito del romanticismo hispano*. Mexico City: Colegio de México, 1955. 158 pp.

502. González del Valle, Francisco. *Cronología herediana, 1803–1839*. Havana: Impr. de Montalvo y Cárdenas, 1938. 331 pp.

503. Ince, Walter Newcombe. *Heredia*. Atlantic Highlands, NJ: Humanities Press, 1979. 151 pp.

504. Lezama Lima, José et al. *José María Heredia*. Toluca, Mex.: Dirección del Patrimionio Cultural y Artístico del Estado de México, 1979. 147 pp.

505. Mejía Ricart, Gustavo Adolfo. *José María Heredia y sus obras*. Havana: Molina, 1941. 364 pp.

506. Páez, Alfonso E. *Recordando a Heredia: estudio crítico*. Havana: Cultural, 1939. 198 pp.

507. Rangel, Nicolás. *Nuevos datos para la biografía de José María Heredia*. Havana: Impr. y Librería "El Universo," 1930. 43 pp.

508. Toussaint, Manuel. *Bibliografía mexicana de Heredia*. Mexico City: Depto. de Información para el Extranjero, Secretaría de Relaciones Exteriores, 1953. 146 pp.

See also #143.

509. *Heredia, Nicolás,* 1855–1901 (novelist, poet). Un hombre de negocios, 1883; Leonela, 1893–1977; Puntos de vista, 1892.

510. *Luaces, Joaquín Lorenzo,* 1826–1867 (playwright, poet). Aristodemo, 1867–1919; Arturo de Osberg, 1867–1983; El becerro de oro, 1859–1985; Comedias, 1984 (Francisco Garzón Céspedes, Carlos Espinosa Domínguez, eds.); Poesías, 1857–1909; Poesías escogidas, 1981 (Sergio Chaple, ed.); Teatro, 1964 (El mendigo rojo [1859], El becerro de oro [1859]).

See also #143.

511. *Madan y García, Augusto E.,* 1853–1915 (playwright, poet). El anillo de Fernando IV, 1877; Bermudo, 1875; El calvario de los tontos, 1880; El cáncer social, 1905; El capitán Amores, 1879; Deber y afecto en contienda, 1877; La escala del crimen, 1877 (with Rafael María Liern y Cerach); Este coche se vende, 1876; Estudiantes y alguaciles, 1880; Galileo, 1875; Genio y figura hasta la sepultura, 1875–1900; El gran suplicio, 1875; La granadina, 1890 (with Rafael María Liern y Cerach); Obras dramáticas, 1879; Pablo y Virginia, 1880; Peraltilla, 1880; Percances matrimoniales, 1876; La perla de Portugal, 1880; La piel del tigre, 1877; El puñal de los celos, 1875; Las redes del amor, 1875; El rey mártir, 1894; El rival de un rey, 1877; Rosa, 1876.

512. *Malpica de la Barca, Domingo,* 1836–1894 (novelist). En el cafetal, 1890–1982.

513. *Manzano, Juan Francisco,* 1797–1854 (playwright, poet). Autobiografía, cartas y versos, 1937–1970 (José L. Franco, ed.); Obras, 1972–1985; Poems by a Slave in the Island of Cuba, 1840 (Richard Robert Madden, tr.); Zafira, 1842–1962.

514. Friol, Roberto. *Suite para Juan Francisco Manzano.* Havana: Editorial Arte y Literatura, 1977. 236 pp.

See also #374.

515. *Martí, José,* 1853–1895 (novelist, playwright, poet, short story writer). Amistad funesta/Lucía Jerez, 1885–1994; Antología, 1981 (Reinaldo Sánchez, ed.); Antología mayor, 1995 (Carlos Ripoll, ed.); Antología mínima, 1972 (Pedro Alvarez Tabío, ed.); Con los pobres

de la tierra, 1991 (Julio E. Miranda, Hugo Achugar, Cintio Vitier, eds.); La edad de oro, 1889–1992; Ensayos y crónicas, 1995 (José Olivio Jiménez, ed.); Escritos desconocidos, 1971 (Carlos Ripoll, ed.); Flor y lava (discursos, juicios, correspondencias), 1910 (Américo Lugo, ed.); Ideario, 1987 (Cintio Vitier, Fina García Marruz, eds.); Ismaelillo, 1882–1994; Letras fieras, 1981–1985 (Roberto Fernández Retamar, ed.); Obra literaria, 1978–1986 (Cintio Vitier, Fina García Marruz, eds.); Obras completas de Martí, 1918; Obras escogidas, 1953–1981; Obras martianas, 1987 (Juan Marinello et al., eds.); Páginas de Martí, 1963 (Fryda Schultz de Mantovani, ed.); Páginas escogidas, 1921–1994 (Various eds.); Páginas literarias (Poesía, cuentos, crónicas y teatro), 1969 (Angel A. Castro, Dorothy Veliz Benson, eds.); Páginas olvidadas de Martí, 1953 (Rafael Heliodoro Valle, ed.); Pensamientos, 1921 (Alfonso Hernández Catá, ed.); Pensamientos y versos, 1991 (Luis G. Villaverde, Alcalá Galiano, eds.); Poesía completa, 1993 (Cintio Vitier, Fina Garcia Marruz, Emilio de Armas, eds.); Poesía de amor, 1985 (Luis Toledo Sande, ed.); Poesía mayor/Poesías, 1928–1985 (Ismaelillo [1882], Versos sencillos [1891], La edad de oro, Versos libres [1913], Flores del destierro, Otros poemas; Juan Marinello, ed.); Poesías completas, 1953 (Rafael Esténger, ed.); Raíz y ala: una antología de Martí para la juventud, 1954–1980 (Anita Arroyo, ed.); Sus mejores páginas, 1950 (Jorge Mañach, ed.); Teatro, 1981 (Rine Leal, ed.); Versos, 1914–1971; Versos libres, 1913–1994; Versos sencillos, 1891–1994.

516. Ancet, Jacques et al. *José Martí*. Madrid: Instituto de Cooperación Iberoamericana, 1995. 107 pp.

517. Arce, Reinerio. *Religión: poesía del mundo venidero—implicaciones teológicas en la obra de José Martí*. Quito: Ediciones CLAI, 1996. 138 pp.

518. Armas, Emilio de. *Un deslinde necesario*. Havana: Editorial Arte y Literatura, 1978. 175 pp. Essay on Martí's *Versos libres* and *Flores del destierro*.

519. Augier, Angel I. *Acción y poesía en José Martí*. Havana: Centro de Estudios Martianos, 1982. 418 pp.

520. Baralt, Blanche Zacharie de. *El Martí que yo conocí*. Havana: Editorial Pueblo y Educación, 1990. 103 pp. Reprint of the 1980 (2d) ed.

521. Becali, Ramón. *Martí corresponsal*. Havana: Editorial Orbe, 1976. 321 pp.

522. Bernal, Emilia. *Martí por sí mismo*. Havana: Impr. Molina, 1934. 63 pp.

523. Carbonell, Néstor Leonelo. *Martí: su vida y su obra*. Havana: Impr. "El Siglo XX," 1923. 226 pp.

524. Cepeda, Rafael. *Lo ético-cristiano en la obra de José Martí*. Matanzas, Cuba: Centro de Información y Estudio Augusto Cotto, 1992. 206 pp.

525. Dill, Hans Otto. *El ideario literario y estético de José Martí*. Havana: Casa de las Américas, 1975. 204 pp.

526. Domínguez Hernández, Marlen A. *José Martí: ideario lingüístico*. Havana: Editorial Pablo de la Torriente, 1990. 68 pp.

527. ———. *Lengua y crítica en José Martí*. Havana: Editorial Pablo de la Torriente, 1990. 111 pp.

528. Esteban, Angel. *José Martí: el alma alerta*. Peligros, Spain: Comares, 1995. 255 pp.

529. Ette, Ottmar. *José Martí*. Tübingen, Ger.: Niemeyer, 1991– [vol. 1–].

530. Fernández de la Torriente, Gastón J. *Temas e imágenes en los "Versos sencillos" de José Martí*. Miami: Ediciones Universal, 1977. 145 pp.

531. Fernández Retamar, Roberto. *José Martí: la encarnación de un pueblo*. Buenos Aires: Almagesto, 1993. 77 pp.

532. ———. *Naturalidad y modernidad en la literatura martiana*. Montevideo: Facultad de Humanidades y Ciencias, Universidad de la República, 1986. 30 pp.

533. Gómez Gómez, Fuco. *Martí: guía de almas—biografía-homenaje*. Havana: [s.n.], 1953. 118 pp.

534. Goodnough, David. *José Martí: Cuban Patriot and Poet*. Springfield, NJ: Enslow Publishers, 1996. 128 pp.

535. Hernández Catá, Alfonso. *Mitología de Martí*. Miami: Mnemosyne Publishing, 1970. 441 pp. Reprint of the 1929 ed.

536. Hernández-Chiroldes, J. Alberto. *Los "Versos sencillos" de José Martí: análisis crítico*. Miami: Ediciones Universal, 1993. 321 pp.

537. Iñiguez, Dalia, ed. *Homenaje en prosa y verso a José Martí*. Havana: Ucar, García, 1953. 58 pp.

538. Jardines, Alexis, and Jorge C. González. *Reflexiones en torno al espiritualismo de José Martí*. Havana: Editorial de Ciencias Sociales, 1990. 48 pp.

539. Jiménez, José Olivio. *José Martí, poesía y existencia*. Mexico City: Editorial Oasis, 1983. 154 pp.

540. ———. *La raíz y el ala: aproximaciones críticas a la obra literaria de José Martí*. Valencia, Spain: Pre-Textos, 1993. 306 pp.

541. Jorge, Elena. *José Martí: el método de su crítica literaria*. Havana: Editorial Letras Cubanas, 1984. 281 pp.

542. Lazo, Raimundo. *Martí y su obra literaria*. Havana: Impr. La Propagandista, 1929. 159 pp.

543. Lizaso, Félix, and Ernesto Ardura. *Personalidad e ideas de José Martí*. Havana: [s.n.], 1954. 73 pp.

544. Llaverías, Joaquín. *Martí en el Archivo Nacional*. Havana: Academia de la Historia de Cuba, 1945. 58 pp.

545. Lolo, Eduardo. *Mar de Espuma: Martí y la literatura infantil*. Miami: Ediciones Universal, 1995. 237 pp.

546. Marinello, Juan. *El caso literario de José Martí: motivos de centenario*. Havana: [s.n.], 1954. 59 pp.

547. ———. *Dieciocho ensayos martianos*. Ed. aum. Havana: Editora Política, 1981. 364 pp. Previous ed. (1965) has title *Once ensayos martianos*.

548. ———. *José Martí*. Madrid: Júcar, 1976. 227 pp. Reprint of the 1972 ed.

549. Marinello, Juan, Ramón Losada Aldana and Trinidad Pérez, eds. *Obras martianas*. Caracas: Biblioteca Ayacucho, 1987. 322 pp.

550. Martí, José. *Cartas familares: selección*. Santiago, Cuba: Editorial Oriente, 1981. 121 pp. Reprint of the 1953 ed.

551. Martí, José, and Daisy Cué, ed. *Visión íntima: cartas escogidas*. Santiago, Cuba: Oriente, 1995. 217 pp.

552. Martí, José, and Félix Lizaso, ed. *Epistolario*. Havana: Editorial Cultural, 1930–1931. 3 vols.

553. Martí, José, Luis García Pascual and Enrique H. Moreno Plá, eds. *Epistolario*. Havana: Editorial de Ciencias Sociales, 1993. 5 vols.

554. Méndez, Manuel Isidro. *Martí: estudio crítico-biográfico*. Havana: Impr. P. Fernández, 1941. 310 pp.

555. Miranda Cancela, Elina. *José Martí y el mundo clásico*. Mexico City: Facultad de Filosofía y Letras, Universidad Nacional Autónoma de México, 1990. 82 pp.

556. Morales, Carlos Javier. *La poética de José Martí y su contexto*. Madrid: Editorial Verbum, 1994. 571 pp.

557. Oraá, Francisco de. *La espada en el sol: contribución a una lectura "poética" de los versos de Martí*. Havana: Unión de Escritores y Artistas de Cuba, 1989. 89 pp.

558. Portuondo, José Antonio. *Martí, escritor revolucionario*. Havana: Editora Política, 1982. 328 pp.

559. Pujol, Louis. *Tres visiones del amor en la obra de José Martí*. Miami: Ediciones Universal, 1989. 85 pp.

560. Rexach, Rosario. *Estudios sobre Martí*. Madrid: Playor, 1985. 176 pp.

561. Ricardo, Yolanda, ed. *Martí en los Henríquez Ureña*. Havana: Instituto de Literatura y Lingüística de la Academia de Ciencias de Cuba, 1995. 248 pp. See also #1531, #1533.

562. Ripoll, Carlos. *Indice universal de la obra de José Martí*. New York: E. Torres, 1971. 263 pp.

563. ———. *José Martí: letras y huellas desconocidas*. New York: E. Torres, 1976. 143 pp.

564. ———. *Páginas sobre José Martí.* New York: Editorial Dos Ríos, 1995. 176 pp.

565. Rotker, Susana. *Fundación de una escritura: las crónicas de José Martí.* Havana: Casa de las Américas, 1992. 290 pp.

566. Saldaña, Excilia. *Flor para amar: apuntes sobre la mujer en la obra de Martí.* Havana: Editorial Gente Nueva, 1980. 69 pp.

567. Santana González, Gilda. *Apuntes para el estudio de la crítica teatral de José Martí.* Havana: Universidad de La Habana, Depto. de Actividades Culturales, 1985. 115 pp.

568. Santí, Enrico Mario. *Pensar a José Martí: notas para un centenario.* Boulder, CO: Society of Spanish and Spanish-American Studies, 1996. 138 pp.

569. Santos Moray, Mercedes. *Martí: amigo y compañero.* Havana: Editorial de Ciencias Sociales, 1983. 216 pp.

570. Schulman, Iván A. *Relecturas martianas: narración y nación.* Atlanta, GA: Rodopi, 1994. 98 pp.

571. ———. *Símbolo y color en la obra de José Martí.* 2a ed. Madrid: Editorial Gredos, 1970. 497 pp.

572. Spain, Ministerio de Cultura. *José Martí: obra y vida.* Madrid: Siruela, 1995. 221 pp.

573. Teja, Ada María. *La poesía de José Martí entre naturaleza e historia: estudios sobre la antitésis y la síntesis.* Cosenza, Italy: Marra, 1990. 228 pp.

574. Val Julián, Carmen, ed. *Soy el amor, soy el verso: José Martí créateur—ouvrage collectif.* Paris: Ellipses, 1995. 159 pp.

575. Vasconcelos, Ramón. *Predestinación de Martí.* Havana: Ucar, García, 1939. 128 pp.

576. Vitier, Cintio, and Fina García Marruz. *Temas martianos.* Río Piedras, P.R.: Ediciones Huracán, 1981. 352 pp. Reprint of the 1969 ed.

See also #300, #449, #1068, #1351.

577. *Matamoros, Mercedes,* 1858–1906 (playwright, poet). Obra poética, 1985; Poesías completas, 1892; Sonetos, 1902.

578. *Medina, Tristán de Jesús,* 1831–1886 (novelist, poet). Narraciones, 1990 (Roberto Friol, ed.).

579. *Mendive y Daumy, Rafael María,* 1821–1886 (playwright, poet). Poesías, 1860–1883; Poesías escogidas, 1977 (Rafael del Valle, ed.).

    580. Chaple, Sergio. *Rafael María de Mendive: definición de un poeta.* Havana: Unión de Escritores y Artistas de Cuba, 1973. 74 pp.

    581. Salazar y Roig, Salvador. *Rafael María de Mendive.* Havana: Impr. de A. Miranda, 1915. 43 pp.

    See also #143.

582. *Meza y Suárez Inclán, Ramón,* 1861–1911 (novelist, playwright, short story writer). Carmela, 1887–1978; Don Aniceto el Tendero, 1889–1961; El duelo de mi vecino, 1886–1980; Flores y calabazas, 1886; Mi tío el empleado, 1887–1993; Novelas breves, 1975 (El duelo de mi vecino [1886], Don Aniceto el Tendero [1889], Ultimas páginas [1891]; Ernesto García Alzola, ed.); Una sesión de hipnotismo (comedia), 1891.

    583. González Freixas, Manuel Alberto. *Sociedad y tipos en las novelas de Ramón Meza y Suárez Inclán.* Miami: Ediciones Universal, 1985. 184 pp.

    See also #314.

584. *Milanés, Jose Jacinto,* 1814–1863 (playwright, poet). Algunas poesías, 1937; Antología lírica, 1975–1990 (Salvador Arias, ed.); Obras, 1846–1865; Obras completas, 1920–1963; Poesía y teatro, 1981 (Salvador Arias, ed.); Poesías, 1920.

    585. González, Tomás. *Delirios y visiones de José Jacinto Milanés.* Havana: Unión de Escritores y Artistas de Cuba, 1988. 95 pp.

    586. UNESCO. *Homenaje a José Jacinto Milanés.* Havana: Comisión Nacional Cubana de la Unesco, 1964. 201 pp.

    See also #143, #373.

587. *Morúa Delgado, Martín,* 1856–1910 (novelist, poet). La familia Unzúazu, 1901–1975; Obras completas, 1957; Sofía, 1891–1977.

588. *Nápoles Fajardo, Juan Cristóbal,* 1829–1861 (playwright, poet). El Cucalambé, 1964–1984 (selección de Rumores del hórmigo; Marino Pérez Durán, ed.); Del epítome a las poesías completas de El Cucalambé, 1992 (Carlos Tamayo Rodríguez, ed.); Poesías completas, 1974–1983 (Jesús Orta Ruiz, ed.); Rumores del hórmigo, 1856–1959.

589. *Palma, José Joaquín,* 1844–1911 (poet). Melancolías, 1912; Patria y mujer, 1916; Poesías, 1882–1962.

590. Azcuy Alón, Fanny. *José Joaquín Palma: toda una vida.* Havana: Academia de la Historia de Cuba, 1948. 112 pp.

591. Morales, José Ramón. *Aproximación poética a J. J. Palma.* Bayamo, Cuba: Ediciones Bayamo, 1995. 112 pp.

592. *Palma, Ramón de,* 1812–1860 (novelist, playwright, poet, short story writer). Aves de paso, 1841; Cuentos cubanos, 1928 (Antonio María Eligio de la Puente, ed.).

593. *Pérez de Zambrana, Luisa,* 1835–1922 (novelist, poet). Angélica y Estrella, 1957; Antología poética, 1977 (Sergio Chaple, ed.); Elegías familiares, 1937; Poesías, 1856–1920; Poesías completas, 1957 (Angel Huete, ed.). See also #490.

594. *Pita y Borroto, Santiago Antonio,* d. 1755 (playwright). El príncipe jardinero y fingido Cloridiano, 1951–1989 (José Juan Arrom, ed.).

595. Smith, Octavio. *Para una vida de Santiago Pita.* Havana: Editorial Letras Cubanas, 1978. 145 pp.

596. *Plácido,* 1809–1844 (poet). Coleción de las mejores poesías de Plácido, 1858; Musa cubana, 1910?; Los poemas más representativos de Plácido, 1976 (Frederick S. Stimson, Humberto E. Robles, eds.); Poesías, 1847; Poesías, 1980 (Roberto Friol, ed.); Poesías completas de Plácido, 1850–1970; Poesías de Plácido, 1855–1904; Poesías escogidas, 1842–1977; Poesías selectas de Plácido, 1930.

597. Casals, Jorge. *Plácido como poeta cubano: ensayo biográfico crítico.* Havana: Ministerio de Educación, Dirección de Cultura, 1944. 199 pp.

598. Castellanos, Jorge. *Plácido: poeta social y político.* Miami: Ediciones Universal, 1984. 141 pp.

599. Figarola-Caneda, Domingo. *Plácido (poeta cubano): contribución histórico-literaria.* Havana: Impr. "El Siglo XX," 1922. 276 pp.

600. García Garófalo y Mesa, Manuel. *Plácido: poeta y mártir.* Mexico City: Ediciones Botas, 1938. 295 pp.

601. Laso de los Vélez, Pedro. *Plácido: su biografía, juicio crítico y análisis de sus más escogidas poesías.* Barcelona: Impr. Barcelonesa, 1875. 174 pp.

602. Pérez del Río, Luis, and Adis Vilorio Iglesias. *¿Es falsa la confesión de Plácido?* Santiago, Cuba: Editorial Oriente, 1994. 85 pp.

See also #143, #373, #374.

603. *Poey, Felipe,* 1799–1891 (poet). Obras literarias de Felipe Poey, 1888.

604. *Sarachaga, Ignacio,* 1852–1900 (playwright). Teatro, 1990 (Rine Leal, ed.).

605. *Sellén, Antonio,* 1838–1889 (poet). Poesías de Antonio Sellén, 1911.

606. *Sellén, Francisco,* 1836–1907 (playwright, poet). Las apuestas de Zuleika, 1901; Cantos de la patria, 1900; Hatuey, 1891; Libro íntimo, 1865; La muerte de Demóstenes, 1926; Poesías, 1890.

607. *Suárez y Romero, Anselmo,* 1818–1878 (novelist). Francisco, el ingenio/Las delicias del campo, 1880–1974.

608. Meson, Danusia Leah. *Historia y ficción: el caso "Francisco".* Buenos Aires: Ediciones de la Flor, 1994. 202 pp.

609. *Tanco Bosmeniel, Felix M.,* 1797–1871 (novelist, poet). Petrona y Rosalía, 1838–1980.

610. *Tejera, Diego Vicente,* 1848–1903 (poet, short story writer). Obras, 1932–1936 (Vol. 1. Poesías—Vol. 2. Prosa literaria); Un poco de prosa, 1895; Poesía y prosa, 1981 (Salvador Bueno, ed.); Poesías, 1893–1932; Poesías completas, 1879; Un ramo de violetas, 1877; Textos escogidos, 1981 (Carlos del Toro, ed.).

611. Tejera, Eduardo J. *Diego Vicente Tejera, 1848–1903: patriota, poeta y pensador cubano—ensayo biográfico y recopilación parcial de su obra poética y política.* Madrid: E. J. Tejera, 1981. 300 pp.

612. *Tolón, Miguel Teurbe,* 1820–1857 (novelist, playwright, poet). ¡A Yumurí!, 1847; Flores y espinas, 1858; Leyendas cubanas, 1856; Luz y sombra, 1856; Lola Guara, 1846; ¡Una noticia!, 1847; Preludios, 1841.

613. Carbonell, José Manuel. *Miguel Teurbe Tolón: poeta y conspirador.* Havana: Siglo XX, 1924. 55 pp.

See also #139.

614. *Uhrbach, Carlos Pío,* 1872–1897 (poet). Camafeos, 1894; Gemelas, 1894 (with Federico Uhrbach); Oro, 1907 (with Federico Uhrbach).

615. *Uhrbach, Federico,* 1873–1932 (poet). Flores de hielo, 1894; Gemelas, 1894 (with Carlos Pío Uhrbach); Oro, 1907 (with Carlos Pío Uhrbach).

616. *Valdés Machuca, Ignacio,* 1800–1851 (playwright, poet). Cantatas, 1829.

617. *Varela, Félix,* 1788–1853 (novelist). Jicoténcal, 1826–1995 (Luis Leal, Rodolfo J. Cortina, eds.); Obras, 1900; Obras de Félix Varela, 1991 (Eduardo Torres-Cuevas, Jorge Ibarra, Mercedes García, eds.).

618. Rexach, Rosario. *Dos figuras cubanas y una sola actitud: Félix Varela y Morales (Habana, 1788-San Agustín, 1853), Jorge Mañach y Robato (Sagua la Grande, 1898-Puerto Rico, 1861).* Miami: Ediciones Universal, 1991. 258 pp.

See also #300.

619. *Varona, Enrique José,* 1849–1933 (playwright, poet). Artículos periodísticos, 1949 (Elías José Entralgo, ed.); Con el eslabón, 1918–1927; De mis recuerdos, 1917; Desde mi belvedere, 1907–1938; Enrique José Varona, 1949 (Medardo Vitier, ed.); Lecturas, 1914; Obras de Enrique José Varona, 1936 (Elías José Entralgo, Medardo Vitier, Roberto Agramonte y Pichardo, eds.); Odas anacreónticas, 1868; Paisajes cubanos, 1879; Poemitas en

prosa, 1921; Poesías escogidas, 1983 (Alberto Rocasolano, ed.);
Textos escogidos, 1968–1974 (Raimundo Lazo, ed); Varona [se-
lecciones], 1943 (José Antonio Fernández de Castro, ed.).

620. Entralgo, Elías José. *Algunas facetas de Varona.* Havana:
Comisión Nacional Cubana de la Unesco, 1965. 321 pp.

621. Entralgo, Elías José, Medardo Vitier and Roberto Agramonte y Pichardo. *Enrique José Varona: su vida, su obra y
su influencia.* Havana: Cultural, 1937. 284 pp.

622. Mañach, Jorge. *Semblante histórico de Varona.* Havana:
Impr. "El Siglo XX," 1949. 34 pp.

623. Sánchez-Boudy, José. *Enrique José Varona y Cuba.* Miami:
Ediciones Universal, 1990. 122 pp.

624. *Vélez y Herrera, Ramón,* 1809–1886 (novelist, playwright, poet).
Los dos novios en los baños de San Diego, 1843; Elvira de
Oquendo/Los amores de una guajira, 1840; Flores de otoño, 1849;
Poesías, 1833–1838; Romances cubanos, 1856.

625. *Villaverde, Cirilo,* 1812–1894 (novelist, short story writer). Cecilia
Valdés/Angel's Hill/The Quadroon, 1935–1962 (Translation of Cecilia Valdés/La loma del Angel [1839–1992]; Sydney G. Gest, tr.);
Dos amores, 1858–1980; El guajiro, 1842–1890; La peineta cal-
ada/La tejedora de sombreros de yarey, 1962–1979; El penitente,
1844–1925; La joven de la flecha de oro y otros relatos, 1840–1984.

626. Alvarez García, Imeldo, ed. *Acerca de Cirilo Villaverde.* Havana: Editorial Letras Cubanas, 1982. 430 pp.

627. González, Reynaldo. *Contradanzas y latigazos.* Nueva ed.,
con un apendice valorativo de Manuel Moreno Fraginals.
Havana: Editorial Letras Cubanas, 1992. 383 pp. Critical in-
terpretation of Cecilia Valdés.

628. Hernández Azaret, Josefa de la Concepción. *Los personajes
femeninos en "Cecilia Valdés".* Santiago, Cuba: Dirección
de Información Científico-Técnica, Universidad de Oriente,
1980. 55 pp.

629. Morúa Delgado, Martín. *Impresiones literarias: las novelas
del señor Villaverde.* Nueva ed. Havana: Impr. Nosotros,
1957. 180 pp.

630. Sánchez, Julio C. *La obra novelística de Cirilo Villaverde.* Madrid: De Orbe Novo, 1973. 215 pp.

631. Santovenia y Echaide, Emeterio S. *Personajes y paisajes de Villaverde.* Havana: [s.n.], 1953. 135 pp.

632. UNESCO. *Homenaje a Cirilo Villaverde.* Havana: Comisión Nacional Cubana de la Unesco, 1964. 345 pp.

633. *Zenea, Juan Clemente,* 1832–1871 (poet). Diario de un mártir y otros poemas, 1871–1972 (Angel Aparicio Laurencio, ed.); Nueva colección de poesías completas, 1909; Poemas selectos, 1944 (Mariano Brull, ed.); Poesía, 1966–1989 (José Lezama Lima, ed.); Poesías, 1855–1936 (Mario Cabrera y Saqui, ed.); Poesías completas, 1872 (Cantos de la tarde [1860], Poesias varias, En dias de esclavitud, Diario de un mártir).

634. Ateneo de La Habana, Comité Pro-Zenea. *Juan Clemente Zenea.* Havana: Rambla, Bouza, 1919. 169 pp.

635. Carbonell, José Manuel. *Juan Clemente Zenea: poeta y mártir.* Havana: Impr. "Avisador Comercial," 1929. 61 pp.

636. Gómez Carbonell, María. *Estudio crítico biográfico de Juan Clemente Zenea.* Havana: Carasa Impresores, 1926. 134 pp.

637. Lezama Lima, José. *Fragmentos irradiadores.* Havana: Editorial Letras Cubanas, 1993. 148 pp. Juan Clemente Zenea—Julián del Casal.

638. Piñeyro, Enrique. *Vida y escritos de Juan Clemente Zenea.* 2a ed. aum. Havana: Consejo Nacional de Cultura, 1964. 329 pp.

639. Vitier, Cintio. *Rescate de Zenea.* Havana: Unión de Escritores y Artistas de Cuba, 1987. 129 pp.

See also #139, #314.

Twentieth Century

640. *Abaroa, Leonardo,* 1939– (short story writer). La altura virgen de Spica, 1987; Con estas otras manos, 1985; País de maravillas, 1992; El triángulo de las Bermudas y otros cuentos de mar-humor, 1988.

641. *Abréu Felippe, José,* 1947– (playwright, poet). Amar así, 1988; Cantos y elegías, 1992; Orestes de noche, 1985; Siempre la lluvia, 1994.

642. *Acosta, Agustín,* 1886–1979 (poet). Ala, 1915–1993; El apóstol y su isla, 1974; Los camellos distantes, 1936; Hermanita, 1923; Las islas desoladas, 1943; Jesús, 1957; Poemas escogidos, 1988 (Alberto Rocasolano, ed.); Poesías escogidas, 1950 (Fidencio Pérez Rosado, ed.); Trigo de luna, 1980; Ultimos instantes, 1941; La zafra, 1926.

    643. Capote, María. *Agustín Acosta: el modernista y su isla.* Miami: Ediciones Universal, 1990. 260 pp.

    644. Coello, Dimas. *Agustín Acosta: entre islas.* Santa Cruz de Tenerife: Orchilla, 1990. 111 pp. Title on cover *Agustín Acosta, poeta nacional de Cuba.*

    645. Forés, Aldo R. *La poesía de Agustín Acosta, poeta nacional de Cuba.* Miami: Ediciones Universal, 1977. 254 pp.

    See also #164, #385.

646. *Acosta, Leonardo,* 1933– (poet, short story writer). Exige tú, que canto yo, 1993; Fantásticos e inquietantes, 1980; Paisajes del hombre, 1967; El sueño del samurai, 1989.

647. *Acosta Pérez, Alberto* (poet). El ángel y la memoria, 1990; ¡Eramos tan puros!, 1991; Monedas al aire, 1996; Todos los días de este mundo, 1990.

648. *Acosta Sánchez, Mercedes* (novelist, poet, short story writer). Aleluya, 1982; Carlos, 1976; Cien pétalos de rosa, 1978; Una mujer difícil, 1981; Por el camino, 1982; Tablao Flamenco, 1990; Ventana al infinito, 1974.

649. *Acosta Tijero, Alberto* (short story writer). La pierna artificial y otros cuentos, 1971–1996.

650. *Agostini, Víctor,* 1908– (novelist, poet, short story writer). Bibijaguas, 1963; Dos viajes, 1965; Filin, 1973; Hombres y cuentos, 1955; Recuento, 1989.

651. *Aguado, Ladislao,* 1971– (poet). Cantar cansa, 1995.

652. *Agüero, Luis,* 1937– (novelist, playwright, poet, short story writer). De aquí para allá, 1962; Desengaño cruel, 1989; Duelo a primera sangre, 1987; La vida en dos, 1967; La vuelta del difunto caballero, 1987.

653. *Agüero, Omega,* 1940– (poet, short story writer). La alegre vida campestre, 1974; El muro de medio metro, 1977.

654. *Aguirre, Mirta,* 1912–1980 (poet, short story writer). Ayer de hoy, 1980; Juegos y otros poemas, 1974–1992; Poemas de la mujer del preso, 1932; Presencia interior, 1938.

   655. Castillo Vega, Marcia, and Olivia Miranda, eds. *Bibliografía de Mirta Aguirre.* Havana: Editorial Letras Cubanas, 1988–1989. 2 vols.

   656. Montero, Susana A. *Obra poética de Mirta Aguirre: dinámica de una tradición lírica.* Havana: Editorial Academia, 1987. 140 pp.

   See also #777.

657. *Alabau, Magaly,* 1945– (poet). Ras, 1987; Sister/Hermana, 1992 (Anne Twitty, tr.).

658. *Alberto, Eliseo,* 1951– (poet). Las cosas que yo amo, 1977; La eternidad por fin comienza un lunes/El gran viaje del Cisne Negro sobre los lagos de hielo de Irlanda, 1992; La fogata roja, 1985; Importará el trueno, 1975; Un instante en cada cosa, 1979.

659. *Alcides, Rafael,* 1933– (novelist, poet, short story writer). Agradecido como un perro, 1983; Nadie, 1993; Noche en el recuerdo, 1989; La pata de palo, 1967; Y se mueren, y vuelven, y se mueren, 1988. See also #113.

660. *Alfonso Barroso, Carlos Augusto,* 1963– (poet). El segundo aire, 1987; La oración del Letrán, 1996.

661. *Alfonso, Domingo,* 1935– (poet). Esta aventura de vivir, 1987; Historia de una persona, 1968; Libro de buen amor, 1979; Poemas del hombre común, 1964; Sueño en el papel, 1959.

662. *Almeida Bosque, Juan* (novelist). Atención!: Recuento!, 1993 (Presidio [1987], Exilio [1987], Desembarco [1988]); La sierra, 1989; La única ciudadana, 1985.

663. *Alónimo, César* (poet). Dispersos, 1991; Espejos, 1994.

664. *Alonso, Dora,* 1910– (novelist, playwright, poet, short story writer). Agua pasada, 1981; Aventuras de Guille, 1969–1991; El

cochero azul, 1975–1993; Cuentos, 1976; Doñita Abeja y doñita Bella, 1976–1985; En busca de la gaviota negra, 1966; La flauta de chocolate, 1980; Gente del mar, 1977; El grillo caminante, 1981; Juega la dama, 1989; Letras, 1980 (Imeldo Alvarez García, ed.); El libro de Camilín, 1979; Once caballos, 1970; Palomar, 1989; Los payasos, 1985; Ponolani, 1966–1979; Suma, 1984; Tierra adentro, 1944; Tierra inerme, 1961–1977; Una, 1977; El valle de la pájara pinta, 1984–1992.

665. *Alonso, Luis Ricardo,* 1929– (novelist, poet). The Candidate, 1972 (Translation of El candidato, 1970–1984, Tana de Gámez, tr.); Los dioses ajenos, 1971; La estrella que cayó una noche en el mar, 1995; El palacio y la furia, 1976; El Supremísimo, 1981; Territorio libre, 1967 (Translation of Territorio libre [1966]; Alan Brown, tr.).

666. *Alonso Yodú, Odette* (poet). Palabra del que vuelve, 1996.

667. *Alvarez Baragaño, José,* 1932–1962 (poet). Cambiar la vida, 1952; Poemas escogidos, 1964; Poesía color de libertad, 1977.

668. *Alvarez Bravo, Armando,* 1938– (poet). El azoro, 1964 (El azoro, Otros poemas, Boy On A Dolphin); Juicio de residencia, 1982; Las lejanías, 1984; Naufragios y comentarios, 1993; Para domar un animal, 1982; El prisma de la razón, 1990; Relaciones, 1973.

669. *Alvarez Conesa, Sigifredo,* 1938– (poet). Casa de madera azul, 1987; Como a una batalla, 1974; Matar el tiempo, 1969; Sobre el techo llueven naranjas, 1988.

670. *Alvarez de los Ríos, Tomás,* 1918– (novelist, short story writer). Las farfanes, 1989; Humo de yaba, 1972; Los triángulos del amor, 1992.

671. *Alvarez Gil, Antonio* (short story writer). Una muchacha en el andén, 1986; Unos y otros, 1990 (Recuerdas, Natalia?, Luna de miel, Tres cerditos, El cielo entre las manos, En el camino, Viento del sur, Piedras en la cuesta, Una casa en medio del mar).

672. *Alvarez Jané, Enrique,* 1941–1984 (novelist, short story writer). Algo que debes hacer, 1977; Macuta La Habana, 1981; Me planto, 1984 (Principios, En mil ochocientos uno, Ratones, ratones, ratones, Cara de niño, Una clase de religión, El tiempo es una esquis, Diez líneas para Victorina, No hay viaje para Miami, Buscahembra, La Cornúa, En el muelle); La muerte es el tema, 1988.

673. *Anhalt, Nedda G. de,* 1934– (novelist, short story writer). El banquete, 1991; El correo del azar, 1984; Crítica apasionada, 1994; Cuentos inauditos, 1994; Rojo y naranja sobre rojo, 1991.

674. *Aparicio, Raúl,* 1913–1970 (novelist, poet, short story writer). Chipojo, 1977; Espejos de alinde, 1968; Frutos del azote, 1961; Hijos del tiempo, 1964; Oficios de pecar y otras narraciones, 1981 (Waldo González López, ed.); Sondeos, 1983.

675. *Aragón, Uva de,* 1944– (poet, short story writer). Entresemáforos, 1981; Eternidad, 1971; Ni verdad ni mentira y otros cuentos, 1977; No puedo más y otros cuentos, 1989; Versos del exilio, 1975–1977.

676. *Arango, Angel,* 1926– (novelist, playwright, poet, short story writer). ¿A dónde van los cefalomos?, 1964; El arco iris del mono, 1980; Coyuntura, 1984; Las criaturas, 1978; El fin del caos llega quietamente, 1971; El planeta negro, 1966; Robotomaquia, 1967; Sider, 1994; Transparencia, 1982.

677. *Arcocha, Juan,* 1927– (novelist). La bala perdida, 1973–1986; Los baños de canela, 1988; A Candle in the Wind, 1967; La conversación, 1986; Los muertos andan solos, 1962; Operación viceversa, 1976–1983; Por cuenta propia, 1970; Tatiana y los hombres abundantes, 1982.

678. *Arenal, Humberto,* 1926– (novelist, playwright, short story writer). Los animales sagrados, 1967; El caballero Charles, 1983; Del agua mansa, 1982; En el centro del blanco, 1989; The Sun Beats Down, 1959 (Translation of El sol a plomo [1958]; Joseph M. Bernstein, tr.); El tiempo ha descendido, 1964; La vuelta en redondo, 1962. See also #268.

679. *Arenas, Reinaldo,* 1943–1990 (novelist, playwright, poet, short story writer). Adiós a Mamá, 1995–1996; The Assault, 1994 (Translation of El asalto [1991]; Andrew Hurley, tr.); Before Night Falls, 1993 (Translation of Antes que anochezca [1992–1994]; Dolores H. Koch, tr.); Cantando en el pozo, 1982; El Central, a Cuban Sugar Mill, 1984 (Translation of El central [1981]; Anthony Kerrigan, tr.); El color del verano/Nuevo jardín de las delicias, 1991; Con los ojos cerrados, 1972; The Doorman, 1991–1994 (Translation of El portero [1989–1990]; Dolores M. Koch, tr.); Farewell to the Sea, 1986–1987 (Translation of Otra vez el mar [1982]; Andrew Hurley, tr.); Final de un cuento, 1991; Graveyard of the Angels, 1987

(Alfred J. MacAdam, tr.); Hallucinations, 1971–1976/The Ill-Fated Peregrinations of Fray Servando, 1987–1994 (Translation of El mundo alucinante [1969–1992]; Andrew Hurley, tr.); Lazarillo de Tormes, 1984; Leprosorio, 1990; La loma del ángel, 1987–1995; Necesidad, libertad, 1986; Old Rosa, 1989–1994 (Translation of La vieja Rosa [1960–1980] and of Arturo, la estrella más brillante [1984]; Ann Tashi Slater, Andrew Hurley, trs.); The Palace of the White Skunks, 1990–1993 (Translation of El palacio de las blanquísimas mofetas [1980–1983]; Andrew Hurley, tr.); Persecución, 1986; Singing From the Well, 1987–1988 (Translation of Celestino antes del alba [1967–1995]; Andrew Hurley, tr.); Termina el desfile, 1981–1986; Viaje a La Habana, 1990–1995; Voluntad de vivir manifestándose, 1989.

680. Arenas, Reinaldo, and Francisco Soto. *Conversación con Reinaldo Arenas*. Madrid: Betania, 1990. 60 pp.

681. Bejar, Eduardo C. *La textualidad de Reinaldo Arenas: juegos de la escritura posmoderna*. Madrid: Editorial Playor, 1987. 264 pp.

682. Hernández-Miyares, Julio E., and Perla Rozencvaig, eds. *Reinaldo Arenas: alucinaciones, fantasía y realidad*. Glenview, IL: Scott, Foresman, 1990. 227 pp.

683. Lugo Nazario, Félix. *La alucinación y los recursos literarios en las novelas de Reinaldo Arenas*. Miami: Ediciones Universal, 1995. 222 pp.

684. Ottmar, Ette, ed. *La escritura de la memoria: Reinaldo Arenas, textos, estudios y documentación*. Frankfurt am Main: Vervuert, 1992. 231 pp.

685. Paulson, Michael G. *The Youth and the Beach: A Comparative Study of Thomas Mann's "Der Tod in Venidig" (Death in Venice) and Reinaldo Arenas' "Otra vez el mar" (Farewell to the Sea)*. Miami: Ediciones Universal, 1993. 87 pp.

686. Rozencvaig, Perla. *Reinaldo Arenas: narrativa de transgresión*. Mexico City: Editorial Oasis, 1986. 124 pp.

687. Sánchez, Reinaldo, ed. *Reinaldo Arenas: recuerdo y presencia*. Miami: Ediciones Universal, 1994. 235 pp.

688. Soto, Francisco. *Reinaldo Arenas: The "Pentagonía"*. Gainesville, FL: University Press of Florida, 1994. 193 pp.

689. Valero, Roberto. *El desamparado humor de Reinaldo Arenas*. Miami: North-South Center, University of Miami, 1991. 412 pp.

See also #413.

690. *Ariel, Sigfredo,* 1962– (poet). Algunos pocos conocidos, 1987; El enorme verano, 1996.

691. *Ariza, René,* 1940– (playwright, poet, short story writer). El regreso de Alicia al país de las maravillas, 1995; La vuelta a la manzana, 1968; Written Even in the Margins/Escrito hasta en los bordes, 1993.

692. *Armand, Octavio,* 1946– (poet). Biografía para feacios, 1980; Como escribir con erizo, 1979–1982; Cosas pasan, 1976; Entre testigos, 1984; Origami, 1987; Piel menos mía, 1979; Refractions, 1994 (Carol Maier, tr.); Superficies, 1980; With Dusk, 1984 (Carol Maier, tr.).

693. Vasco, Juan Antonio. *Conversación con la esfinge: una lectura de la obra de Octavio Armand.* Buenos Aires: Editorial Fraterna, 1984. 249 pp.

694. *Armas, Encarnación de,* 1933– (poet). Beso que desata luz, 1995.

695. *Arozarena, Marcelino,* 1912– (poet). Canción negra sin color, 1966–1983; Habrá que esperar, 1983.

696. *Arroyo, Anita* (short story writer). El caballito verde, 1956 (with Antonio Ortega); Cuentos del Caribe, 1992; El deber ineludible, 1942; El grillo gruñon, 1984; El hombre palabra, 1985; El pájaro de lata, 1946–1973; Las pequeñas muertes, 1992; Raíces al viento, 1974.

697. *Arrufat, Anton,* 1935– (novelist, playwright, poet, short story writer). La caja está cerrada, 1984; El caso se investiga, 1957; En claro, 1962; Escrito en las puertas, 1968; La huella en la arena, 1986; Mi antagonista y otras observaciones, 1963; Las pequeñas cosas, 1988; ¿Qué harás después de mí?, 1988; Repaso final, 1964; Los siete contra Tebas, 1968; Teatro, 1963 (El caso se investiga [1957], El vivo al pollo [1961], El último tren [1963], La repetición [1963], La zona cero [1959]); La rierra permanente, 1987; Todos los domingos, 1965.

698. *Artiles, Freddy,* 1946– (playwright, poet, short story writer). Adriana en dos tiempos, 1972–1979; De dos en dos, 1978; El pavo cantor, 1980; Teatro, 1984.

699. *Atencio Mendoza, Caridad* (poet). Los viles aislamientos, 1996.

700. *Augier, Angel I.,* 1910– (poet). Breve antología, 1963; Canciones para tu historia, 1941; Copa de sol, 1978; Do svidanya, 1971; Isla en el tacto, 1965; Poesía (1928–1978), 1980; Todo el mar en la ola, 1989; Uno, 1932.

701. *Bacardí Moreau, Emilio,* 1844–1922 (novelist, playwright, short story writer). El abismo, 1972; Cuentos de todas las noches, 1972–1983; Doña Guiomar, 1916–1970; Filigrana, 1972; Vía crucis, 1910–1979.

702. *Ballagas, Emilio,* 1908–1954 (poet). Elegía sin nombre y otros poemas, 1936–1981; Júbilo y fuga, 1931–1939; Obra poética, 1984 (Osvaldo Navarro, ed.); Obra poética de Emilio Ballagas, 1955–1969 (Cintio Vitier, ed.); La obra poética de Emilio Ballagas, 1977 (Rogelio de la Torre, ed.); Orbita de Emilio Ballagas, 1965–1972 (Rosario Antuña, ed.); Sabor eterno, 1939.

703. Armas, Emilio de, ed. *Emilio Ballagas.* Havana: Ministerio de Educación, Dirección Nacional de Educación General, 1973. 75 pp.

704. De la Torre, Rogelio A. *La obra poética de Emilio Ballagas.* Miami: Ediciones Universal, 1977. 158 pp.

705. Rice, Argyll Pryor. *Emilio Ballagas: poeta o poesía.* Mexico City: Ediciones Andrea, 1966. 237 pp.

706. *Baquero, Gastón,* 1916– (poet). Autoantología comentada, 1992; Ensayo/Poesía, 1995 (Alfonso Ortega Carmona, Alfredo Pérez Alencart, eds.); La fuente inagotable, 1995 (Autobiographical); Magias e invenciones, 1984; Memorial de un testigo, 1966; Poemas, 1942; Poemas invisibles, 1991; Poesía completa, 1995.

707. Baquero, Gastón, and Felipe Lázaro. *Conversación con Gastón Baquero.* 2a ed. aum. y rev. Madrid: Editorial Betania, 1994. 75 pp.

See also #219.

708. *Barba, Jaime,* 1910– (poet). Bolívar/El sueño que interroga, 1981–1984; Clamor, 1984; La cólera del viento, 1978–1982; El infierno de Ariel, 1986; La llama de cristal, 1982; Más allá de la mies y del sonido, 1974; Los mercaderes del alba, 1976; El paraíso de Ariel, 1987; Por los caminos del aire, 1979; El purgatorio de

Ariel, 1986; Romancero antillano, 1978; Rumor y pulso, 1978–1982; Velamen, 1978–1982.

709. *Barnet, Miguel,* 1940– (novelist, poet). Akeké y la jutía, 1978; Carta de noche, 1982; Gallego, 1981–1988; Mapa del tiempo, 1989; Oficio de angel, 1989–1993; Los perros mudos, 1988; La piedra fina y el pavorreal, 1963; Rachel's Song, 1991 (Translation of La canción de Rachel [1969–1988]; W. Nick Hill, tr.); La sagrada familia, 1967; La vida real, 1986–1989; Viendo mi vida pasar, 1987.

710. *Barquet, Jesús J.,* 1953– (poet). El libro del desterrado, 1994; Un no rompido sueño, 1994; Sagradas herejías, 1985; Sin decir el mar, 1981.

711. *Benet y Castellón, Eduardo,* 1878–1965 (novelist, poet). Bandera blanca, 1941; Birín, 1957–1962; Con la sordina puesta, 1946; Cuando se va la vida, 1949; Del hogar y del aula, 1945; Del remanso y del ensueño, 1938; Un jabuquito de haikáis, 1962; Persiguiendo luceros, 1945; Plumas al viento, 1938; La poesía de Eduardo Benet y Castellón, 1983; La primavera vuelve, 1948; Punto final, 1959; Un respiro, una canción, 1944; El sembrador de esperanzas, 1939; La vida y yo, 1956; Voces de la cima, 1943; Yo, pecador, 1954. See also #139.

712. *Benítez Rojo, Antonio,* 1931– (novelist, short story writer). El escudo de hojas secas, 1969–1972; Estatuas sepultadas y otros relatos, 1984; Heroica, 1976; Los inquilinos, 1976; Sea of Lentils, 1991 (Translation of El mar de las lentejas [1979–1985]; James Maraniss, tr.); La tierra y el cielo, 1978; The Magic Dog and Other Stories, 1990 (Frank Janney, ed.); Tute de reyes, 1967. See also #85.

713. *Bernal, Emilia,* 1884–1964 (novelist, poet). Alma errante, 1916–1990; América, 1938–1990; Como los pájaros, 1922; Exaltación, 1928; Layka froyka, 1925–1931; Negro, 1934; Los nuevos motivos, 1925; Sonetos, 1937; Vida, 1925.

714. Cruz Alvarez, Félix. *La poesía de Emilia Bernal.* Miami: Editorial AIP, 1979. 28 pp.

715. *Bernal Lumpuy, Luis* (novelist, poet, short story writer). El himno de la escoria, 1993; Sueños de un mundo mejor, 1992; Ultimas estrofas del destierro, 1994.

716. *Betancourt, May* (novelist). La casa vacía, 1992; Conspiración, 1995.

717. *Bobes León, Marilyn,* 1955– (poet). La aguja en el pajar, 1979; Hallar el modo, 1989. See also #212.

718. *Bordao, Rafael,* 1951– (poet). Acrobacia del abandono, 1988; The Book of Interferences/El libro de las interferencias, 1995; Escurriduras de la soledad, 1995; Proyectura, 1986.

719. *Borrero de Luján, Dulce Maria,* 1883–1945 (poet). Horas de mi vida, 1912.

720. *Boti y Barreiro, Regino Eladio,* 1878–1958 (poet). Arabescos mentales, 1913; Kodak-ensueño, 1929; El mar y la montaña, 1921–1985; Poesía, 1977; La torre del silencio, 1926.

    721. Armas, Emilio de. *La crítica literaria de Regino Boti.* Havana: Unión de Escritores y Artistas de Cuba, 1985. 185 pp.

    722. Boti y Barreiro, Regino Eladio, Juan Marinello and Nicolás Guillén; Rebeca Ulloa, ed. *Epistolario Boti-Marinello, Boti-Guillén.* Santiago, Cuba: Editorial Oriente, 1985. 120 pp.

    723. Boti y Barreiro, Regino Eladio; José M. Fernández Pequeño and Florentina R. Boti, eds. *Cartas a los orientales, 1904–1926.* Havana: Editorial Letras Cubanas, 1990. 430 pp.

    724. Boti y Barreiro, Regino Eladio, and José Manuel Póveda; Sergio Chaple, ed. *Epistolario Boti-Póveda.* Havana: Editorial Arte y Literatura, 1977. 313 pp.

    725. Sáinz, Enrique. *Trayectoría poética y crítica de Regino Boti.* Havana: Editorial Academia, 1987. 186 pp.

    726. Suarée, Octavio de la. *La obra literaria de Regino E. Boti.* New York: Senda Nueva de Ediciones, 1977. 211 pp.

    See also #385.

727. *Bragado Bretaña, Reinaldo,* 1953– (short story writer). En torno al cero, 1994; La estación equivocada, 1989.

728. *Branly, Roberto,* 1930–1980 (poet). Apuntes y poemas, 1966; Las claves del alba, 1958; Escrituras, 1975; Firme de sangre, 1962; Poesía inmediata, 1968; Siempre la vida, 1978; Vitral de sueños, 1982; Y la orquesta triunfa sobre el aire, 1985.

729. *Brito Fuentes, Mario,* 1955– (short story writer). Cuentos de amor, 1995 (with Enrique Oscar González and Nelson Pérez); En

torno al equilibrio, 1991 (Espiral, La puerta, La carrera, Cuadranautas, Catarsis, En torno al equilibrio).

730. *Brull, Mariano,* 1891–1956 (poet). Canto redondo, 1934; La casa del silencio, 1916; Nada más que, 1954; Poemas en menguante, 1928; Poesía, 1983 (Emilio de Armas, ed.); Tiempo en pena, 1950.

   731. Larraga, Ricardo. *Mariano Brull y la poesía pura en Cuba.* Miami: Ediciones Universal, 1994. 222 pp.

732. *Buesa, José Angel,* 1910– (playwright, poet). Alegría de Proteo, 1948; Año bisiesto, 1981 (Autobiographical); Antología poética total (1936–1980), 1981–1987; Babel, 1936; Canciones de Adán, 1947; Canto final, 1938; La fuga de las horas, 1932; Horario del viento, 1971; Lamentaciones de Proteo, 1947; Mis poemas preferidos, 1971; Muerte diaria, 1943; Los naipes marcados, 1974; Nuevo oasis, 1949–1974; Oasis, 1943–1988; Para ellas, 1982; Poemas en la arena, 1949; Poemas preferidos, 1971; Poemas prohibidos, 1959–1970; Poeta enamorado, 1955–1974; Tiempo en sombra, 1970; Versos de amor, 1959. See also #164.

733. *Buzzi, David,* 1932– (novelist, short story writer). Un amor en La Habana, 1983; Caudillo de difuntos, 1975; Cuando todo cae del cielo, 1978; Los desnudos, 1967–1982; El juicio final, 1977; Mariana, 1970; La religión de los elefantes, 1969–1987; Viejas historias para un mundo nuevo, 1977.

734. *Caballero Menéndez, Atilio Jorge,* 1959– (poet, short story writer). Algunos buenos conocidos, 1990; El azar y la cuerda, 1996; Las canciones recuerdan lo mismo, 1991; Los pasos y los gestos, 1990; El sabor del agua, 1990.

735. *Cabrera Delgado, Luis* (novelist, short story writer). Los calamitosos, 1993; Tía Julita, 1987.

736. *Cabrera Infante, Guillermo,* 1929– (novelist, short story writer). Así en la paz como en la guerra, 1960–1994; Delito por bailar chachachá, 1995; Ella cantaba boleros, 1996; Exorcismos de esti(l)o, 1976–1987; Infante's Inferno, 1984–1990 (Translation of La Habana para un infante difunto [1979–1994]; Suzanne Jill Levine, tr.); Mi música extremada, 1996 (Autobiographical); O, 1975–1986; Three Trapped Tigers, 1971–1990 (Translation of Tres tristes tigres [1965–1994]; Suzanne Jill Levine, tr.); View of Dawn in the Tropics, 1978–1990 (Translation of Vista del

amanecer en el trópico [1974–1994]; Suzanne Jill Levine, tr.); Writes of Passage, 1993 (Translation of Así en la paz como en la guerra [1960–1994]; John Brooksmith, Peggy Boyars, trs.).

737. Alvarez Borland, Isabel. *Discontinuidad y ruptura en Guillermo Cabrera Infante.* Gaithersburg, MD: Hispamérica, 1982. 146 pp.

738. Feal, Rosemary Geisdorfer. *Novel Lives: The Fictional Autobiographies of Guillermo Cabrera Infante and Mario Vargas Llosa.* Chapel Hill, NC: University of North Carolina Press, 1986. 175 pp.

739. Gil López, Ernesto. *Guillermo Cabrera Infante: La Habana, el lenguaje y la cinematografía.* Ed. aum. y rev. Tenerife: ACT, 1991. 323 pp.

740. Hernández-Lima, Dinorah. *Versiones y re-versiones históricas en la obra de Cabrera Infante.* Madrid: Editorial Pliegos, 1990. 183 pp.

741. Jiménez, Reynaldo L. *Guillermo Cabrera Infante y "Tres tristes tigres".* Miami: Ediciones Universal, 1977. 131 pp.

742. Nelson, Ardis L. *Cabrera Infante in the Menippean Tradition.* Newark, DE: Editorial Juan de la Cuesta, 1983. 124 pp.

743. Pereda, Rosa María. *Guillermo Cabrera Infante.* Madrid: Edaf, 1979. 260 pp.

744. Piano, Barbara. *El paisaje anterior.* Caracas: Academia Nacional de la Historia, 1989. 124 pp. Study of parody in the novels of Guillermo Cabrera Infante and Severo Sarduy.

745. Ríos, Julián. *Guillermo Cabrera Infante.* Madrid: Editorial Fundamentos, 1974. 253 pp.

746. Román, Isabel. *La invención en la escritura experimental: del barroco a la literatura contemporánea.* Cáceres, Spain: Universidad de Extremadura, 1993. 104 pp.

747. Souza, Raymond D. *Guillermo Cabrera Infante: Two Islands, Many Worlds.* Austin, TX: University of Texas Press, 1996. 195 pp.

See also #268.

748. *Cabrera, Lydia* (novelist, short story writer). Consejos, pensamientos y notas de Lydia E. Pinbán, 1993 (Isabel Castellanos, ed.); Cuentos negros de Cuba, 1940–1993; Cuentos para adultos

niños y retrasados mentales, 1983; Francisco y Francisca, 1976; Itinerarios del insomnio, 1977; Por qué . . . : cuentos negros de Cuba, 1948–1972; Páginas sueltas, 1994 (Isabel Castellanos, ed.).

749. Castellanos, Isabel, and Josefina Inclán, eds. *En torno a Lydia Cabrera: cincuent[en]ario de "Cuentos negros de Cuba,"* 1936–1986. Miami: Ediciones Universal, 1987. 334 pp.

750. Congreso de Literatura Afro-Americana (1976, Miami, FL); Reinaldo Sánchez and José Antonio Madrigal, eds. *Homenaje a Lydia Cabrera*. Miami: Ediciones Universal, 1978. 349 pp.

751. Gutiérrez, Mariela. *El cosmos de Lydia Cabrera: dioses, animales, y hombres*. Miami: Ediciones Universal, 1991. 137 pp.

752. ———. *Los cuentos negros de Lydia Cabrera: estudio morfológico esquemático*. Miami: Ediciones Universal, 1986. 148 pp.

753. Hiriart, Rosario. *Lydia Cabrera: vida hecha arte*. New York: E. Torres, 1978. 198 pp.

754. Inclán, Josefina. *Ayapá y otras otán iyebiyé de Lydia Cabrera: notas y comentarios*. Miami: Ediciones Universal, 1976. 108 pp.

755. ———. *En torno a "Itinerarios del insomnio: Trinidad de Cuba" de Lydia Cabrera*. Miami: Peninsular Printing, 1978. 38 pp.

756. ———. *Lydia Cabrera: creación y poesía*. Miami: Peninsular Printing, 1981. 29 pp.

757. Perera, Hilda. *Idapo, el sincretismo en los "Cuentos negros" de Lydia Cabrera*. Miami: Ediciones Universal, 1971. 118 pp.

758. Simo, Ana María. *Lydia Cabrera: An Intimate Portrait*. Suzanne Jill Levine, tr. New York: Intar Latin American Gallery, 1984. 22 pp.

759. Soto, Sara. *Magia e historia en los "Cuentos negros," "Por qué" y "Ayapá" de Lydia Cabrera*. Miami: Ediciones Universal, 1988. 162 pp.

760. Valdés-Cruz, Rosa. *Lo ancestral africano en la narrativa de Lydia Cabrera*. Barcelona: Editorial Vosgos, 1974. 114 pp.

See also #85, #159.

761. *Cabrera, Raimundo,* 1852–1923 (novelist, poet, short story writer). Cuentos míos, 1904; Ideales, 1918–1984; Intrigas de un secretario, 1889; Juveniles, 1907; Mis buenos tiempos, 1891–1981 (Autobiographical); Mis malos tiempos, 1920 (Autobiographical); Obras completas, 1900?; Sombras eternas, 1919; Sombras que pasan, 1916–1984.

762. *Cabrisas, Hilarión,* 1883–1939 (playwright, poet). Breviario de mi vida inútil, 1932; La caja de Pandora, 1939–1987; Doreya, 1919; Sed de infinito, 1939–1987.

763. *Cala, Ulises* (playwright). Ciertas tristísimas historias de amor, 1996.

764. *Calleiro, Mary* (playwright, poet, short story writer). A mi manera, 1989; Distancia de un espacio prometido, 1985; Teatro, 1989 (El viejo, Un simple nombre, Los payasos, Los insuficientes); Tiempo sin regreso, 1978; Vagabunda, 1988.

765. *Cano, Joel,* 1966– (playwright). Timeball/El juego de perder el tiempo, 1994.

766. *Carballido Rey, José Manuel,* 1913– (poet, short story writer). Crónicas del Peladero, 1979; Cuentos dispersos, 1978; El gallo pinto, 1965–1977; San Nicolás del Peladero, 1982; Un sarcófago para el Buey de Oro, 1985; El tiempo es un centinela insobornable, 1983.

767. *Cardi, Juan Angel,* 1914– (novelist, short story writer). El American Way of Death, 1980; El caso del beso con sabor a cereza, 1987; Dos casos de un detective, 1983; Una jugada extraordinaria, 1982; La llave dorada, 1989; Un poco de humor cardiano, 1991; Relatos de Pueblo Viejo, 1970; Viernes en plural, 1981.

768. *Cardoso, Onelio Jorge,* 1914–1986 (short story writer). Abrir y cerrar los ojos, 1969; Caballito blanco, 1980–1990; La cabeza en la almohada, 1983; El cuentero, 1958; Cuentos, 1975–1992 (Mónica Mansour, ed.); Cuentos completos, 1962–1981; Cuentos escogidos, 1981–1989; El hilo y la cuerda, 1975; Iba caminando, 1966; La melipona, 1977; Negrita, 1984–1992; La otra muerte del gato, 1964; El perro, 1964; El pueblo cuenta, 1961; Taita, diga Usted cómo, 1945.

769. Bueno, Salvador, ed. *Onelio Jorge Cardoso.* Havana: Casa de las Americas, 1988. 478 pp.

770. Comas Paret, Emilio et al. *El mundo narrativo de Onelio Jorge Cardoso.* [s.l.: s.n., 1987], 32 pp.

771. Gavilán, Angelina, ed. *Onelio Jorge Cardoso.* Havana: Ministerio de Educación, Dirección Nacional de Educación General, 1973. 59 pp.

772. Hernández Azaret, Josefa de la Concepción. *Algunos aspectos de la cuentística de Onelio Jorge Cardoso.* Santiago, Cuba: Editorial Oriente, 1982. 125 pp.

See also #268, #300.

773. *Carmona Ymas, Luis* (playwright). María y José, 1996.

774. *Carpentier, Alejo,* 1904–1980 (novelist, poet, short story writer). Baroque Concerto, 1991 (Translation of Concierto barroco [1974–1993]; Asa Zatz, tr.); The Chase, 1990 (Translation of El acoso [1979–1987]; Alfred MacAdam, tr.); Conferencias, 1987 (Virgilio López Lemus, ed.); Los convidados de plata, 1972; Crónicas del regreso, 1991 (Salvador Arias, ed.); Cuentos, 1976–1991; Explosion in a Cathedral, 1963–1991 (Translation of El siglo de las luces [1962–1992]; John Sturrock, tr.); Los fugitivos, 1990; Guerra del tiempo y otros relatos, 1996; The Harp and the Shadow, 1990 (Translation of El arpa y la sombra [1985–1994]; Thomas Christensen, Carol Christensen, trs.); Historia de lunas, 1990; The Kingdom of This World, 1957–1989 (Translation of El reino de este mundo [1954–1994]; Harriet de Onís, tr.); Letra y solfa, 1976 (Visión de América — Ballet — Cine); The Lost Steps, 1956–1991 (Translation of Los pasos perdidos [1953–1991]; Harriet de Onís, tr.); Obras completas, 1983 (Vol. 1. Ecue-yamba-ó [1933]. La rebambaramba. Cinco poemas afrocubanos. Historia de lunas. Manita en el suelo. El milagro de Anaquillé. Correspondencia con García Caturla.—Vol. 3. Guerra del tiempo. El acoso y otros relatos.—Vol. 4. La aprendiz de bruja. Concierto barroco. El arpa y la sombra.—Vol. 7. La consagración de la primavera [1979].—Vols. 8–9. Crónicas.—Vol. 13. Ensayos.—Vol. 14. Conferencias.—Vol. 15. Letra y solfa: Cine); Razón de ser, 1984; Reasons of State, 1976 (Translation of El recurso del método [1976]; Frances Partridge, tr.); El siglo de las luces, 1962–1992; Tientos, diferencias y otros ensayos, 1964–1987; Viaje a la semilla y otros relatos, 1971; War of Time, 1970 (Translation of Guerra del tiempo [1955–1996]; Frances Partridge, tr.).

775. Absire, Alain. *Alejo Carpentier*. Paris: Editions Julliard, 1994. 175 pp.

776. Acosta, Leonardo. *Música y épica en la novela de Alejo Carpentier*. Havana: Editorial Letras Cubanas, 1981. 130 pp.

777. Alvarez Alvarez, Luis, ed. *Homenaje a Alejo Carpentier y a Mirta Aguirre: valoraciones martianas, comentarios, libros*. Havana: Depto. de Actividades Culturales, Universidad de la Habana, 1981. 287 pp.

778. Arias, Salvador, ed. *Recopilación de textos sobre Alejo Carpentier*. Havana: Casa de las Américas, 1977. 585 pp.

779. Baldran, Jacqueline et al. *Quinze études autour de "El siglo de las luces" de Alejo Carpentier*. Paris: Editions L'Harmattan, 1983. 247 pp.

780. Barroso, Juan. *Realismo mágico y lo real maravilloso en "El reino de este mundo" y "El siglo de las luces."* Miami: Ediciones Universal, 1977. 176 pp.

781. Bravo, Víctor. *Magias y maravillas en el continente literario: para un deslinde del realismo mágico y lo real maravilloso*. Caracas: Ediciones de La Casa de Bello, 1988. 255 pp.

782. Carpentier, Alejo, and Ramón Chao. *Palabras en el tiempo: entrevistas*. Barcelona: Argos Vergara, 1984. 251 pp.

783. Carpentier, Alejo, and Virgilio López Lemus, ed. *Entrevistas*. Havana: Editorial Letras Cubanas, 1985. 548 pp.

784. Collard, Patrick. *Cómo leer a Alejo Carpentier*. Madrid: Ediciones Júcar, 1991. 136 pp.

785. Coloquio sobre Alejo Carpentier (1979, Havana). *Coloquio sobre Alejo Carpentier*. Havana: Unión de Escritores y Artistas de Cuba, 1985. 169 pp.

786. Cristóbal Pérez, Armando. *Un tema cubano en tres novelas de Alejo Carpentier*. Havana: Unión de Escritores y Artistas de Cuba, 1994. 59 pp.

787. Dill, Hans Otto. *Lateinamerikanische Wunder und kreolische Sensibilität: der Erzähler und Essayist Alejo Carpentier*. Hamburg: Kovac, 1993. 394 pp.

788. Durán Luzio, Juan. *Lectura histórica de la novela: el "Recurso del método" de Alejo Carpentier.* Heredia, C.R.: Editorial de la Universidad Nacional, 1982. 136 pp.

789. Fama, Antonio. *Las últimas obras de Alejo Carpentier.* Caracas: Ediciones de La Casa Bello, 1995. 128 pp.

790. Font, María Cecilia. *Mito y realidad en Alejo Carpentier: aproximaciones a "Viaje a la semilla."* Buenos Aires: Editorial R. Alonso, 1984. 55 pp.

791. Fontquerni, Enriqueta. *Les sens cachés du roman: une étude de la signification dans "Le recours de la méthode" d'Alejo Carpentier.* Montreal: Humanitas nouvelle optique, 1990. 222 pp.

792. García-Carranza, Araceli. *Biobibliografía de Alejo Carpentier.* Havana: Editorial Letras Cubanas, 1984. 644 pp. (+ Suppl. published in 1989).

793. Giacoman, Helmy F., ed. *Homenaje a Alejo Carpentier: variaciones interpretativas en torno a su obra.* New York: Las Américas, 1970. 464 pp.

794. Giovannini, Arno. *Entre culturas: "Los pasos perdidos" de Alejo Carpentier.* New York: P. Lang, 1991. 214 pp.

795. Gómez, Francisco A., and José Antonio Tamargo, eds. *Un camino de medio siglo: setenta aniversario de Alejo Carpentier.* Havana: Editorial Orbe, 1976. 94 pp.

796. González, Eduardo. *El tiempo del hombre: huella y labor en cuatro obras de Alejo Carpentier.* Caracas: Monte Avila Editores, 1978. 220 pp.

797. González Echevarría, Roberto. *Alejo Carpentier: The Pilgrim At Home.* Austin, TX: University of Texas Press, 1990. 334 pp. Reprint of the 1977 ed. Spanish ed. entitled *Alejo Carpentier: el peregrino en su patria,* with added chapter, published 1993.

798. González Echevarría, Roberto, and Klaus Müller-Bergh, eds. *Alejo Carpentier: Bibliographical Guide/Alejo Carpentier: guía bibliográfica.* Westport, CT: Greenwood Press, 1983. 271 pp.

799. Harvey, Sally. *Carpentier's Proustian Fiction: The Influence of Marcel Proust on Alejo Carpentier.* London: Tamesis, 1994. 171 pp.

800. Herlinghaus, Hermann. *Alejo Carpentier: persönliche Geschichte eines literarischen Moderneprojekts*. Munchen: Edition Text + Kritik, 1991. 188 pp.

801. Hernández, Shirley. *Aproximación al estudio de Alejo Carpentier*. Montevideo: Túpac Amaru Editorial, 1989. 39 pp.

802. Horta Mesa, Aurelio. *Coordenadas carpenterianas*. Havana: Editorial Pueblo y Educación, 1990. 55 pp.

803. Janney, Frank. *Alejo Carpentier and His Early Works*. London: Tamesis, 1981. 141 pp.

804. King, Lloyd. *Alejo Carpentier: His Euro-Caribbean Vision*. St. Augustine, Trinidad: Research and Publications Fund Committee, University of the West Indies, 1972. 40 pp.

805. Licea Jiménez, Tania Teresa, and Luis Enrique Rodríguez Suárez. *Alejo Carpentier: tres relatos, tres análisis linguoestilísticos*. Havana: Editorial de Ciencias Sociales, 1994. 73 pp. Analysis of *Viaje a la semilla, El camino de Santiago,* and *Semejante a la noche.*

806. Márquez Rodríguez, Alexis. *Lo barroco y lo real-maravilloso en la obra de Alejo Carpentier*. Mexico City: Siglo Veintiuno Editores, 1983. 587 pp.

807. ———. *La obra narrativa de Alejo Carpentier*. Caracas: Universidad Central de Venezuela, 1970. 220 pp.

808. ———. *Ocho veces Alejo Carpentier*. Caracas: Editorial Grijalbo, 1992. 222 pp.

809. Martin, Claire Emilie. *Alejo Carpentier y las crónicas de Indias: orígenes de una escritura americana*. Hanover, NH: Ediciones del Norte, 1995. 220 pp.

810. Mazziotti, Nora, ed. *Historia y mito en la obra de Alejo Carpentier*. Buenos Aires: F. García Cambeiro, 1972. 183 pp.

811. Mocega-González, Esther P. *Alejo Carpentier: estudios sobre su narrativa*. Madrid: Playor, 1980. 153 pp.

812. Müller-Bergh, Klaus. *Alejo Carpentier: estudio biográfico-crítico*. Long Island City, NY: Las Américas, 1972. 220 pp.

813. ———. *Asedios a Carpentier: once ensayos críticos sobre el novelista cubano.* Santiago, Chile: Editorial Universitaria, 1972. 233 pp.

814. Padura, Leonardo. *Colón, Carpentier, la mano, el arpa y la sombra.* Havana: Departamento de Actividades Culturales, Universidad de La Habana, 1987. 43 pp.

815. ———. *Lo real maravilloso: creación y realidad.* Havana: Editorial Letras Cubanas, 1989. 169 pp.

816. Perilli, Carmen. *Imágenes de la mujer en Carpentier y García Márquez: mitificación y demitificación.* Tucumán : Secretaría de Extensión Universitaria, Universidad Nacional de Tucumán, 1990. 271 pp.

817. Pickenhayn, Jorge Oscar. *Para leer a Alejo Carpentier.* Buenos Aires: Plus Ultra, 1978. 175 pp.

818. Plaza, Sixto. *El acá y el allá en la narrativa de Alejo Carpentier.* Buenos Aires: Ediciones Agon, 1984. 71 pp.

819. Puisset, Georges. *Structures anthropocosmiques de l'univers d'Alejo Carpentier.* Montpellier, France: Centre d'études et de recherches sociocritiques, 1987– [vol. 1–].

820. Quiroga, Jorge. *Alejo Carpentier.* São Paulo, Brasiliense, 1984. 100 pp.

821. Rubio de Lértora, Patricia, and Richard A. Young, eds. *Carpentier ante la crítica: bibliografía comentada.* Xalapa, Mex.: Centro de Investigaciones Lingüístico-Literarias, Instituto de Investigaciones Humanísticas, Universidad Veracruzana, 1985. 222 pp.

822. Sánchez-Boudy, José. *La temática novelística de Alejo Carpentier.* Miami: Ediciones Universal, 1969. 208 pp.

823. Schäfer-Sackreuther, Dagmar. *Alejo Carpentiers "Los pasos perdidos" und Johann Wolfgang von Goethes "Italianische Reise": eine intertextuelle Studie.* New York: P. Lang, 1991. 281 pp.

824. Shaw, Donald Leslie. *Alejo Carpentier.* Boston, MA: Twayne, 1985. 150 pp.

825. Smith, Verity. *Carpentier: "Los pasos perdidos."* London: Grant and Cutler, 1983. 78 pp.

826. Solano Salvatierra de Chase, Cida. *Correlación entre algunos procedimientos estilísticos y la temática en la ficción extensa de Alejo Carpentier hasta "El Siglo de las luces."* San José, C.R.: Editorial Texto, 1980. 180 pp. Cover title *Estilística y temática en Alejo Carpentier.*

827. Speratti-Piñero, Emma Susana. *Pasos hallados en "El reino de este mundo."* Mexico City: Colegio de México, 1981. 212 pp.

828. Tusa, Bobs M. *Alejo Carpentier: A Comprehensive Study.* Chapel Hill, NC: Albatros, 1982. 48 pp.

829. Velayos Zurdo, Oscar. *El diálogo con la historia de Alejo Carpentier.* Barcelona: Península, 1985. 152 pp.

830. ———. *Historia y utopía en Alejo Carpentier.* Salamanca: Universidad de Salamanca, 1990. 187 pp.

831. Young, Richard A. *Carpentier: "El reino de este mundo."* London: Grant and Cutler, 1983. 122 pp.

832. Zambrana de Sánchez, Heida. *"El reino de este mundo": correlaciones histórico-literarias.* Río Piedras, P.R.: Editorial Edil, 1992. 104 pp.

See also #44, #45.

833. *Carrión, Miguel de,* 1875–1929 (novelist, short story writer). La esfinge, 1961–1977; Las honradas, 1918–1978; Las impuras, 1919–1978; El milagro, 1903–1977; La última voluntad y otros relatos, 1903–1975 (Mercedes Pereira Torres, ed.).

834. González, Mirza L. *La novela y el cuento psicológicos de Miguel de Carrión.* Miami: Ediciones Universal, 1979. 180 pp.

See also #422.

835. *Casal, Lourdes,* 1938–1981 (poet, short story writer). Alfonso y otros cuentos, 1973; Los fundadores, 1973; Itinerario ideológico (antología), 1982 (María Cristina Herrera, Leonel Antonio de la Cuesta, eds.); Palabras juntan revolución, 1981.

836. *Casas, Luis Angel,* 1928– (novelist, poet, short story writer). Cuentos para la medianoche, 1992; El genio burlón y otros poemas, 1959; Los músicos de la muerte, 1989; Pepe del mar y otros

poemas, 1980; La tiniebla infinita, 1948; Trece cuentos nerviosos, 1990.

837. *Casáus, Víctor,* 1944– (poet, short story writer). Amar sin papeles, 1980; De un tiempo a esta parte, 1984; Entre nosotros, 1977; Maravilla del mundo, 1989; Los ojos sobre el pañuelo, 1984; Para que este pueblo se levantara, 1984 (with Alquimia Peña); Todos los días del mundo, 1966; Voluntario, 1965 (with Sixto Canela, José Solís and Carlos Quintela).

838. *Castellanos, Jesús,* 1879–1912 (novelist, short story writer). La agonía de la garza, 1979; Colección póstuma, 1914–1916 (Vol. 1. Los optimistas. Lecturas y opiniones. Crítica de arte.—Vol. 2. Los argonautas. La manigua sentimental. Cuentos. Crónicas y apuntes—Vol. 3. De la vida internacional); La conjura, 1908–1988; De tierra adentro, 1906. See also #399, #422.

839. *Castillo, Amalia del* (poet). Agua y espejos, 1986; Las aristas desnudas, 1991; Cauce de tiempo, 1981; Géminis deshabitado, 1994; Urdimbre, 1975; Voces del silencio, 1978. See also #166.

840. *Caulfield, Carlota,* 1953– (poet). A las puertas del papel, con amoroso fuego, 1996; Angel Dust/Polvo de ángel, 1990 (Carol Maier, tr.); Fanaim, 1985; Oscuridad divina, 1985–1987; Sometimes I Call Myself Childhood/A veces me llamo infancia, 1985 (Chris Allen, tr.); El tiempo es una mujer que espera, 1986; Thirty-fourth Street and Other Poems, 1987.

841. *Cazorla, Roberto,* 1940– (novelist, poet, short story writer). Con el sol doblado por la frente, 1979; En alas de la sombra, 1978; El epicentro de mi verdad, 1979; Esta calle mundial de indiferencia, 1981; Fuga de ruidos, 1978; La herida exacta, 1978; El mar es el amante de mi rostro, 1979; El mundo es una misa para sordos, 1986; No hay fronteras ni estoy lejos, 1989; El olor silvestre de la fiebre, 1978; Un pedazo de azul en el bolsillo, 1978; Subir de puntos, 1978; También los colores se suicidan, 1980. See also #166.

842. *Cepeda, Josefina de,* 1907– (poet). Grana y armiño, 1935; La llama en el mar, 1954; Palabras en soledad, 1941; Versos, 1936.

843. *Chacón Nardi, Rafaela,* 1926– (poet). Coral del aire, 1982; Del silencio y las vozes, 1978; Treinta y seis nuevos poemas, 1957; Viaje al sueño, 1948–1957.

844. Hernández Menéndez, Mayra. *La poética de Rafaela Chacón Nardi*. Havana: Editorial Letras Cubanas, 1996. 105 pp.

See also #279.

845. *Chavarría, Daniel,* 1933– (novelist). Camagüey completo, 1983–1990 (with Justo E. Vasco); Primero muerto, 1986–1994 (with Justo E. Vasco).

846. *Chaviano Díaz, Daína,* 1957– (novelist, poet, short story writer). El abrevadero de los dinosauros, 1990; Amoroso planeta, 1983–1990; Confesiones eróticas y otros hechizos, 1994; Fábulas de una abuela extraterrestre, 1988; Historias de hadas para adultos, 1986; Los mundos que amo, 1979–1982.

847. *Chericián, David,* 1940– (poet). Arbol de la memoria, 1971; El autor intelectual, 1975–1985; Compay Tito, 1988 (with Excilia Saldaña); Coplas de mundo revuelto, 1988; De donde crece la palma, 1986; Hacia la humana primavera, 1987; Junto aquí, 1983; Los que se van, los que se quedan, 1978; Manecitas de hombre fuerte, 1992; Queriéndolos, nombrándolos, 1971; Rueda la ronda, 1985.

848. *Cid Pérez, José,* 1960– (playwright). Teatro cubano, 1989 (La comedia de los muertos [1953], La rebelión de los títeres (with Dolores Martí de Cid); Esther Sánchez-Grey Alba, ed.); Un tríptico y dos comedias, 1972 (Hombres de dos mundos [1967], Y quiso más la vida [1936], La comedia de los muertos [1953]). See also #295.

849. *Cirules, Enrique,* 1938– (novelist, short story writer). Bluefields, 1988; El corredor de caballos, 1980; En la corriente impetuosa, 1978; Extraña lluvia en la tormenta, 1988; La otra guerra, 1979; Los perseguidos, 1971; La saga de la Gloria City, 1983.

850. *Clavelo, Lise,* 1956– (poet). Anagnórisis, 1994.

851. *Cobián, Ricardo,* 1952– (poet). Un día me quedé sólo, 1993; Estrellas y prisioneros, 1984; Para todos los panes no están todos presente, 1984.

852. *Codina, Norberto,* 1951– (poet). A este tiempo llamarán antiguo, 1975; Lugares comunes, 1987.

853. *Cofiño López, Manuel,* 1936– (novelist, poet, short story writer). Amor a sombra y sol, 1981–1987; Andando por ahí por esas calles,

1982; El anzuelo dorado, 1987; Cuando la sangre se parece al fuego, 1975–1979; Para leer mañana, 1976; Un pedazo de mar y una ventana, 1979; Tiempo de cambio, 1969; La última mujer y el próximo combate, 1971–1987; Y un día el sol es juez, 1976.

854. García Alzola, Ernesto, ed. *Acerca de Manuel Cofiño*. Havana: Editorial Letras Cubanas, 1989. 522 pp.

855. Vidal, Hernán. *Para llegar a Manuel Cofiño: estudio de una narrativa revolucionaria cubana*. Minneapolis, MN: Society for the Study of Contemporary Hispanic and Lusophone African Revolutionary Literatures, 1984. 174 pp.

856. *Collazo, Miguel,* 1936– (novelist, short story writer). El arco de Belén, 1976; Estación central, 1993; Estancias, 1984; El laurel del patio grande, 1978; El libro fantástico de Oaj, 1966; Onoloria y otros relatos, 1988 (Onoloria [1973]); El viaje, 1968–1981.

857. *Consuegra Ortal, Diosdado,* 1944– (novelist, short story writer). Cicerona, 1984; El emperador frente al espejo, 1990; Lo que le pasó al espantapájaros, 1988; La resurrección de las tataguayas, 1985.

858. *Contreras, Félix,* 1939– (poet). Corazón semejante al tuyo, 1983; Cuaderno para el que va a nacer, 1978; Debía venir alguién, 1971; El fulano tiempo, 1969.

859. *Corrales, José* (playwright, poet). Las hetairas habaneras, 1988 (with Manuel Pereiras); Nocturno de cañas bravas, 1994; El palacio de los gritos, 1992–1993; Razones y amarguras, 1978; Temporal, 1993; The Three Marios, 1993 (Circus Maximus—In Absentia); Los trabajos de Gerión, 1980.

860. *Correa, Arnaldo,* 1938– (poet, short story writer). Un caso difícil, 1991; El hombre que vino a matar, 1988; El primer hombre a Marte, 1967; El terror, 1982.

861. *Cos Causse, Jesús,* 1945– (poet). Balada de un tambor y otros poemas, 1987; Como una serenata, 1988; Con el mismo violín, 1970; Las islas y las luciérnagas, 1981; El último trovador, 1975.

862. Ruiz Miyares, Oscar. *Cos Causse: tiempo y poesía*. Santiago, Cuba: Editorial Oriente, 1988. 186 pp.

863. *Crespo, Carlos,* 1947– (poet). Charlot, padre mío, 1996; Corteza y hoja, 1991; El tiempo, Guiomar, 1988.

864. *Cristóbal Pérez, Armando,* 1938– (novelist, poet, short story writer). Aunque no la guerra, 1983; La batalla, 1988; De vida y muerte, 1979; Explosión en tallapiedra, 1980; La ronda de los rubíes, 1973–1990; Siete variaciones policiales, 1975.

865. *Cruz Guerra, Soledad,* 1952– (novelist, poet, short story writer). Adioses y bienvenidas, 1990; Documentos de la otra, 1988–1991; Fábulas por el amor, 1990; Jinete en la memoria, 1989.

866. *Cruz Varela, María Elena,* 1953– (poet). Afuera está lloviendo, 1987; Ballad of the Blood, 1995 (Mairym Cruz-Bernal, Deborah Digges, eds. and trs.); The Exhausted Angel/El ángel agotado, 1991–1992; Guirnalda poética, 1992 (Carmen Rosa Burgos, ed.).

867. *Cuadra, Angel,* 1931– (poet). Angel Cuadra: The Poet in Socialist Cuba, 1994 (Warren Hampton, ed.); A Correspondence of Poems from Jail/Poemas en correspondencia desde prisión (Donald D. Walsh, tr.); Esa tristeza que nos inunda, 1985; Impromptus, 1977; Las señales y los sueños, 1988; Tiempo del hombre, 1977; La voz inevitable, 1994. See also #107.

868. *Cuza Malé, Belkis,* 1942– (poet). Los alucinados, 1962; Cartas a Ana Frank, 1966; Juegos de damas, 1970; Tiempos de sol, 1963; El viento en la pared, 1962; Woman On the Front Lines, 1987 (Translated from Juego de damas [1970]; Pamela Carmell, tr.).

869. *Delgado Novoa, Mayra* (poet). Piedra de toque, 1996.

870. *Delgado-Jenkins, Humberto* (short story writer). Cuentos de tierra, agua, aire y mar, 1995.

871. *Delgado-Sánchez, Joaquín,* 1946– (novelist, poet). Anax, 1987; El rumbo, 1985; El trono del Gólgota, 1994.

872. *Desnoes, Edmundo,* 1930– (novelist, short story writer). El cataclismo, 1965; Inconsolable Memories, 1967–1990; Memories of Underdevelopment, 1990 (Translation of Memorias del subdesarrollo [1965–1988]; No hay problema, 1961–1964. See also #268.

873. *Díaz, Carlos A.,* 1950– (poet). Balada gregoriana, 1988; El jardín del tiempo, 1985; Las puertas de la noche, 1993.

874. *Díaz Castro, Tania,* 1939– (poet). Apuntes para el tiempo, 1964; Everyone Will Have To Listen/Todos me van a tener que oír, 1990 (Pablo Medina, Carolina Hospital, trs.; Spanish ed. [1970]).

875. *Díaz, Jesús,* 1941– (novelist, playwright, short story writer). Los años duros, 1967–1981; Canto de amor y de guerra, 1979; Gritar el amor, 1981; Las iniciales de la tierra, 1987–1992; Las palabras perdidas, 1992; La piel y la máscara, 1996. See also #268.

876. *Díaz, Manuel C.,* 1942– (novelist, short story writer). El año del ras de mar, 1993; Un paraíso bajo las estrellas, 1995.

877. *Díaz Martínez, Manuel,* 1936– (poet). Alcándara, 1991; Los caminos, 1962; El carro de los mortales, 1988; Mientras traza su curva el pez de fuego, 1984; El país de Ofelia, 1965; Poesía inconclusa, 1985; Soledad y otros temas, 1957; La tierra de Saúd, 1967; Vivir es eso, 1968.

878. *Díaz Pimienta, Alexis,* 1956– (short story writer). Cuarto de mala música, 1995; Los visitantes del sábado, 1994.

879. *Díaz Rodríguez, Ernesto,* 1939– (poet). The Bell of Dawn/La campana del alba, 1984–1990; Sea of My Infancy/Mar de mi infancia, 1991 (Ildara Klee, tr.); Un testimonio urgente, escrito en las cárceles de Cuba/Obra poética de un cubano disidente, 1977.

880. *Diego, Eliseo,* 1920– (poet, short story writer). A través de mi espejo, 1981; Un almacén como otro cualquiera, 1978; Cuadernillo de bella sola, 1990; Cuatro de oros, 1991–1993; Los días de tu vida, 1977–1993; Divertimentos, 1946–1993; En la calzada de Jesús del Monte, 1949–1993; En las oscuras manos del olvido, 1942–1979; Entre la dicha y la tiniebla, 1986; Inventario de asombros, 1982; Libro de quizás y de quién sabe, 1989–1993; Muestrario del mundo/Libro de las maravillas de Boloña, 1968–1978; Nombrar las cosas, 1973; Noticias de la quimera, 1975; El oscuro esplendor, 1966; Poems, 1982 (Kathleen Weaver, tr.); Poesía, 1983 (Enrique Sáinz, ed.); Poesía y prosa selectas, 1991 (Aramís Quintero, ed.); Prosas escogidas, 1983; La sed de lo perdido, 1993; El silencio de las pequeñas cosas, 1993; Soñar despierto, 1988; Veintiseis poemas recientes, 1986; Versiones, 1970.

881. Abréu, Mauricio. *Asomado al mundo de Eliseo Diego.* Havana: Ediciones URBE-ARTEX, 1993. 250 pp.

882. Fuentes de la Paz, Ivette. *Nombrar las cosas: sobre la poética de Eliseo Diego.* Havana: Extramuros, 1993. 41 pp.

883. Sáinz, Enrique, ed. *Acerca de Eliseo Diego.* Havana: Editorial Letras Cubanas, 1991. 409 pp.

See also #219.

884. *Domingo, Jorge* (short story writer). Diacronía y otros sucesos, 1996.

885. *Don, Julio Osvaldo* (novelist, short story writer). Cuentos eróticos, 1995; Cuentos pecaminosos, 1988; La fuerza inútil, 1988; Memories of a Masseur, 1994 (Translation of Memorias de un masajista [1990]); Otro puñado de cuentos, 1985; Un puñado de cuentos, 1984; Purunga pura unga, 1986; La rara risa de un exiliado triste, 1987; Wattussi Ura-Cunda, 1988.

886. *Dopico Asencio, Frank Abel,* 1964– (poet). El correo de la noche, 1989; Expediente del asesino, 1991.

887. *Dorr, Nicolás,* 1947– (playwright). El agitado pleito entre un autor y un ángel, 1973; Una casa colonial, 1984; La chacota, 1989 (La chacota, Un viaje entretenido, Confesión en el barrio chino, Vivir en Santa Fé); Cinco farsas y dos comedias, 1978 (El palacio de los cartones [1960], Las pericas [1961], La esquina de los concejales [1963], Maravillosa inercia [1964], Clave de sol [1964], La chacota [1962], Un viaje entretenido, Algo sobre el teatro de Nicolás Dorr); Dramas de imaginación y urgencia, 1987; Teatro, 1963.

888. *Duarte, Carmen,* 1959– (playwright). ¿Cuánto me das marinero?, 1994.

889. *Eguren, Gustavo,* 1925– (novelist, short story writer). El aire entre los dedos, 1989; Al borde del agua, 1972; Alguien llama a la puerta, 1977; Aventuras de Gaspar Pérez de Muela Quieta, 1982; Cuentos, 1988 (Algo para la palidez y una ventana sobre el regreso [1969], Los lagartos no comen queso [1975]); En la cal de las paredes, 1971; La espada y la pared, 1987; Los pingüinos, 1979; La robla, 1967.

890. *Eiranova-Cuza, Florencio* (novelist). El amor en los tiempos de Castro, 1994.

891. *Escandell, Noemí,* 1936– (poet). Ciclos, 1982; Cuadros, 1982; Words/Palabras, 1986 (Joan Dargon, tr.).

892. *Escardó, Rolando,* 1925–1960 (poet). Antología mínima, 1975 (Félix Pita Rodríguez, César Leante, eds.); Libro de Rolando, 1961; Orbita de Rolando Escardó, 1981 (Luis Suurdíaz, ed.); Las

ráfagas, 1961; Rolando Escardó [selecciones], 1981 (Luis Suardíaz, ed.).

893. *Escobar Varela, Angel,* 1957– (poet). Allegro de sonata, 1984–1987; Epílogo famoso, 1985; Malos pasos, 1991; Todavia, 1991; La vía pública, 1987; Viejas palabras de uso, 1978.

894. *Espina Pérez, Darío* (poet, short story writer). A sangre y fuego, 1981; Fabulario y rimas zoológicas, 1983; Ficciones y realidades, 1989; La mujer vista por un poeta, 1995; Los municipios en décimas, 1990 (with Francisco Henríquez and Oscar Pérez Moro); Poemario de historia universal, 1983; Politemas, 1986; Refranero poético, 1984; Sabiduría de los refranes, 1991; Solucionática, 1991; Sonetario y romancero, 1991; Temas literarios, 1986.

895. *Espino Ortega, José Manuel,* 1966– (poet). Barco de sueños, 1991; El cartero llama tres veces, 1992; Rantés vive en la otra puerta, 1996.

896. *Esténger, Rafael,* 1899– (novelist, poet). Cuba en la cruz, 1960; Las máscaras del sueño, 1957; El pulpo de oro, 1954; Retorno, 1945.

897. *Estorino, Abelardo,* 1925– (playwright). Que el diablo te acompañe, 1989; El robo del cochino, 1964; Teatro, 1964 (with Andrés Lizarraga); Teatro, 1984–1987 (El peine y el espejo [1963], El robo del cochino [1964], La casa vieja [1963], La dolorosa historia del amor secreto de Don José Jacinto Milanés, Ni un sí ni un no). See also #288, #289, #291.

898. *Feijóo, Samuel,* 1914– (novelist, poet, short story writer). La alcancía del artesano, 1958; La alegre noticia, 1960; Beth-el, 1949 ; Camarada celeste, 1944; Caminante montés, 1962; Caracol vagabundo, 1949; Carta en otoño, 1957; Concierto, 1947 (with Aldo Menéndez and Alcides Iznaga); Cuentacuentos, 1976; Cuentería, 1982; Cuerda menor, 1964; Gallo campero, 1950; El girasol sediento, 1963; Juan Quinguín en Pueblo Mocho, 1964–1976; Libreta de pasajero, 1964 (Libreta de pasajero, Puntos arcaicos, La hoja del poeta [1957]); Libro de apuntes, 1954; Otros cuentos de Cuentacuentos, 1978; El pájaro de las soledades, 1961; Pleno día, 1974; Poesía, 1984; Poeta en el paisaje, 1949; Polvo que escribe, 1979; Prosa, 1985; Segunda alcancía del artesano, 1962; Ser, 1983; Ser fiel, 1964; Tres novelas de humor, 1977 (Pancho Ruta y Gil Jocuma [1968], La jira descomunal [1968],

Tumbaga [1964]); Viaje de siempre, 1977; Vida completa del poeta Wampampiro Timbereta, 1981–1986 ; Violas, 1958.

899. *Felipe, Carlos,* 1914–1975 (playwright). Teatro, 1959–1988 (El chino [1947], El travieso Jimmy [1951], Réquiem por Yarini [1960], De película [1963]; José A. Escarpanter, José A. Madrigal, eds. [1988]). See also #295.

900. *Felipe, Nersys,* 1936– (novelist, poet, short story writer). Cuentos de Guane, 1976–1995; Cuentos de nato, 1985; Música y colores, 1980; Prenda, 1979; Roman Ele, 1976–1995.

901. *Fernández, Alfredo Antonio,* 1945– (novelist, short story writer). El candidato, 1979–1988; Crónicas de medio mundo, 1983; Del otro lado del recuerdo, 1988; Los profetas de Estelí, 1990; La última frontera, 1985.

902. *Fernández, Amando,* 1949– (poet). Antología personal, 1991; Azar en sombra, 1987; Ciudad, isla invisible, 1994; Espacio mayor, 1991; Lingua franca, 1993; Materia y forma, 1990 ; El minotauro, 1993; Las miradas de Jano, 1995; Museo natural, 1993; Pentagrama, 1987; Perfil de la materia, 1986; La rendición, 1995; El riesgo calculado, 1995; El ruiseñor y la espada, 1989; Los siete círculos, 1990; La túnica dorada, 1995.

903. *Fernández, Arístides,* 1904–1934 (short story writer). Cuentos, 1959–1978.

904. Carreño Rodríguez, Enrique. *Arístides Fernández: narrador y pintor—ensayo.* Matanzas, Cuba: Ediciones Matanzas, 1992. 73 pp.

905. ———. *Transmutaciones relacionables en Arístides Fernández.* Havana: Editorial Letras Cubanas, 1994. 53 pp.

See also #314.

906. *Fernández, Olga,* 1943– (novelist, short story writer). Con mi abuelo y sus amigos, 1988; Mi amigo José Martí, 1991; Niña del arpa, 1989; La otra carga del capitán Montiel, 1990.

907. *Fernández, Pablo Armando,* 1930– (novelist, playwright, poet). Aprendiendo a morir, 1983; Campo de amor y de batalla, 1984; Libro de los héroes, 1964; Los niños se despiden, 1968–1983;

Otro golpe de dados, 1993; Salterio y lamentación, 1953; Un sitio permanente, 1970; El sueño, la razón, 1988; Todo la poesía, 1961–1962; El vientre del pez, 1989–1991.

908. *Fernández Retamar, Roberto,* 1930– (poet). Hacia la nueva, 1989; Palabra de mi pueblo, 1980–1985; Poesía reunida, 1966; Poeta en la Habana, 1992; Revolutionary Poems, 1974 (Joe R. Pereira, ed. and tr.).

909. Fernández Retamar, Roberto. *Entrevisto.* Havana: Unión de Escritores y Artistas de Cuba, 1982. 217 pp.

See also #385.

910. *Fernández-Larrea, Ramón,* 1958– (poet). El libro de las instrucciones, 1991; El libro de los salmos feroces, 1994 ; El pasado del cielo, 1987; Poemas para ponerse en la cabeza, 1989. See also #212.

911. *Ferreira, Ramón,* 1921– (playwright, short story writer). The Gravedigger and Other Stories, 1986 (Translations from Tiburón y otros cuentos [1952] and Los malos olores de este mundo [1969]); Más allá la isla, 1991; Papá, cuéntame un cuento, 1989; Teatro, 1993 (Dónde está la luz, Un color para este miedo, El hombre inmaculado, El mar de cada día).

912. *Ferrer, Eduardo,* 1930– (novelist). Para siempre amor mío, 1995.

913. *Ferrer, Raúl,* 1915– (poet). Décima y romance, 1981; Poemas, 1990; El retorno del maestro, 1990; El romancillo de las cosas negras y otros poemas escolares, 1947; Viajero sin retorno, 1979.

914. *Ferrer, Rolando,* 1925–1976 (playwright). Teatro, 1963–1983.

915. *Florit, Eugenio,* 1903– (poet). A pesar de todo, 1987; Antología penúltima, 1970; Antología personal, 1992; Antología poética, 1956; Asonante final y otros poemas, 1956; De tiempo y agonía, 1974; Doble acento, 1937; Hábito de esperanza, 1965; Hasta luego, 1991–1992; Lo que queda, 1995; Las noches, 1988; Obra poética, 1967; Obras completas, 1982; Poema mío, 1947; Reino, 1938; Treinta y dos poemas breves, 1927; Trópico, 1930; Versos pequeños, 1979.

916. Collins, María Castellanos. *Tierra, mar y cielo en la poesía de Eugenio Florit.* Miami: Ediciones Universal, 1976. 66 pp.

917. Saa, Orlando. *La serenidad en las obras de Eugenio Florit.* Miami: Ediciones Universal, 1973. 118 pp.

918. Vega Queral, María Victoria. *La obra poética de Eugenio Florit: temática y estilo.* Miami: Ediciones Universal, 1987. 104 pp.

See also #385.

919. *Friol, Roberto,* 1928– (poet). Alción al fuego, 1968; Turbión, 1988.

920. Biblioteca Nacional José Martí. *Un ejemplar trabajador de la cultura: homenaje a Roberto Friol por sus más de treinta años de trabajo investigativo.* Havana: La Biblioteca, 1987. 63 pp.

921. *Frómeta, Zoelia,* 1960– (poet). Pasos de ciegos, 1995.

922. *Fuentes Gómez, René* (poet). Los gallinazos, 1996.

923. *Fuentes, Norberto,* 1943– (novelist, short story writer). Cazabandido, 1970; Condenados de Condado, 1968–1991; El último santuario, 1992.

924. *Fundora de Rodríguez Aragón, Raquel* (poet). El canto del viento, 1983; Nostalgia inconsolable, 1973; Sendero de ensueños, 1990.

925. *Galiano, Alfredo* (short story writer). De las palabras y el silencio, 1996.

926. *Galindo Lena, Carlos,* 1929– (poet). Hablo de tierra conocida, 1964; Mortal como una paloma en pleno vuelo, 1988 (Francisco de Oraá, ed.); Rosas blancas para el Apocalipsis, 1991.

927. *Galliano, Alina,* 1950– (poet). En el vientre del trópico, 1994; Entre el párpado y la mejilla, 1980; La geometría de lo incandescente (en fija residencia), 1992; Hasta el presente, 1989.

928. *García Alzola, Ernesto,* 1914– (poet, short story writer). Diálogo con la vida, 1947; Martí va con nosotros, 1953; El paisaje interior, 1956–1977; Siempre cantando primavera, 1983.

929. *García Benítez, Francisco,* 1913–1988 (poet). Cuidado que le doy un sonetazo, 1980; Rumores y visiones, 1991.

930. *García, Clara A.* (playwright, poet). Grímpolas de mi alma, 1973–1991; Obras dramáticas y históricas, 1988.

931. *García Marruz, Fina,* 1923– (poet). Las miradas perdidas, 1951; Poesías escogidas, 1984; Viaje a Nicaragua, 1987 (with Cintio Vitier); Visitaciones, 1970.

  932. Arcos, Jorge Luis. *En torno a la obra poética de Fina García Marruz.* Havana: Unión de Escritores y Artistas de Cuba, 1990. 239 pp.

  See also #219.

933. *García Méndez, Luis Manuel,* 1954– (novelist, poet, short story writer). Aventuras esclavas de don Antonín del Corojo y Crónica del Nuevo Mundo según Iván el Terrible, 1989; Los amados de los dioses, 1987; Los forasteros, 1987; Habanecer, 1987–1990; Sin perder la ternura, 1987.

934. *García Ramos, Reinaldo,* 1944– (poet). El buen peligro, 1987; Caverna fiel, 1993.

935. *García Tuduri, Mercedes,* 1904– (poet). Alas, 1935; Andariega de Dios, 1983; Arcano, 1947; Ausencia, 1968. See also #161.

936. *García Vega, Lorenzo,* 1926– (poet, short story writer). Cetrería del títere, 1960; Collages de un notario, 1993; Espaciones para lo huyuyo, 1993; Espirales del cuje, 1951; Poemas para penúltima vez (1948–1989), 1991; Ritmos acribillados, 1972; Rostros del reverso, 1977; Suite para la espera, 1948; Variaciones a como veredicto para el sol de otras dudas, 1993. See also #219.

937. *Garzón Céspedes, Francisco,* 1947– (playwright, poet, short story writer). Amor, donde sorprenden gaviotas, 1980; Cantos a la revolución, al pueblo, y al amor, 1985; Desde los órganos de puntería, 1971.

938. *Gayol Mecías, Manuel,* 1945– (short story writer). El jaguar es un sueño de ámbar y otros cuentos, 1992; Retablo de la fábula, 1989.

939. *Gaztelu, Angel,* 1914– (poet). Gradual de laudes, 1955–1987; Poemario, 1994.

  940. Lezama Lima, José. *El padre Gaztelu en la poesía.* Mexico City: Ediciones del Equilibrista, 1987. 141 pp. Reprint of the 1955 ed.

  See also #219, #385.

941. *Geada, Rita,* 1937– (poet, short story writer). Cuando cantan las pisadas, 1967; Desvelado silencio, 1959; Esta lluvia de fuego que

nos quema, 1988; Mascarada, 1970; Poemas escogidos, 1969; Vertizonte, 1977–1980.

See also #161, #166.

942. *Gil, Lourdes* (poet). Blanca aldaba preludia, 1989; Empieza la ciudad, 1993; Neumas, 1977; Vencido el fuego de la especie, 1983.

943. *Giraudier, Antonio* (poet). Aceros guardados, 1966; Acorde y asombro, 1969; Bajel último y otras obras, 1989; Calles de la tarde, 1989; Green Against Linen and Other Poems, 1957 (Samuel Weisberg, tr.); Leyenda de una noche del Caribe, 1989 ; Nueva York, 1988; Poemas para avivar un ocaso, 1994; Prosa y verso, 1962 (Una mano en el espacio [1955], Bordes [1956], La cerca [1958], Las piedras mágicas [1959], Piénsame [1960], La voz de Víctor Luang); Vigil, Sor Juana Inés, Martí, 1989.

944. *Goldarás, José Raúl,* 1912– (poet). Hail America/Salve América, 1986; Irisado mensaje, 1991; Suavidades, 1941; Tres Goldarás en la poesía del siglo XX, 1981 (with José López Goldarás and Roberto L. Goldarás).

945. *Gómez Franca, Lourdes,* 1933– (poet). Era una lágrima que se amaba en silencio, 1975; El niño de guano, 1993 ; Poemas íntimos, 1964; The Thorns Are Green My Friend, 1989.

946. *Gómez-Vidal, Oscar,* 1923– (poet, short story writer). Definiciones, 1979; Diez cuentos de ciudad amarga, 1975; El otro mundo de Tina, 1975; Poemas del hombre y su sombra, 1995; Retorno a Iberia, 1989; Sabes la noticia . . . ? Dios llega mañana, 1978 (Actos y milagros, Los senos de María Ordaneta, Dos más dos son cinco, El vendedor de arena, La llamaban Eva, Vocalomanía, El barman, Borrón y cuenta nueva, Angel y la mosca, Los inocentes, El tridente, La última noticia).

947. *González de Cascorro, Raúl,* 1922– (novelist, playwright, poet, short story writer). Aquí se habla de combatientes y de bandidos, 1975; Arboles sin raíces, 1960; Un centavo de sol para su alma, 1983; Cincuentenario y otros cuentos, 1952; Concentración pública, 1963; Despedida para el perro lobo, 1980; El fusil, 1979; Gente de la Playa Girón, 1962–1975; El hijo de Arturo Estévez, 1975; Historias de brigadistas, 1979; Jinetes sin cabeza, 1975; Muerte del bandido, 1989; Piezas de museo, 1970; La razón de los muertos, 1985; Romper la noche, 1976; La semilla, 1965; Traición en Villa Feliz, 1978 (Una paloma para Graciela, Arboles sin raíces

[1960], La muchacha vestida de limpio, Traición en Villa Feliz); Vamos a hablar de El Mayor, 1978; La ventana y el tren, 1978; Vidas sin domingo, 1956.

948. *González Díaz, Juan,* 1948– (poet, short story writer). Nosotros, los de entonces, 1994 (La misma noche, Mambises del siglo XX, Manolo y el capitán, En el campamento de Cayajabo, Una brigada vanguardia, Entre el bullicio del gentío, Al leer un cuento, Esta fiesta en el central, De cuando Richard no se despertó, Bebiendo cervezas,La rubita aquella); Tocar en la aldaba, 1992.

949. *González, Enrique Oscar,* 1947– (short story writer). Círculos, 1994; Cuentos de amor, 1995 (with Mario Brito Fuentes and Nelson Pérez).

950. *González Esteva, Orlando,* 1952– (poet). El ángel perplejo, 1975; De la poesía, 1979; Elogio del garabato, 1994 ; El pájaro tras la flecha, 1988.

951. *González, Miguel* (poet). Cuba y Ofelia, 1992; Don Quijote en América, 1988; Sangre en Cuba, 1960.

952. *González, Nicolás Roberto,* 1961– (poet). Es mayo y quiero cantar, 1995.

953. *González, Omar,* 1950– (novelist, poet, short story writer). Al encuentro, 1975; Nieve roja, 1981; Nosotros los felices, 1978; Poemas rotos, 1985; El propietario, 1978; Secreto a voces, 1985; Tobogán del océano, 1991.

954. *González Sánchez, Ronel,* 1971– (poet). Dictado del corazón, 1993; Reflexiones de un equilibrista, 1990; Todos los signos del hombre, 1992.

955. *Guerra, Félix,* 1939– (poet, short story writer). Amor de los pupitres, 1992; El sueño del yaguar, 1987.

956. *Guerra, Wendy,* 1970– (poet). Cabeza rapada, 1996; Tlatea a oscuras, 1987.

957. *Guillén, Nicolás,* 1902–1989 (poet). Antología clave, 1971; Antología mayor, 1990 (Angel I. Augier, ed.); Antología poética, 1987 (Gustavo Bonifacini, ed.); Antología poética, 1987 (Oscar Hermes Villordo, ed.); Cantos para soldados y sones para turistas,

1937–1985; Che comandante, 1967; Coplas de Juan Descalzo, 1979 ; El corazón con que vivo, 1975; Cuba, amor y revolución, 1972–1973 (Winston Orrillo, ed.); Cuba libre, 1948 (Translation of selections from El son entero [1947–1982]; Langston Hughes, Ben Frederic Carruthers, trs.); The Daily Daily, 1989 (Translation of El diario que a diario [1972]; Vera M. Kutzinski, tr.); Elegías, 1977 (Elegía a un soldado vivo—Elegía a Jacques Roumain [1947], Elegía a Jesús Menéndez [1951], Elegía cubana, Elegía a Emmett Till, Elegía camagüeyana); En la guerra de España, 1988 (Antonio Merino, ed.); España, 1937–1976; Isla de rojo coral, 1993; Latinamericasón, 1974 (De Poemas de amor [1964], De Tengo [1964], De El gran zoo [1967], De Poemas para el Che [1968], De La rueda dentada [1969]); Las grandes elegías, 1984–1992 (Angel I. Gautier, ed.); El libro de las décimas, 1980; El libro de los sones, 1982 (Angel I. Gautier, ed.); El libro de los sonetos, 1984 (Angel I. Augier, ed.); Man-Making Words (Selected Poems), 1972–1975 (Robert Márquez, David Arthur McMurray, eds. and trs.); Motivos del son, 1930–1980; Música de cámara, 1979; New Love Poetry/Nueva poesía de amor, 1994 (Keith Ellis, ed and tr.); Nicolás Guillén, 1950 (José Luis Varela, ed.); Nicolás Guillén, 1964 (Claude Couffon, ed.); Nicolás Guillén, 1973 (Abel Enrique Prieto, ed.); Nicolás Guillén, 1981 (Cristóbal Garcés Lara, ed.); Nicolás Guillén (antología poética), 1987 (Gustavo Bonifacini, ed.); Nicolás Guillen/Antología poética de Nicolás Guillén, 1987 (Oscar Hermes Villordo, ed.); Nueva antología, 1979–1986 (Angel I. Augier, ed.); Obra poética, 1974–1985 (Angel I. Augier, ed.); Páginas vueltas, 1980–1988; La paloma de vuelo popular, 1958–1979; ¡Patria o muerte!: The Great Zoo and Other Poems, 1972–1973 (Translation of El gran zoo y otros poemas [1925–1969]; Robert Márquez, ed. and tr.); Poemas de amor, 1964; Poemas manuables, 1975 ; Por el mar de las Antillas anda un barco de papel, 1978; ¿Por qué imperialismo?, 1976; Prosa de prisa, 1975–1987 (Angel Augier, ed.); Sol de domingo, 1982; Sóngoro cosongo y otros poemas, 1931–1981; Summa poética, 1976–1990 (Luis Iñigo Madrigal, ed.); Sus mejores poemas, 1959; Tengo, 1974 (Richard J. Carr, tr.); Todas las flores de abril, 1992 (Juan Nicolás Padrón Barquín, ed.); West Indies, Ltd., 1934–1976.

958. Aguirre, Mirta. *Un poeta y un continente*. Havana: Editorial Letras Cubanas, 1982. 139 pp.

959. Antuña, María Luisa, and Josefina García-Carranza, eds. *Bibliografía de Nicolás Guillén*. Havana: Instituto Cubano del Libro, 1975. 379 pp.

960. Augier, Angel I. *Nicolás Guillén*. Havana: Instituto Cubano del Libro, 1971. 318 pp.

961. ———. *Nicolás Guillén: estudio biográfico-crítico*. Havana: Unión de Escritores y Artistas de Cuba, 1984. 539 pp.

962. ———. *Nicolás Guillén: notas para un estudio biográfico-crítico*. 2a ed., rev. Santa Clara, Cuba: Universidad Central de Las Villas, 1965– [Vol. 1–].

963. ———. *La Revolución Cubana en la poesía de Nicolás Guillén*. Havana: Editorial Letras Cubanas, 1979. 54 pp.

964. Boti y Barreiro, Regino Eladio. *Homenaje a Nicolás Guillén en su octogésimo cumpleaños*. Havana: Unión de Escritores y Artistas de Cuba, 1982. 103 pp.

965. Cossío Esturo, Adolfina. *Rhythmic Effects in Nicolás Guillén's Poetry*. Santiago, Cuba: Dirección de Información Científica y Técnica, Universidad de Oriente, 1979. 39 pp.

966. Ellis, Keith. *Cuba's Nicolás Guillén: Poetry and Ideology*. Buffalo, NY: University of Toronto Press, 1985. 251 pp. Reprint of the 1983 ed.

967. ———. *Nicolás Guillén: poesía e ideología—perfil libre*. Havana: Unión de Escritores y Artistas de Cuba, 1987. 387 pp.

968. Fernández Retamar, Roberto. *El son de vuelo popular*. Havana: Editorial Contemporáneos, 1979. 62 pp. Reprint of the 1972 ed.

969. Irish, J. A. George. *Nicolás Guillén: Growth of a Revolutionary Consciousness*. New York: Caribbean Research Center, City University of New York, 1990. 144 pp.

970. Kubayanda, Josaphat Bekunuru. *The Poet's Africa: Africanness in the Poetry of Nicolás Guillén and Aimé Césaire*. New York: Greenwood Press, 1990. 176 pp.

971. Mansour, Mónica. *Análisis textual e intertextual: "Elegía a Jesús Menéndez" de Nicolás Guillén*. Mexico City: Facultad de Filosofía y Letras, Universidad Autónoma de México, 1980. 93 pp.

972. Márquez, Roberto, Alfred Melon and Keith Ellis. *Tres ensayos sobre Nicolás Guillén*. Havana: Unión de Escritores y Artistas de Cuba, 1980. 94 pp.

973. Martínez Estrada, Ezequiel. *La poesía afrocubana de Nicolás Guillén*. Montevideo: Arca, 1966. 92 pp.

974. Martínez Estrada, Ezequiel, and Horacio Salas. *La poesía de Nicolás Guillén: seguido de una antología del poeta*. Buenos Aires: Calicanto Editorial, 1977. 151 pp.

975. Morejón, Nancy. *Nación y mestizaje en Nicolas Guillén*. Havana: Unión de Escritores y Artistas de Cuba, 1982. 332 pp.

976. ———, ed. *Recopilación de textos sobre Nicolas Guillén*. Havana: Casa de las Américas, 1974. 429 pp.

977. Ruffinelli, Jorge. *Poesía y descolonización: viaje por la poesía de Nicolás Guillén*. Jalapa, Mex.: Universidad Veracruzana, 1985. 176 pp.

978. Ruscalleda Bercedóniz, Jorge María. *La poesía de Nicolás Guillén: cuatro elementos esenciales*. Río Piedras, P.R.: Editorial Universitaria, Universidad de Puerto Rico, 1975. 310 pp.

979. Santana, Joaquín G. *Nicolás Guillén: juglar americano—un poeta por la Revolución*. Havana: Editora Política, 1989. 311 pp.

980. Sardinha, Carl Dennis. *The Poetry of Nicolás Guillén: An Introduction*. London: New Beacon Books, 1976. 80 pp.

981. Smart, Ian. *Nicolás Guillén: Popular Poet of the Caribbean*. Columbia, MO: University of Missouri Press, 1990. 187 pp.

982. Tous, Adriana. *La poesía de Nicolás Guillén*. Madrid: Ediciones Cultura Hispánica, 1971. 159 pp.

983. Varela, José Luis, ed. *Nicolás Guillén*. Madrid: Edinter, 1950. 95 pp.

984. White, Clement A. *Decoding the Word: Nicolás Guillén as Maker and Debunker of Myth*. Miami: Ediciones Universal, 1993. 219 pp.

985. Williams, Lorna Valerie. *Self and Society in the Poetry of Nicolás Guillén*. Baltimore, MD: Johns Hopkins University Press, 1982. 177 pp.

See also #36, #300.

986. *Güirao, Ramón,* 1908–1949 (poet). Bongó, 1934; Poemas, 1947.

987. *Gutiérrez Fernández, Jorge Luis,* 1969– (poet). Luna de lana, 1995.

988. *Henríquez, Bruno,* 1947– (poet, short story writer). Aventura en el laboratorio, 1987; Por el atajo, 1991.

989. *Henríquez, Francisco* (poet). Jardines de la rima, 1993–1994; Los municipios en décimas, 1990 (with Darío Espina Pérez and Oscar Pérez Moro); Reflejos, 1986; Vivencias del campo cubano, 1994 (with Oscar Pérez-Moro).

990. *Heras León, Eduardo,* 1940– (short story writer). A fuego limpio, 1980; Acero, 1977–1989; Cuestión de principio, 1986–1993; La guerra tuvo seis nombres, 1968–1970; La nueva guerra, 1989; Los pasos en la hierba, 1970–1990.

991. *Hernández Catá, Alfonso,* 1885–1940 (novelist, playwright, poet, short story writer). El ángel de Sodoma, 1928; Bajo la luz, 1923; El bebedor de lágrimas, 1926–1969; La casa de las fieras, 1922; El corazón, 1923; El cristiano errante, 1927; Cuatro libras de felicidad, 1933; Cuentos, 1966; Cuentos olvidados, 1982 (Jorge Febles, ed.); Cuentos pasionales, 1907–1920; Cuentos y noveletas, 1983 (Salvador Bueno, ed.); Don Cayetano el informal, 1978; Don Luis Mejía, 1925; El drama de la señorita Occidente, 1921; Escala, 1931; El fabricante de recuerdos, 1928; Los frutos ácidos y otros cuentos, 1915–1953; El gigante, 1922; Juegos fatuos, 1919; La juventud de Aurelio Zaldívar, 1911–1950; El laberinto, 1924; Libro de amor, 1924 (El drama de la señorita Occidente, Bajo la luz, El sembrador de sal, Girasol); La madrastra, 1919–1955; Una mala mujer, 1922; Manicomio, 1931; Martierra, 1928; La muerte nueva, 1922; La niña débil, 1931; La noche clara, 1928; Novela erótica, 1909 (Novela erotica, El pecado original, La distancia); Pelayo González, 1909–1922; Piedras preciosas, 1927; El placer de sufrir, 1921; La puerta falsa, 1931; Los siete pecados, 1920; Sus mejores cuentos, 1936; El tercer Fausto, 1923 ; El viaje sin fin, 1926; La voluntad de Dios, 1921–1930.

  992. Aragón, Uva de. *Alfonso Hernández Catá: un escritor cubano, salmantino y universal.* Salamanca: Universidad Pontificia de Salamanca, 1996. 179 pp.

  993. Fernández de la Torriente, Gastón F. *La novela de Hernández-Catá: un estudio desde la psicología.* Madrid: Playor, 1976. 131 pp.

  994. Mañach, Jorge, Juan Marinello and Antonio Barreras. *Recordación de Alfonso Hernández Catá.* Havana: La Verónica, 1941. 47 pp.

995. Meruelo González, Anisia. *Las novelas cortas de Alfonso Hernández Catá.* Montevideo: Geminis, 1973. 185 pp.

See also #399.

996. *Hernández Espinosa, Eugenio,* 1937– (playwright). Teatro, 1989 (El sacrificio, María Antonia [1979], La Simona [1977], Mi socio Manolo).

997. *Hernández, Jorge Luis,* 1946– (novelist, short story writer). El jugador de Chicago, 1985; Más bien de la memoria que del tiempo, 1994 ; Un tema para el griego, 1987.

998. *Hernández, Leopoldo M.,* 1921– (novelist, playwright, short story writer). Piezas cortas, 1990 (Sombras [1957], El infinito es negro [1959], En el parque [1961], Mañana el sol [1963], El mudo [1961], Infierno y duda [1967], No negocie, Sr. Presidente [1977], Cheo [1975], Los pobres ricos [1979]); Siempre tuvimos miedo, 1988; Y salieron del humo, 1994.

999. *Hernández Novás, Raúl,* 1948– (poet). Al más cercano amigo, 1987; Animal civil, 1988; Da capo, 1982; Embajador en el horizonte, 1982; Enigma de las aguas, 1982; Sonetos a gelsomina, 1991.

1000. *Hernández Rivera, Sergio Enrique,* 1921– (poet). Alabanzas, recuerdos, 1982; Compadecido bosque, 1964; De distintas maneras, 1990; Defensa de la golondrina, 1956; Forastero de la sombra, 1948; Mis siete palabras, 1948; Revolución es también eso, 1975.

1001. *Herrera, Georgina,* 1936– (poet). Gentes y cosas, 1974; Grande es el tiempo, 1989; Granos de sol y luna, 1978.

1002. *Herrera Ysla, Nelson,* 1947– (poet). El amor es una cosa esplendorosa, 1983; Escrito con amor, 1979; La tierra que hoy florece, 1978.

1003. *Hiriart, Rosario* (novelist, poet, short story writer). Albahaca, 1993; Las horas, 1995; Malpartida, 1993; Nuevo espejo de paciencia (y otros juegos literarios), 1988; Tu ojo, cocodrilo verde, 1984.

1004. *Ibaceta, Herminia D.* (poet). El amor resucitado, 1992; Amor y filosofía, 1992; Canto a Cuba, 1973; Ondas del eco, 1983.

1005. *Ibarzábal, Federico de,* 1894–1954 (novelist, poet, short story writer). El balcón de Julieta, 1916; La charca, 1938; Derelictos (y otros cuentos), 1939; Gente del "Heraldo," 1917; Gesta de héroes,

1918; La isla de los muertos y otros relatos, 1983 (Enrique Saínz, ed.); Nombre del tiempo, 1946; Tam-tam, 1941.

1006. *Iglesia, Alvaro de la,* 1859–1940 (novelist, short story writer). Adoración, 1894–1906; Cuentos, 1901; Pepe Antonio, 1903–1979.

1007. *Iglesias, Elena,* 1940– (poet, short story writer). Campo Raso, 1983; Cuenta el caracol, 1995; Mundo de aire, 1978; Península, 1977.

1008. *Iglesias Kennedy, Daniel,* 1950– (novelist). El gran incendio, 1989; La hija del cazador, 1995; La ranura del horizonte en llamas, 1987.

1009. *Iglesias Pérez, Luis* (poet). Tratado sobre la falsificación del oro, 1996.

1010. *Isidrón, Chanito,* 1903– (poet). Camilo y Estrella, 1989; Manuel García, rey de los campos de Cuba, 1989; Obra humorística, 1991 (Aldo Isidron del Valle, ed.).

    1011. Isidrón del Valle, Aldo. *Dos estilos y un cantar: El Indio Naborí y Chanito Isidrón.* Havana: Editorial Letras Cubanas, 1982. 173 pp.

    See also #1143.

1012. *Iznaga, Alcides,* 1910– (novelist, poet). Las cercas caminaban, 1970; Concierto, 1947 (with Aldo Menéndez and Samuel Feijóo); Cuentos y narraciones, 1990; Felipe y su piel, 1954; Hojas evasivas, 1956; La roca y la espuma, 1965; Los valedontes, 1953–1981.

1013. *James Figarola, Joel,* 1941– (novelist, short story writer). El caballo bermejo, 1987; Hacia la tierra del fin del mundo, 1982; Sobre muertos y dioses, 1989; Los testigos, 1973.

1014. *Jamís, Fayad,* 1930–1988 (poet). Abrí la verja de hierro, 1973; Breve historia del mundo, 1980?; Cuatro poemas en China, 1961; Cuerpos, 1966; Los párpados y el polvo, 1954–1981; La pedrada, 1972–1985; Por esta libertad, 1962–1977; Los puentes, 1962–1989; Sólo el amor, 1983; Tintas, 1980; Vagabundo del alba, 1959; La victoria de Playa Girón, 1964.

1015. *Jiménez, Ghiraldo,* 1892– (poet). La selva interior, 1919–1991.

1016. *Jorge, Guillermo J.* (poet). El cuadro, 1990; Selecciones de Samir (décimas inútiles), 1996.

1017. *Kozer, José,* 1940– (poet, short story writer). Antología breve, 1981; The Ark Upon the Number, 1982–1989; Bajo este cien, 1983; Carece de causa, 1988; El carillón de los muertos, 1987; De Chepén a La Habana, 1973 (with Isaac Goldemberg); De donde oscilan los seres en sus proporciones, 1990; La garza sin sombras, 1985; Jarrón de las abreviaturas, 1980; Nueve láminas (glorieta) y otros poemas, 1984; La rueca de los semblantes, 1980; Trazas del lirondo, 1993; Y así tomaron posesión en las ciudades, 1978.

1018. *Labrador Ruiz, Enrique,* 1902– (novelist, poet, short story writer). Anteo, 1940; Carne de quimera, 1947–1983; Cartas a la carte, 1991; Conejito Ulán, 1963; Cresival, 1936; Cuentos, 1970; El gallo en el espejo, 1953; Grimpolario, 1937; El laberinto de sí mismo, 1933–1983; Manera de vivir, 1941; Papel de fumar, 1945; La sangre hambrienta, 1950; Trailer de sueños, 1949.

1019. Labrador Ruiz, Enrique, and Reinaldo Sánchez. *Labrador Ruiz—tal cual: conversaciones.* Miami: Hispamerican Books, 1984. 95 pp. Spine title *Enrique Labrador Ruiz: conversaciones con Reinaldo Sánchez.*

1020. Molinero, Rita. *La narrativa de Enrique Labrador Ruiz.* Madrid: Playor, 1977. 262 pp.

1021. Sánchez, Reinaldo, ed. *Homenaje a Enrique Labrador Ruiz: textos críticos sobre su obra.* Montevideo: Editorial Ciencias, 1981. 84 pp.

1022. Villaronda, Guillermo. *Tres novelas distintas y un solo autor verdadero.* Havana: La Verónica, 1941. 30 pp.

1023. *Lago González, David,* 1950– (poet). Los hilos del tapiz, 1978–1994.

1024. *Larcada, Luis Ignacio* (short story writer). The Crystal Piano, 1987 (Translation of El piano de cristal [1986]); La imagen que no se deteriora, 1988; La península y la isla, 1986; Tierra del sur, 1993 (El algarrobo, El naranjo, La vid).

1025. *Lauro Pino, Alberto,* 1959– (poet). Con la misma furia de la primavera, 1987; Cuaderno de antinoo, 1994; Los tesoros del duende, 1987.

1026. *Lázaro, Felipe,* 1948– (poet). Las aguas, 1979; Despedida del asombro, 1974; Los muertos están cada día más indóciles, 1986.

1027. *Leante, César,* 1928– (novelist, short story writer). Calembour, 1988; Capitán de cimarrones, 1982; Desnudo femenino y otros cuentos, 1995; Los guerrilleros negros, 1976–1980; Muelle de caballería, 1973; Padres e hijos, 1967; Propiedad horizontal, 1978; La rueda y la serpiente, 1969; Tres historias, 1977 (El perseguido [1964], Una pistola y dos granadas, Una lápida para Enrique). See also #268.

1028. *León, Emilio J.,* 1924– (poet). Empinando chiringa, 1990 (with René León); Erospoemas y otros, 1988; Los hijos de las tinieblas, 1983; Recuerdos, 1985 (with René León); Ripios y parodias, 1986.

1029. *León, René,* 1935– (poet). Ayer, 1986; De todo un poco, 1988–1994; Empinando chiringa, 1991 (with Emilio J. León); Juracán, 1991; Mi triste corazón, 1993; Pensando en tí, 1990; Recorriendo el camino, 1994; Recuerdos, 1985 (with Emilio J. León).

1030. *LeRiverend, Pablo,* 1907– (poet). Algunos poemas de Pablo Le Riverend, 1985; Un aliento de poros, 1977; Cantos del dilatado olvido, 1964; Cielo de piedra, 1964; Con una salvedad congruente, 1979; Cuentos, 1983; De un doble, 1975–1979; Donde sudan mis labios, 1979; Espuma para los días, 1985; Glosas martianas, 1964; Hijo de Cuba soy, me llaman Pablo, 1980; Ir tolerando el látigo del tiempo, 1978–1983; Itinerario penúltimo, 1970; Jaula de sombras, 1977; Los ojos trepanados, 1978; Pena trillada, 1966; Por más señas, 1974; Postumo, relativamente . . . , 1982; Sobre esta clara piel octogenaria, 1987–1991.

1031. *Leyva Guerra, Juan,* 1938– (novelist, poet, short story writer). A la vuelta de abril, 1982; Animalia, 1977; Dónde dice asimismo debe decir pesimismo, 1991; El soldadito rubio, 1974; Zapatero remendón, 1981.

1032. *Leyva Portal, Waldo,* 1943– (poet). Con mucha piel de gente, 1982; De la ciudad y sus héroes, 1976; Diálogo de uno, 1988; El polvo de los caminos, 1984. Reprint of the 1955 ed.

1033. *Lezama Lima, José,* 1910–1976 (novelist, poet, short story writer). Algunos tratados en La Habana, 1971; Analecta de reloj, 1953; Cangrejos, golondrinas, 1977 (Autorretrato poético, Cangrejos, golondrinas, Fugados, Para un final presto, El patio morado, Juego de las decapitaciones); Confluencias, 1988 (Abel Enrique Prieto, ed.); Cuentos, 1987–1994 (Various eds.); Las eras imaginarias,

1971–1982; Esferaimagen, 1970–1979; La expresión americana y otros ensayos, 1969; Fascinación de la memoria (textos inéditos), 1994 (Iván González Cruz, ed.); Fragmentos a su imán, 1978; Imagen y posibilidad, 1981–1992 (Ciro Bianchi Ross, ed.); Las imágenes posibles, 1970–1979; Introducción a los vasos órficos, 1971; Juego de las decapitaciones, 1944–1984; La Habana, 1991 (José Prats Sariol, ed.); Lezama Lima, 1968 (Poesía: Muerte de Narciso [1937], Enemigo rumor [1941], Aventuras sigilosas [1945], La fijeza [1949], Dador [1960], Poemas no recojidos en libros. Cuentos: El patio morado, Juego de las decapitaciones. Ensayos: las imágenes posibles, Sierpe de Don Luis de Góngora, Sucesivas a las coordenadas habaneras. Novelas: Paradiso, Fronesis; Armando Alvarez Bravo, ed.); Muerte de Narciso, 1937–1988 (Various eds.); Obras completas, 1975 (Novela, Poesía completa, Ensayos, Cuentos); Oppiano Licario, 1977–1989 (Various eds.); Paradiso, 1974–1988 (Translation of Paradiso [1966–1993]; Gregory Rabassa, tr.); Orbita de José Lezama Lima, 1966 (Armando Alvarez Bravo, ed.); Poesía, 1992 (Emilio de Armas, ed.); Poesía completa, 1988; Posible imagen de José Lezama Lima [poesías], 1969–1972 (José A. Goytisolo, ed.); El reino de la imagen [selecciones], 1981 (Julio Ortega, ed.); Relatos, 1976–1988; Suerpe de Don Luis de Góngora, 1960–1979; Tratados en La Habana, 1958–1970.

1034. Arcos, Jorge Luis. *La solución unitiva: sobre el pensamiento poético de José Lezama Lima.* Havana: Editorial Academia, 1990. 86 pp.

1035. Bejel, Emilio. *José Lezama Lima: Poet of the Image.* Gainesville, FL: University of Florida Press, 1990. 178 pp.

1036. Bello Valdés, Mayerín. *Dos hilos de Ariadna: lecturas de "Para un final presto" y "El patio morado."* Havana: Editorial Letras Cubanas, 1996. 105 pp.

1037. Camacho Rivero de Gingerich, Alina L. *La cosmovisión poética de José Lezama Lima en "Paradiso" y "Oppiano Licario."* Miami: Ediciones Universal, 1990. 169 pp. Reprint of the 1911 ed.

1038. González, Reynaldo. *Lezama Lima: el ingenuo culpable.* Havana: Editorial Letras Cubanas, 1988. 164 pp.

1039. Lezama Lima, José, and Ciro Bianchi Ross, ed. *José Lezama Lima: diarios 1939–49, 1956–58.* Mexico City: Ediciones Era, 1994. 134 pp.

1040. Lezama Lima, José, Félix Guerra and Emilio Bejel, ed. *José Lezama Lima: amo al coro cuando canta—entrevistas.* Boulder, CO: Society of Spanish and Spanish-American Studies, 1994. 31 pp.

1041. Lezama Lima, José, and Eloísa Lezama Lima, ed. *Cartas, 1939–1976.* Madrid: Orígenes, 1979. 291 pp.

1042. Llopiz Cudel, Jorge Luis. *La región olvidada de José Lezama Lima.* Havana: Abril, 1994. 59 pp.

1043. Marqués de Armas, Pedro. *Fascículos sobre Lezama.* Havana: Editorial Letras Cubanas, 1994. 33 pp.

1044. Márquez, Enrique. *José Lezama Lima: bases y génesis de un sistema poético.* New York: P. Lang, 1991. 224 pp.

1045. Molinero, Rita. *José Lezama Lima; o, El hechizo de la búsqueda.* Madrid: Playor, 1989. 185 pp.

1046. Moreno-Durán, Rafael Humberto, ed. *Lezama Lima.* Barcelona: Montesinos, 1982. 102 pp.

1047. Pellón, Gustavo. *José Lezama Lima's Joyful Vision: A Study of "Paradiso" and Other Prose Works.* Austin, TX: University of Texas Press, 1989. 151 pp.

1048. Pérez León, Roberto. *Lezama: en la desmesura de la imagen.* Havana: Depto. de Actividades Culturales, Universidad de La Habana, 1987. 53 pp.

1049. Rensoli Laliga, Lourdes. *Lezama Lima: una cosmología poética.* Havana: Editorial Letras Cubanas, 1990. 143 pp.

1050. Rodríguez, Israel. *La estructura metafórica en "Paradiso": realismo e irrealismo en los tropos del trópico.* Elizabeth, NJ: American Press, 1983. 28 pp.

1051. Rodríguez Feo, José, and José Lezama Lima. *Mi correspondencia con Lezama Lima.* Mexico City: Ediciones Era, 1991. 182 pp. Reprint of the 1989 ed.

1052. Simón, Pedro, ed. *Recopilación de textos sobre José Lezama Lima.* Havana: Casa de las Américas, 1970. 375 pp.

1053. Souza, Raymond D. *The Poetic Fiction of José Lezama Lima.* Columbia, MO: University of Missouri Press, 1983. 149 pp.

1054. Ulloa, Justo C., ed. *José Lezama Lima: textos críticos.* Miami: Ediciones Universal, 1979. 156 pp.

1055. Villa, Alvaro de, and José Sánchez-Boudy. *Lezama Lima, peregrino inmóvil: "Paradiso" al desnudo—un estudio crítico de "Paradiso."* Miami: Ediciones Universal, 1974. 219 pp.

1056. Zaldívar, Gladys. *Novelística cubana de los años 60: "Paradiso," "El mundo alucinante."* Miami: Ediciones Universal, 1977. 75 pp.

See also #187, #219.

1057. Lima, Chely, 1957– (novelist, poet, short story writer). Los asesinos las prefieren rubias, 1990 (with Alberto Serret); Brujas, 1990; Confesiones nocturnas, 1994; La desnudez y el alba, 1989 (with Alberto Serret); Espacio abierto, 1983 (with Alberto Serret); Monólogo con lluvia, 1981; Rock sucio, 1992; Terriblemente iluminados, 1988; Tiempo nuestro, 1980; Triángulos mágicos, 1994.

1058. Llerena, Edith, 1936– (poet). Canciones para la muerte, 1982; Canto a España, 1979; Las catedrales del agua, 1981; El libro de los animales, 1983–1990; Los oficios, 1979–1982; La piel de la memoria, 1976; Resacas del amar, aires y lunas, 1992.

1059. López, Agustín (poet). Canto de la noche y sonetos mitológicos, 1985; Poemas de resaca, 1987; Sonetos de amor, de la vida y de la muerte, 1984; Sonetos quevedescos, 1985; Sus últimos poemas (María Arniella de López, ed.), 1991.

1060. López, César, 1933– (poet, short story writer). Ambito de los espejos, 1986; Apuntes para un pequeño viaje, 1966; La búsqueda y su signo, 1971–1989; Ceremonias y ceremoniales, 1988; Circulando el cuadrado, 1963–1986; Consideraciones, 1990–1993; Doble espejo para muerte denigrante, 1991; Primer libro de la ciudad, 1967; Quiebra de la perfección, 1983; Segundo libro de la ciudad, 1971–1989; Silencio en voz de muerte, 1963.

1061. López Lemus, Virgilio, 1946– (poet). Hacia la luz y hacia la vida, 1981; El pan de Aser, 1987; La sola edad, 1990.

1062. *López Morales, Eduardo,* 1939– (poet). Acerca del estado y del sueño, 1987; Antología, 1960; Camino a hombre, 1974; Cuaderno de un escolar sencillo, 1980; Elogio de la razón poética, 1982; Ensayo sobre el entendimiento humano, 1969.

1063. *Lorente, Luis,* 1948– (poet). Café nocturno, 1985; Como la noche incierta, 1991 (with Aramís Quintero); Las puertas y los pasos, 1976.

1064. *Lorenzo Fuentes, José,* 1928– (novelist, short story writer). Brígida pudo soñar/Los ojos del papel/El tiempo es el diablo, 1985–1990 [1985 ed. incorrectly attributed to Ricardo Bofill Pagés]; Después de la gaviota y otros cuentos, 1968–1988; Maguaraya arriba, 1963; Mesa de tres patas, 1980 (Tarde de papalotes, Los alquimistas del Capri, Mesa de tres patas); La piedra de María Ramos, 1986; El sol, ese enemigo, 1963; El vendedor de días, 1967; Viento de enero, 1968. See also #268.

1065. *Loveira, Carlos,* 1882–1928 (novelist). Los ciegos, 1922–1980; Generales y doctores, 1920–1984; Los inmorales, 1919–1980; Juan Criollo, 1927–1987; La última lección, 1924.

    1066. Marqués, Sarah. *Arte y sociedad en las novelas de Carlos Loveira.* Miami: Ediciones Universal, 1977. 240 pp.

    See also #422.

1067. *Loynaz, Dulce María,* 1903–1997 (novelist, poet). Alas en la sombra, 1992; Antología lírica, 1993; Bestiarium, 1991–1993; Canto a la mujer, 1993; Carta de amor a Tut-Ank-Amen, 1953; Dulce María Loynaz, 1992; Dulce María Loynaz (una poética de la soledad y el silencio), 1993; Ensayos, 1992; Finas redes, 1993; Jardín, 1951–1993; Juegos de agua, 1947; La novia de Lázaro, 1991–1993; Obra lírica, 1955 (Versos, 1920–1938, Juegos de agua, Poemas sin nombre); Poemas escogidos, 1993; Poemas náufragos, 1991; Poems Without a Name, 1993 (Translation of Poemas sin nombre [1953]; Harriet de Onís, tr.); Poesía completa, 1993; Poesías escogidas, 1984; Ultimos días de una casa, 1958–1993; Un verano en Tenerife, 1958–1994; Versos (1920–1938), 1938–1950; Yo fuí (feliz) en Cuba, 1993.

    1068. Aldaya, Alicia González Recio, ed. *Tres poetas hispanoamericanos: Dulce Maria Loynaz, Jaime Torres Bodet, José Martí.* Madrid: Playor, 1978. 128 pp.

1069. Baquero, Gastón. *Acercamiento a Dulce María Loynaz.* Madrid: Ediciones de Cultura Hispánica, Instituto de Cooperación Iberoamericana, 1993. 47 pp.

1070. Boza Masdival, Aurelio. *Dulce María Loynaz: poesía, ensueño y silencio.* Havana: Universidad de La Habana, 1948. 26 pp.

1071. Cuéllar, Aida. *Ala y raiz en el "Jardín" de Dulce María Loynaz.* Havana: Sociedad de Artes y Letras Cubanas, 1950. 30 pp.

1072. Loynaz, Dulce María, and Aldo Martínez Malo. *Confesiones de Dulce María Loynaz: entrevista.* Pinar del Río, Cuba: Hnos. Loynaz, 1993. 72 pp. Cronología, Bibliografía selecta, Poesía, Novela (Jardín), Viajes: Un verano en Tenerife, Conferencias, artículos, Semblanzas.

1073. Núñez, Ana Rosa, ed. *Homenaje a Dulce María Loynaz: obra literaria, poesía y prosa, estudios y comentarios.* Miami: Ediciones Universal, 1993. 415 pp.

1074. Simón, Pedro, ed. *Dulce María Loynaz.* Havana: Casa de las Américas, 1991. 834 pp.

1075. Spain, Ministerio de Cultura. *Dulce María Loynaz.* Madrid: El Ministerio, 1993. 177 pp.

1076. *Macau, Miguel Angel,* 1886–1971 (novelist, playwright, poet). Antología, 1944; Arpas amigas, 1906 (with José G. Villa); Biognosis, 1953; Cancionero folklórico, 1886; Clotilde Tejidor, 1958; Flores del trópico, 1912–1936; Harpas de alba, 1930–1938; Impresiones del camino, 1911–1942; Lírica saturnal, 1912–1943; Mi vía crucis, 1947 (Autobiographical); Obras dramáticas, 1913–1950 (La justicia en la inconciencia, Julián [1910], La partida); Pasajes en claroscuro, 1954; Peregrinaje ocioso, 1937; Ritmos del ideal, 1920–1949; Soledad, 1933–1940; Spoliarium, 1940–1948; Teatro, 1924–1957 (La herencia maldita, La fuerza incontrastable, La encina); Véspero radiante, 1961; Y se salvaba el amor, 1959.

1077. *Machado Pérez, Eloy,* 1940– (poet). El callejón del suspiro, 1993; Camán lloró, 1984.

1078. *Manzano Díaz, Roberto,* 1949– (poet). Puerta al camino, 1992; Tablillas de barro, 1996.

1079. *Marcos, Miguel de,* 1894–1954 (novelist, short story writer). Así es la vida, 1979; Cuentos pantuflares/Fábula de la vida apacible, 1943–1980; Fotuto, 1948–1976; Itinerario, 1956; Lujuria, 1915; Papaíto Mayarí, 1947.

1080. *Marín, Thelvia,* 1926– (playwright, poet). Desde mí, 1957; Una gran moneda sin escudos, 1973; Grito de paz, 1964; Reina de la noche, 1989.

1081. *Marinello, Juan,* 1898–1977 (poet). Domingos, 1985; Ensayos, 1977 (Imeldo Alvarez García, ed.); Escritos sociales, 1980 (Mirta Aguirre, ed.); Liberación, 1927; Meditación americana, 1959–1963; Poesía, 1977; Poesía, 1989 (Emilio de Armas, ed.); Recopilación de textos, 1979.

   1082. Antuña, María Luisa, and Josefina García Carranza. *Bibliografía de Juan Marinello.* Havana: Editorial Orbe, 1975. 473 pp.

   1083. Augier, Angel I., ed. *Orbita de Juan Marinello.* Havana: Unión de Artistas y Escritores de Cuba, 1968. 414 pp.

   1084. Marinello, Juan, and Luis Pavón, ed. *Cartas a Pepilla.* Havana: Editora Política, 1990. 166 pp. Correspondence with María Josefa Vidaurreta de Marinello.

   1085. Pérez, Trinidad and Pedro Simón, eds. *Recopilación de textos sobre Juan Marinello.* Havana: Casa de las Américas, 1979. 781 pp.

1086. *Mario, José,* 1940– (novelist, poet). El grito, 1960; Muerte del amor por la soledad, 1965; No hablemos de la desesperación, 1970–1983; Trece poemas, 1988.

1087. *Mario, Luis* (poet). Cuba en mis versos, 1993; Desde mis domingos, 1973; Esta mujer, 1983;--la misma, 1989; Un poeta cubano (poemas y décimas), 1971; Prófugo de la sal, 1978; Y nació un poema, 1975.

1088. *Márquez, Enrique,* 1952– (poet). Borrowed Time/Lo esperado y lo vivido, 1984 (Kate Wheeler, tr.); Cinco variaciones sobre la existencia, 1973 (with Ana Rosa Núñez and Félix Cruz Alvarez); Esquema tentativo del poema, 1973; Res, 1973 (with Ana Rosa Núñez and Félix Cruz Alvarez).

1089. *Márquez-Sterling, Manuel,* 1931– (novelist). Hondo corre el Cauto, 1990; La salsa del diablo, 1994.

1090. *Martí Fuentes, Adolfo,* 1922– (poet). El árbol del retorno, 1993; Alrededor del punto, 1971–1982; Contrapunto, 1980; La hora en punto, 1983; Libro de Graciela, 1985; Por el ancho camino, 1979; Puntos cardenales, 1980.

1091. *Martín, Juan,* 1954– (poet). Hasta que el tiempo estalle, 1987; Soliloquios del amor y la muerte, 1990.

1092. *Martínez Coronel, José Antonio* (short story writer). Los hijos del silencio, 1996.

1093. *Martínez Matos, José,* 1930– (novelist, poet). La casa del tiempo, 1983; Los conquistadores, 1978; Días de futuro, 1964; Juracán, 1974; La llanura, 1964; La luna sobre el rocío, 1987; Más allá del tiempo, 1982; Los oficios, 1970.

1094. *Martínez, Milton M.* (novelist). Espacio y albedrío, 1991; Los otros marielitos, 1983; Sitio de máscaras, 1987.

1095. *Martínez Villena, Rubén,* 1899–1934 (poet, short story writer). Antología, 1971; Mensaje lírico civil, 1978; Un nombre, prosa literaria, 1940; Poesía y prosa, 1978; Poesías, 1955; La pupila insomne, 1943–1960; Rubén Martínez Villena [selecciones], 1972 (Roberto Fernández Retamar, ed.).

   1096. Núñez Machín, Ana. *Rubén Martínez Villena.* Havana: Editorial de Ciencias Sociales, 1988. 458 pp.

1097. *Matas, Julio,* 1931– (playwright, short story writer). Aquí cruza el ciervo, 1990; Catálogo de imprevistos, 1963; La crónica y el suceso, 1964–1990; Erinia, 1971; El extravío, 1990; Juegos y rejuegos, 1992; Transiciones, migraciones, 1993.

1098. *Matías, Manuel* (novelist). Las chilenas, 1991; Día de yo y noches de vino y rosas, 1989.

1099. *Medina Hernández, Reinaldo,* 1961– (short story writer). Bar de Ida, 1994 (El cocodrilo, Se mueren los Rubén, Baltasar, el triste, Ojos de María, Viajero nocturno, El mar, Una foto en la calle 44, Bar de Ida).

1100. *Méndez Alpízar, L. Santiago* (poet). Plaza de armas, 1996.

1101. *Méndez Capote, Renée,* 1901– (novelist, short story writer). Apuntes, 1927; Dos niños en la Cuba colonial, 1966–1979;

Episodios de la epopeya, 1968–1974; Hace muchos años, una joven viajera, 1983–1990; Memorias de una cubanita que nació con el siglo, 1963–1990; Por el ojo de la cerradura, 1977–1981; Relatos heróicos, 1965; El remolino y otros relatos, 1982.

1102. *Méndez, Roberto,* 1958– (poet). Carta de relación, 1988; Desayuno sobre la hierba con máscaras, 1991; Manera de estar solo, 1989.

1103. *Menéndez Alberdi, Adolfo,* 1906–1987 (poet). El alba compartida, 1964; Canciones a fines, 1947; Emocionario doliente, 1938; Escala, 1945; Frutas cubanas, 1982; Juegos de islasol, 1976; Libro de las jueguinvenciones, 1976; Paloma del viento libre, 1992; Poemas del pueblo, 1960; Que el amor inventa, 1983; Las raíces con nombres y apellidos, 1975; El sueño inevitable, 1950; Zona del canto, 1983.

1104. *Menéndez Gallo, Rogelio* (short story writer). En una esquina del ring, 1992; Tesico y los pecados capitales, 1980.

1105. *Milián, José,* 1946– (playwright). Mamico omi omo, 1965; Vade reto y otras obras, 1990; ¿Y quién va a tomar café?, 1987.

1106. *Mir, Francisco,* 1953– (poet). Las hojas clínicas, 1985; Pianista en el restaurant, 1990; Proyecto de olvido y esperanza, 1981; Sinfonía fantástica, 1993.

1107. *Miranda, Julio E.,* 1945– (poet). Anotaciones de otoño, 1987; Casa de Cuba, 1990; El guardián del museo, 1992; El libro tonto, 1968; Maquillando el cadáver de la revolución, 1977; No se hagan ilusiones, 1970; Parapoemas, 1979; Poesía, paisaje y política, 1992; El poeta invisible, 1981; Rock urbano, 1989; Sobre vivientes, 1992; Vida del otro, 1982.

1108. *Montalvo, Berta G.* (poet). Donde se ocultan las sombras, 1995; Gotas de rocio, 1992; Miniaturas, 1990; Para mi gaveta, 1989.

1109. *Montaner, Carlos Alberto,* 1943– (novelist, poet, short story writer). Los combatientes, 1969; De la literatura considerada como una forma de urticaria, 1980; The Edge of the Abyss, 1973 (Translation of Instantáneas al borde del abismo [1970]; Bob L. Robinson, tr.); Perromundo, 1972–1985; Trama, 1987; The Witches' Poker Game and Other Stories, 1973 (Translation of Póker de brujas [1968–1978]; Bob L. Robinson, tr.).

1110. Fernández de la Torriente, Gastón J., ed. *La narrativa de Carlos Alberto Montaner: estudios sobre la nueva literatura hispanoamericana.* Madrid: Cupsa, 1978. 262 pp.

1111. *Montenegro, Carlos,* 1900– (novelist, short story writer). Aviones sobre el pueblo, 1937; Dos barcos, 1934; Los héroes, 1941; Hombres sin mujer, 1938–1990; El renuevo y otros cuentos, 1929.

1112. Baptista Gumucio, Mariano. *Montenegro el desconocido.* La Paz, Bolivia: Ultima Hora, 1979. 380 pp.

1113. *Montero, Reinaldo,* 1952– (playwright, poet, short story writer). Con tus palabras, 1987; Donjuanes, 1986; En el año del cometa, 1986; Fabriles, 1988; Memoria de las lluvias, 1989.

1114. *Montes Huidobro, Matías,* 1931– (novelist, playwright, poet, short story writer). La anunciación y otros cuentos cubanos, 1967; Exilio, 1988; Funeral en Teruel, 1989–1990; Obras en un acto, 1991; Ojos para no ver, 1979; Qwert and the Wedding Gown, 1992 (Translation of Desterrados al fuego [1975]; John Mitchell, Ruth Mitchell de Aguilar, trs.); Segar a los muertos, 1980; La vaca de los ojos largos, 1967. See also #166, #296.

1115. *Morales, Alberto Edel,* 1961– (poet). Viendo los autos pasar hacia occidente, 1994.

1116. *Morante, Rafael,* 1931– (novelist, short story writer). Amor más acá de las estrellas, 1987; Desterrado en el tiempo, 1990; La memoria metálica, 1993.

1117. *Morejón, Nancy,* 1944– (poet). Amor, ciudad atribuída, 1964; Elogio de la danza, 1982; Octubre imprescindible, 1982; Ours the Earth, 1990 (Joe R. Pereira, ed. and tr.); Paisaje célebre, 1993; Parajes de una época, 1979; Piedra pulida, 1986; Poemas, 1980; Richard trajo su flauta y otros argumentos, 1967; Where the Island Sleeps Like a Wing, 1985 (Kathleen Weaver, tr.).

1118. *Morell, Miriam* (novelist). El fulgor de las estrellas, 1991; Las palmas son novias que esperan, 1987.

1119. *Muller, Alberto,* 1939– (novelist, poet, short story writer). Monólogo con Yolanda, 1995; Tierra metalizada, 1985; Todos heridos por el norte y por el sur, 1981; USA, tierra condenada, 1980.

1120. *Muñoz Caravaca, Ricardo,* 1964– (playwright). Nostalgias de escenario, 1994 (La gran temporada, Rosas de María Fonseca, A la vuelta: año mil novecientos tanto).

1121. *Muñoz, Elías Miguel* (novelist, poet, short story writer). Ladrón de la mente, 1995; No fue posible el sol, 1989; Los viajes de Orlando Cachumbambé, 1984; Viajes fantásticos, 1994.

1122. *Muñoz Maceo, Lucía,* 1953– (poet). Pongo de este lado los sueños, 1989; Sobre hojas que nadie ve, 1994.

1123. *Nadereau, Efraín,* 1940– (poet). Bodegón con frutas y otros temas, 1989; Dulce es la canción de los talleres, 1983; Esto de hacer cantos, 1987; La isla que habitamos, 1973; La otra mitad del mundo, 1982. See also #217.

1124. *Navarro Luna, Manuel,* 1897–1966 (poet). Cartas de la ciénaga, 1930; Corazón adentro, 1922; Doña Martina, 1951–1961; Odas, 1977; Odas mambisas, 1961; Poemas, 1963; Los poemas mambises, 1959; Poesía y prosa, 1980 (Joaquín González Santana, ed.); Pulso y onda, 1933–1962; Ritmos dolientes, 1919; Siluetas aldanas, 1925; Surco, 1928; La tierra herida, 1960.

> 1125. Garzón, Xiomara, ed. *En torno a Navarro Luna.* Santiago, Cuba: Editorial Oriente, 1976. 226 pp.

> 1126. Rocasolano, Alberto. *Apuntes para un estudio acerca de Manuel Navarro Luna.* Havana: Editorial Letras Cubanas, 1979. 53 pp.

> 1127. Santana, Joaquín G. *Furia y fuego en Manuel Navarro Luna.* Havana: Unión de Escritores y Artistas de Cuba, 1975. 255 pp.

1128. *Navarro, Noel,* 1931– (novelist, short story writer). Brillo de sol sobre el acero, 1981; Los caminos de la noche, 1967; El círculo de fuego, 1986; Los días de nuestra angustia, 1962; Donde cae la luna, 1977; La huella del pulgar, 1972; El nivel de las aguas, 1980; El plano inclinado, 1968; El retrato, 1978; El sol de mediodía, 1992; Techo y sepultura, 1984; La última campaña de un elegido, 1979; Zona de silencio, 1971.

1129. *Navarro, Osvaldo,* 1946– (poet). El caballo de Mayaguara, 1984–1990; Clarividencia, 1988; Combustión interna, 1985; De regreso a la tierra, 1974; Los días y los hombres, 1975; Espejo de conciencia, 1980; Las manos en el fuego, 1981; Nosotros dos, 1984.

1130. *Niggemann, Clara,* 1910– (poet). Canto al apóstol, 1953; Como un ardiente río, 1985; En la puerta dorada, 1973; Otoño en Glendale, 1982; Remolino de fuego, 1980.

1131. *Nogueras, Luis Rogelio,* 1944–1985 (novelist, poet). Cabeza de zanahoria, 1967; El cuarto círculo, 1976–1979 (with Guillermo Rodríguez Rivera); La forma de las cosas que vendrán, 1989; Imitación de la vida, 1981; Nada del otro mundo, 1988; Nosotros, los sobrevivientes, 1981–1990; Las quince mil vidas del caminante, 1977; El último caso del inspector, 1983; Y si muero mañana, 1978–1984.

1132. *Novás Calvo, Lino,* 1905–1983 (novelist, poet, short story writer). Cayo Canas, 1946; En los traspatios, 1946; La luna nona y otros cuentos, 1942; Maneras de contar, 1970; El negrero, 1933–1956; No sé quién soy, 1945; Obra narrativa, 1990; El otro cayo, 1959.

    1133. Roses, Lorraine Elena. *Voices of the Storyteller: Cuba's Lino Novás Calvo.* Westport, CT: Greenwood Press, 1986. 155 pp.

    1134. Souza, Raymond D. *Lino Novás Calvo.* Boston, MA: Twayne, 1981. 146 pp.

1135. *Núñez, Ana Rosa,* 1926– (poet). Cartas al tiempo, 1993 (Mario G. Beruvides, ed.); Cinco variaciones sobre la existencia, 1973 (with Félix Cruz Alvarez and Enrique Márquez); Chrysanthemums/Crisantemo, 1990 (Jay H. Leal, tr.); Un día en el verso, 1959; Escamas del Caribe/Haikus de Cuba, 1971; Los oficia-leros, 1973; Res, 1973 (with Félix Cruz Alvarez and Enrique Márquez); Los siete lunas de enero, 1967; Sol de un solo día, 1973–1993; Uno y veinte golpes por América, 1991; Verde sobre azul, 1987; Viaje al Cazabe, 1970.

    1136. Rubido, Esperanza et al. *Ambito de la poesía de Ana Rosa Núñez.* Miami: Editorial Cartel, 1987. 46 pp.

    See also #161.

1137. *Núñez, Serafina,* 1913– (poet). Isla en el sueño, 1938; Mar cautiva, 1937; Los reinos sucesivos, 1992; Vigilia y secreto, 1941.

1138. *Ochoa Romero, Quintín,* 1952– (poet). Cofre de estrellas, 1992; Sobre un giro de espejos, 1988.

1139. *Oliver Labra, Carilda,* 1924– (poet). Al sur de mi garganta, 1949; Antología poética, 1992; Calzada de Tirry 81, 1987–1993 (Rafael Alcides, ed.); Desaparece el polvo, 1984; Se me ha perdido un hombre, 1991; Las sílabas y el tiempo, 1983; Sonetos, 1990; Tú eres mañana, 1979.

1140. *Oraá, Francisco de,* 1929– (poet). Bodas, 1989; Bodegón de las llamas, 1978; Ciudad, ciudad, 1979; Con figura de gente y en uso de razón, 1969; Desde la última estación, 1982; Es necesario, 1964; Haz una casa para todos, 1986; Por nefas, 1966; La rosa en la ceniza, 1990.

1141. *Oraá, Pedro,* 1931– (poet). Apuntes para una mitología de La Habana, 1971; Las destrucciones por el horizonte, 1968; El instante cernido, 1953; Sitio y sucesiones, 1981; La voz a tierra, 1956–1975.

1142. *Orovio, Helio,* 1938– (poet). Contra la luna, 1970; La cuerda entre los dedos, 1991; El huracán y la palma, 1980.

1143. *Orta Ruiz, Jesús,* 1922– (poet). Al son de la historia, 1986; Boda profunda, 1957; Cantos breves, 1978; De Hatuey a Fidel, 1960; Entre, y perdone Usted—, 1973–1983; Entre el reloj y los espejos, 1990; Marcha triunfal del ejército rebelde y poemas clandestinos y audaces, 1959; Pase de lista en décimas a la medida de sus nombres, 1973; El pulso del tiempo, 1966; Sueño reconstruido, 1962; Viajera peninsular, 1990. See also #1011.

1144. *Ortal-Miranda, Yolanda* (poet). The Sleepwalker's Ballad/Balada sonámbula de los desterrados del sueño, 1991 (Denise Smith, Mark Cerosaletti, trs.).

1145. *Ortega, Gregorio,* 1926– (novelist, short story writer). Del Guatao a Hong Kong, 1986; Los dinausaros y otros relatos, 1993 (Luis Alonso Girgado, ed.); Estado de gracia, 1992; Kappaüà, 1982–1994; La red y el tridente, 1985; Reportaje de las vísperas, 1967–1982; Una de cal y otra de arena, 1957–1983.

1146. *Ortiz Domínguez, Pedro,* 1942– (short story writer). Carta al rey, 1990; Comer con los indios, 1992; La hora tercia, 1987; Marta en la ventana, 1990; Primer encuentro, 1986.

1147. *Ortiz Hernández, Ernesto* (poet). Obelisco del hereje, 1996.

1148. *Otero, Lisandro,* 1932– (novelist, poet, short story writer). Arbol de la vida, 1990–1992; Bolero, 1986–1991; En ciudad semejante, 1970–1977; General a caballo, 1980–1993; Pasión de Urbino, 1966–1993; La situación, 1963–1982; Temporada de ángeles, 1983–1989; Trazado, 1976. See also #268, #289.

1149. *Pacheco Sosa, Sindo,* 1956– (novelist, short story writer). María Virginia está de vacaciones, 1994; Oficio de hormigas, 1990.

1150. *Padilla, Heberto,* 1932– (novelist, poet). A Fountain, A House of Stone, 1991 (Alastair Reed, Alexander Coleman, trs.); Fuera del juego, 1968–1982; Heroes Are Grazing in My Garden, 1984 (Translation of En mi jardín pastan los héroes [1981–1984]; Andrew Hurley, tr.); El justo tiempo humano, 1962–1972; Legacies (Selected Poems), 1982 (Translation of El hombre junto al mar [1981]; Alastair Reid, Andrew Hurley, trs.); Poetry and Politics/Poesía y política (Selected Poems), 1974; Provocaciones, 1973; Self-Portrait of the Other, 1990 (Translation of La mala memoria [1989–1992]; Alexander Coleman, tr.; Autobiographical); Sent Off the Field (A Selection of Poetry), 1972 (John Michael Cohen, tr.); Subversive Poetry: The Padilla Affair, 1972. See also #413.

1151. *Padrón Barquín, Juan Nicolás,* 1950– (poet). Aventuras de Elpidio Valdez, 1979; Crónica de la noche, 1994; Peregrinaciones, 1991; Tergiversaciones, 1985.

1152. *Padura, Leonardo,* 1955– (novelist, short story writer). Fiebre de caballos, 1988; Pasado perfecto, 1991; Según pasan los años, 1989–1992.

1153. *Palacios Hoyos, Esteban J.,* 1928– (short story writer). Descargas de un matancero de pueblo chiquito, 1990; El libertador de los cubanos, 1988.

1154. *Pardo, Angel* (poet). Ancestro, 1989; Behind Bars at Boniato/Entre rejas de Boniato, 1989 (Stephanie M. Joe, tr.); Horizonte a la deriva, 1989; Neomambí, 1989.

1155. *Pausides, Alex,* 1951– (poet). Ah mundo amor mío, 1978; Cuaderno del artista adolescente, 1993; Habitante del viento, 1996; Malo de magia, 1990.

1156. *Pavón, Luis,* 1930– (poet). Aquiles y la pólvora, 1990; Descubrimientos, 1967; El tiempo y sus banderas desplegadas, 1984.

1157. *Paz, Senel,* 1950– (novelist, short story writer). Fresa y chocolate, 1994–1995; El lobo, el bosque y el hombre nuevo, 1991; Los muchachos se divierten, 1989; El niño aquel, 1980; Un rey en el jardín, 1983–994.

1158. *Pedroso, Regino,* 1896–1983 (poet). Antología poética, 1939; Bolívar, sinfonía de libertad, 1945; El ciruelo de Yuan Pei Fu, 1955; Más allá canta el mar, 1939; Nosotros, 1933–1984; Obra poética, 1975; Poemas, 1966–1975; Poesías, 1984 (Félix Pita Rodríguez, ed.); Regino Pedroso [selecciones], 1973–1975 (Emilio de Armas, Osvaldo Navarro, Petra Ballagas, eds.); Sobre la marea de los siglos, 1987; Sólo acero, 1979.

1159. *Peña, Humberto J.,* 1928– (short story writer). Espinas al viento, 1983; El hijo del hijo, 1991; El viaje más largo, 1974; Ya no habrá más domingos, 1971.

1160. *Peñabaz, Manuel* (novelist). Miami, Casablanca del Caribe, 1991; La trampa, 1983.

1161. *Pereira, Manuel,* 1948– (novelist). El Comandante Veneno, 1977–1979; La prisa sobre el papel, 1987; La quinta nave de los locos, 1988; El ruso, 1980–1982; Toilette, 1993.

1162. *Perera, Hilda,* 1926– (novelist, short story writer). Cuentos de Adli y Luas, 1960; Cuentos de Apolo, 1947–1983; Cuentos para chicos y grandes, 1976–1991; Felices pascuas, 1977; La fuga de los juguetes, 1986; La jaula del unicornio, 1990; Kike, a Cuban Boy's Adventures in America, 1992 (Translation of Kike [1984–1993]; Warren Hampton, Hilda González, trs.); Mai, 1983–1992; Mañana es 26, 1960; Mumú, 1990; La noche de Ina, 1993; Pepín y el abuelo, 1983–1993; Perdido, 1994; Plantado, 1981–1985; Podría ser una vez, 1981; Los Robledal, 1987; El sitio de nadie, 1972.

> 1163. Alzaga, Florinda. *Ensayo sobre "El sitio de nadie" de Hilda Perera.* Miami: Ediciones Universal, 1975. 47 pp.

> 1164. Detjens, Wilma Else. *Teresa y los otros: voces narrativas en la novelística de Hilda Perera.* Miami: Ediciones Universal, 1993. 83 pp.

1165. *Pérez, Ada Elba,* 1961– (poet). La cara en el cristal, 1994.

1166. *Pérez Olivares, José,* 1949– (poet). A imagen y semejanza, 1987; Caja de Pandora, 1987; Cristo entrando en Bruselas, 1994; Examen del guerrero, 1992; Me llamo Antoine Doinel, 1992; Papeles personales, 1985; Proyecto para tiempos futuros, 1993. See also #212.

1167. *Pérez, Ricardo Alberto* (poet). Nietzsche dibuja a Cósima Wagner, 1996.

1168. *Pérez Sarduy, Pedro,* 1943– (novelist, poet, short story writer). Cumbite and Other Poems/Cumbite y otros poemas [1987], 1990; Surrealidad, 1967.

1169. *Pérez-Cruz, Ignacio Hugo,* 1940– (poet). Graciela, 1993; Parque de las avenidas, 1983.

1170. *Pérez-Moro, Oscar* (poet). Así es mi tierra, 1973; Lira criolla, 1987; Los municipios en décimas, 1990 (with Darío Espina Pérez and Francisco Henríquez); Ríos y palmas, 1985; Rumores de mi bohio, 1972; Vivencias del campo cubano, 1994 (with Francisco Henríquez).

1171. *Pichardo, Francisco Javier,* 1873–1941 (playwright, poet). Poesías escogidas, 1985 (Luis Suardíaz, ed.); Voces nómadas, 1908.

1172. *Pichardo, Manuel Serafín,* 1865–1937 (poet). Canto a Villaclara, 1907; La ciudad blanca, 1894; Cuba a la república, 1902.

1173. *Pichardo Moya, Felipe,* 1892–1957 (playwright, poet). Canto de la isla, 1942; Caverna, costa y meseta, 1945; La ciudad de los espejos, 1925–1992; Poesías, 1959; La zafra, 1926.

1174. *Picó, Fernando* (novelist, short story writer). Don Quijote en motora y otras andanzas, 1993; The Red Comb, 1994 (Translation of La peineta colorada [1991]; Argentina Palacios, tr.).

1175. *Piedra, Joaquín Enrique* (novelist, poet). Sabino, el último balsero, 1995; Sangre bajo las banderas, 1986; Unica palabra, 1954.

1176. *Piedra-Bueno, Andrés de,* 1903–1958 (poet). Antología poética, 1960 (Yolanda Lleonart, ed.); Don Bosco, 1941; En el camino, 1926; Lápida heroica, 1927–1929; Obras completas, 1939;

Pascualita, 1933; Poemas de Piedra-Bueno, 1983 (Yolanda Lleonart, Oscar Fernández de la Vega, eds.); Tabaco, 1944; Vas spirituale, 1924; Versos de Andrés de Piedra-Bueno, 1939; Yolandia, 1939.

1177. *Piñera, Virgilio,* 1912–1979 (novelist, playwright, poet, short story writer). Algunas verdades sospechosas, 1992 (Jorge Angel Pérez Sánchez, ed.); Una broma colosal, 1988; Una caja de zapatos vacía, 1986 (Luis F. González-Cruz, ed.); Cold Air, 1985 (Translation of Aire frío [1959–1990]; Maria Irene Fornes, tr.); Cold Tales, 1988 (Translation of Cuentos fríos [1956–1989]; Mark Schafer, tr.); Cuentos, 1964–1983; Cuentos de la risa del horror, 1994 (Efraín Rodríguez Santana, ed.); Dos viejos pánicos, 1968; El que vino a salvarme, 1970; Un fogonazo, 1987; Muecas para escribientes, 1987–1990; El no, 1994; Pequeñas maniobras, 1963–1986; Poesía y prosa, 1944; Presiones y diamantes, 1967–1986; René's Flesh, 1992 (Translation of La carne de René [1952–1985]; Mark Schafer, tr.); Teatro completo, 1961 (Electra Garrigó [1941], Jesús [1950], Falsa alarma [1948], La boda [1958], El flaco y el gordo [1959], Aire frío [1959], El filántropo [1960]); Teatro inconcluso, 1990 (Rine Leal, ed.); La vida entera, 1969.

1178. Garrandés, Alberto. *La poética del límite: sobre la cuentística de Virgilio Piñera.* Havana: Editorial Letras Cubanas, 1994. 134 pp.

1179. Torres, Carmen. *La cuentística de Virgilio Piñera: estrategias humorísticas.* Madrid: Pliegos, 1989. 133 pp.

See also #219, #268.

1180. *Pita, Juana Rosa,* 1939– (poet). Aires etruscos, 1987; El arca de los sueños, 1978; Las cartas y las horas, 1977; Crónicas del Caribe, 1983; Una estación en tren, 1994; Eurídice en la fuente, 1979; Florencia nuestra, 1992; Manual de magia, 1979; Mar entre rejas, 1977; Pan de sol, 1976; Plaza sitiada, 1987; El sol tatuado, 1986; Sips of Light/Sorbos de luz, 1990 (Mario de Salvatierra, tr.); Transfiguración de la armonía, 1993; Viajes de Penélope, 1980.

1181. *Pita, Julio Ramón* (novelist). El ojo del rey, 1996.

1182. *Pita Rodríguez, Félix,* 1909– (poet, short story writer). Aquiles Serdán 18, 1988; Cantigas, 1979; Cuentos, 1960; De sueños y memorias, 1985; Elogio de Marco Polo, 1974; Félix Pita Rodríguez (poesía y prosa), 1978; Hiroshima, 1962; Historia tan natural, 1971; Niños de Vietnam, 1974; Poemas y cuentos, 1965–1975 (Poesía dispersa, Corcel de fuego [1948], Las crónicas [1961–1963], Las noches [1940], Cuentos completos [1963], Cuentos dispersos); La pipa de cerezo y otros cuentos, 1987; Poesía, 1978; Prosa, 1978; Proyectos del lirio, 1988–1992; Recordar el futuro, 1985; San Abul de Montecallado, 1945; Solamente a morir, 1976; Tarot de la poesía, 1976; Tobías, 1955.

1183. Chaple, Sergio. *De veleros y recuerdos: una nueva lectura de "Tobías."* Havana: Editorial Letras Cubanas, 1992. 39 pp.

1184. González Bolaños, Aimée. *La narrativa de Félix Pita Rodríguez.* Havana: Editorial Letras Cubanas, 1985. 379 pp.

1185. Santos Moray, Mercedes. *La doble aventura.* Havana: Editorial Letras Cubanas, 1983. 117 pp.

1186. *Portilla, Juan Ramón de la* (novelist, short story writer). Hechos en casa, 1995; Olvida ese tango, 1996.

1187. *Póveda, José Manuel,* 1888–1926 (novelist, poet). José Manuel Póveda, 1975 (Alberto Rocasolano, ed.); Obra poética, 1988 (Alberto Rocasolano, ed.); Proemios de cenáculo, 1948; Prosa, 1980–1981; Versos precursores, 1928.

1188. Póveda, Alcibiades S. *José Manuel Póveda: renovacion y modernismo.* Santiago, Cuba: Ediciones Caseron, 1989. 45 pp.

1189. Rocasolano, Alberto. *El último de los raros: estudios acerca de José Manuel Póveda.* Havana: Editorial Letras Cubanas, 1982. 382 pp.

1190. *Prado, Pura del,* 1931– (poet). Canto a Martí, 1956; Color de orisha, 1972; De codo en el arcoiris, 1952; Idilio del girasol, 1975; Otoño enamorado, 1972; La otra orilla, 1972; El río con sed, 1956; Los sábados y Juan, 1953. See also #161.

1191. *Prats, Delfín,* 1945– (poet). El esplendor y el caos, 1991; Para festejar el ascenso de Icaro, 1987.

1192. *Prieres, Manuel,* 1942– (novelist, poet). Desheredados, 1976; Senderos de rocío y sal, 1992.

1193. *Prieto González, José Manuel* (short story writer). Nunca antes habías visto el rojo, 1996.

1194. *Querejeta Barceló, Alejandro,* 1947– (novelist, poet). Arena negra, 1989; Cartas interrumpidas, 1993; Crónicas infieles, 1992; Los términos de la tierra, 1985.

1195. *Quiñones, Serafín,* 1942– (short story writer). A pie de obra, 1990; Al final del terraplén el sol, 1971.

1196. *Quintero, Aramís,* 1948– (poet). Cálida forma, 1987; Como la noche incierta, 1991 (with Luis Lorente); Diálogos, 1981; Días del aire, 1982; Fábulas y estampas, 1982; Letras mágicas, 1991; Maíz regado, 1981.

1197. *Ramos, José Antonio,* 1885–1946 (novelist, playwright). Caniquí, 1936–1977; Coaybay, 1926–1980; Cuando el amor muere, 1911; En las manos de Dios, 1933; Entreactos, 1913; FU-3001, 1944; El hombre fuerte, 1915; Humberto Fabra, 1908–1984; Las impurezas de la realidad, 1929–1979; Liberta, 1911; La recurva, 1984; Satanás, 1913; Teatro, 1989 (Francisco Garzón Céspedes, ed.); Teatro cubano, 1983 (Esther Sánchez-Grey Alba, ed.); Tembladera, 1918; El traidor, 1941. See also #295.

1198. *Ramy, Manuel Alberto,* 1940– (short story writer). Margarita y otros cuentos de San Marién del Mar, 1995.

1199. *Renteros, Exora* (novelist). Pensar es un pecado, 1994.

1200. *Ríos, Soleida,* 1950– (poet). De la sierra, 1977; Entre mundo y juguete, 1987.

1201. *Rivera, Frank* (novelist, poet, short story writer). Construcciones, 1979; Cuentos cubanos, 1992; Las sábanas y el tiempo, 1984–1986.

1202. *Rivero, Isel,* 1941– (poet). El banquete, 1981; Fantasías de la noche, 1959; Night Rained Here, 1976; Tundra, 1963. See also #166.

1203. *Rivero, José Rolando* (poet). Santa palabra, 1996.

1204. *Rivero, Raúl,* 1945– (poet). Cierta poesía, 1982; Corazón que ofrecer, 1980; Escribo de memoria, 1987; Papel de hombre, 1970; Poesía pública, 1983; Poesía sobre la tierra, 1973.

1205. *Riverón Morales, Rogelio M.,* 1964– (short story writer). Los equivocados, 1992; Subir al cielo y otras equivocaciones, 1996.

1206. *Riverón Rojas, Ricardo,* 1949– (poet). La luna en un cartel, 1991; La próxima persona, 1993 (Este soy yo, Dicen, aquí en familia, El libro de María, Cuaderno naif, Para decir que palabras, El otro en el espejo); Y dulce era la luz como un venado, 1989.

1207. *Robles, Mireya,* 1934– (novelist, poet). En esta aurora, 1978; Hagiografía de Narcisa la Bella, 1985; Time, the Artisan/Tiempo artesano, 1973–1977.

1208. *Rocasolano, Alberto,* 1935– (poet). A cara y cruz, 1970; Diestro en soledades y esperanzas, 1967; Es de humanos, 1976; Ese sueño que fuímos, 1991; Fundar la gloria, 1988; Permiso para el alto navegar, 1992; Porque tenemos héroes, 1982.

1209. *Rodríguez, Antonio Orlando,* 1956– (short story writer). Los caminantes caminan caminos, 1992; Cuentos de cuando La Habana era chiquita, 1983; Querido Drácula, 1989; Siffig y el vramontono 45-A, 1978; Strip-tease, 1985; El sueño, 1984–1994.

1210. *Rodríguez, Héctor L.* (short story writer). Cuentos de Miami, 1995.

1211. *Rodríguez, Luis Felipe,* 1888–1947 (novelist, playwright, poet, short story writer). Ciénaga y otros relatos, 1937–1984; La conjura de la ciénaga, 1924–1969; La copa vacía, 1926; Don Quijote de Hollywood, 1936; Marcos Antilla/Relatos de Marcos Antilla, 1932–1972; El negro que se bebió la luna, 1978 (El negro que se bebió la luna, Cómo opinaba Damián Paredes [1916], Flores de ilusión, La pascua de la tierra natal [1928]; Eduardo Heras León, ed.); Poemas del corazón amoroso, 1920.

1212. *Rodríguez, Reina María,* 1952– (poet). Cuando una mujer no duerme, 1982; La gente de mi barrio, 1975; Para un cordero blanco, 1984. See also #212.

1213. *Rodríguez Rivera, Guillermo,* 1943– (novelist, poet). Cambio de impresiones, 1966; En carne propria, 1983; El cuarto círculo, 1976–1979 (with Luis Rogelio Nogueras); Para salir del siglo XX, 1994 (Cambio de impresiones [1966], Respuestas y preguntas, El libro rojo [1970], Canta, En carne propria [1983], Para salir del siglo XX).

1214. *Rodríguez, Rolando,* 1940– (novelist). Cuba 1930/República angelical, 1988–1995.

1215. *Rodríguez Santana, Efraín,* 1953– (poet). Conversación sombría, 1991; El hacha de miel, 1993; Vindicación de los mancebos, 1983; El zig-zag y la flecha, 1984–1987.

1216. *Rodríguez Santos, Justo,* 1915– (poet). La belleza que el cielo no amortaja, 1950; El diapason del ventisquero, 1975; La epopeya del Moncada, 1963; Luz cautiva, 1938; Los naipes conjurados, 1979; Las óperas del sueño, 1981. See also #219.

1217. *Rodríguez Tosca, Alberto,* 1962– (poet). Otros poemas, 1992; Todas las jaurías del rey, 1988.

1218. *Rojas, Agustín de,* 1949– (novelist). El año 2000, 1990; Catarsis y sociedad, 1993; Espiral, 1982; Una leyenda del futuro, 1985.

1219. *Ruano, Luis Felipe* (poet). Petrarca furioso, 1996.

1220. *Sabourín Fornaris, Jesús,* 1928– (poet). Desde lejos y aquí, 1991; Elegías combatientes y otros poemas, 1988; Hallazgo del hombre, 1982.

1221. *Salado, Minerva,* 1944– (poet). Al cierre, 1972; El juguetero prodigioso, 1986; País de noviembre, 1987; Palabras en el espejo, 1987; Tema sobre un paseo, 1978.

1222. *Salcines, Claro Misael* (short story writer). Compañero de mesa, 1996.

1223. *Saldaña, Excilia,* 1946– (poet, short story writer). Cantos para un mayito y una paloma, 1983; Compay Tito, 1988 (with David Chericián); Kele kele, 1987; Mi nombre, 1991; La noche, 1989; El refranero de la víbora, 1989.

1224. *Sales, Miguel,* 1951– (poet). Desde las rejas, 1976; Desencuentros, 1995.

1225. *Sánchez Galarraga, Gustavo,* 1892–1934 (playwright, poet). Las alamedas románticas, 1927; Arabescos, 1920; La barca sonora, 1917; Cancionero español, 1923; La copa amarga, 1920; Copos de sueño, 1918; Las espinas del rosal, 1927; Flores de agua, 1921; La fuente matinal, 1915; Glosas del camino, 1920; El héroe, 1942 (Virgil Alexander Warren, James Obed Swain, eds.); Huerto cerrado, 1924; Humo azul, 1923; El jardín de Margarita, 1917; Momentos líricos, 1920; Motivos sentimentales, 1919; Música triste, 1920; Recogimiento, 1920; Senderos de luna, 1924.

1226. *Sánchez Mejías, Rolando,* 1959– (poet, short story writer). Collage en azul adorable, 1991; Derivas, 1994; Escrituras, 1994; La noche profunda del mundo, 1993.

1227. *Sánchez Ochoa, Magaly,* 1940– (novelist). Fabia Tabares asomada al espejo, 1996; La milla, 1996; Mata, 1996.

1228. *Sánchez-Boudy, José,* 1927– (novelist, playwright, poet, short story writer). Aché, babalú ayé, 1975; Acuara ochún de caracoles verdes, 1987; Afro-Cuban Poetry de Oshún a Yemayá: The Afro-Cuban Poetry of José Sánchez-Boudy in English Translation, 1978 (Claudio Freixas, ed. and tr.); Alegrías de coco, 1970; Candelario Soledá, guaracha y látigo, 1986; El corredor Kresto, 1976; Crocante de maní, 1973; Los cruzados de la aurora, 1972; Cuba and Her Poets: The Poems of José Sánchez-Boudy, 1974 (Woodrow W. Moore, ed. and tr.); Cuentos a luna llena, 1971; Cuentos blancos y negros, 1983; Cuentos de la niñez y otros, 1983; Cuentos del hombre, 1969; Cuentos grises, 1966; Dile a Catalina, 1990; Ekué abanakué ekué, 1977; Fulastres y fulastones y otras estampas cubanas, 1987; El héroe, 1980; El hombre que era dos, 1980; Homo sapiens: teatro del absurdo, 1971; Leyendas de azúcar prieta, 1977; Lilayando, 1971; Lilayando pal tu, 1978; Mi barrio y mi esquina, 1989; Niquín el cesante, 1980; Orbus terrarum, 1974; Patrióticas, 1986; El picúo, el fisto, el barrio y otras estampas cubanas, 1977; Poemas de otoño e invierno, 1967; Poemas del silencio, 1969; Potaje y otro mazote de estampas cubanas, 1988; Pregones, 1975; La rebelión de los negros, 1980; Ritmo de solá, 1967; Los sarracenos del ocaso, 1977; La soledad de la Playa Larga, 1975; Tiempo congelado, 1979; Tres tiros un viernes santo, 1980; Tus ojos Cuba, sosiego, viento y ola, 1988.

1229. León, René. *La poesía negra de José Sánchez-Boudy.* Miami: Ediciones Universal, 1977. 37 pp.

1230. Suárez, Laurentino, ed. *La narrativa de José Sánchez-Boudy: tragedia y folklore.* Miami: Ediciones Universal, 1983. 192 pp.

1231. *Santana, Ernesto* (short story writer). Bestiario pánico, 1996.

1232. *Santayana, Manuel J.,* 1953– (poet). De la luz sitiada, 1980; Las palabras y las sombras, 1992.

1233. *Sarduy, Severo,* 1937– (novelist, playwright, poet). Barroco, 1974; Big Bang, 1974; Christ on the Rue Jacob, 1995 (Translation of El Cristo de la rue Jacob [1987–1994]; Suzanne Jill Levine,

Carol Maier, trs.); Cobra, 1972–1986; Cocuyo, 1990; Colibrí, 1984–1988; Epitafios, 1994; For Voice, 1985 (Translation of Para la voz [1978]; Philip Barnard, tr.); From Cuba With a Song, 1994 (Translation of De dónde son los cantantes [1967–1993]; Suzanne Jill Levine, tr.); Gatico-Gatico, 1994; Gestos, 1963–1973; Maitreya, 1987 (Translation of Maitreya [1978–1981]; Suzanne Jill Levine, tr.); Pájaros de la playa, 1993; Un testigo fugaz y disfrazado, 1985–1993; Un testigo perenne y delatado, 1993.

1234. Aguilar Mora, Jorge et al. *Severo Sarduy.* Madrid: Editorial Fundamentos, 1976. 202 pp.

1235. Cabanillas, Francisco. *Escrito sobre Severo: una relectura de Severo Sarduy.* Miami: Ediciones Universal, 1995. 105 pp.

1236. González Echevarría, Roberto. *La ruta de Severo Sarduy.* Hanover, NH: Ediciones del Norte, 1987. 274 pp.

1237. Guerrero, Gustavo. *La estrategia neobarroca: estudio sobre el resurgimiento de la poética barroca en la obra narrativa de Severo Sarduy.* Barcelona: Edicions del Mall, 1987. 212 pp.

1238. Macé, Marie Anne. *Severo Sarduy.* Paris: L'Harmattan, 1992. 173 pp.

1239. Méndez Rodenas, Adriana. *Severo Sarduy: el neobarroco de la transgresión.* Mexico City: Universidad Nacional Autónoma de México, 1983. 165 pp.

1240. Montero, Oscar. *The Name Game: Writing/Fading Writer in "De dónde son los cantantes."* Chapel Hill, NC: University of North Carolina Press, 1988. 149 pp.

1241. Pérez, Rolando. *Severo Sarduy and the Religion of the Text.* Lanham, MD: University Press of America, 1988. 49 pp.

1242. Sánchez-Boudy, José. *La temática novelística de Severo Sarduy: "De dónde son los cantantes."* Miami: Ediciones Universal, 1985. 102 pp. Cover title *La temática narrativa de Severo Sarduy..*

See also #744.

1243. *Sarusky, Jaime,* 1931– (novelist, short story writer). La búsqueda, 1961–1982; Rebelión en la octava casa, 1967–1979; Un testigo fugaz y disfrazado, 1985–1993; Un testigo perenne y delatado, 1993.

1244. *Saunders, Rogelio* (poet). Polyhimnia, 1996.

1245. *Savariego, Berta,* 1946– (novelist, short story writer). Fiesta de abril, 1981; La mandolina y otros cuentos, 1988.

1246. *Serpa, Enrique,* 1899–1968 (novelist, poet, short story writer). Aletas de tiburón, 1963–1975; Contrabando, 1938–1982; Felisa y yo, 1937; La manigua heroica, 1978; La miel de las horas, 1925; Noche de fiesta, 1951; La trampa, 1956–1980; Vitrina, 1940.

1247. *Serret, Alberto,* 1947– (poet, short story writer). Los asesinos las prefieren rubias, 1990 (with Chely Lima); Consultorio terrícola, 1988; Cordeles de humo, 1987; Cuento para un ojo perdido, 1993; El desnudez y el alba, 1989 (with Chely Lima); Un día de otro planeta, 1986; En plena desnudez, 1988; Espacio abierto, 1983 (with Chely Lima); Figuras soñadas y cantadas, 1981; Jaula abierta, 1980; Sortilegio para caminantes, 1992. See also #217.

1248. *Sicilia Martínez, Alberto,* 1966– (poet). El camión verde, 1994.

1249. *Silverio, Nicasio,* 1930– (poet). Afán del agua, 1994.

1250. *Smith, Octavio,* 1921– (poet). Andanzas, 1987; Crónicas, 1974; Del furtivo destierro, 1946; Estos barrios, 1966; Lejos de la casa marina, 1981. See also #219.

1251. *Soler Puig, José,* 1916– (novelist, playwright). Anima sola, 1986; Bertillón 166, 1986 (Translation of Bertillón 166 [1960–1982]; Harold Spencer, tr.); El caserón, 1976–1990; El derrumbe, 1964–1981; En el año de enero, 1963; Una mujer, 1987; Un mundo de cosas, 1982–1989; El nudo, 1983; The Slow-Rising Bread, 1987 (Translation of El pan dormido [1975–1990]; Jane McManus, tr.). See also #300.

1252. *Solís, Cleva,* 1926– (poet). A nadie espera el tiempo, 1961; Las mágicas distancias, 1961; Los sabios días, 1984; Vigilia, 1957.

1253. *Sosa de Quesada, Arístides,* 1908– (novelist, playright, poet). Ayer sin fecha, 1957; Brasas en la nieve, 1971; Errante, 1967; Un extraño en la familia, 1958; La patria y la vida, 1944; Tardes de Aristafael, 1954; Wan Pu, relato de una vida, 1951; Zumo y sueños, 1988.

1254. *Sosa González, Manuel* (poet). Saga del tiempo inasible, 1996.

1255. *Suardíaz, Luis,* 1936– (poet). Como quien vuelve de un largo viaje, 1975; Haber vivido, 1966; Un instante que sostiene toda la luz, 1988; Leyenda de la Justa Belleza, 1978; Nuevos cuadernos de clase, 1989; Siempre habrá poesía, 1983; Todo lo que tiene fin es breve, 1983.

1256. *Suárez, Adolfo,* 1936– (poet). Donde el poeta opina, 1970; Ella siente llegar el mediodía, 1988; Letras fieras, 1975; Sucesos de la tarde, 1980.

1257. *Suárez León, Carmen,* 1951– (poet). El patio de mi casa, 1994.

1258. *Tallet, José Zacharías,* 1893–1962 (poet). Orbita de José Z. Tallet, 1969 (Helio Orovio, ed.); Poesía y prosa, 1979; La semilla estéril, 1951; Vivo aún, 1978.

1259. *Tápanes Estrella, Raúl,* 1938– (short story writer). Enigmas, 1987; La escapada, 1992; Traición a la sangre, 1991.

1260. *Tauler López, Arnoldo,* 1937– (novelist). Cagüeyro, 1984; Las cáscaras del hombre, 1979; Las centinelas de la aurora, 1988; Cuentos de Seboruco, 1979; La puesta en marcha, 1989; La sangre regresada, 1978; Los siete pasos del sumario, 1978.

1261. *Tejera, Nivaria,* 1930– (novelist, poet). El barranco, 1959–1989; La barrera fluídica/París escarabajo, 1976; La gruta, 1952; Innumerables voces, 1964; Luz de lágrimas, 1951; Rueda del exiliado, 1983; Sonámbulo del sol, 1972; Y martelar, 1983.

1262. *Terry Valdespino, Miguel,* 1963– (playwright). Laberinto de lobos, 1994.

1263. *Toledo Sande, Luis,* 1950– (poet, short story writer). De raíz y memoria, 1993; Flora cubana, 1980; Libro de Laura y Claudia, 1993; Precisa recordar, 1976.

1264. *Tomás, Lourdes* (short story writer). Las dos caras de D., 1985; Fray Servando alucinado, 1994.

1265. *Tomás, Mercedes* (poet). La palabra total, 1994.

1266. *Torralbas, José Mariano,* 1962– (poet, short story writer). Estaciones de luz, 1991; La otra cara, 1991.

1267. *Torréns de Garmendia, Mercedes,* 1886–1965 (poet). Esquila en el poniente, 1951; La flauta del silencio, 1946; Fragua de estrellas, 1935; Fuente sellada, 1956; Jardines del crepúsculo, 1948; Jazminero en la sombra, 1942.

1268. *Torrente, Aurelio N.,* 1924– (novelist, poet). Chubascos del exilio, 1977; Lidia María: la historia de una mujer, decidida y valiente que amó a su patria, 1994.

1269. *Torres, Omar,* 1945– (novelist, poet). Al partir, 1986; Apenas un bolero, 1981; Conversación primera, 1975; De nunca a siempre, 1981; Fallen Angels Sing, 1991; Tiempo robado, 1978.

1270. *Torriente Brau, Pablo de la,* 1901–1936 (novelist, short story writer). Aventuras del soldado desconocido cubano, 1940–1990; Batey, 1930 (with Gonzalo Mazas Garbayo); Cuentos de Batey, 1962; Humor y pólvora, 1984 (Mercedes Santos Moray, ed.); Muchachos . . . !, 1978; El periodista Pablo: crónicas y otros textos 1930–1936, 1989 (Víctor Casaus, ed.); Pluma en ristre, 1949–1965 (Raúl Roa, ed.); Realengo 18, 1962–1979.

1271. Casáus, Víctor. *Pablo, con el filo de la hoja.* Havana: Unión de Escritores y Artistas de Cuba, 1983. 235 pp.

1272. Santos Moray, Mercedes. *Las aventuras del almirante.* Havana: Editorial Gente Nueva, 1987. 319 pp.

1273. Torriente, Loló de la. *Torriente-Brau: retrato de un hombre.* Havana: Instituto del Libro, 1968. 234 pp.

1274. Torriente Brau, Pablo de la, and Víctor Casáus, ed. *Cartas cruzadas.* Havana: Editorial Letras Cubanas, 1981. 602 pp.

1275. *Torriente, Loló de la,* 1907–1983 (novelist, short story writer). Los caballeros de la marea roja, 1984; Imagen en dos tiempos, 1982 (Autobiographical); Mi casa en la tierra/ Testimonio desde dentro, 1956–1985; Narraciones de Federica y otros cuentos, 1988.

1276. *Travieso, Julio,* 1940– (novelist, short story writer). Los corderos beben vino, 1970; Cuando la noche muera, 1983; Días de guerra, 1967; Larga es la lucha, 1982; Para matar al lobo, 1971–1990; El polvo y el oro, 1993; El prisionero, 1979.

1277. *Triana, José,* 1931– (playwright, poet). Ceremonial de guerra, 1990; Cuaderno de familia, 1989; Medea en el espejo, 1960–1991;

La noche de los asesinos, 1965–1991; Palabras comunes, 1991; La muerte del ñeque, 1964; Oscuro el enigma, 1993; El parque de la fraternidad, 1962.

1278. Campa, Román V. de la. *José Triana: ritualización de la sociedad cubana.* Minneapolis, MN: Institute for the Study of Ideologies and Literature, 1979. 124 pp.

1279. Taylor, Diana, ed. *En busca de una imagen: ensayos críticos sobre Griselda Gambaro y José Triana.* Ottawa, Ont.: Girol Books, 1989. 195 pp.

See also #292, #413.

1280. *Triff, Eduardo* (novelist, poet). El descalabro, 1995; El dharma del hombre, 1990; Donde reposan las hachas, 1994; Hombre pequeño, 1943; El maestro y Li, 1993; Momentos, 1954.

1281. *Ulloa, Yolanda,* 1947– (poet). Los cantos de Benjamín, 1975.

1282. *Valdés Ginebra, Arminda,* 1923– (poet). Equilibrio del ansia, 1993; Renuevo tras la lluvia, 1993; Sigo zurciendo las medias de mi hijo, 1991; Sombras imaginarias, 1989; Vigilia del aliento, 1990.

1283. *Valdés, Marta* (poet). Cancionero proprio, 1995.

1284. *Valdés Torres, René* (poet). A solas con Casandra, 1995.

1285. *Valdés Vivó, Raúl,* 1929– (novelist, playwright). El bonzo de Kyoto, 1993; La brigada y el mutilado, 1974; Naranjas en Saigón, 1977; Los negros ciegos, 1971–1976; Reacción disociativa, 1986.

1286. *Valdés, Zoé,* 1959– (novelist, poet). La hija del embajador, 1995; La nada cotidiana, 1995; Respuesta para vivir, 1986; Sangre azul, 1994; Todo para una sombra, 1986.

1287. *Valero, Roberto,* 1955– (novelist, poet). Desde un oscuro ángulo, 1982; Dharma, 1985; En fin, la noche, 1984; Este viento de cuaresma, 1994; No estaré en tu camino, 1991; Venias, 1990.

1288. *Valladares, Armando,* 1937– (poet). Against All Hopes, 1986–1991 (Translation of Contra toda esperanza, 1985–1990; Andrew Hurley, tr.); El alma de un poeta, 1988; Cavernas del silencio, 1983; El corazón con que vivo, 1980–1984; Desde mi silla de ruedas, 1976–1985.

1289. *Valle, Gerardo del*, 1898–1983 (poet, short story writer). Un cuarto fambá y diecinueve cuentos más, 1967; Retazos, 1951. See also #85.

1290. *Valle Ojeda, Amir*, 1967– (short story writer). En el nombre de Dios, 1990; Yo soy el malo, 1989.

1291. *Vallés Calaña, Lirca* (short story writer). Relatos de la costa de los esclavos, 1994.

1292. *Valls, Jorge*, 1933– (playwright, poet). A la paloma nocturna y otros poemas, 1984; Coloquio del azogamiento, 1989; Filo, contrafilo y punta, 1991; Mi enemigo, mi hermano: cantar del recuento, Cuba (1952–1984), 1989; Twenty Years and Forty Days, 1986 (Autobiographical); Where I Am There Is No Light and It Is Barred/Donde estoy no hay luz y está enrejado, 1981–1984 (Autobiographical); The Wild Dogs/Los perros jíbaros, 1983.

1293. *Valls, Juan Carlos*, 1965– (poet). Los animales del corazón, 1994; Los días de la pérdida, 1995.

1294. *Vasco, Justo E.*, 1943– (novelist, short story writer). Completo Camagüey, 1983–1990 (with Daniel Chavarría); El muro, 1990; Primero muerto, 1986–1994 (with Daniel Chavarría).

1295. *Vázquez Díaz, René* (novelist, playwright, poet, short story writer). Difusos mapas, 1994; La era imaginaria, 1987; La isla del Cundeamor, 1995; La precocidad de los tiempos, 1982; Querido traidor, 1993; Trovador americano, 1978; El último concierto, 1992.

1296. Martínez, Elena M. *El discurso dialógico de "La era imaginaria" de René Vázquez*. Madrid: Editorial Betania, 1991. 100 pp.

1297. *Vázquez Pérez, Rubén*, 1940– (novelist). Aventura peligrosa, 1982; El caso de Ivonne Isabey, 1980; El impostor, 1977; La venganza del muerto, 1983; Pasión de historia y otras historias de pasión, 1987–1994.

1298. *Vega Chapú, Arístides*, 1962– (poet). Ultimas revelaciones en las postales del viajero, 1994.

1299. *Vega, Jesús,* 1954– (short story writer). Wunderbar, maravilloso!, 1994.

1300. *Vega Queral, María Victoria* (novelist, poet). The Tamarind Tree/El tamarindo, 1993; Violeta, 1991.

1301. *Venegas Yero, Camilo,* 1967– (poet). Los trenes no vuelven, 1994.

1302. *Vián Altarriba, Ivette* (poet, short story writer). Curundán y Basula, 1992; Mi amigo Muk Kum; Siete cuentinos, 1992.

1303. *Vian, Enid,* 1948– (novelist, poet, short story writer). Che, miembro del río, 1986; Cuentos de sol y luna, 1975; De las rastrirrañas y las miñocorras, 1992; Las historias de Juan Yendo, 1984; La inmensa mujer, el hombrecito y la madreselva, 1987.

1304. *Victoria, Carlos,* 1950– (novelist). Puente en la oscuridad, 1994; Las sombras en la playa, 1992; La travesía secreta, 1994.

1305. *Vidal Ortiz, Guillermo,* 1952– (novelist, short story writer). Los iniciados, 1986; Matarile, 1993; Se permuta esta casa, 1987.

1306. *Viera, Félix Luis,* 1945– (novelist, poet, short story writer). Cada día muero 24 horas, 1989; Con tu vestido blanco, 1989; En el nombre del hijo, 1983–1989; Las llamas en el cielo, 1983; Una melodía sin ton ni son bajo la lluvia, 1977; Poemas de amor y de olvido, 1994; Precio del amor, 1990; Prefiero los que cantan, 1988; Y me han dolido los cuchillos, 1991.

1307. *Vieta, Ezequiel,* 1922– (novelist, playwright, short story writer). Aquelarre, 1954–1991; Baracutey, 1983; Libro de los epílogos, 1963; Mi llamada es—, 1982; Pailock, el prestidigitador, 1966–1991; Swift, la lata de manteca, 1980; Teatro, 1966; Vivir en Candonga, 1966.

    1308. Garrandés, Alberto. *Ezequiel Vieta y el bosque cifrado.* Havana: Editorial Letras Cubanas, 1993. 222 pp.

    1309. Murrieta Rodríguez, Fabio. *La esperanza de Pailock.* Havana: Editorial Letras Cubanas, 1994. 57 pp.

1310. *Villa, Antonio* (novelist). Morir en La Habana, 1995.

1311. *Villanueva, Manuel* (poet). Detrás de la esperanza, 1995.

1312. *Villar Buceta, María,* 1898–1977 (poet). Poesía y carácter, 1978; Unanisimo, 1927.

1313. *Villaronda, Guillermo,* 1912– (poet). Búsqueda y clamor, 1948; La canción sembrada, 1963; Centro de orientación, 1940; La fiesta del Bambulaé y otros poemas de Puerto Rico, 1963; Hontanar, 1938; Mástil, 1935; Niña muchacha, 1941; Poemas a Walt Disney, 1943.

1314. *Villaverde, Fernando,* 1938– (playwright, poet, short story writer). Cosas de viejos, 1991; Crónicas del Mariel, 1992; Cuaderno de caligrafía, 1994; Los labios pintados de Diderot y otros viajes imaginarios, 1993.

1315. *Vitier, Cintio,* 1921– (novelist, poet). Antología poética, 1981; Canto llano, 1956; De mi provincia, 1945; De peña pobre, 1978–1990; Escrito y cantado, 1954–1959; Experiencia de la poesía, 1944; Extrañeza de estar, 1945; La fecha al pie, 1981; El hogar y el olvido, 1949; Hojas perdidizas, 1988; La luz del imposible, 1957; Nupcias, 1953–1993; Palabras a la aridez, 1989; Los papeles de Jacinto Finalé, 1984; Poemas, 1938; Poemas de mayo y junio 1988, 1990; Prosas leves, 1993; Rajando la leña está, 1986; Sustancia, 1950; Versos de la nueva casa, 1993; Viaje a Nicaragua, 1987 (with Fina García Marruz); Vísperas y testimonios, 1988.

   1316. Díaz Quiñones, Arcadio. *Cintio Vitier: la memoria integradora.* San Juan: Editorial Sin Nombre, 1987. 167 pp.

See also #219.

1317. *X, Marilola,* 1906–1990 (poet). Cantos de amanecer, 1934; Fruto dorado, 1942; Poemas, 1991 (Daer Pozo-Ramírez, ed.).

1318. *Xenes, Nieves,* 1859–1915 (poet). Poesías, 1915–1984.

1319. *Yáñez, Mirta,* 1947– (poet, short story writer). El diablo son las cosas, 1988; La Habana es una ciudad bien grande, 1980; La hora de los mameyes, 1983; Todos los negros tomamos café, 1976; Las visitas y otros poemas, 1970–1986.

1320. *Zaldívar, Gladys,* 1937– (poet, short story writer). La baranda de oro, 1981; The Keeper of the Flame/Fabulación de Eneas, 1979 (Elias L. Rivers, tr.).; Viene el asedio, 1987; El Visitante, 1971; Zéjeles para el clavel, 1981.

DOMINICAN REPUBLIC

A. BIBLIOGRAPHIES AND BIO-BIBLIOGRAPHIES

General

1321. Collado, Miguel. *Apuntes bibliográficos sobre la literatura dominicana*. Santo Domingo: Biblioteca Nacional, 1993– [vol. 1–].

1322. Lugo, Américo. *Bibliografía*. Santo Domingo: Cuna de América, 1906. 115 pp.

1323. Waxman, Samuel Montefiore. *A Bibliography of the Belles-Lettres of Santo Domingo*. Cambridge, MA: Harvard University Press, 1931. 31 pp.

General: Sixteenth to Nineteenth Centuries

1324. Vallejo de Paredes, Margarita. *Apuntes biográficos y bibliográficos de algunos escritores dominicanos del siglo XIX*. Santo Domingo: Publicaciones ONAP, 1995. 2 vols.

General: Twentieth Century

1325. Olivera, Otto. *Bibliografía de la literatura dominicana, 1960–1982*. Lincoln, NE: Society of Spanish and Spanish-American Studies, 1984. 86 pp.

1326. Tarazona, Enrique. *Guía bibliográfica: ciento veintitres escritores dominicanos vivos*. Santo Domingo: Biblioteca Nacional, 1983. 139 pp.

B. DICTIONARIES AND ENCYCLOPEDIAS

1327. Gerón, Cándido. *Diccionario de autores dominicanos, 1492–1992*. Santo Domingo: Editora Alfa y Omega, 1992. 395 pp.

C. ANTHOLOGIES

General

1328. Alcántara Almánzar, José, ed. *Antología de la literatura dominicana*. Santo Domingo: Editora Taller, 1988. 439 pp. Reprint of the 1972 ed.

1329. Báez Díaz, Tomás ed. *Antología de escritores banilejos*. Santo Domingo: Editora de Colores, 1991– [vol. 1–].

1330. Gómez de Michel, Fiume. *Manual de literatura dominicana y americana: antología, guía de análisis y comentarios*. Santo Domingo: Universidad Autónoma de Santo Domingo, 1984. 511 pp. Reprint of the 1980 ed.

1331. Vallejo de Paredes, Margarita et al., eds. *Antología literaria dominicana*. Santo Domingo: Instituto Tecnológico de Santo Domingo, 1981. 5 vols.

General: Twentieth Century

1332. Ateneo Insular (Moca, Dominican Republic); Bruno Rosario Candelier, ed. *El movimiento interiorista: antología del Ateneo Insular*. Moca, D.R.: Ateneo Insular, 1995. 378 pp.

1333. Coiscou Weber, Rodolfo, ed. *La generación del 48 en la literatura dominicana*. Santo Domingo: Casa Weber, 1985. 114 pp.

1334. ———. *El postumismo: sus creadores, Domingo Moreno Jimenes, Andrés Avelino y Rafael Augusto Zorrilla*. Santo Domingo: Editora Libros y Textos, 1985. 86 pp.

1335. Fernández-Rocha, Carlos, and Danilo de los Santos. *Lecturas dominicanas*. Madrid: Playor, 1977. 372 pp.

1336. Francisco, Ramón, ed. *Literatura dominicana 60 [i.e., sesenta]*. Santiago, D.R.: Universidad Católica Madre y Maestra, 1969. 257 pp.

1337. Mujeres en Desarrollo (Dominican Republic). *La era de Trujillo: décimas, relatos y testimonios*. Santo Domingo: Las Mujeres, 1989. 189 pp.

1338. Universidad Tecnológica del Cibao (Dominican Republic). *Antología de "los nuevos."* La Vega, D.R.: La Universidad, 1988. 76 pp.

Poetry

1339. Baeza Flores, Alberto, ed. *Poesía dominicana: las mejores poesías de amor.* Barcelona: Editorial Bruguera, 1955. 124 pp.

1340. Beiro Alvarez, Luis and Huchi Lora, eds. *La décima escrita en la República Dominicana: antología histórica.* Santo Domingo: Fundación Barceló Pro Cultura, 1994. 203 pp.

1341. Bisonó, Pedro, ed. *Cantos al amor: antología de la poesía amorosa dominicana.* Santo Domingo: Publicaciones América, 1986. 222 pp.

1342. Cocco-DeFilippis, Daisy, ed. *Sin otro profeta que su canto: antología de poesía escrita por dominicanas.* Santo Domingo: Editora Taller, 1988. 231 pp.

1343. Contín Aybar, Pedro René, ed. *Antología poética dominicana.* 2a ed. Santo Domingo: Librería Dominicana, 1951. 310 pp.

1344. ———. *Poesía dominicana.* Santo Domingo: J. D. Postigo, 1969. 211 pp.

1345. Díaz de Soñé, Inés, ed. *Antología biográfica de poetas petromacorisanos.* San Pedro de Macorís, D,.R.: Universidad Central del Este, 1982. 318 pp.

1346. Fernández Mejía, Abel, ed. *Poesía dominicana: desde sus inicios hasta la muerte del último tirano.* Santo Domingo: Editorial Tiempo, 1987. 115 pp.

1347. Lloréns, Vicente, ed. *Antología de la poesía dominicana, 1844–1944.* 2a ed. aum. Santo Domingo: Sociedad Dominicana de Bibliófilos, 1984. 348 pp.

1348. Mejía Ricart, Gustavo Adolfo. *Antología de poetas dominicanos.* Ciudad Trujillo: La Palabra de Santo Domingo, 1954– [vol. 1–].

1349. Nolasco, Flérida de. *La poesía folklórica en Santo Domingo.* Santiago, D.R.: Editorial El Diario, 1946. 367 pp.

1350. Rodríguez Demorizi, Emilio. *Del romancero dominicano.* 2a ed. Barcelona: Gráf. M. Pareja, 1979. 115 pp.

1351. ———, ed. *Martí y Máximo Gómez en la poesía dominicana*. Santo Domingo: Editora Taller, 1984. 205 pp. Reprint of the 1953 ed.

1352. Townsend, Francis Edward, ed. *Quisqueya: An English-Spanish Version of the Poetry of Santo Domingo/Una antología bilingüe de la poesía de Santo Domingo*. 2d ed. Bogotá: [s.n.], 1964. 63 pp.

Poetry: Sixteenth to Nineteenth Centuries

1353. Bazil, Osvaldo, ed. *Parnaso dominicano : compilación completa de los mejores poetas de la República de Santo Domingo*. Barcelona: Maucci, 1917. 223 pp.

1354. Castellanos, José, ed. *Lira de Quisqueya: poesías dominicanas*. Santo Domingo: Editora de Santo Domingo, 1974. 328 pp. Reprint of the 1874 ed.

1355. Mota, Fabio E., and Emilio Rodríguez Demorizi, eds. *Cancionero de la Restauración*. Santo Domingo: Editora del Caribe, 1963. 213 pp.

Poetry: Twentieth Century

1356. Cocco-DeFilippis, Daisy, and Emma Jane Robinett, eds. and trs. *Poems of Exile and Other Concerns/Poemas del exilio y de otras inquietudes: A Bilingual Selection of the Poetry Written by Dominicans in the United States*. New York: Alcance, 1988. 146 pp.

1357. Coiscou Weber, Rodolfo, ed. *La poesía sorpendida: antología poética*. Santo Domingo: Casa Weber, 1985. 48 pp.

1358. Concurso Nacional de Décimas (1992, Santo Domingo). *Décimas premiadas*. Santo Domingo: Centro Dominicano de Estudios de la Educación, 1993. 78 pp.

1359. Conde, Pedro, ed. *Antología informal: la joven poesía dominicana*. Santo Domingo: Editora Nacional, 1970. 110 pp.

1360. Fernández Spencer, Antonio, ed. *Nueva poesía dominicana*. Santo Domingo: Publicaciones América, 1983. 331 pp. Reprint of the 1953 ed.

1361. Gutiérrez, Franklin, ed. *Antología histórica de la poesía domini-cana del siglo XX (1912–1995)*. New York: Edidiones Alcance, 1995. 446 pp.

1362. Juliá, Julio Jaime, ed. *Nueva antología de poetas mocanos*. Santo Domingo: Editora Corripio, 1988. 174 pp. Revision of *Antología de poetas mocanos* (1977).

1363. Martínez, Frank, ed. *Juego de imágenes: antología de jóvenes po-etas dominicanos, 1980–1995*. Santo Domingo: Ediciones Ho-jarasca, 1995. 203 pp.

1364. Mateo, Andrés L., ed. *Poesía de post guerra: joven poesía do-minicana*. Santo Domingo: Editora Alfa y Omega, 1981. 119 pp.

1365. Medrano, Marianela, and Mateo Morrison, ed. *Seis mujeres po-etas: homenaje a Salomé Ureña*. Santo Domingo: Editora Uni-versitaria, 1989. 102 pp.

1366. Pérez, Isael et al. *Colectivo de escritores romaneses: antología*. Santo Domingo: Biblioteca Nacional, 1986. 126 pp.

1367. Raful, Tony, and Pedro Peix, eds. *El síndrome de Penélope en la poesía dominicana: antología básica*. Santo Domingo: Biblioteca Nacional, 1986. 349 pp.

1368. Rodríguez Demorizi, Emilio, ed. *Poesía popular dominicana*. Santiago, D.R.: Universidad Católica Madre y Maestra, 1979. 300 pp. Reprint of the 1973 (2d) ed.

1369. Rueda, Manuel, and Lupo Hernández Rueda, eds. *Antología panorámica de la poesía dominicana contemporánea, 1912–1962*. Santiago de los Caballeros, D.R.: Universidad Católica Madre y Maestra, 1972– [vol.1–].

1370. Santos Moray, Mercedes, ed. *Meridiano 70 [i.e., setenta]: poesía social dominicana siglo XX*. Havana: Casa de las Américas, 1978. 280 pp.

1371. Villegas, Víctor, ed. *Antología de poetas petromacorisanos*. San Pedro de Macorís, D.R.: Universidad Central del Este, 1982. 335 pp.

Fiction

1372. Henríquez Ureña, Max, ed. *Veinte cuentos de autores dominicanos.* Santo Domingo: Secretaría de Estado de Educación, Bellas Artes y Cultos, 1995. 285 pp. Reprint of a 1938 ms.

1373. Hernández Contreras, Domingo, ed. *Antología del cuento psicológico de la República Dominicana.* Santo Domingo: Universidad Iberoamericana, 1995. 273 pp.

1374. Lloréns, Vicente, ed. *Antología de la prosa dominicana, 1844–1944.* 2a ed. Santo Domingo: Sociedad Dominicana de Bibliófilos, 1987. 474 pp.

1375. Peix, Pedro, ed. *La narrativa yugulada.* 2a ed. Santo Domingo: Editora Taller, 1987. 661 pp.

1376. Rodríguez Demorizi, Emilio, ed. *Tradiciones y cuentos dominicanos.* Santo Domingo: J. D. Postigo, 1969. 275 pp.

Fiction: Twentieth Century

1377. Cartagena Portalatín, Aída, ed. *Narradores dominicanos: antología.* Caracas: Monte Avila Editores, 1969. 153 pp.

1378. Cocco-De Filippis, Daisy, and Franklin Gutiérrez, eds. *Stories from Washington Heights and Other Corners of the World/Historias de Washington Heights y otros rincones del mundo.* New York: Latino Press, 1994. 204 pp.

1379. Cocco-DeFillipis, Daisy, ed. *Combatidas, combativas y combatientes: antología de cuentos escritos por mujeres dominicanas.* Santo Domingo: Editora Taller, 1992. 446 pp.

1380. Coiscou Weber, Rodolfo, ed. *Voces en el sendero: cuentos.* Santo Domingo: Casa Weber, 1987. 54 pp.

1381. Díaz Grullón, Virgilio et al. *La nueva narrativa dominicana.* Santo Domingo: Casagrande, 1978. 256 pp.

1382. Hernández Contreras, Domingo, ed. *Cuentos de perros humanos: mini antología de los autores Juan Bosch [et al.].* [Santo Domingo]: Sociedad Democrática de Bibliófilos, 1993. 119 pp.

1383. Moscoso Puelló, Francisco Eugenio, Ramón Marrero Aristy and Manuel A. Ariama. *La novela de la caña.* Santo Domingo: Editora de Santo Domingo, 1981. 713 pp. *Cañas y bueyes* (F. E. Moscoso Puelló), *Over* (R. Marrero Aristy), *El terrateniente* (M. Ariama.)

1384. Nolasco, Sócrates, ed. *El cuento en Santo Domingo: selección antológica.* Santo Domingo: Biblioteca Nacional, 1986. 204 pp. Reprint of the 1957 ed.

1385. Rodríguez Demorizi, Emilio, ed. *Cuentos de política criolla.* Santo Domingo: Librería Dominicana, 1977. 240 pp. Reprint of the 1963 ed.

1386. Valdez, Pedro Antonio, ed. *Ultima flor del naufragio: antología de novísimos cuentistas dominicanos.* Santo Domingo: Ediciones Hojarasca, 1995. 142 pp.

D. HISTORY AND CRITICISM

General

1387. Balaguer, Joaquín. *Historia de la literatura dominicana.* Santo Domingo: Editora Corripio, 1992. 370 pp. Reprint of the 1972 (5th) ed.

1388. ———. *Semblanzas literarias.* Santo Domingo: Editora Corripio, 1990. 325 pp. Reprint of the 1985 (2d rev.) ed.

1389. ———. *Letras dominicanas.* Santo Domingo: Editora Corripio, 1990. 351 pp. Reprint of the 1985 ed. which was originally published in 1950 under title *Literatura dominicana.*

1390. Bazil, Darío. *Poetas y prosistas dominicanos.* Santo Domingo: Editora Cosmos, 1978. 235 pp.

1391. Congreso Crítico de Literatura Dominicana (1993, Santo Domingo); Diógenes Céspedes, Soledad Alvarez and Pedro Vergés, eds. *Ponencias del Congreso Crítico de Literatura Dominicana.* Santo Domingo: Editora de Colores, 1994. 290 pp.

1392. Contín Aybar, Néstor. *Historia de la literatura dominicana.* San Pedro de Macorís, D.R.: Universidad Central del Este, 1982– [vol. 1–].

1393. Francisco, Ramón. *Crític-a-demás*. Santo Domingo: Publicaciones América, 1987. 265 pp.

1394. Henríquez Ureña, Max. *Panorama histórico de la literatura dominicana*. 2a ed., rev. y ampliada. Santo Domingo: [s.n.], 1965– [vol. 1–2–].

1395. Matos, Esthervina. *Estudios de literatura dominicana*. Ciudad Trujillo: Pol Hermanos, 1955. 387 pp.

1396. Mejía, Abigail. *Historia de la literatura dominicana*. 7a ed., rev. y aum. Ciudad Trujillo: Impr. Dominicana, 1951. 179 pp.

1397. Vicioso G., Abelardo. *El freno hatero en la literatura dominicana*. Santo Domingo: Universidad Autónoma de Santo Domingo, 1983. 379 pp.

General: Sixteenth to Nineteenth Centuries

1398. Alcántara Almánzar, José, ed. *Los escritores dominicanos y la cultura*. Santo Domingo: Instituto Tecnológico de Santo Domingo, 1990. 226 pp.

1399. Balaguer, Joaquín. *Los próceres escritores*. Santo Domingo: Editora Corripio, 1989. 306 pp. Reprint of the 1947 ed.

1400. Henríquez Ureña, Pedro. *La cultura y las letras coloniales en Santo Domingo*. Buenos Aires: Universidad de Buenos Aires, 1936. 191 pp.

1401. Vicioso G., Abelardo. *Santo Domingo en las letras coloniales, 1492–1800*. Santo Domingo: Universidad Autónoma de Santo Domingo, 1979. 355 pp.

General: Twentieth Century

1402. Céspedes, Diógenes. *Estudios sobre literatura, cultura e ideologías*. San Pedro de Macorís, D.R.: Universidad Central del Este, 1983. 253 pp.

1403. Di Pietro, Giovanni. *Temas de literatura y de cultura dominicanas*. Santo Domingo: Instituto Tecnológico de Santo Domingo, 1993. 146 pp.

1404. Incháustegui Cabral, Héctor. *De literatura dominicana siglo veinte*. Santiago, R. D.: Universidad Católica Madre y Maestra, 1973. 413 pp. Reprint of the 1968 ed.

1405. Lockward Artiles, Antonio. *Romper el cerco*. Santo Domingo: Editora Universitaria, 1985. 148 pp.

1406. Mateo, Andrés L. *Manifiestos literarios de la República Dominicana*. Santo Domingo: Editora Taller, 1984. 81 pp.

1407. Pérez, Odalis G., ed. *Las ideas literarias en la República Dominicana: entrevistas*. Santo Domingo: Editora Amigo del Hogar, 1993. 200 pp.

1408. Rosario Candelier, Bruno. *Ensayos críticos: análisis de textos dominicanos contemporáneos*. Santiago, D.R.: Pontificia Universidad Católica Madre y Maestra, 1982. 301 pp.

1409. ————. *Valores de las letras dominicanas*. Santiago, D.R.: Pontificia Universidad Católica Madre y Maestra, 1991. 433 pp.

1410. Vicioso, Sherezada. *Algo que decir: ensayos sobre literatura femenina, 1981–1991*. Santo Domingo: Editora Búho, 1991. 143 pp.

Poetry

1411. Alcántara Almánzar, José. *Estudios de poesía dominicana*. Santo Domingo: Editora Alfa y Omega, 1979. 435 pp.

1412. Caamaño de Fernández, Vicenta. *El negro en la poesía dominicana*. Santo Domingo: Centro de Estudios Avanzados de Puerto Rico y el Caribe, 1989. 288 pp.

1413. Lebrón Saviñón, Mariano. *Luces del trópico: conferencias y notas acerca de la literatura en la República Dominicana y un panorama de la poesía negra*. Buenos Aires: [s.n.], 1949. 108 pp.

1414. Nolasco, Flérida de. *Rutas de nuestra poesía*. Ciudad Trujillo: Impr. Dominicana, 1953. 155 pp.

1415. Pérez, Carlos Federico. *Evolución poética dominicana*. Santo Domingo: Editora Taller, 1987. 271 pp. Reprint of the 1956 ed.

1416. Rosario Candelier, Bruno. *La creación mitopoética: símbolos y arquetipos en la lírica dominicana.* Santiago, D.R.: Pontificia Universidad Católica Madre by Maestra, 1989. 252 pp.

1417. ————. *Lo popular y lo culto en la poesía dominicana.* Santiago, D.R.: Pontificia Universidad Católica Madre y Maestra, 1977. 372 pp.

Poetry: Sixteenth to Nineteenth Centuries

1418. Pensón, César Nicolás. *Reseña histórico-crítica de la poesía en Santo Domingo.* Santo Domingo: Editora Taller, 1980. 495 pp. Reprint of the 1892 ed.

Poetry: Twentieth Century

1419. Baeza Flores, Alberto. *La poesía dominicana en el siglo XX: historia, crítica, estudio comparativo y estilístico.* Santiago, D.R.: Pontificia Universidad Católica Madre y Maestra, 1976–1986. 4 vols.

1420. ————. *Los poetas dominicanos del 1965; una generación importante y distinta.* Santo Domingo: Biblioteca Nacional, 1985. 484 pp.

1421. Cabral, Manuel del, ed. *Diez poetas dominicanos: tres poetas con vida y siete desenterrados.* Santo Domingo: Publicaciones América, 1980. 189 pp.

1422. Céspedes, Diógenes. *Lenguaje y poesía en Santo Domingo en el siglo XX.* Santo Domingo: Editora Universitaria, Universidad Autónoma de Santo Domingo, 1985. 450 pp.

1423. Cocco-DeFilppis, Daisy. *Estudios semióticos de poesía dominicana.* Santo Domingo: Editora Taller, 1984. 174 pp.

1424. Hernández Rueda, Lupo. *La generación del 48 en la literatura dominicana.* Santiago, D.R.: Pontificia Universidad Católica Madre y Maestra, 1981. 537 pp.

1425. Santos Moray, Mercedes. *Poesía sobre la pólvora.* Santiago, Cuba: Editorial Oriente, 1980. 72 pp.

Fiction

1426. Amarante, Héctor. *Esquema para el estudio de la novela dominicana.* Lima: ANEA, 1987. 136 pp. Cover title *La novela dominicana.*

1427. Caamaño de Fernández, Vicenta. *La lengua campesina en la narrativa costumbrista dominicana.* Santo Domingo: Centurion, 1976. 207 pp.

1428. Montero, Jenny. *La cuentística dominicana.* Santo Domingo: Biblioteca Nacional, 1986. 221 pp.

1429. Pimentel, Miguel A. *Ideología de la novela criolla, 1880–1944.* Santo Domingo: Editora Universitaria, Universidad Autónoma de Santo Domingo, 1986. 225 pp.

1430. Rosario Candelier, Bruno. *Tendencias de la novela dominicana.* Santiago, D.R.: Departamento de Publicaciones, Pontificia Universidad Católica Madre y Maestra, 1988. 378 pp.

1431. Sommer, Doris. *One Master for Another: Populism as Patriarchal Rhetoric in Dominican Novels.* Lanham, MD: University Press of America, 1983. 280 pp.

Fiction: Sixteenth to Nineteenth Centuries

1432. Cruz, Josefina de la. *La sociedad dominicana de finales de siglo a través de la novela.* Santo Domingo: Editora Cosmos, 1978. 300 pp.

Fiction: Twentieth Century

1433. Goico Castro, Manuel de Jesús. *La prosa artística en Santo Domingo.* Santo Domingo: Editora Corripio, 1982. 111 pp.

1434. Graciano, Berta. *La novela de la caña: estética e ideología.* Santo Domingo: Editora Alfa y Omega, 1990. 131 pp.

1435. Rosario Candelier, Bruno. *La imaginación insular: mitos, leyendas, utopías y fantasmas en la narrativa dominicana.* Santo Domingo: Taller, 1984. 190 pp.

Drama

1436. Ginebra, Danilo, ed. *Panorama del teatro dominicano.* Santo
Domingo: Editora Corripio, 1984– [vol. 1–].

1437. Molinaza, José. *Historia crítica del teatro dominicano.* Santo
Domingo: Universidad Autónoma de Santo Domingo, 1984–
[vols. 1–2–]. Vol. 1. 1492–1844.—Vol. 2. 1844–1930.

E. INDIVIDUAL AUTHORS

Sixteenth to Nineteenth Centuries

1438. *Angulo Guridi, Alejandro,* 1823–1906 (novelist, poet). Los
amores de los indios, 1843; La joven Carmela, 1841; La venganza
de un hijo, 1842 (with Francisco Javier Blanchie).

1439. *Angulo Guridi, Francisco Javier,* 1816–1884 (novelist, playwright, poet). Ensayos poéticos, 1843.

1440. *Billini, Francisco Gregorio,* 1844–1898 (novelist, playwright).
Baní/Engracia y Antoñita, 1892–1988.

    1441. Rodríguez Demorizi, Emilio. *Baní y la novela de Billini.*
    Santo Domingo: Editora del Caribe, 1964. 320 pp.

1442. *Bonó, Pedro Francisco,* 1828–1906 (novelist). El montero, 1989
(Emilio Rodríguez Demorizi, ed.).

1443. *Deligne, Gastón Fernando,* 1861–1913 (playwright, poet). Gala-
ripsos, 1908–1963; Páginas olvidadas, 1944–1982 (Emilio Rodríguez Demorizi, ed.).

    1444. Amiama Tío, Fernando A. *Contribución a la bibliografía
    de Gastón Fernando Deligne.* Ciudad Trujillo: L. Sánchez
    Andujar, 1944. 28 pp.

    1445. Cestero, Manuel Florentino. *Ensayos críticos: Gastón F.
    Deligne.* Santo Domingo: Secretaría de Educación, 1974.
    64 pp.

    1446. Mejía Ricart, Gustavo Adolfo. *Gastón Fernando Deligne:
    el poeta civil.* Ciudad Trujillo: Editores Pol, 1944. 267 pp.

1447. *Deligne, Rafael Alfredo,* 1863–1902 (playwright, poet, short story writer). En prosa y en verso, 1902; La justicia y el azar, 1894; Milagro, 1896; Vidas tristes, 1901.

1448. *Galván, Manuel de Jesús,* 1834–1910 (novelist, poet). The Cross and the Sword, 1954–1975 (Translation of Enriquillo [1882–1990]; Robert Graves, tr.).

    1449. Conde, Pedro. *Notas sobre el "Enriquillo."* Santo Domingo: Ediciones de Taller, 1978. 68 pp.

    1450. Piña Contreras, Guillermo. *"Enriquillo": el texto y la historia.* Santo Domingo: Editora Alfa y Omega, 1985. 164 pp.

1451. *Muñoz del Monte, Francisco,* 1800–1868 (poet). Poesías, 1880.

1452. *Ortea, Virginia Elena,* 1866–1903 (novelist, playwright, short story writer). Las feministas, 1897; Mi hermana Catalina, 1897; Risas y lágrimas, 1901–1978.

1453. *Pellerano Castro, Arturo Bautista,* 1865–1916 (playwright, poet). Alma criolla, 1916; Antonia, 1895; Criollas, 1907–1927; De casa, 1907–1927; De mala entraña, 1902; La última cruzada, 1888.

1454. *Pensón, César Nicolás,* 1855–1901 (playwright, poet, short story writer). Cosas añejas, 1891–1990.

1455. *Pérez, José Joaquín,* 1845–1900 (playwright, poet, short story writer). Fantasías indígenas y otros poemas, 1877–1989 (José Alcántara Almánzar, ed.); La lira de José Joaquín Pérez, 1928; Obra poética, 1970 (Carlos Federico Pérez, ed.).

1456. *Ureña de Henríquez, Salomé,* 1850–1897 (poet). Anacaona, 1970; Cantos a la patria, 1970; Poesías, 1920; Poesías completas, 1950–1992 (Various eds.); Poesías de Salomé Ureña de Henríquez, 1880; Poesías escogidas, 1960.

    1457. Herrera, César A. *La poesía de Salomé Ureña en su función social y patriótica.* 2a ed. Santo Domingo: Biblioteca Nacional, 1988. 38 pp.

    1458. Rodríguez Demorizi, Emilio. *Salomé Ureña y el Instituto de Señoritas: para la historia de la espiritualidad dominicana.* Ciudad Trujillo: Impresora Dominicana, 1960. 427 pp.

1459. Rodríguez Demorizi, Silveria R. de. *Salomé Ureña de Hen-ríquez*. Santo Domingo: Editora Taller, 1984. 45 pp. Reprint of the 1944 ed.

See also #1365.

Twentieth Century

1460. *Alcántara Almánzar, José,* 1946– (short story writer). Callejón sin salida, 1975; La carne estremecida, 1989–1991; Las máscaras de la seducción, 1983; Mutanville, 1980 (with Arturo Rodríguez Fernández); El sabor de lo prohibido, 1993; Testimonios y profanaciones, 1978; Viaje al otro mundo, 1973.

1461. *Alfonseca, Miguel,* 1942–1994 (poet, short story writer). Arribo a la luz, 1965; El enemigo, 1970; La guerra y los cantos, 1966.

1462. *Alix, Juan Antonio,* 1833–1918 (poet). Décimas, 1927–1969; Décimas dominicanas de ayer y de hoy, 1973–1986 (with Antonio Zacarías Reyes Ledesma and José Rafael Heredia Paulino); Décimas inéditas, 1966–1982; Décimas políticas, 1977.

1463. Balaguer, Joaquín. *Juan Antonio Alix.* Santiago, D.R.: Biblioteca Popular Dominicana, 1977. 76 pp.

1464. Modesto, Tomás. *¿Es popular la poesía de Juan Antonio Alix?* Santo Domingo: Biblioteca Nacional, 1987. 83 pp.

1465. *Almánzar Rodríguez, Armando,* 1935– (poet, short story writer). Cuentos en cortometraje, 1993; Infancia feliz, 1978; Límite, 1967–1979; Selva de agujeros negros para "Chichí la Salsa", 1985.

1466. *Amarante, Héctor,* 1944– (novelist, short story writer). Ritos, 1981.

1467. *Arias, Aurora,* 1962– (poet). Piano lila, 1994; Vivienda de pájaro, 1986.

1468. *Avilés Blonda, Máximo,* 1931–1988 (playwright, poet). Cantos a Helena, 1970; Centro del mundo, 1962–1970; Del comienzo a la mitad del camino de la vida, 1976; Del comienzo al final de la vida, 1989; Llueve y es que es mayo, Dulce Señora, 1988; Las manos vacías, 1959; Los profetas, 1978–1987; Teatro, 1968 (La otra estrella en el cielo [1963], Yo, Bertolt Brecht [1966], Pirámide 179 [1968]); Trío, 1957 (with Lupo Hernández Rueda and Rafael Valera Benítez); Vía crucis, 1983.

1469. *Balaguer, Joaquín,* 1907– (poet). Antología poética bilingüe (1921–1992), 1995 (Claude Couffon, ed. and tr.); Azul en los charcos, 1941; Los carpinteros, 1985–1993; Cruces iluminadas, 1974–1993; La cruz de cristal, 1976–1993; Huerto sellado, 1980; Psalmos paganos, 1922; La venda transparente, 1988–1993; Voz silente, 1992–1993.

    1470. Gerón, Cándido. *Hacia una interpretación de la poesía de Joaquín Balaguer.* Santo Domingo: C. Gerón, 1991. 294 pp.

1471. *Barinas Coiscou, Sócrates,* 1915– (poet, short story writer). Antología lírica, 1993; Cuentos de la frontera, 1994; Dolida piel americana, 1970; Holocausto y poemas de las últimas espigas, 1989; Juan sin tiempo, 1994; Medalliones místicos, 1986; Las siete palabras de mi cáliz, 1986.

1472. *Bazil, Osvaldo,* 1884–1946 (poet). Arcos votivos, 1907; Cabezas de América, 1933; Campanas de la tarde, 1922; La cruz transparente, 1939; Huerto de inquietud, 1926; Osvaldo Basil, 1985 (Domingo Porfirio Rojas Nina, ed.); Remos en la sombra, 1945; Rosales en flor, 1906; Tarea literaria y patricia, 1943.

1473. *Beras Goico, Freddy* (novelist, short story writer). Juan de los Palotes, 1993; El libro de las excusas con su ñapa, 1970–1981; Lo mejor de La Multona, 1981.

1474. *Bermúdez, Federico Ramón,* 1884–1921 (playwright, poet). Los humildes, 1916–1986; Las liras del silencio, 1923; Oro virgen, 1910; Todas las poesías de Federico Bermúdez, 1986.

1475. *Bosch, Juan,* 1909– (novelist, short story writer). Camino real, 1933–1984; Cuento de Navidad, 1956–1988; Cuentos, 1983; Cuentos escritos antes del exilio, 1975–1992; Cuentos escritos en el exilio, 1962–1994; Cuentos selectos, 1993; Dos pesos de agua, 1941; La mañosa, 1936–1992; Más cuentos escritos en el exilio, 1964–1994; La muchacha de La Guaira, 1955; Obras completas, 1989; Ocho cuentos, 1947; El oro y la paz, 1975–1992; Textos culturales y literarios, 1988–1989.

    1476. Fernández Olmos, Margarite. *La cuentística de Juan Bosch: un análisis estético-cultural.* Santo Domingo: Editora Alfa y Omega, 1982. 182 pp.

    1477. Gerón, Cándido. *Juan Bosch: vida y obra narrativa.* Santo Domingo: Editora Alfa y Omega, 1993. 300 pp.

1478. Gutiérrez, Franklin, ed. *Aproximaciones a la narrativa de Juan Bosch.* New York: Ediciones Alcance, 1989. 165 pp.

1479. Ocaña, Antonio. *Un hombre llamado Juan Bosch.* Santo Domingo: Alfa y Omega, 1995. 366 pp.

1480. Ossers Cabrera, Manuel Augusto. *La expresividad en la cuentística de Juan Bosch: análisis estilístico.* Santo Domingo: Editora Alfa y Omega, 1989. 255 pp.

1481. Rosario Candelier, Bruno. *La narrativa de Juan Bosch.* Santo Domingo: Editora Alfa y Omega, 1989. 275 pp.

See also #1382.

1482. *Bueno, Martha,* 1962– (novelist). Elena Varela, 1995.

1483. *Cabral, Manuel del,* 1907– (novelist, playwright, poet, short story writer). Los anti-tiempo, 1967; Antología clave, 1957; Antología tierra, 1949; Antología tres, 1987; Biografía de un silencio, 1940; La carabina piensa, 1976–1991; Carta a Compadre Mon, 1987; Carta a Rubén, 1951; Catorce mudos de amor, 1962–1963; Cédula del mar, 1981; Chinchina busca el tiempo, 1945–1980; Color de agua, 1935; Compadre Mon, 1942–1981; Cuentos, 1976; Cuentos cortos con pantalones largos, 1981; De este lado del mar, 1949; Doce poemas negros, 1935; Dos cantos continentales y unos temas eternos, 1956; Egloga 2000, 1970; El escupido, 1970–1987; La espada metafísica, 1989–1990; Historia de mi voz, 1964–1974; Los huéspedes secretos, 1974–1988; La isla ofendida, 1965–1978; El jefe y otros cuentos, 1979; Obra poética completa, 1976–1987; Ocho gritos, 1937; Palabra, 1977; Pedrada planetaria, 1927–1958; Pilón, 1929; Poemas de amor y sexo, 1974; El presidente negro, 1973–1990; Los relámpagos lentos, 1966; Sangre mayor, 1945; Segunda antología tierra, 1952; Sexo no solitario, 1970; Sexo y alma, 1956; Treinta parabolas, 1956; Trópico negro, 1941; Veinte cuentos, 1951.

1484. *Cabrera, Fernando,* 1964– (poet). Planos del ocio, 1990; The Tree/El árbol, 1993 (Charlene E. Santos, tr.).

1485. *Caro, Néstor,* 1917– (novelist, playwright, short story writer). Cielo negro, 1949–1973; Desde un tambor solitario, 1979.

1486. *Cartagena Portalatín, Aída,* 1918–1994 (novelist, poet, short story writer). Del sueño al mundo, 1945–1995; En la casa del tiempo, 1984; Escalera para Electra, 1970–1980; From Desolation

to Compromise/Del desconsuelo al compromiso, 1988 (Emma
Jane Robinett, Daisy Cocco-DeFilippis, trs.); Llámale verde,
1945; Mi mundo el mar, 1953–1955; Una mujer está sola, 1955;
Tablero, 1978; La tarde en que murió Estefanía, 1983; La tierra escrita, 1967; Víspera del sueño, 1944–1995; Una voz desatada,
1962; Yania Tierra, 1995 (Translation of Yania Tierra [1981]; M.
J. Fenwick, Rosabelle White, trs.).

1487. Sosa, José Rafael, ed. *Mujer y literatura: homenaje a Aída
        Cartagena Portalatín.* Santo Domingo: Universidad
        Autóonma de Santo Domingo, 1986. 148 pp.

1488. *Castillo, Efraím,* 1940– (novelist, playwright, short story writer).
      Confín del polvo, 1994; La cosecha, 1984; Curriculum, 1982; Inti
      huaman/Eva Again, 1984; Viaje de regreso, 1968.

1489. *Castro, Tomás,* 1959– (poet). Amor a quemarropa, 1984–1986;
      Bodas de tinta, 1987; Entre la espada y el espejo, 1986–1990; En-
      trega inmediata y otros incendios, 1985; Epigramas del encubri-
      miento de América, 1992; Hábeas Corpus, 1994; Vuelta al cantar
      de los cantares, 1986.

1490. *Cestero, Tulio Manuel,* 1877–1955 (novelist, playwright, poet,
      short story writer). Citerea, 1907; Ciudad romántica, 1911–1978;
      Escritos de Tulio Manuel Cestero, 1985 (Julio Jaime Julia, ed.);
      Hombres y piedras, 1916; La sangre/Una vida bajo la tiranía,
      1915–1980; Sangre de primavera, 1903–1908.

1491. *Coiscou Weber, Rodolfo,* 1926– (poet). Los cuatro y el capitán,
      1986; Entonces, buen hombre, 1983; La luz herida, 1981; Presen-
      cia del ángel, 1987; Retorno al origen sin origen, 1993; Se están
      comiendo a Margarita y otros canibalismos, 1986; El vedrinismo,
      1983; Velero del regreso, 1948.

1492. *Colón Ruiz, José O.,* 1934– (novelist, poet). Amor a primera vista,
      1993; Centilar de mi arce, 1980; Cuando florece el amor, 1988;
      Gotitas de rocío, 1982; Paleto, 1990; Poesía para computadoras,
      1984.

1493. *Contreras, Hilma,* 1913– (novelist, poet, short story writer). Cua-
      tro cuentos, 1953; Entre dos silencios, 1987; Facetas de la vida,
      1993; El ojo de Dios, 1962; La tierra está bramando, 1986.

1494. Biblioteca Nacional (Dominican Republic). *Hilma Con-
        treras: una vida en imágenes, 1913–1993—[exhibición],*

Biblioteca Nacional, Santo Domingo, del 8 al 12 de diciembre de 1993. Santo Domingo: La Biblioteca, 1993. 1 vol. (unpaged).

1495. *Cruz, Giovanny* (playwright). Amanda, 1993; "—En un acto," 1985; La virgen de los narcisos, 1993.

1496. *Cruz Vélez, José Manuel de la* (novelist). Un pueblo lleno de ira, 1994.

1497. *Damirón, Rafael,* 1882–1956 (novelist, playwright, poet, short story writer). Ay de los vencidos!, 1925–1983; La cacica, 1944–1983; Cronicones de antaño, 1949–1983; Estampas, 1938–1984; Hello, Jimmy!, 1945; Revolución, 1942–1983.

1498. *David, León,* 1945– (poet). Adentro, 1986; Compañera, 1980; Guirnalda (antología poética), 1994 (Nelson Julio Minaya, ed.); Huellas sobre la arena, 1986; Intento de bandera, 1991; Narraciones truculentas de poetas, filósofos y mujeres, 1980; Parábola de la verdad sencilla, 1985; Poemas, 1979; Poemas del hombre anodino, 1984; Poemas del hombre nuevo, 1986; Trovas del tiempo añejo, 1986.

1499. *Delgado Pantaleón, Mélida,* 1885–1967 (playwright, poet, short story writer). La cítara campestre cibaeña, 1989 (Hugo Eduardo Polanco Brito, ed.); La criolla, 1930–1989.

1500. *Díaz Carela, Cecilio,* 1948– (novelist, poet). Anacaona flor de oro, 1992; El día que intentaron hundir la isla, 1993; Tira pulla electoral, 1993.

1501. *Díaz Grullón, Virgilio,* 1924– (novelist, poet, short story writer). Los algarrobos también sueñan, 1977; Crónicas de altocerro, 1966–1994; De niños, hombres y fantasmas, 1981–1991; Un día cualquiera, 1958–1981; El escritor ante su obra [antología], 1986; Más allá del espejo, 1975–1983.

1502. *Díaz Ordóñez, Virgilio,* 1895–1968 (novelist, poet, short story writer). Del árbol del olvido, 1973 (Julio Jaime Julia, ed.); Figuras de barro, 1930; Jerónimo, 1969; Poesías completas, 1980; Sonetos, 1971.

1503. *Díaz, Vigil,* 1880–1961 (poet). Del sena al Ozama, 1922; Galeras de Pafos, 1921; Góndolas, 1913; Miserere patricio, 1915; Música de ayer, 1925–1952; Orégano, 1949.

1504. *Disla, Reynaldo* (playwright). Bolo Francisco, 1985; Función de hastío y otras piezas, 1993 (Un comercial para Máximo Gómez, La cárcel encantada, Detrás de la puerta, Función de hastío, Dos pasos de paz, dos pasos de guerra).

1505. *Domínguez Charro, Francisco,* 1918–1943 (novelist, playwright, poet, short story writer). América en genitura épica, 1942; Poesía junta, 1979; Romance del espigal, 1943; Tierra y ámbar, 1940.

1506. *Domínguez, Franklin,* 1931– (playwright, poet). Un amigo desconocido nos aguarda, 1958; La broma del senador, 1958; La espera, 1959; Obras premiadas, 1993 (Los borrachos, El primer voluntario de junio, Lisístrata odia la política [1981], Drogas, Omar y los demás); Se busca un hombre honesto, 1965; Teatro, 1968 (Espigas maduras [1958], Antígona-Humor [1961], Los actores [1968], El encuentro [1968]); El último instante, 1958.

1507. *Echavarría, Colón,* 1898- (novelist, poet, short story writer). Canción de amor, 1967; Cancionero galante, 1946; Cantares, 1963; La epopeya de la raza, 1936–1946; Frutos del amor prohibido, 1950; Jíbaro en San Juan, 1965; Más palos que bombos, 1968; Palabras desconocidas, 1951; Pirámides, 1930; Puños y regatones, 1970; El soldado de San Cristóbal, 1953; Los soldados de la patria, 1957; Sonetos de Colón Echavarría, 1934; Los sonetos de la muerte viva, 1973; Sonetos de neurastenia, 1959; Los sonetos de piedra, 1942; Sonetos en pública subasta, 1963–1972; Tambor de negros, 1946; Tertulia de sonetos, 1972; La última copa del festín, 1958.

1508. *Espinal, Cayo Claudio,* 1955– (poet). Banquetes de aflicción, 1979; Comedio (entre gravedad y risa), 1993; Utopía de los vínculos, 1982.

1509. *Fernández Mejía, Abel,* 1931– (poet, short story writer). Adolescente y nubes, 1958; Cuentos para ser disparados, 1992; Piedra y tierra, 1975–1977.

1510. *Fernández Spencer, Antonio,* 1922–1995 (poet). Bajo la luz del día, 1953–1958; Como naciendo aún, 1994; Diario del mundo, 1970; En la aurora, 1986; Noche infinita, 1967; Obras poéticas, 1986–1990; Poemas sin misterio, 1988; El regreso de Ulises, 1985; Tengo palabras, 1980; Los testigos, 1962; Vendaval interior, 1944.

1511. Villegas, Víctor. *Antonio Fernández Spencer: poeta y humanista.* Santo Domingo: [s.n.], 1995. 33 pp.

1512. *Ferreras, Ramón Alberto* (novelist, poet). Chapeo, 1974–1982; Cofresí, el intrépido, 1992; Desde el vientre de mi madre, 1991; Dominicanos, 1974; Las Mirabal, 1976–1982; Negros, 1983; Versos verídicos, 1990.

1513. *Fiallo, Fabio,* 1865–1942 (playwright, poet, short story writer). El balcón de Psiquis, 1935; La canción de una vida, 1992 (José Enrique García, ed.); Canciones de la tarde, 1920; Cantaba el ruiseñor, 1910; Cuentos frágiles, 1908–1992; Las manzanas de Mefisto, 1934–1992; Obras completas, 1980 (La canción de una vida [1926], Cuentos frágiles [1908], Nacionalismo auténtico, Estudios acerca de su vida y de sus obras); Poems of the Little Girl in Heaven, 1937 (Translation of Poemas de la niña que está en el cielo [1935]; Margaret B. Hurley, tr.); Poesías, 1931; Primavera sentimental, 1902; Sus mejores versos, 1938.

1514. *García Godoy, Federico,* 1857–1924 (novelist, poet, short story writer). Antología, 1951 (Joaquín Balaguer, ed.); Trilología patriótica, 1982 (Rufinito [1908], Alma dominicana [1911], Guanuma [1914]; Franklin García Godoy, ed.).

1515. *García Guerra, Iván,* 1938– (playwright, poet, short story writer). La guerra no es para nosotros, 1979; Teatro, 1982 (Más allá de la búsqueda [1967], Don Quijote de todo el mundo [1969], Un héroe más para la mitología [1964], Los hijos del Fénix [1965], Fábula de los cinco caminantes [1968], Muerte del héroe, Los tiranos, Interioridades).

1516. *García, José Enrique,* 1948– (poet, short story writer). Contando lo que pasa, 1986; Cuando la miraba pasar, 1987; En el camino y en la casa, 1985; El fabulador y otros poemas, 1980–1989; Huellas de la memoria, 1994; Meditaciones alrededor de una sospecha, 1977; Ritual del tiempo y los espacios, 1982.

1517. *García Romero, Rafael,* 1957– (short story writer). El agonista, 1986; Bajo el acoso, 1987; Historias de cada dia, 1995.

1518. *Gatón Arce, Freddy,* 1920–1994 (poet). Andanzas y memorias, 1990; La canción de la hetera, 1992; Cantos comunes, 1983; Celebraciones de cuatro vientos, 1987; De paso y otros poemas, 1984; Era como entonces, 1988; Estos días de tíbar, 1983; La guerillera Sila Cuásar, 1991; La leyenda de la muchacha, 1962; Magino Quesada, 1966; Mirando el lagarto verde, 1985; La moneda del príncipe, 1993; Poblana, 1965; El poniente, 1982; Retiro hacia la luz, 1980; Los ríos hacen voca, 1986; Son guerras y amores, 1980; Vlía, 1944; Y con ayer tanto tiempo, 1981.

1519. Castro, Tomás. *A propósito de Freddy Gatón Arce: homenaje póstumo.* Santo Domingo: [s.l.], 1995. 50 pp.

1520. Rivera, María del Carmen Prosdocimi de. *La poesía de Freddy Gatón Arce: una interpretación.* Santo Domingo: Ediciones Siboney, 1983. 157 pp.

1521. *Gautreaux Piñeyro, Bonaparte,* 1937– (novelist, short story writer). Al final del arcoiris, 1982; Atisbando, 1986; La ciudad clandestina y los secretos del general, 1980; Cuentos del abuelo Julio, 1980; La muerte de Raquel Martínez, 1991; El viaje de don Enrique, 1993.

1522. *Gerón, Cándido,* 1950– (poet). El amor es una derrota en silencio, 1991; Asombro de los tiempos, 1973; Aún después del tiempo, 1984; Caminos del alba, 1993; Canto a Orlando, 1976; Canto infinito a Salvador Allende, 1979; Canto triste para una niña que nunca conocí, 1980; Elida del Alba, 1985; Etnaris, 1984; Euridice, 1981; Hasta ahora, 1987; Los horizontes del deseo, 1991; Huellas de dolor, 1974; El invincible de los tiempos, 1982; Minerva, en el temblor de las mudas paredes, 1983; Opinión pasional, 1994; París ya no es lo mismo, 1989; Los primeros pasos de un oficio, 1988.

1523. *Giró, Valentín,* 1883–1949 (poet). Jacinto Dionisio Flores (Fray Luis), 1935; Sinfonía heroica en honor del Generalísimo Trujillo, 1941.

1524. *Goico Alix, Juan,* 1891–1958 (poet). Los poemas del insomnio y otros poemas, 1937–1971.

1525. *Gómez, Miguel Angel,* 1958– (poet, short story writer). Cuentos, 1981 (with Avelino Stanley Rondón); Las manos de la muerte son de seda, 1989.

1526. *Gómez Rosa, Alexis,* 1950– (poet). Cabeza de alquiler, 1990; Contra la pluma la espuma, 1990; High Q/High Quality, 1985; New York City en tránsito de pie quebrado, 1993; Oficio de post-muerte, 1977; Opio territorio, 1990; Pluróscopo, 1977; Tiza y tinta, 1991.

1527. *Grimaldi Silié, Eleanor* (poet, short story writer). Cristal de ilusiones, 1995; Poesías para tí, 1983.

1528. *Guzmán Carretero, Octavio,* 1915–1948 (poet). Solazo, 1939–1986.

1529. *Henríquez i Carvajal, Federico,* 1848–1952 (novelist, playwright, poet, short story writer). Baní, 1939; Cuentos, 1950; Del amor i del dolor, 1926; Discursos y conferencias, 1970; Etica i estética, 1929; Guarocuya, 1924; La hija del hebreo, 1877; Ideario, 1960–1963 (Alberto Baeza Flores, ed.); Mi album de sonetos, 1927; El poema de la historia, 1948; Romances históricos, 1937; Un siglo de conducta y valor, 1969 (Autobiographical).

1530. *Henríquez, Rafael Américo,* 1899–1968 (poet). Briznas de cobre, 1977; Rosa de tierra y otros poemas, 1944–1989.

1531. *Henríquez Ureña, Max,* 1885–1968 (novelist, playwright, poet). Anforas, 1914; El arzobispo Valera, 1944; Cuentos insulares, 1947; Fosforescencias, 1930; Garra de luz, 1958; La independencia efímera, 1938–1967; El retorno de los galeones, 1930–1963.

> 1532. Fernández Pequeño, José M. *Periplo santiagüero de Max Henríquez Ureña.* Santiago, Cuba: Ediciones Caserón, 1989. 57 pp.
>
> See also #561.

1533. *Henríquez Ureña, Pedro,* 1884–1946 (playwright, poet, short story writer). Antología, 1950–1992 (Max Henríquez Ureña, ed.); Cuentos de la Nana Lupe, 1966–1989; De mi patria, 1974 (Jorge Tena Reyes, ed.); Desde Washington, 1915–1975; Diario, 1989 (Enrique Zuleta Alvarez, ed.); Ensayos, 1965–1976 (José Rodríguez Feo, José Alcántara Almánzar, eds.); Homenaje a Pedro Henríquez Ureña en el centenario de su nacimiento [selecciones]), 1985 (Rodolfo Coiscou Weber, ed.); Horas de estudio, 1910; Memorias, 1989 (Enrique Zuleta Alvarez, ed.); El nacimiento de Dionisos, 1916; Obra crítica, 1960–1981 (Emma Susana Speratti Piñero, ed.); Obra dominicana, 1988; Obras completas de Pedro Henríquez Ureña, 1976 (Juan Jacobo de Lara, ed.); Páginas escogidas, 1946 (José Luis Martínez, ed.); Pedro Henríquez Ureña, 1967 (Carmelina de Castellanos, Luis Alberto Castellanos, eds.); Pedro Henríquez Ureña, 1991 (Javier Lasarte Valcárcel, ed.); Pedro Henríquez Ureña, 1993 (Tomás Mallo, ed.); Pedro Henríquez Ureña en los Estados Unidos, 1961 (Alfredo A. Roggiano, ed.); Plenitud de España, 1940–1979; Poesías juveniles, 1949–1984; Tres cuentos de Pedro Henríquez Ureña, 1981.

> 1534. Alvarez, Soledad. *La magna patria de Pedro Henríquez Ureña.* Santo Domingo: Editora Taller, 1981. 132 pp.

1535. Carilla, Emilio. *Pedro Henríquez Ureña: signo de América.* Santo Domingo: Universidad Nacional Pedro Henríquez Ureña, 1985. 151 pp.

1536. ———. *Pedro Henríquez Ureña y otros estudios.* Buenos Aires: R. Medina, 1949. 163 pp.

1537. Coiscou Weber, Rodolfo, ed. *Homenaje a Pedro Henríquez Ureña en el centenario de su nacimiento.* Santo Domingo: Casa Weber, 1985. 47 pp.

1538. Durán, Diony. *La flecha de anhelo.* Havana: Editorial Letras Cubanas, 1992. 288 pp.

1539. ———. *Literatura y sociedad en la obra de Pedro Henríquez Ureña.* Havana: Editorial Letras Cubanas, 1994. 317 pp.

1540. Febres, Laura. *Pedro Henríquez Ureña: crítico de América.* Caracas: Casa de Bello, 1989. 165 pp.

1541. Goico Castro, Manuel de Jesús. *Pedro Henríquez Ureña.* Santo Domingo: Biblioteca Nacional, 1986. 231 pp.

1542. Henríquez Ureña, Max. *Hermano y maestro.* Ciudad Trujillo: Librería Dominicana, 1950. 54 pp.

1543. Henríquez Ureña, Pedro, and Alfonso Reyes. *Epistolario íntimo, 1906–1946.* Santo Domingo: UNPHU, 1981– [vol. 1–3–].

1544. Juliá, Julio Jaime, ed. *El libro jubilar de Pedro Henríquez Ureña.* Santo Domingo: Universidad Nacional Pedrio Henríquez Ureña, 1984. 2 vols.

1545. Ramos, José, ed. *Pedro Henríquez Ureña: homenaje con motivo del centenario de su nacimiento.* Caracas: Casa de Bello, 1985. 67 pp.

1546. Rodríguez Demorizi, Emilio. *Dominicanidad de Pedro Henríquez Ureña.* Santo Domingo: Editora Taller, 1984. 84 pp.

1547. Vargas, José Rafael, ed. *La integridad humanística de Pedro Henríquez Ureña: antología.* Santo Domingo: Universidad Autónoma de Santo Domingo, 1984. 371 pp.

See also #561.

1548. *Hernández Franco, Tomás Rafael,* 1904–1952 (poet, short story writer). Canciones del litoral alegre, 1936–1953; Capitulario, 1921; Cibao, 1951–1986; De amor, inquietud, cansancio, 1923; El hombre que había perdido su eje, 1926; Rezos bohemios, 1921; Yelidá, 1942–1985.

1549. *Hernández Núñez, Angela* (poet, short story writer). Alótropos, 1989; Desafío, 1985; Edades de asombro, 1992; Los fantasmas prefieren la luz, 1986; Las mariposas no temen a los cactus, 1985–1988; Masticar una rosa, 1993; Tizne y cristal, 1987.

1550. *Hernández Rueda, Lupo,* 1930– (poet). Círculo, 1979; Como naciendo aún, 1953–1994; Con el pecho alumbrado, 1988; Crónica del sur, 1965; Cuanza, 1984; Del tamaño del tiempo, 1978; Dentro de mi conmigo, 1967; Muerte y memoria, 1963; Por ahora: antología poética, 1975; Por el mar de tus ojos, 1993; Santo Domingo vertical, 1962; El tiempo que espero, 1972; Trio, 1957 (with Máximo Avilés Blonda and Rafael Valera Benítez).

1551. *Hernández-Mejía, Edgar,* 1948– (poet). A partir de nuestros designios y otras obras poéticas, 1982; El histórico Cristo sin rostro, 1990; Imágenes del litoral, 1973; Voz de medio mundo, 1975.

1552. *Incháustegui Cabral, Héctor,* 1912–1979 (playwright, poet, short story writer). Canciones para matar un recuerdo, 1944; Casi de ayer, 1952; De vida temporal, 1944; Diario de la guerra, 1967; Los dioses ametrallados, 1967; En soledad de amor herido, 1943; Filoctetes, 1964; Hipólito, 1964; Imágenes de Héctor Incháustegui Cabral, 1980 (José Alcántara Almánzar, ed.); Las ínsulas extrañas, 1952; Miedo en un puñado de polvo, 1964; Muerte en "El Edén", 1951; Poemas de una sola angustia, 1940–1978; Por Copacabana buscando, 1964; El pozo muerto, 1960–1980; Prometeo, 1960–1964; Rebelión vegetal y otros poemas menos amargos, 1956; Rumbo a la otra vigilia, 1942; La sombra del tamarindo, 1984; Soplo que se va y que vuelve, 1946; Versos, 1950.

1553. *James Rawlings, Norberto,* 1945– (poet). Hago constar, 1983; La provincia sublevada, 1972; Sobre la marcha, 1969; Vivir, 1981.

1554. *Javier, Adrián,* 1967– (poet). Bolero del esquizo, 1994; El oscuro rito de la luz, 1988.

1555. *Jesús, Dionisio de,* 1959– (poet). Axiología de las sombras, 1984; Celebración del ausente, 1991; La infinita presencia de la sangre, 1988; Oráculo del suicida, 1985.

1556. *Lacay Polanco, Ramón,* 1924– (novelist, short story writer). Antología, 1994; La mujer de agua, 1949; No todo está perdido, 1966; Punto Sur, 1958; Rosa de Soledad, 1986.

1557. *Lamarche, Juan Bautista,* 1894–1957 (poet). A la sombra de los olivos, 1953; Cancionero de las Españas, 1955; El espejo invisible, 1955; El libro de la luna y la noche, 1955; Paisajes y cromos, 1955; Patria recóndita, 1937; Poemas del humo, la marinería y el arrabal, 1954; Tierra, sangre y sombra, 1955; Treinta sonetos a Trujillo, 1955.

1558. *Lebrón Saviñón, Carlos* (poet, short story writer). Canto iluminado, 1985; Nacimiento de auroras, 1979; Qué importa, soy feliz, 1994.

1559. *Lebrón Saviñón, Mariano,* 1922– (playwright, poet). Tiempo en la tierra, 1982; Triángulos, 1943 (with Domingo Moreno Jimenes and Alberto Baeza Flores).

1560. *Lockward Artiles, Antonio,* 1943– (novelist, poet, short story writer). Ay! Ay! Se me muere Rebeca, 1979; Espíritu intranquilo, 1966; Hotel Cosmos, 1966; Los poemas del ferrocarril central, 1971; Yo canto al tanque de lastre del Regina Express, 1981.

1561. *Lockward, Yoryi,* 1912– (poet). Acúcheme uté, 1941–1982.

1562. *López, José Ramón,* 1866–1922 (novelist, playwright, short story writer). José Ramón López, 1991 (Cuentos puertoplateños [1904], Ensayos y artículos, Diario).

1563. *Lora, Huchi* (poet). Las décimas de Huchi Lora, 1992 (Luis Beiro Alvarez, ed.).

1564. *Lugo, Américo,* 1870–1952 (playwright, short story writer). A punto largo, 1900; Antología, 1949 (Vetilio Alfau Durán, ed.); Antología de Américo Lugo, 1976 (Julio Jaime Juliá, ed.); Camafeos, 1918; Ensayos dramáticos, 1906 (El avaro, Víspera de boda, En la peña pobre, Elvira); Heliotropo, 1939; Obras escogidas, 1993 (Roberto Cassá, ed.).

1565. *Lugo, Ludín,* 1916– (novelist, poet). El caballero de la ciudad, 1981; Canoas de falso piso, 1993.

1566. *Madera, Teonilda* (poet). Corazón de jade con lágrimas de miel, 1995.

1567. *Marcallé Abréu, Roberto,* 1948– (novelist, short story writer). Alternativas para una existencia gris, 1987; Cinco bailadores sobre la tumba caliente del licenciado, 1978; Las dos muertes de José Inirio, 1972; Espera de penumbres en el viejo bar, 1980; El minúsculo infierno del señor Lukas, 1973; Sábado de sol después de las lluvias, 1978–1984; Ya no están estos tiempos para trágicos finales de historias de amor, 1982–1984.

1568. *Mármol, José,* 1960– (poet). Deus ex machina, 1994; Encuentro con las mismas otredades, 1985–1989; Lengua del paraíso, 1993; La invención del día, 1989; El ojo del arúspice, 1984.

1569. *Marrero Aristy, Ramón,* 1912–1959 (novelist, short story writer). Balsié, 1938–1994; Over, 1939–1994. See also #1383.

1570. *Martínez, Carmen Natalia,* 1917–1976 (novelist, playwright, poet). Alma adentro, 1939–1981; Llanto sin término por el hijo nunca llegado, 1960; Poesías, 1981; La victoria, 1992.

1571. *Mateo, Andrés L.,* 1946– (novelist, poet). La balada de Alfonsina Bairán, 1985–1994; La otra Penélope, 1982; Pisar los dedos de Dios, 1979–1986.

1572. *Medina, Oquendo,* 1956– (poet). Conversaciones con Pedro y otros poemas, 1993; Imágenes de luces y de sombra, 1986.

1573. *Mieses Burgos, Franklin,* 1907–1976 (playwright, poet). Antología poética, 1948; Clima de eternidad, 1944–1986; Franklin Mieses Burgos (antología), 1953–1986 (Freddy Gatón Arce, ed.); El héroe, 1954; Presencia de los días, 1948–1951; Seis cantos para una sola muerte, 1948; Sin rumbo ya y herido por el cielo, 1944.

1574. *Mieses, Juan Carlos,* 1947– (playwright, poet). La cruz y el cetro, 1985; Flagellum dei, 1987; Gaia, 1992; Urbi et orbi, 1984.

1575. *Miller, Jeanette,* 1944– (poet, short story writer). Estadías, 1985; Fichas de identidad, 1985; Fórmulas para combatir el miedo, 1972.

1576. *Miolán, Angel* (novelist). Hombres de Cayo Confite, 1993; Páginas dispersas, 1970.

1577. *Mir, Pedro,* 1913– (novelist, poet, short story writer). Amén de mariposas, 1969; Buen viaje, Pancho Valentín, 1981; Countersong to Walt Whitman and Other Poems, 1993 (Translation of Contra-canto a Walt Whitman [1952–1976]; Jonathan Cohen, Donald D. Walsh, trs.); Cuando amaban las tierras comuneras, 1978; La gran hazaña de Límber y después Otoño, 1977; Hay un país en el mundo y otros poemas, 1948–1994; Homenaje a Pedro Mir (antología), 1983; El huracán Neruda, 1975–1983; El lapicida de los ojos morados, 1993; Poemas de buen amor y a veces de fantasía, 1969; Poesías (casi) completas, 1994; Primeros versos, 1993; Seis momentos de esperanza, 1951–1962; Tres leyendas de colores, 1969; Viaje a la muchedumbre, 1971–1981.

1578. *Molinaza, José,* 1951– (playwright, poet). Crepúsculo sur, 1985; Sueños de Penélope, 1977; Ultimo verso, 1972.

1579. *Monclús, Miguel Angel* (novelist). Cachón, 1944–1993.

1580. *Mora Serrano, Manuel,* 1933– (short story writer). Cucarachas, 1993; Decir samán, 1984; Goeíza, 1980; Juego de dominó, 1973.

1581. *Morel, Tomás,* 1913– (poet). Del llano i de la loma, 1937–1987; Mi pueblo y otros poemas, 1990.

1582. *Moreno Jimenes, Domingo,* 1894–1986 (poet). Advenimiento, 1941; América hacia el hombre, 1946; América-mundo, 1935; Antología, 1949–1970; Antología mínima, 1943–1973; Antología poética, 1949; Burbujas en el vaso de una vida breve, 1948; El caminante sin camino, 1935; Canto a la ceiba de Colón, 1925–1958; Canto al Atlántico, 1941; Cuatro (qué sé yo) estambres, 1942; Decrecer, 1927; Del gemido a la fragua, 1975; El diario de la aldea, 1925–1940; Días sin lumbre, 1931; Elixiris, 1929; Embiste de raza, 1936; Emocionadamente, 1945; Evangelio americano, 1942; Exalté el ideal y sufrí ante la vida, 1944; Fogata sobre el signo, 1940; Indice de una vida, 1941; Mi vieja se muere, 1925–1939; Moderno apocalipsis, 1934; Obras poéticas, 1975; Palabras en el agua, 1945; Palabras sin tiempo, 1932; El poema de la hija reintegrada, 1938–1965; Poemario de la cumbre y el mar, 1942; Promesa, 1916; Psalmos, 1921; Santa Berta y otros poemas, 1959; Sentir es la norma, 1939; Sésamo, 1931; Siete vías poéticas, 1947; Los surcos opuestos, 1931; Tres pasos en la sombra, 1946; Triángulos, 1943 (with Alberto Baeza Flores and Mariano Lebrón Saviñon); Vuelos y duelos, 1916.

1583. Lantigua, José Rafael. *Domingo Moreno Jimenes: biografía de un poeta.* 4a ed. rev. Santo Domingo: Editora Taller, 1994. 192 pp.

1584. Tanasescu, Horia. *La milenaria vida de Domingo Moreno Jimenes: Lao Tsém, el budhismo Zen, y un poeta dominicano.* Santo Domingo: Publicaciones América, 1974. 77 pp.

See also #1334.

1585. *Morrison, Mateo,* 1947– (poet). Anniversary of Pain/Aniversario del dolor, 1986 (Spanish ed. [1973]); Apropos of Images/A propósito de imágenes, 1991; Si la casa se llena de sombras, 1986; Visiones del amoroso ente, 1990; Visiones del transeúnte, 1984.

1586. *Naranjo, Manuel,* 1954– (novelist, poet). Compás diverso, 1995; Potestad de la niebla, 1989; Quitapuela, 1994.

1587. *Natalia, Carmen,* 1917–1976 (novelist, playwright, poet). Poesías, 1976; La victoria, 1992.

1588. *Nina, Diógenes,* 1941– (poet). Apricina, bestia del paraíso, 1987; Metamorfosis del silencio, 1989; Permutable Republic/República permutable, 1979 (Marion Mehlman, tr.).; El secreto de los ciclos, 1991.

1589. *Nina, Juan Bautista,* 1959– (poet). Evocaciones de los tiempos en fin de siglo, 1992; Manja y otros poemas de amor, 1990; Otra mirada al horizonte, 1993; La tierra no resiste más heridas, 1989.

1590. *Nolasco, Sócrates,* 1884–1970 (short story writer). Cuentos cimarrones, 1958; Cuentos del sur, 1931; El diablo ronda en los Guayacanes, 1967; Obras completas, 1994 (Carlos Esteban Deive, ed.).

1591. *Objío, Nelson Eddy* (poet). Arcoiris en sonetos, 1991; Cánticos a mi patria, 1988; Un hombre acosado, 1979; Poemas para un nuevo continente, 1983.

1592. *Pantaleón, Adalgisa* (poet). Mi silencio roto, 1995.

1593. *Peix, Pedro,* 1952– (novelist, poet, short story writer). El brigadier/La fábula del lobo y el sargento, 1981; Los despojos del cóndor, 1983; El fantasma de la calle El Conde, 1988; Las locas de la Plaza de los Almendros, 1978; La noche de los buzones blancos, 1980; El paraíso de la memoria, 1985; El placer está en el último piso, 1974; Pormenores de una servidumbre, 1985.

1594. *Peña de Bordas, Virginia de,* 1930– (poet, short story writer). La eracra de oro, 1978; La princesa de los cabellos platinados, 1978; Seis novelas cortas, 1978; Toeya, 1952.

1595. *Peralta Romero, Rafael,* 1948– (poet, short story writer). Un chin de caramelo, 1992; Diablo azul, 1992; Las piedras sobre las flores, 1985; Punto por punto, 1983.

1596. *Perdomo, Apolinar,* 1882–1918 (playwright, poet). Cantos de Apolo, 1943–1986.

1597. *Pereyra, Emilia* (novelist). El crimen verde, 1994.

1598. *Pérez Alfonseca, Ricardo,* 1892–1950 (playwright, poet). Canto a la independencia, 1920–1976; Finis patria, 1914–1976; Palabras de mi madre y otros poemas, 1925.

1599. *Pérez, Faustino A.,* 1945– (short story writer). Chisporroteo, 1984; Ese libro se llama, 1994.

1600. *Pérez, Isael,* 1961– (poet). Burócratas del polvo, 1984; Contemporáneos del tiempo, 1995.

1601. *Pérez, Mario Emilio* (short story writer). Brincando por la vida, 1988; Cuentos de vividores, 1986; Estampas dominicanas, 1971–1983; !Hogar!, fuñío hogar, 1983; Más brincos por la vida, 1993; El miedo cerró las puertas, 1970; Personajes migueletes, 1981; ¿Quién entiende a las mujeres?, 1995; Traicionero aguardiente, 1985.

1602. *Perozo, César N.* (short story writer). Horas de buen humor, 1925–1993.

1603. *Piñeyro, Frank J.* (novelist). Náufragos del odio, 1995.

1604. *Prestol Castillo, Freddy* (novelist). El masacre se pasa a pie, 1973–1989; Pablo Mama, 1985.

    1605. Grullón, Iván. *La matanza de los haitianos en "El masacre se pasa a pie" y "Mi compadre el General Sol."* Santo Domingo: Editora de la Universidad Autónoma de Santo Domingo, 1989. 50 pp.

1606. *Raful, Tony,* 1951– (poet). Abril, nacen alas delante de tus ojos, 1980; Las bodas de Rosaura con la primavera, 1991; La dorada mosca del fuego, 1988; Gestión de alborada, 1973; Pájaros y horizontes sitiados, 1984; La poesía y el tiempo, 1973; Ritual onírico de la ciudad y otras memorias, 1983; Visiones del escriba, 1981.

1607. *Reyes Vásquez, Radhamés,* 1952– (poet). El bolero, memoria histórica del corazón, 1994; La muerte en el combate, 1973.

1608. *Risco Bermúdez, René del,* 1937–1972 (poet, short story writer). Cuentos y poemas completos, 1981; En el barrio no hay banderas, 1974; El viento frío y otros poemas, 1967–1985.

1609. *Rivera, Martha,* 1960– (poet). Geometría del vértigo, 1995; Twenty Century y otros poemas, 1985; Transparencias de mi espejo, 1985.

1610. *Rodríguez Fernández, Arturo,* 1948– (novelist, short story writer). La búsqueda de los desencuentros, 1974; Espectador de la nada, 1986; Mutanville, 1980 (with José Alcántara Almánzar); Subir como una marea, 1980.

1611. *Rodríguez Soriano, René,* 1950– (short story writer). Blasfemia angelical, 1995 (with Ramón Tejada Holguín); Canciones para una niña gris metal, 1983; Muestra gratis, 1986; No les guardo rencor, Papá, 1989; Probablemente es virgen todavía, 1993 (with Ramón Tejada Holguín); Raíces, 1977–1981; Su nombre, Julia, 1991; Textos destetatos a destiempo con sabor de tiempo y de canción, 1979; Todos los juegos el juego, 1986.

1612. *Román, Sabrina,* 1956– (poet). Carrusel de mecedoras, 1989–1994; De un tiempo a otro tiempo, 1978; Imagen repetida en múltiples septiembres, 1986; Palabra rota, 1984.

1613. *Rueda, Manuel,* 1921– (playwright, poet, short story writer). Con el tambor de las islas, 1975; Congregación del cuerpo único, 1989; La criatura terrestre, 1963; Las edades del viento, 1979; Las noches, 1949–1953; Papeles de Sara y otros relatos, 1985; Por los mares de la dama, 1976; La prisionera del Alcázar, 1976; El Rey Clinejas, 1979–1985; Teatro, 1968 (La trinitaria blanca [1957–1992], La tía Beatriz hace un milagro, Vacaciones en el cielo, Entre alambradas); Tríptico, 1949.

1614. Borrel Garrido, Sandra, and Maril Núñez Yangüela. *Pluralismo: Manuel Rueda.* Santo Domingo: Editora Taller, 1988. 66 pp.

1615. *Salvador Gautier, Manuel,* 1930– (novelist). El atrevimiento, 1993; La convergencia, 1993; Monte adentro, 1993; Pormenores del exilio, 1993; Tiempo para héroes, 1993.

1616. *Sánchez Beras, César,* 1962– (poet). Con el pie forzado, 1994; Memorias del retorno, 1992; Travesía a la quinta estación, 1994.

1617. *Sánchez, Enriquillo,* 1947– (poet). Convicto y confeso I, 1990; Musiquito, 1993; Pájaro dentro de la lluvia, 1985; Por la cumbancha de Maguita, 1985.

1618. *Sánchez Lamouth, Juan,* 1929–1968 (poet). Brumas, 1954; Canto a la Provincia de Trujillo y otros poemas, 1960; Canto a las legiones de Trujillo y otros poemas, 1959; Cincuenta cantos a Trujillo y una oda a Venezuela, 1958; Cuaderno para una muerte en primavera, 1956; Doscientos versos para una sola rosa, 1956; Elegía de las hojas caídas y diez poemas sin importancia, 1955; Granada rota, 1960; Memorial del bosque, 1956; Otoño y poesía, 1959; Poemas de Juan Sánchez Lamouth, 1981 (Mateo Morrison, ed.); El pueblo y la sangre, 1958; Resplandor del relámpago (obra completa), 1992 (Julio Jaime Juliá, ed.); Sinfonía vegetal a Juan Pablo Duarte y otros poemas, 1967.

1619. *Sanz Lajara, J. M.,* 1917–1963 (novelist, short story writer). Antología de cuentos, 1994 (Andrés L. Mateo, ed.); El candado, 1959; Caonex, 1949; Cotopaxi, 1949; El misterio del golfo, 1934; El príncipe y la comunista, 1937; Viv, 1961.

1620. *Scheker Hane, Luis,* 1907– (poet). Lapislázuli, 1943–1990; Trazos en las brumas lejanas, 1984.

1621. *Sención, Viriato,* 1941– (novelist, short story writer). La enana Celania y otros cuentos, 1994; They Forged the Signature of God, 1995 (Translation of Los que falsificaron la firma de Dios [1992–1993]; Asa Zatz, tr.).

1622. *Serulle, Haffe,* 1947– (playwright, poet). Bianto y su señor, 1984; Los caminos de la infancia futura, 1985; Los caminos del fuego, 1985; Los caminos del pan, 1986; La danza de Mingó, 1977; Duarte, 1976; El hatero del seibo (Pedro Santana), 1976; El otro abril, 1986; El salto de la sangre, 1986; Las tinieblas del dictador, 1978; Voy a matar al presidente, 1972–1974; El vuelo de los imperios, 1983.

1623. *Smester, Rosa,* 1859–1945 (short story writer). Prosas, 1931–1987.

1624. *Stanley Rondón, Avelino,* 1959– (novelist, short story writer). Catedral de la libido, 1994; Cuentos, 1981 (with Miguel Angel Gómez); Los disparos, 1988; Equis, 1986; La máscara del tiempo, 1996.

1625. *Suriel, Orlando* (poet). La búsqueda del tiempo, 1986; Desde la sima, 1993; El ser y la nada, 1986.

1626. *Suro, Rubén,* 1916– (poet). Poemas de una sola intención, 1978–1984.

1627. *Tarazona, Enrique,* 1944– (novelist). El doble muerte de un radical de ahora, 1979; El historiólogo, 1992; El homo de las imágenes, 1979.

1628. *Tejada Holguín, Ramón* (short story writer). Blasfemia angelical, 1995 (with René Rodríguez Soriano); Probablemente es virgen todavía, 1993 (with René Rodríguez Soriano).

1629. *Toribio, Tirso,* 1936– (novelist). La muerte de Jacinto Mendoza, 1995.

1630. *Torres, Luis Alfredo,* 1935– (poet). Alta realidad, 1970; Linterna sorda, 1958; Oscuro litoral, 1980.

1631. *Valdez, Diógenes,* 1943– (novelist, short story writer). Del imperio del caos al reino de la palabra, 1986; Lucinda Palmares, 1981–1984; La pinacoteca de un burgués, 1992; El silencio del caracol, 1978; La telaraña, 1980; Los tiempos revocables, 1984; Todo puede suceder un día, 1984.

1632. *Valera Benítez, Rafael,* 1928– (poet). Canciones australes, 1979; Los centros peculiares, 1964; La luz descalza y elegías, 1966; Trio, 1957 (with Máximo Avilés Blonda and Lupo Hernández Rueda).

1633. *Vassallo, Margarita* (poet). Dos pasos detrás de la memoria, 1993; Ecos de mi sombra, 1991; Manantiales de silencio, 1994.

1634. *Veloz Maggiolo, Marcio,* 1936– (novelist, playwright, poet, short story writer). Los ángeles de hueso, 1967–1985; Apearse de la máscara, 1986; La biografía difusa de sombra castañeda, 1980–1984; El buen ladrón, 1960–1962; Creonte, 1963; Cuentos, recuentos y casicuentos, 1986; De abril en adelante, 1975–1984; La fértil agonía del amor, 1982; Florbella, 1986; Intus, 1962; El jefe iba descalzo, 1993; Judas, 1962; Materia prima, 1988; Nosotros los suicidas, 1965; Novelas cortas, 1980–1994; La palabra reunida, 1982; Poemas en ciernes, 1986; Retorno a la palabra, 1986; Ritos de cabaret, 1991; El sol y las cosas, 1957; La vida no tiene nombre, 1965.

1635. *Ventura, Miriam,* 1957– (poet). Claves para fantasmas, 1995; Poemas de la noche, 1986; Trópico acerca del otoño, 1987.

1636. *Vicioso G., Abelardo,* 1930– (poet). Cien poemas de intenso vivir, 1990; La lumbre sacudida, 1958.

1637. *Vicioso, Sherezada,* 1948– (poet). Un extraño ulular traía el viento, 1985; Internamiento, 1992; Viaje desde el agua, 1981; Volver a vivir, 1986.

1638. *Villegas, Víctor,* 1924– (poet). Botella en el mar, 1984; Charlotte Amalie, 1977–1994; Cosmos, 1986; Diálogos con Simeón, 1977–1994; Juan Criollo y otras antielegías, 1982; La luz en el regreso, 1993; Poco tiempo después, 1991; Poesía de Víctor Villegas, 1986.

 1639. Cuevas, Julio. *Visión crítica en torno a la poesía de Víctor Villegas.* Santo Domingo: Biblioteca Nacional, 1985. 106 pp.

1640. *Weber, Delia,* 1900– (playwright, poet, short story writer). Apuntes, 1949–1993; Los bellos designios, 1949–1991; Dora y otros cuentos, 1952; Encuentro, 1939; Espigas al sol, 1959; Pensamiento inédito, 1987; Poemas a mi madre, 1982; Los viajeros, 1944.

PUERTO RICO

A. BIBLIOGRAPHIES AND BIO-BIBLIOGRAPHIES

General

1641. Bravo, Enrique R. *An Annotated, Selected Puerto Rican Bibliography/Bibliografía puertorriqueña selecta y anotada*. New York: Urban Center, Columbia University, 1972. 229 pp.

1642. Ellowitch, Azi. *Hidden Treasures: An Annotated Bibliography of Puerto Rican, Nuyorican, and Caribbean Literature for Use in Adult Basic Education*. New York: Institute for Literacy Studies, City University of New York, 1991. 61 pp.

1643. Foster, David William. *Puerto Rican Literature: A Bibliography of Secondary Sources*. Westport, CT: Greenwood Press, 1982. 232 pp.

1644. González, Nilda. *Bibliografía de teatro puertorriqueño: siglos XIX y XX*. Río Piedras, P.R.: Editorial Universitaria, Universidad de Puerto Rico, 1979. 223 pp.

1645. Hill, Marnesba D., and Harold B. Schleifer. *Puerto Rican Authors: A Bibliographic Handbook*. Metuchen, NJ: Scarecrow Press, 1974. 267 pp.

1646. Pedreira, Antonio Salvador. *Bibliografía puertorriqueña, 1493–1930*. New York: B. Franklin, 1974. 707 pp. Reprint, with a new introd., of the 1932 ed.

1647. ———. *Curiosidades literarias de Puerto Rico*. San Juan: Biblioteca de Autores Puertorriqueños, 1939. 48 pp.

1648. Piñeiro de Rivera, Flor. *A Century of Puerto Rican Children's Literature/Un siglo de literatura infantil puertorriqueña*. Río Piedras, P.R.: Editorial de la Universidad de Puerto Rico, 1987. 139 pp.

1649. Rivera, Guillermo. *A Tentative Bibliography of the Belles-Lettres of Porto Rico*. Cambridge, MA: Harvard University Press, 1931. 61 pp.

General: Sixteenth to Nineteenth Centuries

1650. Géigel y Zeñón, José, and Abelardo Morales Ferrer. *Bibliografía puertorriqueña*. Barcelona: Editorial Araluce, 1934. 453 pp.

1651. Sama, Manuel María. *Bibliografía puerto-riqueña*. Mayagüez, P.R.: Tip. Comercial-Marina, 1887. 159 pp.

General: Twentieth Century

1652. Hernández de Trelles, Carmen Dolores. *De aquí y de allá: libros de Puerto Rico y del extranjero*. San Juan: Biblioteca de Autores Puertorriqueños, 1988. 195 pp.

1653. Ortiz Salichs, Ana M. *Guía a cuentos de Puerto Rico*. Ponce, P.R.: Centro de Estudios Puertorriqueños, 1992. 353 pp.

B. DICTIONARIES AND ENCYCLOPEDIAS

1654. Arana Soto, Salvador. *Catálogo de poetas puertorriqueños*. San Juan: Sociedad de Autores Puertorriqueños, 1968. 257 pp. (with suppl. [39 pp.] published in 1972).

1655. Braschi, Wilfredo. *Perfiles puertorriqueños*. San Juan: Biblioteca de Autores Puertorriqueños, 1978. 186 pp.

1656. Rivera de Alvárez, Josefina. *Diccionario de literatura puertorriqueña*. 2a ed. rev. y aum. y puesta al día hasta 1967. San Juan: Instituto de Cultura Puertorriqueña, 1974–1979. 2 vols. in 3.

C. ANTHOLOGIES

General

1657. Agosto Otero, Milagros, and Pedro Juan Avila, eds. *Antología de autores manatieños*. Manatí, P.R.: Club Altrusa de Manatí, 1993. 148 pp.

1658. Alegría, Ricardo E., ed. *El tema del café en la literatura puertorriqueña*. San Juan: Instituto de Cultura Puertorriqueña, 1965. 67 pp.

1659. Babín, María Teresa, and Stan Steiner, eds. *Borinquen: An Anthology of Puerto Rican Literature*. New York: Vintage, 1974. 515 pp.

1660. Fernández Juncos, Manuel. *Antología portorriqueña: prosa y verso*. New York: Barnes and Noble, 1959. 343 pp. Reprint of the 1923 (2d, rev. ed.).

1661. Hernández Aquino, Luis. *El modernismo en Puerto Rico: poesía y prosa*. San Juan: Editorial Universitaria, Universidad de Puerto Rico, 1977. 212 pp. Reprint of the 1967 ed.

1662. Laguerre, Enrique Arturo, and Esther Melón de Díaz, eds. *El jíbaro de Puerto Rico: símbolo y figura—antología*. Sharon, CT: Troutman Press, 1991. 249 pp. Reprint of the 1968 ed.

1663. Martínez Masdeu, Edgar, and Esther Melón de Díaz, eds. *Literatura puertorriqueña: antología general*. Río Piedras, P.R.: Editorial Edil, 1990. 2 vols. Reprint of the 1972 (2d, rev.) ed.

1664. Rivera de Alvarez, Josefina, and Manuel Alvarez Nazario, eds. *Antología general de la literatura puertorriqueña: prosa, verso, teatro*. Madrid: Partenón, 1982– [vol. 1–].

1665. Rosa-Nieves, Cesáreo, ed. *El costumbrismo literario en la prosa de Puerto Rico: antología*. San Juan: Editorial Cordillera, 1971. 2 vols. Vol. 1. Siglo XIX.—Vol. 2. Siglo XX.

General: Sixteenth to Nineteenth Centuries

1666. Colón, Emilio M., ed. *Primicias de las letras puertorriqueñas*. San Juan: Instituto de Cultura Puertorriqueña, 1970. 516 pp. Includes *Aguinaldo puertorriqueño* [1843], *Album puertorriqueño* [1844], *El cancionero de Borinquen* [1846].

1667. Matos Paoli, Francisco, ed. *Aguinaldo puertorriqueño de 1843*. Ed. conmemorativa del centenario. San Juan: Junta Editora de la Universidad de Puerto Rico, 1946. 206 pp.

1668. Reyes Dávila, Marcos F. and María del Carmen Currás, eds. *La tierra prometida: antología crítica de la literatura puertorriqueña, 1493–1898*. Hato Rey, P.R.: Borikén Libros, 1986. 534 pp.

General: Twentieth Century

1669. Santiago, Roberto, ed. *Boricuas: Influential Puerto Rican Writings—An Anthology*. New York: One World, 1995. 357 pp.

Poetry

Poetry: General

1670. Barradas, Efraín, ed. *Para entendernos: inventario poético puertorriqueño, siglos XIX y XX*. San Juan: Instituto de Cultura Puertorriqueña, 1992. 458 pp.

1671. Barreto, Lydia Zoraida, ed. *Poemario de la mujer puertorriqueña*. San Juan: Instituto de Cultura Puertorriqueña, 1976– [vol. 1–].

1672. Corchado Juarbe, Carmen. *El indio en la poesía puertorriqueña: desde 1847 hasta la generación del sesenta—antología*. Río Piedras, P.R.: ESMACO, 1993. 352 pp. Companion volume to her *El indio: su presencia en la poesía puertorriqueña* (#1778).

1673. Fernández Méndez, Eugenio, ed. *Antología de la poesía puertorriqueña*. San Juan: Cultural Puertorriqueña, 1983. 172 pp. Reprint of the 1968 ed.

1674. Gil de Rubio, Víctor M., ed. *Puerto Rican Poems/Poemas puertorriqueños*. Barcelona: Ediciones Rumbos, 1968. 157 pp.

1675. Gómez Tejera, Carmen, Ana María Losada and Jorge Luis Porras Cruz, eds. *Poesía puertorriqueña*. Mexico City: Editorial Orión, 1990. 425 pp. Reprint of the 1955 ed.

1676. Gutiérrez, Fernando, ed. *Poetas puertorriqueños*. Barcelona: Editorial Bruguera, 1954. 128 pp.

1677. Hadjopoulos, Theresa Ortiz de, ed. *Antología de la poesiá de la mujer puertorriqueña: desde los comienzos hasta el presente*. New York: Peninsula, 1981. 248 pp.

1678. Hernández Aquino, Luis, ed. *Cantos a Puerto Rico: antología siglos XIX y XX*. San Juan: Instituto de Cultura Puertorriqueña, 1967. 218 pp.

1679. ————. *Poesía puertorriqueña*. Río Piedras, P.R.: Universidad de Puerto Rico, 1954. 129 pp.

1680. ————. *Poetas de Lares: antología*. San Juan: Instituto de Cultura Puertorriqueña, 1966. 123 pp.

1681. Instituto de Cultura Puertorriqueña. *Poetas aguadillanos: antología poética*. San Juan: El Instituto, 1967. 91 pp.

1682. López de Vega, Maximiliano, ed. *Las cien mejores poesías de Puerto Rico: joyas poéticas del arte boricua*. Río Piedras, P.R.: Editorial Edil, 1993. 309 pp. Reprint of the 1970 ed.

1683. Marrero, Carmen, ed. *Antología de décimas populares puertorriqueñas*. San Juan: Editorial Cordillera, 1974. 196 pp. Reprint of the 1971 ed.

1684. ————. *Poemas de amor en la lírica puertorriqueña*. San Juan: Editorial Cordillera, 1971. 161 pp.

1685. Matilla Rivas, Alfredo and Iván Silén, eds. *The Puerto Rican Poets/Los poetas puertorriqueños*. New York: Bantam, 1972. 238 pp.

1686. Morales, Jorge Luis, ed. *Las cien mejores poesías líricas de Puerto Rico*. Río Piedras, P.R.: Editorial Edil, 1988. 248 pp. Reprint of the 1973 ed.

1687. Moreira, Rubén Alejandro, ed. *Antología de poesía puertorriqueña*. Hato Rey, P.R.: Triptico Editores, 1992– [vol. 1–]. Vol. 1. Romanticismo.

1688. Ríos, Laura, ed. *Antología general de la poesía puertorriqueña: tradición y originalidad*. Hato Rey, P.R.: Boriken Libros, 1982. 680 pp.

1689. Rosa-Nieves, Cesáreo. *Aguinaldo lírico de la poesía puertorriqueña*. 2a ed. rev. Río Piedras, P.R.: Editorial Edil, 1971. 3 vols. Vol. 1. Románticos y parnasianos.—Vol. 2. Los modernistas.—Vol. 3. Postmodernistas y vanguardistas.

1690. ————, ed. *Antología de décimas cultas de Puerto Rico*. San Juan: Editorial Cordillera, 1975. 221 pp. Reprint of the 1971 ed.

1691. Vargas Pérez, Ramón, ed. *Antología de poetas de San Sebastián (pepinianos)*. San Sebastián, P.R.: R. Vargas Pérez, 1977. 232 pp.

Poetry: Sixteenth to Nineteenth Centuries

1692. Carreras, Carlos Noriega, ed. *Antología completa de poetas puertorriqueños*. San Juan: Puerto Rico Ilustrado, 1922. 3 vols.

1693. Limón de Arce, José. *Poetas arecibeños, 1832–1904*. Arecibo, P.R.: H. C. del Pozo, 1926. 292 pp.

1694. Monge, José María, Manuel María Sama and Antonio Ruiz Quiñones, eds. *Poetas puerto-riqueños*. Mayagüez, P.R.: M. Fernández, 1879. 388 pp.

1695. Torres Rivera, Enrique, ed. *Parnaso portorriqueño: antología esmeramente seleccionada de los mejores poetas de Puerto Rico*. Barcelona: Maucci, 1920. 351 pp. Reprint of the 1910 ed.

Poetry: Twentieth Century

1696. Báez Fumero, José Juan, Francisco Lluch Mora and María de los Milagros Pérez, eds. *Poetas de Yauco: antología*. Yauco, P.R.: Respetable Logia Hijos de la Luz, 1991. 369 pp.

1697. Barradas, Efraín, and Rafael Rodríguez, eds. *Herejes y mitificadores: muestra de poesía puertorriqueña en los Estados Unidos*. Carmen Lilianne Marín, tr. Río Piedras, P.R.: Ediciones Huracán, 1980. 166 pp.

1698. Cancel Negrón, Ramón, and Manuel Pareja Flamán, eds. *Antología de la joven poesía universitaria de Puerto Rico*. San Juan: Editorial Campos, 1959. 192 pp.

1699. Concurso de Trovadores Ron Bacardí (First, 1984, Caguas, P.R., etc.). *Primer Concurso de Trovadores Ron Bacardí: antología de décimas improvisadas*. San Juan: Bacardí Corp., 1986. 47 pp.

1700. González, José Raúl et al. *En la mirilla: poesías*. San Juan: Comunicaciones Piso Trece, 1992. 59 pp. Poetry by José Raúl González, Ivy Andino, Rolando Guardiola, Alan Figueroa, and Iriselma Robles.

1701. Labarthe, Pedro Juan, ed. *Antología de poetas contemporáneos de Puerto Rico*. Mexico City: Editorial Clásica, 1946. 349 pp.

1702. López-Adorno, Pedro, ed. *Papiros de Babel: antología de la poesía puertorriqueña en Nueva York*. Río Piedras, P.R.: Editorial de la Universidad de Puerto Rico, 1991. 509 pp.

1703. Luiña de Latimer, Angélica, and René Torres Delgado, eds. *Selecciones palesianas*. San Juan: Colección Hipatia, 1981. 48 pp. Poetry by Vicente Palés Anés, Consuelo Matos de Palés, Luis Palés Matos, Vicente Palés Matos, and Gustavo Palés Matos.

1704. Marzán, Julio, ed. *Inventing a Word: An Anthology of Twentieth-Century Puerto Rican Poetry*. New York: Columbia University Press, 1980. 184 pp.

1705. Melendes, Joserramón ed. *Poesiaoi: antolojía de la sospecha*. Río Piedras, P.R.: Qease, 1978. 2 vols.

1706. Morales, Jorge Luis, ed. *Ríos al mar: poesía puertorriqueña presente*. Río Piedras, P.R.: Instituto Nacional de Bellas Letras, 1986. 296 pp.

1707. Pérez de Jesús, Dhennis Antonio, ed. *Fulgor poético: antología*. Aguadilla, P.R.: Ediciones Dhearez, 1990. 61 pp.

1708. Reyes Dávila, Marcos F. and Manuel de la Puebla, eds. *Antología de poesía puertorriqueña*. Río Piedras, P.R. [etc]: Ediciones Mairena [etc.], 1983–1986. 3 vols.

1709. Reyes Dávila, Marcos F., ed. *Guajana: tres décadas de poesía 1962–1992*. San Juan: Editorial Guajana, 1992. 485 pp. Cover title *Hasta el final del fuego*

1710. Rivera, María Zoraida et al. *Cuatro vertientes en una cascada: poemas*. Río Piedras, P.R.: Jay-Ce Printing, 1989. 89 pp.

1711. Rodríguez Bou, Ismael, ed. *Versos del hombre y de la vida*. Mexico City: Editorial Orion, 1958. 221 pp.

1712. Rodríguez Nietzsche, Vicente, ed. *Albizu en dos generaciones: poemas*. San Juan: Instituto de Cultura Puertorriqueña, 1994. 69 pp.

1713. Romero García, Luz Virginia, ed. *Veinte poetas modernistas puertorriqueños: antología*. San Juan: Instituto de Cultura Puertorriqueña, 1988. 88 pp.

1714. Rosa-Nieves, Cesáreo, ed. *Voz folklórica de Puerto Rico.* Sharon, CT: Troutman Press, 1991. 128 pp. Reprint of the 1967 ed.

1715. Rosario Quiles, Luis Antonio, ed. *Poesía nueva puertorriqueña: antología.* San Juan: Producciones Bondo, 1971. 232 pp.

1716. Sotomayor, Aurea María, ed. *De lengua, razón y cuerpo: nueve poetas contemporáneas puertorriqueñas—antología y ensayo crítico.* San Juan: Instituto de Cultura Puertorriqueña, 1987. 254 pp.

1717. Valbuena Briones, Angel and Luis Hernández Aquino, eds. *Nueva poesía de Puerto Rico.* Madrid: Ediciones Cultura Hispánica, 1952. 388 pp.

Fiction

Fiction: General

1718. Arce de Vázquez, Margot, and Mariana Robles de Cardona, eds. *Lecturas puertorriqueñas.* 9a ed. Sharon, CT: Troutman Press, 1991. 424 pp. Previous ed. by Margot Arce de Vázquez, Laura Gallego, and Luis de Arrigoitia.

1719. Laguerre, Enrique Arturo, ed. *Antología de cuentos puertorriqueños.* Mexico City: Editorial Orión, 1989. 175 pp. Reprint of the 1954 ed.

1720. Rosa-Nieves, Cesáreo, and Félix Franco Oppenheimer, eds. *Antología general del cuento puertorriqueño.* San Juan: Editorial Edil, 1970. 2 vols. Reprint of the 1959 ed.

1721. Silva de Muñoz, Rosita, ed. *Antología puertorriqueña.* 3a ed. rev. Madrid: Artes Gráf. Corrales, 1975. 279 pp. First ed. (1928) has title *Antología de cuentos.*

Fiction: Sixteenth to Nineteenth Centuries

1722. Carreras, Carlos Noriega, ed. *Florilegio de cuentos puertorriqueños.* San Juan: Puerto Rico Ilustrado, 1924. 171 pp.

Fiction: Twentieth Century

1723. Acevedo, Ramón Luis, ed. *Del silencio al estallido: narrativa femenina puertorriqueña.* Río Piedras, P.R.: Editorial Cultural, 1991. 259 pp.

1724. Alfonso, Vitalina and Emilio Jorge Rodríguez, eds. *Cuentos para ahuyentar el turismo: dieciseis autores puertorriqueños.* Havana: Editorial Arte y Literatura, 1991. 340 pp.

1725. Barradas, Efraín, ed. *Apalabramiento: diez cuentistas puertorriqueños de hoy.* Hanover, NH: Ediciones del Norte, 1983. 250 pp.

1726. Escalera Ortiz, Juan, ed. *Antología del cuento español, hispanoamericano y puertorriqueño: siglo XX.* 3a ed. Madrid: Editorial Playor, 1990. 655 pp.

1727. Instituto de Cultura Puertorriqueña. *Tipos puertorriqueños: prosa costumbrista del siglo 20.* San Juan: El Instituto, 1968. 48 pp.

1728. Ledesma, Moisés, ed. *Cuentos de Puerto Rico.* 2a ed. New York: [s.n.], 1980. 174 pp.

1729. Marqués, René, ed. *Cuentos puertorriqueños de hoy.* Río Piedras, P.R.: Editorial Cultural, 1990. 287 pp. Reprint of the 1959 ed.

1730. Meléndez, Concha. *El arte del cuento en Puerto Rico.* 4a ed. aum. San Juan: Editorial Cordillera, 1975. 446 pp.

1731. ———, ed. *Literatura de ficción en Puerto Rico: cuento y novela.* San Juan: Editorial Cordillera, 1971. 195 pp.

1732. Rosado, José Angel, ed. *El rostro y la máscara: antología alterna de cuentistas puertorriqueños contemporáneos.* San Juan: Editorial de la Universidad de Puerto Rico, 1995. 203 pp.

1733. Solá, María M., ed. *Aquí cuentan las mujeres: muestra y estudio de cinco narradoras puertorriqueñas.* Río Piedras, P.R.: Ediciones Huracán, 1990. 177 pp. Rosario Ferré, Magali García Ramis, Carmen Lugo Filippi, Lourdes Vázquez, Ana Lydia Vega.

1734. Vega, José Luis, ed. *Reunión de espejos: cuentos escritos durante los últimos diecisiete años por trece narradoras y narradores puertorriqueños.* Río Piedras, P.R.: Editorial Cultural, 1988. 303 pp. Reprint of the 1983 ed.

1735. Vélez, Diana Lourdes, ed and tr. *Reclaiming Medusa: Short Stories by Contemporary Puerto Rican Women.* San Francisco, CA: Spinsters/Aunt Lute, 1988. 161 pp.

1736. Wagenheim, Kal, ed. *Cuentos: An Anthology of Short Stories from Puerto Rico.* New York: Schocken Books, 1978. 170 pp.

Drama

Drama: General

1737. Morfi, Angelina. *Antología de teatro puertorriqueño.* San Juan: Ediciones Juan Ponce de León, 1970– [vol. 1–]. Vol. 1. La cuarterona (A. Tapia y Rivera), Héroe y mártir (S. Brau), Un jíbaro (R. Méndez Quiñones), El héroe galopante (N. R. Canales).

Drama: Twentieth Century

1738. Dávila Santiago, Rubén, ed. *Teatro obrero en Puerto Rico, 1900–1920: antología.* Río Piedras, P.R.: Editorial Edil, 1985. 359 pp. La emancipación del obrero, Rebeldías (R. del Romeral), Himno del Primero de mayo (Pietro Gori), Primero de mayo, boceto dramático . . . Redención (José Ramón Limón de Arce [Edmundo Dantés], Cómo se prostituyen las pobres. En el campo, amor libre (Luisa Capetillo), El rompe-huelga, El poder del obrero; o, La mejor venganza (Antonio Milián), Prólogo a M. González, Arte y rebeldía (Jesús Ma. Santiago), Los crímenes sociales, Pelucín el limpiabotas, o, La obra del sistema capitalista (Magdaleno González).

1739. González, Lydia Milagros. *Textos para teatro de El Tajo del Alacrán.* San Juan: Instituto de Cultura Puertorriqueña, 1980. 234 pp.

D. HISTORY AND CRITICISM

General

1740. Babín, María Teresa. *Jornadas literarias: temas de Puerto Rico.* Barcelona: Ediciones Rumbos, 1967. 351 pp.

1741. Cabrera, Francisco Manrique. *Historia de la literatura puertorriqueña.* Río Piedras, P.R.: Editorial Cultural, 1986. 384 pp. Reprint of the 1956 ed.

1742. Conferencia Nacional de Literatura Puertorriqueña (First, 1983, Newark, NJ); Asela Rodriguez-Seda de Laguna, ed. *Images and*

Identities: The Puerto Rican in Two World Contexts. New Brunswick, NJ: Transaction Books, 1987. 276 pp.

1743. Díaz de Fortier, Matilde. *La crítica literaria en Puerto Rico, 1843–1915.* San Juan: Instituto de Cultura Puertorriqueña, 1980. 430 pp.

1744. González, José Luis. *Literatura y sociedad en Puerto Rico: de los cronistas de Indias a la generación del 98.* Mexico City: Fondo de Cultura Económica, 1976. 246 pp.

1745. Lloréns, Washington. *El humorismo, el epigrama y la sátira en la literatura puertorriqueña.* San Juan: Instituto de Cultura Puertorriqueña, 1960. 54 pp.

1746. Lluch Mora, Francisco. *Miradero: ensayos de crítica literaria.* San Juan: Editorial Cordillera, 1966. 260 pp.

1747. Martínez Masdeu, Edgar, ed. *Veintidós conferencias de literatura puertorriqueña.* San Juan: Librería Editorial Ateneo, 1994. 406 pp.

1748. Méndez, José Luis. *Para una sociología de la literatura puertorriqueña.* Havana: Casa de las Américas, 1982. 141 pp.

1749. Nolasco, Sócrates. *Escritores de Puerto Rico.* Manzanillo, Cuba: Editorial "El Arte," 1953. 232 pp.

1750. Pedreira, Antonio Salvador. *La actualidad del jíbaro.* Río Piedras, P.R.: Universidad de Puerto Rico, 1935. 49 pp.

1751. Quintana de Rubero, Hilda E., María Cristina Rodríguez and Gladys Vila Barnés, eds. *Personalidad y literatura puertorriqueñas.* 6a ed. rev. San Juan: Editorial Plaza Mayor, 1994. 379 pp.

1752. Rivera de Alvarez, Josefina. *Historia de la literatura puertorriqueña.* San Juan: Editorial del Depto. de Instrucción Pública, 1969. 2 vols.

1753. ———. *Literatura puertorriqueña: su proceso en el tiempo.* Madrid: Ediciones Partenón, 1983. 953 pp.

1754. Rosa-Nieves, Cesáreo. *Ensayos escogidos: apuntaciones de crítica literaria sobre algunos temas puertorriqueños.* San Juan: [s.n.], 1970. 176 pp.

1755. ————. *Historia panorámica de la literatura puertorriqueña, 1589–1969*. San Juan: Editorial Campos, 1963. 2 vols.

1756. ————. *La lámpara del faro: variaciones críticas sobre temas puertorriqueños—ensayos*. San Juan: Editorial Club de La Prensa, 1957–1960. 2 vols.

1757. ————. *Plumas estelares en las letras de Puerto Rico*. San Juan: Universidad de Puerto Rico, 1967–1971. 2 vols. Vol. 1. Siglo XIX.—Vol. 2. Siglo XX (1907 a 1945).

1758. Silén, Juan Angel. *Las bichas: una interpretación crítica de la literatura femenista y femenina en Puerto Rico*. Río Piedras, P.R.: Valdivia y Alvarez Dunn, 1992. 222 pp.

1759. ————. *Literatura, ideología y sociedad en Puerto Rico*. San Juan: Editorial Edil, 1979. 155 pp.

1760. Silva, Ana Margarita. *El jíbaro en la literatura de Puerto Rico*. 2a ed. corr. y aum. San Juan: Silva, 1957. 165 pp.

General: Sixteenth to Nineteenth Centuries

1761. Olivera, Otto. *La literatura en periódicos y revistas de Puerto Rico: siglo XIX*. Río Piedras, P.R.: Editorial de la Universidad de Puerto Rico, 1987. 410 pp.

1762. Rosa-Nieves, Cesáreo. *El romanticismo en la literatura puertorriqueña, 1843–1880*. San Juan: Instituto de Cultura Puertorriqueña, 1972. 30 pp. Reprint of the 1960 ed.

General: Twentieth Century

1763. Alegría, José S. *Cincuenta años de literatura puertorriqueña*. San Juan: Academia Puertorriqueña de la Lengua, 1955. 65 pp.

1764. Colberg, Juan Enrique. *Cuatro autores clásicos contemporáneos de Puerto Rico: Concha Meléndez, Miguel Meléndez Muñoz, José A. Balseiro, Cesáreo Rosa-Nieves*. San Juan: Editorial Cordillera, 1966. 261 pp.

1765. Díaz Quiñones, Arcadio. *El almuerzo en la hierba: Lloréns Torres, Palés Matos, René Marqués*. Río Piedras, P.R.: Ediciones Huracán, 1982. 168 pp.

1766. Fernández Olmos, Margarite. *Sobre la literatura puertorriqueña de aquí y de allá: aproximaciones feministas*. Santo Domingo: Editora Alfa y Omega, 1989. 136 pp.

1767. Gelpí, Juan G. *Literatura y paternalismo en Puerto Rico*. San Juan: Editorial de la Universidad de Puerto Rico, 1993. 201 pp.

1768. Martínez Masdeu, Edgar. *La crítica puertorriqueña y el modernismo en Puerto Rico*. San Juan: Instituto de Cultura Puertorriqueña, 1977. 302 pp.

1769. Ortega, Julio. *Reapropiaciones: cultura y nueva escritura en Puerto Rico*. Río Piedras, P.R.: Editorial de la Universidad de Puerto Rico, 1991. 252 pp.

1770. Rivera-Avilés, Sotero. *La generación del '60: aproximaciones a tres autores*. San Juan: Instituto de Cultura Puertorriqueña, 1976. 82 pp. Carmelo Rodríguez Torres, Jorge María Ruscalleda Barcedóniz, Salvador López González.

1771. Silén, Juan Angel. *La generación de escritores de 1970 en Puerto Rico, 1950–1976*. Río Piedras, P.R.: Editorial Cultural, 1977. 103 pp.

1772. Sociedad de Autores Puertorriqueños. *Escritores contemporáneos de Puerto Rico*. San Juan: La Sociedad, 1978. 224 pp.

1773. Sotomayor, Aurea María. *Hilo de Aracne: literatura puertorriqueña hoy*. San Juan: Editorial de la Universidad de Puerto Rico, 1995. 318 pp.

1774. Torre, José Ramón de la. *Cuatro puertas a una fábula y otros ensayos*. San Juan: Publicaciones Yuquiyú, 1991. 112 pp.

1775. Umpierre, Luz María. *Nuevas aproximaciones críticas a la literatura puertorriqueña contemporánea*. Río Piedras, P.R.: Editorial Cultural, 1983. 132 pp.

1776. Zayas Micheli, Luis O. *Mito y política en la literatura puertorriqueña*. Madrid: Partenón, 1981. 192 pp.

Poetry

Poetry: General

1777. Cadilla de Martínez, María. *La poesía popular en Puerto Rico*. Madrid: Universidad de Madrid, 1933. 367 pp.

1778. Corchado Juarbe, Carmen. *El indio: su presencia en la poesía puertorriqueña*. Río Piedras, P.R.: Editorial de la Universidad de Puerto Rico, 1985. 285 pp. Sequel *El indio en la poesía puertorriqueña* (#1672).

1779. Escabí, Pedro C. and Elsa M. Escabí. *La décima: vista parcial del folklore*. Río Piedras, P.R.: Editorial Universitaria, Universidad de Puerto Rico, 1976. 520 pp.

1780. Franco Oppenheimer, Félix. *Imagen de Puerto Rico en su poesía*. Nueva ed. San Juan: Editorial Universitaria, Universidad de Puerto Rico, 1972. 260 pp. First ed. (1964) has title *Imagen y visión edénica de Puerto Rico en su poesía*.

1781. Jiménez de Báez, Yvette. *La décima popular en Puerto Rico*. Mexico City: Universidad Veracruzana, 1964. 446 pp.

1782. Lluch Vélez, Amalia. *La décima culta en la literatura puertorriqueña*. Río Piedras, P.R.: Editorial de la Universidad de Puerto Rico, 1988. 209 pp.

1783. Malaret, Augusto. *Medallas de oro*. 5a ed. aum. Mexico City: Editorial Orión, 1966. 209 pp. Manuel Fernández Juncos, Salvador Brau, Román Baldorioty de Castro, José Gautier Benítez, Francisco Gonzalo Marín.

1784. Puebla, Manuel de la, ed. *Historia y significado del Atalayismo*. San Juan: Ediciones Mairena, 1994. 152 pp.

1785. Rosa-Nieves, Cesáreo. *La poesía en Puerto Rico: historia de los temas poéticos en la literatura puertorriqueña*. San Juan: Editorial Edil, 1969. 301 pp. Reprint of the 1958 ed.

Poetry: Sixteenth to Nineteenth Centuries

1786. Rivera Rivera, Eloísa. *La poesía en Puerto Rico antes de 1843*. 2a ed., rev. y aum. San Juan: Instituto de Cultura Puertorriqueña, 1981. 365 pp.

Poetry: Twentieth Century

1787. González, Josemilio. *La poesía contemporánea de Puerto Rico, 1930–1960*. San Juan: Instituto de Cultura Puertorriqueña, 1986. 531 pp. Reprint of the 1972 ed.

1788. ———. *Los poetas puertorriqueños de la década de 1930*. San Juan: Instituto de Cultura Puertorriqueña, 1972. 30 pp. Reprint of the 1960 ed.

1789. González, Rubén. *Crónica de tres décadas: poesía puertorriqueña actual—de los sesenta a los ochenta*. Río Piedras, P.R.: Editorial de la Universidad de Puerto Rico, 1989. 230 pp.

1790. González Torres, Rafael Antonio. *Puerto Rico: poesía e identidad espiritual*. San Juan: R. A. González Torres, 1994. 219 pp.

1791. Hernández Aquino, Luis. *Nuestra aventura literaria: los ismos en la poesía puertorriqueña, 1913–1948*. Río Piedras, P.R.: Editorial de la Universidad de Puerto Rico, 1980. 270 pp. Reprint of the 1966 (2d, rev.) ed.

1792. Laguerre, Enrique Arturo. *La poesía modernista en Puerto Rico*. San Juan: Editorial Coquí, 1969. 217 pp.

1793. Melendes, Joserramón. *Postemporáneos*. Río Piedras, P.R.: Qease, 1994. 134 pp.

1794. Puebla, Manuel de la, ed. *Poesía militante puertorriqueña*. San Juan: Instituto de Cultura Puertorriqueña, 1979. 2 vols.

1795. Rodríguez Pagán, Juan Antonio. *Lorca en la lírica puertorriqueña*. Río Piedras, P.R.: Editorial Universitaria, Universidad de Puerto Rico, 1981. 359 pp.

1796. Sarramía, Tomás. *Los juegos florales en Puerto Rico: crónica de un centenario*. Manati, P.R.: ARTCUMA, 1990. 111 pp.

Fiction

Fiction: General

1797. Beauchamp, José Juan. *Imagen del puertorriqueño en la novela: en Alejandro Tapia y Rivera, Manuel Zeno Gandía y Enrique A. Laguerre*. Río Piedras, P.R.: Editorial Universitaria, Universidad de Puerto Rico, 1976. 184 pp.

1798. Gómez Tejera, Carmen. *La novela en Puerto Rico: apuntes para su historia*. San Juan: Junta Editora, Universidad de Puerto Rico, 1947. 138 pp.

1799. Quiles de la Luz, Lillian. *El cuento en la literatura puertorriqueña.* San Juan: Editorial de la Universidad de Puerto Rico, 1968. 293 pp.

1800. Umpierre, Luz María. *Ideología y novela en Puerto Rico: un estudio de la narrativa de Zeno, Laguerre y Soto.* Madrid: Playor, 1983. 151 pp.

Fiction: Twentieth Century

1801. Alfonso, Vitalina. *Narrativa puertorriqueña actual: realidad y parodia.* Havana: Editorial Letras Cubanas, 1994. 49 pp.

1802. Arana de Love, Francisca. *La novela de Puerto Rico durante la primera década del Estado Libre Asociado, 1952–1962.* 2a ed. Barcelona: Vosgos, 1976. 93 pp. First ed. (1969) has title *Los temas fundamentales de la novela puertorriqueña durante la primera década de Puerto Rico como Estado Libre Asociado a los Estados Unidos.*

1803. Casanova Sánchez, Olga. *La novela puertorriqueña contemporánea: los albores de un decir—hasta 1975.* San Juan: Instituto de Cultura Puertorriqueña, 1986. 290 pp.

1804. Daroqui, María Julia. *Las pesadillas de la historia en la narrativa puertorriqueña.* Caracas: Monte Avila Editores, 1993. 131 pp.

1805. Falcón, Rafael. *Lo afronegroide en el cuento puertorriqueño.* Miami: Ediciones Universal, 1993. 82 pp.

1806. —————. *La emigración puertorriqueña a Nueva York en los cuentos de José Luis González, Pedro Juan Soto y José Luis Vivas Maldonado.* New York, NY: Senda Nueva de Ediciones, 1984. 175 pp.

Drama

Drama: General

1807. Pasarell, Emilio Julio. *Orígenes y desarrollo de la afición teatral en Puerto Rico.* 2a impresión, rev. Río Piedras, P.R.: Editorial Universitaria, Universidad de Puerto Rico, 1970. 2 vols.

Drama: Sixteenth to Nineteenth Centuries

1808. Girón, Socorro, ed. *Puerto Rico en su teatro popular, 1880–1899.* Ponce, P.R.: S. Girón, 1985. 543 pp.

Drama: Twentieth Century

1809. Arriví, Francisco. *Conciencia puertorriqueña del teatro contem-poráneo, 1937–1956.* San Juan: Instituto de Cultura Puertor-riqueña, 1967. 207 pp.

1810. ⸻. *Evolución del autor dramático puertorriqueño a partir de 1938.* San Juan: Instituto de Cultura Puertorriqueña, 1961. 42 pp.

1811. Collins, J. A. *Contemporary Theater in Puerto Rico: The Decade of the Seventies.* Río Piedras, P.R.: Editorial Universitaria, Uni-versidad de Puerto Rico, 1982. 261 pp.

1812. García del Toro, Antonio. *Mujer y patria en la dramaturgia puer-torriqueña: proyecciones del sentimiento patrio en la figura de la mujer como protagonista de la dramaturgia puertorriqueña.* Madrid: Playor, 1987. 267 pp.

1813. Montes Huidobro, Matías. *Persona, vida y máscara en el teatro puertorriqueño.* San Juan: Centro de Estudios Avanzados de Puerto Rico y el Caribe, 1986. 631 pp.

1814. Morfi, Angelina. *Historia crítica de un siglo de teatro puertor-riqueño.* San Juan: Instituto de Cultura Puertorriqueña, 1993. 569 pp. Reprint of the 1980 ed.

1815. Phillips, Jordan Blake. *Contemporary Puerto Rican Drama.* New York: Plaza Mayor Ediciones, 1972. 220 pp.

1816. Ramos-Perea, Roberto. *Perspectiva de la nueva dramaturgia puertorriqueña: ensayos sobre el nuevo teatro nacional.* San Juan: Ateneo Puertorriqueño, 1989. 93 pp.

1817. Vientós Gastón, Nilita. *Apuntes sobre teatro.* San Juan: Instituto de Cultura Puertorriqueña, 1989. 96 pp.

E. INDIVIDUAL AUTHORS

Sixteenth to Nineteenth Centuries

1818. *Abril y Ostaló, Mariano,* 1861–1935 (poet). Amorosas, 1900.

    1819. Silva, Ana Margarita. *Mariano Abril y Ostaló: su vida y su obra, 1861–1935.* San Juan: Editorial Club de la Prensa, 1966. 174 pp.

1820. *Alvarez Marrero, Francisco,* 1847–1881 (playwright, poet). Antología, 1966 (Cesário Rosa-Nieves, ed.); Obras literarias, 1882.

1821. *Amy, Francisco Javier,* 1837–1912 (poet, short story writer). Antología poética, 1968; Ecos y notas, 1884; Letras de molde, 1890; Predicar en desierto, 1907.

1822. *Benítez, María Bibiana,* 1783–1873 (playwright, poet). La cruz del Morro, 1862; Décima, 1863; Diálogo alegórico, 1858; La ninfa de Puerto Rico, 1833; Soneto, 1839.

   1823. Girón, Socorro. *Vida y obra de María Bibiana y Alejandrina Benítez.* 2a ed., rev. e aum. Ponce, P.R.: [s.n.], 1991. 305 pp.

   1824. Arrillaga, María. *Los silencios de María Bibiana Benítez.* San Juan: Instituto de Cultura Puertorriqueña, 1985. 70 pp.

1825. *Betances, Ramón Emeterio,* 1827–1898 (novelist, poet). Betances, poeta [selecciones], 1986 (Luis Hernández Aquino, ed.); Obras del doctor Ramón Emeterio Betances, 1978 (Epistolario, La virgen de Borinquen [1859], Epostolario íntimo; Ada Suárez Díaz, ed.).

   1826. Cabrera, Francisco Manrique et al. *Ramón Emeterio Betances.* San Juan: Instituto de Cultura Puertorriqueña, 1980. 99 pp.

1827. *Bonafoux y Quintero, Luis,* 1855–1918 (novelist, short story writer). El avispero, 1882–1989; Bilis, 1908–1990; Bombos y palos, 1907–1990; Casi críticas, 1914–1991; Clericanallas, 1909; Coba, 1889–1989; Esbozos novelescos, 1894–1990; La España de Bonafoux [selecciones], 1990 (José Luis Cano, ed.); Los españoles en París, 1913–1995; Gotas de sangre, 1910; Huellas literarias, 1894–1990; Literatura de Bonafoux, 1887–1989 (Various eds.); Melancolía, 1901; Mosquetazos de Aramis, 1885–1988; París al día, 1900–1994; Por el mundo arriba, 1909–1993; Príncipes y majestades, 1910; Risas y lágrimas, 1900; Ultramarinos, 1882–1988; Yo y el plagiario de Clarín/Tiquis-miquis, 1888–1989.

   1828. Cautiño Jordán, Eduardo. *La sátira en la obra de Luis Bonafoux Quintero.* San Juan: Instituto de Cultura Puertorriqueña, 1985. 218 pp.

   1829. Girón, Socorro. *Bonafoux y su época.* Ponce, P.R.: S. Girón, 1987. 243 pp.

1830. *Brau, Salvador,* 1842–1912 (novelist, playwright, poet). De la superficie al fondo, 1874; Héroe y mártir, 1871; Hojas caídas, 1909; Los horrores del triunfo, 1887; ¿Pecadora?, 1887–1975; La vuelta al hogar, 1877–1975.

>   1831. Córdova Landrón, Arturo. *Salvador Brau: su vida y su época.* San Juan: Editorial Coquí, 1968. 152 pp. Reprint of the 1949 ed.

>   1832. Cortón, Antonio. *Un poema de Brau (Mi campo Santo).* San Juan: Tip. Boletín Mercantil, 1905. 26 pp.

>   1833. Fernández Méndez, Eugenio. *Salvador Brau y su tiempo.* San Juan: Universidad de Puerto Rico, 1956. 120 pp.

>   See also #1737, #1783.

1834. *Corchado y Juarbe, Manuel,* 1840–1884 (playwright, poet, short story writer). Las barricadas, 1870–1882; Desde la comedia al drama, 1885; Dios, 1869; Historias de ultra-tumba, 1872; María Antonieta, 1880; Obras completas, 1985 (Vicente Geigel Polanco, ed.); Páginas sangrientas, 1875.

>   1835. Cadilla de Martínez, María. *Alturas paralelas: ensayos biográficos sobre d. Rafael del Valle Rodríguez y d. Manuel M. Corchado Juarbe.* San Juan: Impr. Venezuela, 1941. 162 pp.

>   1836. Enamorado-Cuesta, José. *Manuel María Corchado y Juarbe: auténtico liberal puertorriqueño.* San Juan: Editorial Puerto Rico Libre, 1955. 82 pp.

1837. *Daubón, José Antonio,* 1840–1922 (poet). Cosas de Puerto Rico, 1904; El negro José, 1886; Poesías, 1900.

1838. *Diego, José de,* 1866–1918 (poet). Antología poética, 1966–1977 (Juan Martínez Capó, Luis Ripoll, eds.); El caballero de la raza, 1966–1972; Cantos de pitirre, 1949–1975; Cantos de rebeldía, 1916–1975; José de Diego [poesías], 1975–1989; José de Diego [selecciones], 1959; José de Diego y su poesía, 1972; Jovillos, 1890–1971; Obras completas, 1966–1970 (Poesía: Jovillos [1890], Pomarrosas [1904], Cantos de rebeldía [1916], Cantos de pitirre [1949]. Prosa: Nuevas campañas, El plebiscito).

>   1839. Arce de Vázquez, Margot. *La obra literaria de José de Diego.* San Juan: Instituto de Cultura Puertorriqueña, 1967. 673 pp.

1840. Gotay, Modesto, ed. *José de Diego: caballero del idioma y de la raza,* 1867–1918 — *comentarios y biografía.* Barcelona: Rumbos, 1958. 124 pp.

1841. Meléndez, Concha. *José de Diego en mi memoria.* 2a ed., rev. San Juan: Editorial Cordillera, 1970. 153 pp.

1842. Rodríguez Escudero, Néstor A. *José de Diego: el caballero de la patria.* Aguadilla, P.R.: N. A. Rodríguez Escudero, 1992. 293 pp.

1843. Torres Delgado, René. *José de Diego.* Río Piedras, P.R.: Editorial Cultural, 1982. 102 pp.

1844. ———. *Voz de José de Diego.* Boston, MA: Florentia Publishers, 1977. 118 pp.

1845. *Domínguez, José de Jesús,* 1843–1898 (playwright, poet). Antología, 1963 (Ana María Losada, ed.); Las huríes blancas, 1886; Odas elegíacas, 1883.

1846. *Eulate Sanjurjo, Carmela,* 1871–1961 (novelist, poet). Marqués y marquesa, 1911; La muñeca, 1895–1987 (Angel M. Aguirre, ed.).

1847. Silva, Ana Margarita. *Carmela Eulate Sanjurjo: puertorriqueña ilustre.* San Juan: Biblioteca de Autores Puertorriqueños, 1966. 217 pp.

1848. *Ferrer Hernández, Gabriel,* 1847–1900 (playwright, poet). Anhelos y esperanzas, 1962; Consecuencias, 1892; Herir en el corazón, 1883.

1849. *Gautier Benítez, José,* 1848–1880 (poet). El Album de Cecilia, 1965 (Socorro Girón, ed.); Facsímiles de su obra, 1965 (Socorro Girón, ed.); Poesías, 1880–1967.

1850. Curet de De Anda, Miriam. *La poesía de José Gautier Benítez.* Río Piedras, P.R.: Editorial Universitaria, Universidad de Puerto Rico, 1980. 158 pp.

1851. Gautier Benítez, José, and Socorro Girón, ed. *Epístolas.* Madrid: Oficina Gráf. Madrileña, 1956. 101 pp.

1852. Girón, Socorro. *Vida y obra de José Gautier Benítez.* San Juan: Instituto de Cultura Puertorriqueña, 1980. 565 pp.

1853. Rosa-Nieves, Cesáreo. *Vida y obra poética de José Gautier Benítez*. Nueva ed. Río Piedras. P.R.: Editorial Edil, 1975. 228 pp.

See also #1783.

1854. *González García, Matías,* 1866–1938 (novelist, poet, short story writer). Carmela, 1903–1966; Cosas, 1898; Cosas de antaño, 1918–1953; Cosas de ogaño, 1922–1953; Cuentos, 1960–1992 (Juan Martínez Capó, ed.); El escándalo, 1894; Gestación, 1905–1938; La primera cría, 1892–1992.

1855. *Hostos, Eugenio María de,* 1839–1903 (novelist, poet). Antología, 1952 (Eugenio Carlos de Hostos, ed.); Cuento, teatro, poesía, ensayo, 1992 (Julio César López, ed.); Diario, 1990 (Julio César López et al, eds.); Hostos [selecciones], 1944 (Pedro de Alba, ed.); Ideario, 1966 (Carlos N. Carreras, ed.); Meditando, 1909; Obra literaria selecta, 1988 (Julio César López, ed.); Obras, 1976–1988 (Camila Henríquez Ureña, ed.); Obras completas, 1839–1969 (Vols. 1–2. Diario.—Vol. 3. Páginas íntimas.—Vol. 4. Cartas.—Vol. 5. Madre isla.—Vol. 6. Mi viaje al sur.—Vol. 7. Temas sudamericanos.—Vol. 8. La peregrinación de Bayoán [1863], Vol. 9. Temas cubanos.—Vol. 10. La cuna de América.—Vol. 11. Crítica.—Vol. 12–13. Forjando el porvenir americano.—Vol. 14. Hombres e ideas.—Vol. 15. Lecciones de derecho constitucional.—Vol. 16. Tratado de moral.—Vol. 17. Tratado de sociología.—Vol. 18–20. Ensayos didácticos); Obras completas, 1988 (Literatura—La peregrinación de Bayoán [1863]; Julio César López, Vivian Quiles Calderín, Pedro Alvarez Ramos, eds.—Crítica; Julio César López, Vivian Quiles Calderín, Marcos F. Reyes Dávila, eds.—Ensayos didácticos.—Hombre e ideas); Páginas escogidas, 1952 (José F. Forgione, ed.); La tela de araña, 1992 (Argimiro Ruano, ed.); Textos, 1982 (José Luis González, ed.).

1856. Blanco-Fombona, Rufino. *Hostos*. Montevideo: C. García, 1945. 129 pp.

1857. Bosch, Juan. *Mujeres en la vida de Hostos*. 3a ed. aum. San Juan: Editorial Marien, 1988. 72 pp.

1858. Carreras, Carlos Noriega. *Ideario de Hostos*. San Juan: Editorial Cordillera, 1966. 250 pp.

1859. Géigel Polanco, Vicente. *Ensayos hostosianos*. Boston, MA: Florentia Publishers, 1976. 89 pp.

1860. Lugo-Guernelli, Adelaida. *Eugenio María de Hostos: ensayista y crítico literario.* San Juan: Instituto de Cultura Puertorriqueña, 1970. 207 pp.

1861. Mora, Gabriela. *Hostos intimista: introducción a su "Diario."* San Juan: Instituto de Cultura Puertorriqueña, 1976. 58 pp.

1862. Roméu y Fernández, Raquel. *Eugenio Maria de Hostos: antillanista y ensayista.* Madrid: Facultad de Filosofía y Letras, Seminario de Estudios Americanistas, 1959. 170 pp.

1863. Sáinz, JoAnn Borda de. *Eugenio María de Hostos: Philosophical System and Methodology—Cultural Fusion.* New York: Senda Nueva de Ediciones, 1989. 240 pp.

1864. *Marín, Pachín,* 1863–1897 (poet, short story writer). Antología, 1958 (María Teresa Babín, ed.); Cinco narraciones, 1972 (Cesáreo Rosa-Nieves, Patria Figueroa de Cifedo, eds.); En la arena, 1898–1944; Pachín Marín, 1989; Romances, 1892.

1865. Figueroa de Cifredo, Patria. *Pachín Marín: héroe y poeta.* San Juan: Instituto de Cultura Puertorriqueña, 1967. 220 pp.

See also #1783.

1866. *Marín, Ramón,* 1832–1902 (playwright, poet). El hijo del amor, 1872; Obra completa, 1989 (Socorro Girón, ed.).

1867. *Matos Bernier, Félix,* 1869–1937 (poet). Cromos ponceños, 1896; Isla de arte, 1907; Páginas sueltas, 1897; Pedazos de roca, 1894; Puesta de sol, 1903; Recuerdos benditos, 1895.

1868. Díaz de Olano, Carmen R. *Félix Matos Bernier: su vida y su obra.* San Juan: Biblioteca de Autores Puertorriqueños, 1956. 196 pp.

1869. *Méndez Quiñones, Ramón Avelino,* 1847–1889 (playwright, poet). Una jíbara, 1881; Un jíbaro, 1878; Los jíbaros progesistas, 1882; La vuelta de la feria, 1882.

1870. Girón, Socorro. *Vida y obra de Ramón Méndez Quiñones.* San Juan: Instituto de Cultura Puertorriqueña, 1991. 540 pp. Reprint of the 1983 ed.

See also #1737.

1871. *Mercado, José Ramón,* 1863–1911 (poet). Mi equipaje, 1901; Virutas, 1900.

1872. *Monge, José María,* 1840–1891 (poet). Poesía y prosa, 1897.

1873. *Muñoz Rivera, Luis,* 1859–1916 (poet). Luis Muñoz Rivera (poesías), 1961; Obras completas, 1960–1968 (Eugenio Fernández Méndez, Lidio Cruz Monclova, eds.); Tropicales, 1902.

1874. *Padilla, José Gualberto,* 1829–1896 (poet). Antología, 1961 (Miriam Curet de Anda, ed.); En el combate, 1913–1969; En la muerte de Corchado, 1885; Para un palacio un caribe/Desengaños de la vida, 1874–1956; Rosas de pasión, 1912; Zoopoligrafía, 1855.

1875. *Rodríguez de Tío, Lola,* 1843–1924 (poet). Cantares, nieblas y congojas, 1968; Claros de sol, 1968; Obras completas, 1968 (Mis cantares [1876], Claros y nieblas [1885], Mi libro de Cuba [1893], Trabajos inéditos en prosa); Ofrendas, 1968; Poesías, 1960; Poesías patrióticas, poesías religiosas, 1968.

    1876. Mendoza Tío, Carlos F. *Contribución al estudio de la obra poética de Lola Rodríguez de Tío,* 1843–1924. San Juan: [s.n.], 1974. 262 pp.

    1877. ———, ed. *Lola Rodríguez de Tío.* San Juan: Mendoza Tío, 1978. 387 pp.

    1878. Rodríguez de Tío, Lola, and Ricardo Palma. *Diecisiete cartas inéditas con otras éditas, 1894–1907.* Lima: [s.n.], 1968. 92 pp.

1879. *Soler y Martorell, Manuel,* 1863–1897 (poet). Nuevo cancionero de Borinquen, 1872.

1880. *Tapia y Rivera, Alejandro,* 1826–1882 (novelist, playwright, poet). A orillas del Rhin, 1880–1962; El bardo de Guamaní, 1862; La cuarterona, 1867–1993; Cuentos y artículos varios, 1938; Enardo and Rosael, 1952 (Translation of Enardo y Rosael [1880]; El heliotropo, 1860; Historia de un hombre que resucitó en el cuerpo de su enemigo, 1872–1945; La leyenda de los veinte años, 1874–1975; Mis memorias/Puerto Rico, como lo encontré y como lo dejo, 1928–1986 (Alejandro Tapia y Díaz, ed.); Obras completas, 1968 (Vol. 1. Novela. Cofresí [1876], La antigua sirena [1862], Póstumo II el transmigrado.—Vol. 2. Teatro. Vasco Nuñez de Balboa [1872], La parte del león [1878], Roberto d'Evreux [1857], Bernardo de Palissy [1862], Camoes [1868], Hero y Leandro [1878], La cuarterona [1867]. Vol. 3. Biblioteca histórica de Puerto Rico); La palma del cacique, 1852–1986; Póstumo (I–II), 1872–1975; La sataniada, 1878–1975.

1881. Martín, José Luis. *Análisis estilístico de "La sataniada" de Tapia*. San Juan: Instituto de Cultura Puertorriqueña, 1958. 198 pp.

See also #1737, #1797.

1882. *Tío Segarra, Bonocio,* 1839–1905 (poet). Poesía, 1983 (Carlos F. Mendoza Tío, ed.).

1883. *Valle Atiles, Francisco del,* 1852–1928 (novelist). Inocencia, 1884.

1884. *Vidarte, Santiago,* 1828–1848 (poet). Poesías, 1965.

Twentieth Century

1885. *Abréu Adorno, Manuel,* 1955–1984 (poet, short story writer). Llegaron los hippies y otros cuentos, 1978; No todas las suecas son rubias, 1991.

1886. *Agostini de del Río, Amelia,* 1886– (playwright, poet, short story writer). A la sombra del arce, 1965; Canto a San Juan de Puerto Rico y otros poemas, 1974; Duerme hijo, 1978; Hasta que el sol se muera, 1969; Más acá de la muerte, 1980; Nuestras vidas son los ríos, 1974; Puertorriqueños en Nueva York, 1970; Quiero irme gozosa, 1981; Rosa de los vientos, 1980; Seis voces y dos sainetes más, 1978; Viñetas de Puerto Rico, 1965.

1887. *Agrait, Gustavo,* 1909– (poet, short story writer). El extraño caso de—¿quién?, 1991; Ocho casos extraños y dos cosas más, 1972; Variaciones sobre temas obsesivos, 1969.

1888. *Ajón León, Alberto* (short story writer). Pesquisas en Castalia, 1996.

1889. *Alegría, José S.,* 1887–1965 (poet, short story writer). El alma de la aldea, 1956–1972; Cartas a Florinda, 1958; Crónicas frívolas, 1938; Retablos de la aldea, 1949–1991; Rosas y flechas, 1958.

1890. *Arana, Felipe N.,* 1902–1962 (poet, short story writer). Florecillas silvestres, 1927; Grito de la tierra honda, 1960; Música aldeana, 1934; El plato del día, 1955; Sementera, 1945.

1891. *Arana Soto, Salvador,* 1908– (poet, short story writer). Aguas desnudas y otras intemperies, 1976; Aguas turbias y otras sinra-

zones, 1988; Entelequias enlatadas, 1977; Estampas puertorriqueñas, 1979 (Don Quijote en Santurce [1977], La camisa volan-
tona [1965], Negro y amargo [1969]); Exactamente nada y otros
disparates, 1984–1986; Historia de mis libros, 1984; Indes-
cifrando, 1982; Maldita luz (y otras divagaciones), 1971; Papá
Buyuyo, 1967; Primeros versos, 1981; El signo, el ademán, el
gesto (antología poética), 1986 (Reynaldo Marcos Padua, ed.); Ultimas prosas y demás desatinos, 1983.

1892. *Arrillaga, María,* 1940– (novelist, poet). Cascada de sol, 1977;
Frescura, 1981; Vida en el tiempo, 1974.

1893. *Arriví, Francisco,* 1915– (playwright, poet). Canticle for a Memory, 1993 (Clementine Rabassa, tr.); Ceiba (Areyto, Cemí, Coquí),
1980; Entrada por las raíces, 1964; Máscara puertorriqueña, 1971
(Bolero y plena [1960], Sirena [1960], Vejigantes [1958]); Teatro,
1953 (Una sombra menos [1940], Club de solteros [1940]); Teatro
mental, 1990 (Sirena [1960], Escultor de la sombra [1965], Poema
al infinito); Tres piezas de teatro puertorriqueño, 1968 (Club de
solteros [1940], María Soledad [1947], Vejigantes [1958]); Vía
poética, 1978 (Isla y nada [1958], Fronteras [1960], Ciclo de lo
ausente [1962], Escultor de la sombra [1965], En la tenue geografía [1971]).

1894. *Arroyo Vicente, Arminda* (poet). Cuando la noche va cayendo,
1994; Mar del Sur, 1984; Palomas del tiempo, 1988; La rosa in-
mersa en la sombra, 1988.

1895. *Babín, María Teresa,* 1910– (playwright, poet, short story writer).
La barca varada, 1982; Fantasía boricua, 1957–1982; La hora col-
mada, 1960; Las voces de tu voz, 1962.

1896. *Balseiro, José Agustín,* 1900– (novelist, playwright, poet, short
story writer). Al rumor de la fuente, 1922; El ala y el beso, 1983;
La copa de Anacreonte, 1924; En vela mientras el mundo duerme,
1953; Flores de primavera, 1919; La gratitud humana, 1969;
Música cordial, 1926; Obra selecta de José Agustín Balseiro, 1990
(María Teresa Babín, ed.); Las palomas de Eros, 1924; La pureza
cautiva, 1946; La ruta eterna, 1926; El sueño de Manón, 1922;
Vísperas de sombra y otros poemas, 1959. See also #1764.

1897. *Bauzá, Guillermo,* 1916– (novelist, playwright, poet, short story
writer). La canción de los cincuenta, 1974; Canción de pesadum-
bre, 1965; Con los brazos abiertos, 1963; Los cuatro ejes, 1964;

Cuentos de misterio y fantasía, 1967 (El tribunal de la conciencia, El alma no muere, El complejo de Edipo, Nuevo encuentro, Palingenisia, La voz, La mujer del otro, Murió el presidente, Murió en la cruz); Diario en verso, 1984; Don Cristóbal, 1963; Don Juan, 1973; El filo del ensueño, 1962; La guerra, 1969; La loba, 1964; El periodista inmortal, 1989; Racismo, 1964; El triángulo, 1964; Vidas inconclusas, 1963.

1898. *Bauzá, Obdulio,* 1907– (poet). La canción de los olivos, 1958; La casa solariega, 1954; Las hogueras de cal, 1947; Selected Poems, 1961 (Helen Wohl Patterson, tr.); Las voces esperadas, 1956–1960.

1899. *Belaval, Emilio S.,* 1903– (playwright, short story writer). Areyto, 1948; Circe o el amor, 1963; Cuentos de la Plaza Fuerte, 1963–1977; Los cuentos de la universidad, 1935–1977; Cuentos para colegiales, 1918–1923; Cuentos para fomentar el turismo, 1946–1985; La muerte, 1953; La vida, 1959.

> 1900. Sánchez, Luis Rafael. *Fabulación e ideología en la cuentística de Emilio S. Belaval.* San Juan: Instituto de Cultura Puertorriqueña, 1979. 268 pp.

1901. *Blanco, Antonio Nicolás,* 1887–1945 (poet). Alas perdidas, 1921–1928; Antología, 1959 (Luis Hernández Aquino, ed.); El jardín de Pierrot, 1914; Muy sencillo, 1919.

1902. *Blanco, Tomás,* 1900– (novelist, poet, short story writer). The Child's Gifts: A Twelfth Night Tale/Los aguinaldos del Infante: glosa de epifanía, 1954–1994 (Harriet de Onís, tr.); Los cinco sentidos, 1955–1968; Cuentos sin ton ni son, 1970; La dragontea, 1956; Letras para música, 1964; Los vates, 1949–1981.

1903. *Bobadilla, José,* 1955– (poet). Abalorios, 1982; Salmos, 1994.

1904. *Braschi, Wilfredo,* 1918– (short story writer). Metrópoli, 1968; La primera piedra, 1977 (La primera piedra, Un zurcido en la sotana, El hombre que hacía bailar los peces, El vino verde, Cuando llegan las tinieblas, Marinero en tierra, Moisés Turcio, alcalde vitalicio, Dos centavos, Tulia Tula Tell y unos ojos color de miel, El milagro del padre Marcelo).

1905. *Burgos, Julia de,* 1914–1953 (poet). Antología poética, 1967–1987; Canción de la verdad sencilla, 1939–1982; Julia de Burgos: amor y soledad, 1994 (Manuel de la Puebla, ed.); Julia de Burgos: periodista en Nueva York, 1992 (Juan Antonio Rodríguez Pagán, ed.); Julia de Burgos: poesías, 1990–1995; El mar y tú, 1954–1986; Obra poética, 1961 (Consuelo Burgos, Juan Bautista Pagán, eds.); Poema en veinte surcos, 1938–1982; Roses in the Mirror/Rosas en el espejo, 1992 (Carmen D. Lucca, tr.); Song of the Simple Truth: The Complete Poems of Julia de Burgos, 1995 (Jack Agüeros, tr.); Yo misma fuí mi ruta, 1986 (María Magdalena Solá, ed.).

1906. Congreso Internacional Julia de Burgos (1993, San Juan); Edgar Martínez Masdeu, ed. *Actas*. San Juan: Ateneo Puertorriqueño, 1993. 440 pp.

1907. González, Josemilio. *Julia; o, La intimidad de los instantes*. San Juan: Ateneo Puertorriqueño, 1992. 66 pp.

1908. Jiménez de Báez, Yvette. *Julia de Burgos: vida y poesía*. San Juan: Editorial Coquí, 1966. 210 pp.

1909. Martínez Masdeu, Edgar. *Cronología de Julia de Burgos*. San Juan: Ateneo Puertorriqueño, 1992. 54 pp.

1910. Puebla, Manuel de la, ed. *Julia de Burgos*. Río Piedras, P.R.: Ediciones Mairena, 1986. 175 pp. Reprint of the 1985 ed. which had title *Homenaje a Julia de Burgos*.

1911. Rodríguez Pagán, Juan Antonio. *Julia de Burgos: tres rostros de Nueva York—y un largo silencio de piedra*. Humacao, P.R.: Oriente, 1987. 247 pp.

1912. Vicioso, Sherezada. *Julia de Burgos: la nuestra*. Santo Domingo: Editora Alfa y Omega, 1987. 37 pp.

See also #2000.

1913. *Cabrera, Francisco Manrique,* 1908–1974 (poet). Francisco Manrique Cabrera: [selecciones], 1984; Huella-sombra y cantar, 1943; Poemas de mi tierra tierra, 1936–1983.

1914. González, Josemilio. *Poesía y lengua en la obra de Francisco Manrique Cabrera*. Río Piedras, P.R.: Editorial Cultural, 1976. 155 pp.

1915. *Cabrera, José Antonio* (poet). Aura en las cumbres, 1972; Cantos de mi azul, 1981; Enséñame a volar, 1982; La flor del Génesis,

1971; Ilán y Guaniquina, 1978; El instante, 1980; Mitacha, 1975; Los muñecos de cera, 1973; On the Visions of the Master's Hair/La caballera del maestro, 1987 (José Abad Ramos, tr.).

1916. *Cadilla Ruibal, Carmen,* 1908– (poet, short story writer). Ala y ancla, 1940; Alfabeto del sueño, 1970; Antología poética, 1941; Canciones en flauta blanca, 1934; Cien sinrazones, 1962; Entre el silencio y Dios, 1966; Litoral del sueño, 1937; Lo que tú y yo sentimos, 1933; Monólogos de un muchacho campesino, 1948–1963; Litoral del sueño, 1937; Mundo sin geografía, 1948–1963; Raíces azules, 1936; Los silencios diáfanos, 1931; Tierras del alma, 1969; Voz de las islas íntimas, 1939.

1917. *Cajigas, Billy,* 1944– (poet). Mi corazón para cuatro mujeres, 1992; El rebaño, 1990.

1918. *Canales, Nemesio R.,* 1878–1923 (novelist, playwright, poet, short story writer). Antología nueva de Canales, 1974 (Servando Montaña Peláez, ed.); El héroe galopante, 1935–1981; Meditaciones acres, 1974 (Servando Montaña Peláez, ed.); Nuevos paliques y otras páginas, 1965; Obras completas, 1992 (Servando Montaña Peláez, ed.); Paliques, 1913–1974.

> 1919. Babín, María Teresa. *Genio y figura de Nemesio R. Canales.* San Juan: Biblioteca de Autores Puertorriqueños, 1978. 78 pp.

> 1920. Montaña Peláez, Servando. *Nemesio Canales: lenguaje y situación.* San Juan: Universidad de Puerto Rico, 1973. 254 pp.

> 1921. Quiñones, Samuel R. *Nemesio R. Canales: el humorista de Puerto Rico.* San Juan: Senado de Puerto Rico, 1961. 129 pp.

1922. *Cancel Negrón, Ramón* (poet, short story writer). Intracendencias, 1989; Socialidades y politicadas, 1992.

1923. *Carreras, Carlos Noriega,* 1890–1959 (playwright, poet, short story writer). El caballero del silencio, 1940; Juan Ponce de León, 1934 (with José Ramírez Santibáñez); Luna verde, y otros cuentos, 1958; El ruiseñor extraviado, 1959; La sortija de agua, 1957.

1924. *Carrero, Jaime,* 1931– (novelist, playwright, poet, short story writer). A cuchillo de palo, 1992; Here the Angels/Aquí los ángeles, 1960 (Gilbert Neiman, ed. and tr.); El hombre que no sudaba, 1982; Los nombres, 1972; Raquelo tiene un mensaje, 1970;

Teatro, 1973 (Flag Inside, Capitán F4C, Pipo Subway no sabe reír, El caballo de Ward); Tyrannosaurus Rex, Amen Amen/ Tiranosauro rey, amén amén, 1963.

1925. *Cartaña, Luis,* 1942– (poet). Canciones olvidadas, 1977–1988; Estos humanos dioses, 1967; La joven resina, 1971; Límites al mar, 1978; La mandarina y el fuego, 1983; Permanencia del fuego, 1989; Poesías completas, 1993; Sobre la música, 1982.

1926. *Casas, Myrna,* 1934– (playwright). Absurdos en soledad, 1964–1987; Cristal roto en el tiempo, 1961–1987; Eugenia Victoria Herrera, 1964; El impromptu de San Juan, 1974; La trampa, 1974–1987; Tres, 1987.

1927. *Castro Ríos, Andrés,* 1942– (poet). Estos poemas, 1967 (with Vicente Rodríguez Nietzsche); Libro de glosas, 1980; Lírica colérica, 1977 (with Etnairis Rivera, Vicente Rodríguez Nietzsche, and Angelamaría Dávila Malavé); Muerte fundada, 1967; Receta de mujer, 1994; Transeúnte de niebla, 1991.

1928. *Chiesa de Pérez, Carmen,* 1914– (novelist, poet). El aborto, 1991; Alma brava, 1992; Diálogos, 1983; Príncipe, autobiografía de un perro, 1963–1980; Septiembre, en floración de luna, 1984; Una sonrisa y varios destellos, 1993; La telaraña, 1969.

1929. *Coll Vidal, Antonio,* 1898– (playwright, poet). Un hombre de cuarenta años, 1928; Mediodía, 1919; Trovas de amor, 1916.

1930. *Córdova Iturregui, Félix,* 1944– (novelist, poet, short story writer). Militancia contra la soledad, 1987; Para llenar de días el día, 1985; El rabo de lagartija de aquel famoso señor rector y otros cuentos de orilla, 1986–1988; Sobre esta difícil tierra, 1993.

1931. *Corretjer, Juan Antonio,* 1908– (poet). Aguinaldo escarlata, 1974–1984; Alabanza en la torre de Ciales, 1953–1980; Amor de Puerto Rico, 1937; El buen borincano, 1945 (Lamento borincano, El buen borincano, La tierra de Borinquen, Los hijos de Borinquen); El cumplido, 1979; Día antes, 1973; Los días contados, 1984; Don Diego en el cariño, 1956; El estado del tiempo, 1983; Genio y figura, 1961; Juan Antonio Corretjer [poesías], 1976; El leñero, 1944–1972; Obras completas, 1977; Para que los pueblos canten, 1976; Paso a Venezuela, 1976; Pausa para el amor, 1967–1976; Poesía y revolución, 1981; Los primeros años, 1950; Primeros libros poéticos, 1990; La sangre en huelga, 1966; Yerba bruja, 1957–1992.

1932. Delgado, Juan Manuel. *Juan Antonio Corretjer*. [San Juan]: Editorial Guazabara, 1985. 64 pp.

1933. Medina López, Ramón Felipe. *Juan Antonio Corretjer: poeta nacional puertorriqueño—cuarenta años de poesía, 1927–1967*. San Juan: Instituto de Cultura Puertorriqueña, 1984. 207 pp.

1934. Melendes, Joserramón. *La poesía inebitable [sic]: ensayo de interpretación de los primeros libros poéticos de Juan Antonio Corretjer*. Río Piedras, P.R.: Qease, 1989. 70 pp.

1935. Puebla, Manuel de la, ed. *Homenaje a Juan Antonio Corretjer*. Río Piedras, P.R.: Ediciones Mairena, 1983. 172 pp.

1936. *Cortés Cabán, David,* 1952– (poet). Al final de las palabras, 1985; Poemas y otros silencios, 1981; Una hora antes, 1990.

1937. *Cox, Mario* (novelist). Amor libre sin libertinaje, 1989; La prostituta inmaculada, 1995.

1938. *Cruz-Bernal, Mairym* (poet). Poemas para no morir, 1995.

1939. *Cuchí Coll, Isabel,* 1904– (novelist, playwright, poet, short story writer). La espera, 1984; Frutos de mi pensamiento, 1971; Mi periodismo, 1973; Mujer, 1945–1972; My Puertorrican Poppa, 1974 (Translation of La familia de Justo Malgenio [1963–1974]; Jean H. de Porrata-Doria, tr.); Oro nativo, 1936; Un patriota y un pirata, 1973; Teatro escolar, 1990 (La muñeca, Sueño de Navidad, Cofresí [1976], El patriota, El seminarista [1971], La novia del estudiante [1948], La familia de Justo Malgenio [1963]); Trece novelas cortas, 1965–1974; El sexto sentido, 1986; The Student's Sweetheart, 1973 (Translation of La novia del estudiante [1948]).

1940. *Cuevas, Clara* (novelist, playwright, poet, short story writer). Amor ultraterrestre, 1976; La cárcel del tiempo, 1970; La extraña paradoja de mi vida, 1978; Kaleidoscopio del amor, 1970; Magia de amor, 1970; Mare magnum, 1976; Puente entre dos mundos, 1976; The Vultures of the Soul/Los buitres del alma, 1976.

1941. *Dávila, José Antonio,* 1898–1941 (poet). Almacén de baratijas, 1941; Motivos de Tristán, 1957–1972; Poemas, 1964; Prosa, 1971 (Vicente Geigel Polanco, ed.); Pueblito de antes, 1941; Vendimia, 1940–1975.

1942. Ramos Mimoso, Adriana. *Vida y poesía en José Antonio Dávila*. 2a ed. rev. Río Piedras, P.R.: Editorial de la Universidad de Puerto Rico, 1986. 418 pp.

1943. *Dávila Malavé, Angelamaría,* 1944– (poet). Animal fiero y tierno, 1977–1981; Lírica colérica, 1977 (with Etnairis Rivera, Vicente Rodríguez Nietzsche, and Angel Castro Ríos).

1944. *Dávila, Virgilio,* 1869–1943 (poet). Aromas del terruño, 1916–1991 (Cesáreo Rosa-Nieves, ed.); Autobiografía, 1989; Obras completas, 1964–1970; Tipos de ahora, 1989; Un libro para mis nietos, 1928–1971 (Cesáreo Rosa-Nieves, ed.); Patria, 1903–1971 (Cesáreo Rosa-Nieves, ed.); Pueblito de antes, 1917–1974 (Cesáreo Rosa-Nieves, ed.); Tipos de ahora, 1989; Viviendo y amando, 1912–1975 (Cesáreo Rosa-Nieves, ed.).

1945. Orama Padilla, Carlos. *Virgilio Dávila: su vida y su obra.* 2a ed. San Juan: Editorial Cordillera, 1964. 179 pp.

1946. *Delgado, Ana María,* 1925– (novelist). La mitad de un día, 1989; The Room In-Between, 1995 (Translation of Habitación de por medio [1987]; Sylvia Ehrlich Lipp, tr.).

1947. *Delgado, Juan Manuel* (poet). Grito al yanqui y otros gritos, 1986; Trova borincana para el quinto centenario, 1993.

1948. *Díaz Alfaro, Abelardo Milton,* 1919– (poet, short story writer). Mi isla soñada, 1967–1986; Terrazo, 1947–1990.

1949. *Díaz Montero, Aníbal,* 1911– (novelist, short story writer). Andy's Bar, 1978 (El Andy's Bar, La inyección, El profesor, El toro Lucero, El gran campeón, En estreno, Estreno en el Tapia, La canción, El jugador, La piedra de Angelina, El informante, Martín, el soldado, La deuda); La biblioteca encantada, 1957–1974; La brisa mueve las guajanas, 1953–1979; Cerro y llanura, 1964–1991; Mocho y azada, 1979 (Piedras blancas, La venganza, El papujo, El berrendo, Carbón y poesía, El macho completo, Capitán, El alambiquero, El platanar, La parcela, Las recetas, El macanmero, Mis recuerdos); Una mujer y una sota, 1955–1970; Nico el Pinche, 1975–1986; Recordando, 1982; Veredas de la finca, 1968; Young Peter and His Friends, 1969–1980 (Translation of Pedruquito y sus amigos [1950–1983]).

1950. *Díaz Válcarcel, Emilio,* 1929– (novelist, short story writer). El asedio y otros cuentos, 1958; Cuentos, 1983; Dicen que de noche tú no duermes, 1985–1987; El hombre que trabajó el lunes, 1966–1987 (El hombre que trabajó el lunes, La culpa, María, El alcalde, Sol negro); En el mejor de los mundos (Autobiographical), 1991; Hot Soles in Harlem, 1993 (Translation of Harlem todos los días [1978–1987]; Tanya F. Fayen, tr.); Inventario, 1975; Mi mamá me ama, 1981–1988; Napalm, 1971; Panorama, 1971; Proceso en diciembre, 1963; Schemes in the Month of March, 1979 (Translation of Figuraciones en el mes de marzo [1972–1988]; Nancy A. Sebastiani tr.); Taller de invenciones, 1993.

1951. *Diego Padró, José Isaac de,* 1899–1973 (novelist, poet, short story writer). Un cencerro de dos badajos, 1969; En babia, 1940–1961; Escaparate iluminado, 1959; El hombrecito que veía en grande, 1973; El minotauro se devora a sí mismo, 1965; Ocho epístolas mostrencas, 1952; El tiempo jugó conmigo, 1960; La última lámpara de los dioses, 1921–1950.

    1952. Soto, Pedro Juan et al, eds. *En busca de J. I. de Diego Padró.* Río Piedras, P.R.: Editorial de la Universidad de Puerto Rico, 1990. 392 pp.

1953. *Espada Rodríguez, José,* 1892– (poet). Campanadas, 1932 (with Tulio A. Cestero Burgos and Francisco Muñíz Bou); Canto a los argonautas y otros poemas, 1958; Ella y la montaña, 1960; Verso y prosa (antología), 1990.

1954. *Esteves, José de Jesús,* 1882–1918 (poet). Poemas selectos, 1954 (Luis A. Duprey, ed.); Rosal de amor, 1917–1980.

1955. *Esteves, Sandra María,* 1948– (poet). Bluestown Mockingbird Mambo, 1990; Tropical Rains, 1984; Yerba buena, 1980.

1956. *Feliciano Mendoza, Ester,* 1918– (poet, short story writer). Arco Iris, 1951; Cajita de música, 1968–1983; Coqui, 1957–1982; Homenaje póstumo, 1988; Ilán-ilán, 1985; Islamar, 1988; Nanas, 1945–1980; Romancero de la Conquista, 1985; Ronda del mar, 1981; Sinfonía de Puerto Rico, 1968–1979; Voz de mi tierra/Voz de la tierra mía, 1956.

1957. *Fernández Gill, Alicia* (poet). Cantaré la rosa, 1980; Ese perfil que avanza, 1989; Espejitos de luna, 1988 (with Manuel de la Puebla).

1958. *Fernández Juncos, Manuel,* 1846–1928 (novelist, poet, short story writer). Antología de sus obras, 1965 (José Antonio Torres Morales, ed.); Cuentos y narraciones, 1907–1926. See also #1783.

1959. *Fernández Méndez, Eugenio,* 1924– (poet). Poesía viva, 1992; Tras siglos, 1958.

1960. *Ferré, Rosario,* 1940– (novelist, poet, short story writer). Antología personal, 1994; La batalla de las vírgenes, 1993; La caja de cristal, 1978; La cucarachita Martina, 1990; Los cuentos de Juan Bobo, 1981; Las dos Venecias, 1992; Fábulas de la garza desangrada, 1982; The House on the Lagoon, 1995; La mona que le pisaron la cola, 1981; Sitio a Eros, 1980–1986; Sonatinas, 1989; Sweet Diamond Dust, 1989 (Translation of Maldito amor [1986–1994]); The Youngest Doll, 1991 (Translation of Papeles de Pandora [1976–1992]). See also #1733.

1961. *Figueroa Laureano, Roberto* (poet). Efluvios de mi lira, 1971; Entre lo serio y la broma—el amor, 1994.

1962. *Flax, Hjalmar,* 1942–(poet). Ciento cuarenta y cuatro poemas en dos libros, 1969 (with Arturo Trías); Confines peligrosos, 1985; Los pequeños laberintos, 1978; Razones de envergadura, 1995; Tiempo adverso, 1982.

1963. *Fonfrías, Ernesto Juan,* 1909– (novelist, poet, short story writer). Al calor de la lumbre, 1936; Conversao en el batey, 1956–1958; Cosecha, 1956; Espigas de oro, 1962; Guasima, 1957–1963; Juan es su nombre, 1969; El martirio de una familia humilde, 1986; Presencia de la verdad, 1976; Raíz y espiga, 1963–1970; Sementera, 1962; Una voz en la montaña, 1958.

    1964. Lloréns, Washington. *Comentarios a refranes, modismos, locuciones de "Conversao en el batey" de Ernesto Juan Fonfrías.* San Juan: Club de la Prensa, 1962. 36 pp.

1965. *Franco Oppenheimer, Félix,* 1912– (poet). Antología poética (1950–1972), 1976; Aquí, presente, 1976; Contornos, 1960–1978; La curva de las tardes, 1990; Del tiempo y su figura, 1956–1970; Estas cosas así fueron, 1966–1970; El hombre y su angustia, 1950–1973; Horas del tiempo, 1993; Imágenes, 1957–1985; Los lirios del testimonio, 1964–1971; La presencia ignorada, 1978–1980; Prosas sin clave, 1971; Ser, 1992.

    1966. González Torres, Rafael Antonio. *La obra poética de Félix Franco Oppenheimer: estudio temático-analítico-estilístico.* Río Piedras, P.R.: Editorial Universitaria, Universidad de Puerto Rico, 1981. 246 pp.

1967. Hernández Sánchez, Jesús. *Félix Franco Oppenheimer: poeta del dolor—vida y obra, bibliografía, antología.* San Juan: Editorial Yaurel, 1964. 107 pp.

1968. *Freire de Matos, Isabel* (poet, short story writer). La brujita encantada y otros cuentos, 1979; La casita misteriosa y otros cuentos, 1978; Isla para los niños, 1981 (with Francisco Matos Paoli); Ritmos de tierra y mar, 1988–1992.

1969. *Galib, Hamid* (poet). Aleluya para un clavel, 1976; Contravida, 1992; Estrellanza, 1991; Los presagios, 1991; Revoque, 1990–1991; Solemnidades, 1985.

1970. *Gallego, Laura,* 1924– (poet). Obra poética, 1972; Presencia, 1952; Que voy de vuelo, 1979.

1971. *García Damiani, José Luis,* 1955– (poet, short story writer). Cuensias del reflejo, 1992; Voz en el verso, eco en el cuento, 1990.

1972. *García del Toro, Antonio* (playwright). Donde reinan las arpías, 1991 (Metamorfosis de una pena, Hotel melancolía [1989], Donde reinan las arpías, Un aniversario de larga duración/Long-Playing de nuestra historia, Los que se van se divierten con las flores del camino); La primera dama, 1992; Ventana al sueño, 1993.

1973. *García Ramis, Magali,* 1946– (novelist, short story writer). La familia de todos nosotros, 1976–1990; Felices días, tío Sergio, 1986–1992. See also #1733.

1974. *Géigel Polanco, Vicente,* 1904–1979 (poet). Bajo el signo de Géminis, 1963; Canto de tierra adentro, 1965; Canto del amor infinito, 1962; Palabras de nueva esperanza, 1969.

1975. *Gerena Brás, Gaspar,* 1909– (poet). Mientras muere la tarde, 1929; Trillogía lírica, 1969 (Aljibe [1959], Los sonetinos del mar [1963], Las cenizas tienen alas).

1976. *Gómez Costa, Arturo,* 1896– (poet). Cantos al viejo San Juan, 1981; Creadora voz, 1978; Las luces en extasis, 1970; Puerto Rico heroico, 1960; San Juan: ciudad fantástica de América, 1957.

1977. *González González, Samuel* (poet). Entre calles y amores, 1995; Paréntesis, 1990.

1978. *González, José Luis,* 1926– (novelist, short story writer). Antología personal, 1990; Ballad of Another Time, 1987 (Translation of Balada de otro tiempo [1978–1988]; Asa Zatz, tr.); Las caricias del tigre, 1984–1991; Chau Bogart, 1989; Cinco cuentos de sangre, 1945; Cuento de cuentos y once más, 1973; En este lado, 1954; En la sombra, 1943; En Nueva York y otras desgracias, 1973–1981; La galería y otros cuentos, 1972–1989; Historia de vecinos y otras historias, 1993; El hombre en la calle, 1948; La llegada, 1980; La luna no era de queso, 1988 (Autobiographical); Mambrú se fué a la guerra y otros relatos, 1972–1975; El oído de Dios, 1984–1986; La tercera llamada y otros relatos, 1983; Todos los cuentos, 1992; Todos los relatos, 1992; Veinte cuentos y Paisa [1950], 1973–1986.

> 1979. Díaz Quiñones, Arcadio. *Conversación con José Luis González.* Río Piedras, P.R.: Ediciones Huracán, 1977. 159 pp.

> 1980. Universidad Veracruzana, Centro de Investigaciones Lingüístico-Literarias. *Textos de/sobre José Luis González.* Xalapa, Mex.: El Centro, 1979. 47 pp.

> See also #85, #1806.

1981. *Grau Archilla, Raúl,* 1910– (poet). Arpa de luz, 1984; Caléndula y otras flores poéticas, 1981; Desde mi inmóvil soledad, 1990; Destierro de lo inútil, 1962; Golondrinas, 1956; Ipomea azul, 1983; Noche, tu poema, 1952; Normatides, 1962; Psalterio, 1962; Raíces, 1977; Regreso de la noche, 1964; Taj Majal a una sombra, 1974; Vértigo de la nube, 1954.

1982. *Hernández Aquino, Luis,* 1907– (novelist, poet). Agua de remanso, 1939; Antología poética, 1974 (José Emilio González, ed.); Del tiempo cotidiano, 1961; Entre la elegía y el réquiem, 1968; Isla para la angustia, 1943; Luis Hernández Aquino, 1988 (Luis Hernández Cruz, ed.); Memoria de Castilla, 1956; La muerte anduvo por el Guasio, 1959–1971; Poemas de la vida breve, 1940; Voz en el tiempo, 1952 (Margot Arce de Vázquez, ed.).

1983. *Hernández, José P. H.,* 1892–1922 (poet). Antología, 1956 (Manuel Siaca Rivera, ed.); Cantos de la sierra, 1925; José P.H. Hernández [selecciones], 1992; Obra poética, 1966 (Manuel Siaca Rivera, ed.); Poesías, 1965 (Emilio M. Colón, ed.); El último combate, 1921.

1984. Siaca Rivera, Manuel. *José P. H. Hernández: vida y obra.* San Juan: Editorial Coquí, 1965. 127 pp.

1985. *Hernández Sánchez, Jesús* (poet). Campus, 1958; Fidel Castro, 1959; The Gorgeous Caribbean/La magia del Caribe, 1992.

1986. *Hernández Sánchez, Roberto* (short story writer). Las aventuras de Juan Bobo, 1995; Aventuras en el closet mágico, 1986–1990; La cárcel de cristal, 1987; Nuevos cuentos de Juan Bobo, 1987; El sembrador de números y otros cuentos, 1985; Yo soy el otro, 1979–1990.

1987. *Jesús, Aida María de,* 1945– (poet). A veinticinco años después de la marea, 1988; Diario para los tiempos y las cosas, 1987; Poemas para tí, 1965; Transeúnte, 1990.

1988. *Joglar Cacho, Manuel,* 1898– (poet). Antología selecta de la poesía de Manuel Joglar Cacho, 1987 (Josemilio González, ed.); La canción que va contigo, 1967–1974; Canto a los ángeles, 1958; Cien campanas en una sola torre, 1986; Creación última, 1988; Donde cae y no cae la noche, 1978; En el carro de los muertos, 1979; En una sola torre, 1987; En voz baja, 1944; Espejo del agua fugitivo, 1982; Faena íntima, 1955–1970; Manuel Joglar Cacho: [selecciones], 1976; La morada del hombre, 1984; Poema inconcluso, 1988; Poema para que no se duerma el niño, 1971–1978; La sed del agua, 1965; Soliloquies of Lazarus/ Soliloquios de Lázaro, 1956–1963 (Helen Wohl Patterson, tr.); Vuela un pájaro, 1975.

1989. *Juliá Marín, Ramón,* 1878–1917 (novelist, poet). La gleba, 1912–1962; Tierra adentro, 1911–1962.

1990. *Labarthe, Pedro Juan,* 1906–1966 (novelist, playwright, poet). Atalaya, 1932; Cirios, 1945; Claustro verde, 1937; De mi yo, 1956; Estrías de sueños, 1936; Interrogatorio a la muerte, 1961; Mary Smith, 1958; Pueblo, gólgota del espíritu, 1938; Reclinatorio, 1944; Y me voy preguntando, 1959.

1991. *Laguerre, Enrique Arturo,* 1906– (novelist, playwright, poet, short story writer). Benevolent Masters, 1986 (Translation of Los amos benévolos [1976–1990]; Gino Parisi, tr.); Cauce sin río, 1962–1991; El fuego y su aire, 1970; Los gemelos, 1992; Infiernos privados, 1986; The Labyrinth, 1960–1984 (Translation of El laberinto [1959–1974]; William Rose, tr.); La llamarada, 1935–1990; Obras completas, 1962–1974 (La llamarada [1935], Solar Montoya [1941],

El treinta de febrero [1943], La resaca [1949], Los dedos de la mano [1951], La ceiba en el tiesto [1956], El laberinto [1959], La resentida [1944]); Por boca de caracoles, 1990; Solar Montoya, 1941–1983; El treinta de febrero, 1943–1978.

1992. Casanova Sánchez, Olga. *La crítica social en la obra novelística de Enrique A. Laguerre*. Río Piedras, P.R.: Editorial Cultural, 1975. 190 pp.

1993. García Cabrera, Manuel. *Laguerre y sus polos de la cultura iberoamericana*. San Juan: Biblioteca de Autores Puertorriqueños, 1978. 75 pp.

1994. Irizarry, Estelle. *Enrique A. Laguerre*. Boston, MA: Twayne, 1982. 165 pp.

1995. Montserrat Gámiz, María del Carmen. *Enrique A. Laguerre y "Los amos benévolos."* San Juan: Instituto de Cultura Puertorriqueña, 1987. 582 pp.

1996. Morfi, Angelina. *Enrique A. Laguerre y su obra "La resaca" : cumbre en su arte de novelar*. San Juan: Instituto de Cultura Puertorriqueña, 1964. 194 pp.

1997. Ortega-Vélez, Ruth E. *La mujer en la obra de Enrique A. Laguerre*. Río Piedras, P.R.: Editorial de la Universidad de Puerto Rico, 1989. 141 pp.

See also #1797, #1800.

1998. *Lair, Clara,* 1895–1973 (poet). Arras de cristal, 1937–1983; Más allá del poniente, 1950–1983; Obra poética, 1979 (Vicente Géigel Polanco, ed.); Poesías, 1961; Trópico amargo, 1950–1983.

1999. Cuchí Coll, Isabel. *"Arras de cristal" y Clara Lair*. Ciudad Trujillo: Cromos, 1938. 1 vol. (unpaged).

2000. ———. *Dos poetisas de América: Clara Lair, Julia de Burgos*. Barcelona: [s.n.], 1970. 46 pp. Reprint of the 1965 ed.

2001. *Landrón, Eric,* 1953– (poet). Piropazos, 1991; Pupilazos, 1978.

2002. *Licelott Delgado, Edna* (poet). Voces bajas de pausas en un amor gigante, 1987–1990; Y cuando digo todos, 1970.

2003. *Lloréns Torres, Luis,* 1878–1944 (playwright, poet). Antología, 1986 (Arcadio Díaz Quiñones, ed.); Obras completas, 1967–1984 (Vol. 1. Poesía: Al pie de la Alhambra [1899], Sonetos sinfónicos [1914], Voces de a campana mayor [1935], Alturas de América [1940].—Vol. 2. Prosa y teatro: América [1898], El grito de Lares [1927].—Vol. 3. Artículos de revistas y periódicos); La prosa de Luis Lloréns Torres, 1986 (Daisy Caraballo Abreu, ed.).

2004. Figueroa Berrios, Edwin et al. *Luis Lloréns Torres en su centenario.* Río Piedras, P.R.: Editorial Universitaria, Universidad de Puerto Rico, 1983. 67 pp.

2005. Hadjopoulos, Theresa Ortiz de. *Luis Lloréns Torres: A Study of His Poetry.* New York: Plus Ultra, 1977. 134 pp.

2006. Lloréns, Washington. *Los grandes amores del poeta Luis Lloréns Torres.* San Juan: Editorial Campos, 1959. 47 pp.

2007. Marrero, Carmen. *Luis Lloréns Torres (1876–1944): vida y obra, bibliografía, antología.* 2a ed. aum. San Juan: Editorial Cordillera, 1968. 187 pp.

2008. Ortiz García, Nilda S. *Vida y obra de Luis Lloréns Torres.* San Juan: Instituto de Cultura Puertorriqueña, 1977. 299 pp.

See also #1765.

2009. *Lluch Mora, Francisco,* 1924– (poet). Antología poética, 1984; Canto de despedida a Juan Ramón Jiménez, 1965; Canto desesperado a la ceniza, 1955; Cartapacio de amor, 1961; Decimario primero, 1976; Del asedio y la clausura, 1950; Del barro a Dios, 1954; Diapason negro, 1960; La huella del latido, 1994; La lumbre y el ocaso, 1973; Momento de alegría, 1959; Variaciones sobre un mismo tema, 1976.

2010. Cautiño Jordán, Eduardo. *La personalidad literaria de Francisco Lluch Mora.* San Juan: Ediciones Mairena, 1994. 135 pp.

2011. *Lomar, Martha,* 1893– (playwright, poet). La canción de la hora, 1959; Por aquí pasa un hombre, 1939; Silabario de espuma, 1963; Vejez sonora, 1931–1963.

2012. *López de Victoria y Fernández, Magda,* 1900– (poet). Amor, 1956; Clarinadas en tiempos de mi isla, 1966; De mi templo interior, 1956; De Puerto Rico al corazón de América, 1943; Hijos, 1940; Tú, hombre, 1959.

2013. *López González, Salvador,* 1937– (poet). A media asta, 1979; Hijos del trabajo, 1990; La sombra de barro, 1976. See also #1770.

2014. *López, Julio César* (poet). Al amor, 1980; Borrones y borradores, 1979; Cien desvarios de la noche amante, 1989; Cuaderno de los desconciertos, 1973; Doble fondo, 1975; Escalas de la semilla, 1975; Estaciones de la vigilia, 1990; Fogatas del tiempo, 1972; Peregrino de sombras, 1967; Poemas de tránsito y otras dolencias, 1985.

2015. *López Ramírez, Tomás,* 1946– (novelist, short story writer). Cordial magia enemiga, 1971; Juego de las revelaciones, 1976; Tristes aunque breves ceremonias, 1991.

2016. *López Suria, Violeta,* 1926– (poet, short story writer). Amorosamente, 1960; Antología poética, 1970; Argénida, supiste, 1984; Las nubes dejan sombras, 1965; Obsesión de Heliotropo, 1965 (Obsesión de Heliotropo, El teléfono de copa, El hongo en el paraguas, El caldo, El parapeto, Autobiografía de trapo, El reloj desnudado, Mariposas de Taiwan, Cuando el parque era parque, Ambos a dos, El cojín, La peinilla, La única, La fuente seca, La balada y el árbol, El espejo ahumado, La barra, Aguaviva, El gusano, Soneto en cuento); La piel pegada al alma, 1962; Poemas a la Cáncora, 1963; Polvorín de Santa Elena, 1992; Resurrección de Eurídice, 1963; Sentimiento de un viaje, 1955; Unas cuantas estrellas en mi cuarto, 1957; Violeta López Suria [selecciones], 1995.

2017. *Lugo Filippi, Carmen,* 1940– (short story writer). Vírgenes y mártires/Scaldada y Cuervo, S.A., presentan . . . , 1981–1991 (with Ana Lydia Vega). See also #1733.

2018. *Lugo, Samuel,* 1905– (poet). Antología poética, 1971; Donde caen las claridades, 1934; Ronda de la llama verde, 1949; Yumbra, 1943.

2019. *Lugo Toro, Sigfredo* (poet). Aljibe, 1964; Caracol, corno de nácar, 1990; Memorias, anatomía de lo insólito, 1993; Quinqué, 1965.

2020. *Maldonado Villalobos, Irma Antonia* (poet). Fuga de sombras, 1991; Incontenible, 1988.

2021. *Marcano Montañez, Jaime* (poet). Del amor y las gaviotas, 1995; Invitación a la ternura, 1991; Poemas de amor, 1977.

2022. *Margenat, Hugo,* 1934–1957 (poet). Intemperie, 1955; Lámpara apagada, 1954; Mundo abierto, 1958; Obras completas, 1974; Ventana hacia lo último, 1961.

2023. *Marqués, René,* 1919–1979 (novelist, playwright, poet, short story writer). El apartamiento, 1966–1971; Carnaval afuera, carnaval adentro, 1971; La casa sin reloj, 1962–1971; Los casos de Ignacio y Santiago, 1960; Cuatro cuentos de mujeres, 1959–1967; David y Jonatán, 1970; The Docile Puerto Rican, 1976 (Translation of Ensayos [1953–1972]; Barbara Bockus Aponte, tr.); En una ciudad llamada San Juan, 1960–1983; Ese mosaico fresco sobre aquel mosaico antiguo, 1975; El hombre y sus sueños, 1971; Inmersos en el silencio, 1976; Juan Bobo y la dama de ocidente, 1956–1989; Juventud, 1958; The Look, 1983 (Translation of La mirada [1975]; Charles Pilditch, tr.); Mariana/El alba, 1968; El niño y su mundo, 1954; Otro día nuestro, 1955; The Oxcart, 1969 (Translation of La carreta [1952–1991]; Charles Pilditch, tr.); Peregrinación, 1944; Purificación en la calle del Cristo, 1963–1983; Sacrificio en el monte Moriah, 1969–1976; El sol y los MacDonald, 1950–1971; Teatro, 1959–1986 (Los soles truncos [1963], Un niño azul para esa sombra [1970], La muerte no entrará en el palacio [1958]); Tito y Berenice, 1970; Vía Crucis del hombre puertorriqueño, 1971; La víspera del hombre, 1959–1990.

2024. Caballero Wangüemert, María del Milagro. *La narrativa de René Marqués*. Madrid: Editorial Playor, 1986. 318 pp.

2025. Diéguez Caballero, Ileana. *Lo trágico en el teatro de René Marqués*. Havana: Depto. de Actividades Culturales, Universidad de la Habana, 1985. 80 pp.

2026. Espinosa Torres, Victoria. *El teatro de René Marqués y la escenificación de su obra "Los soles truncos."* Mexico City: Facultad de Filosofía y Letras, Universidad Nacional Autónoma de México, 1969. 579 pp.

2027. Festival de Teatro (Sixteenth, 1982–1983, San Juan). *Ateneo Puertorriqueño presenta XVI Festival de Teatro en homenaje a René Marqués, septiembre 1982 a marzo 1983*. San Juan: Ateneo Puertorriqueño, 1983. 56 pp. Cover title *Homenaje a René Marqués*.

2028. Martin, Eleanor J. *René Marqués*. Boston, MA: Twayne, 1979. 168 pp.

2029. Palmer Bermúdez, Neyssa S. *Las mujeres en los cuentos de René Marqués*. Río Piedras, P.R.: Editorial de la Universidad de Puerto Rico, 1988. 103 pp.

2030. Peterson, Vernon Lynn. *Idea y representación literaria en la narrativa de René Marqués*. Madrid: Editorial Pliegos, 1986. 191 pp.

2031. Pilditch, Charles R. *René Marqués: A Study of his Fiction*. New York: Plus Ultra, 1977. 245 pp.

2032. Reynolds, Bonnie Hildebrand. *Space, Time, and Crisis: The Theatre of René Marqués*. York, SC: Spanish Literature Publishing, 1988. 120 pp.

2033. Rodríguez Ramos, Esther. *Los cuentos de René Marqués*. Río Piedras, P.R.: Editorial Universitaria, Universidad de Puerto Rico, 1976. 202 pp.

2034. Vientós Gastón, Nilita, ed. *Homenaje a René Marqués*. San Juan: Editorial Sin Nombre, 1979. 163 pp.

See also #1765.

2035. *Martínez Tolentino, Jaime* (playwright, short story writer). Cuentos fantásticos, 1983; Desde el fondo del caracol y otros cuentos taínos, 1992; La imagen del otro, 1980.

2036. *Matos Paoli, Francisco,* 1915– (poet). El acorde, 1988; Antología minuto, 1978–1981 (Luis Cartaña, ed.); Antología poética, 1972 (Cardo labriego [1937], Habitante del eco [1944], Teoría del olvido [1944], Canto a Puerto Rico [1952], Luz de los hértoes [1954], Criatura del rocío [1954], Canto de la locura [1962], El viento y la paloma [1960]; José Emilio González, ed.); La caída del clavel, 1979; Cancionero, 1970–1983; El cerco de Dios (antología), 1995 (Manuel de la Puebla, ed.); El engaño a los ojos, 1974; Contra la interpretación, 1989; Criatura del rocío, 1958; Los crueles espejos, 1980; Dación y milagro, 1976; Decimario de la Virgen, 1990; Diario de un poeta, 1973–1987 (Autobiographical); La distancia vencida, 1990; La frontera y el mar, 1987; Habitante del eco, 1944; Hacia el hondo vuelo, 1983; Isla para los niños, 1981 (with Isabel

Freire de Matos); Jardín vedado, 1980; Loor del espacio, 1977; Luz de los héroes, 1954–1992 (Isabel Freire de Matos, ed. [1992]); La marea sube, 1971; La orilla situada, 1974; Las pausas blancas, 1986; Las pequeñas muertes, 1989; Primeros libros poéticos, 1982 (Cardo labriego y otros poemas [1937], Habitante del eco [1944], Teoría del olvido [1944], Canto a Puerto Rico [1952], Criatura del rocío [1954], Canto de la locura [1962]; Joserramón Melendes, ed.); Rapto en el tiempo, 1978; Razón del humo, 1986; Rielo del instante, 1975; Romancillos para adolescentes, 1985; Rostro en la estela, 1973; La semilla encendida, 1971; Sombra verdadera, 1980; Song of Madness and Other Poems, 1985 (Translation of Canto de la locura [1962–1983]; Frances R. Aparicio, tr.); Testigo de la esperanza, 1974; Unción de la tierra, 1975; Variaciones del mar, 1973; Vestido para la desnudez, 1984; El viento y la paloma, 1969; Ya se oye el cenit, 1977.

2037. Ciordia Muguerza, Javier. *Entre el delirio y el órden: preámbulo a Matos Paoli.* Ponce, P.R.: Universidad de Puerto Rico, 1994. 391 pp.

2038. Encarnación, Angel Manuel. *El "Cancionero I" de Francisco Matos Paoli.* San Juan: Instituto de Cultura Puertorriqueña, 1988. 133 pp.

2039. González Torres, Rafael Antonio. *La búsqueda de lo absoluto; o, La poesía de Francisco Matos Paoli.* San Juan: Editorial Andina, 1978. 157 pp.

2040. Matos Paoli, Francisco, and Héctor J. Martell Morales, ed. *El poeta don Francisco Matos Paoli: entrevista.* Ponce, P.R.: Editorial Creación, 1978. 52 pp.

2041. Matos Paoli, Francisco, and Manuel de la Puebla, ed. *Francisco Matos Paoli: poeta esencial—entrevista.* Río Piedras, P.R.: Ediciones Mairena, 1985. 50 pp.

2042. *Mattos Cintrón, Wilfredo* (novelist). El cerro de los buitres, 1984–1992; El cuerpo bajo el puente, 1989; Las dos caras de Jano, 1995.

2043. *Medina López, Ramón Felipe* (poet). Andina de la Alborada, 1978; Arbol de palabras, 1987; Cantos de Dios airado, 1969; Del tiempo al tiempo, 1973; Prodigio del tiempo, 1977; El ruiseñor bajo el cielo, 1956; Te hablo a tí, 1971; El veintisiete, 1973.

2044. *Meléndez, Concha,* 1892–1981 (poet). Antología de Concha Meléndez, 1995 (Mariano A. Feliciano Fabre, ed.); Antología y cartas de sus amigos, 1995 (Mariano A. Feliciano Fabre, ed.); Obras completas, 1971; Psiquis doliente, 1923. See also #1764.

2045. *Meléndez Muñoz, Miguel,* 1884–1966 (novelist, short story writer). Cuentos de la carretera central, 1941–1982; Cuentos del cedro, 1937–1987; Cuentos y estampas, 1958; Ensayos, 1927 (El niño, la escuela y el hogar, El pauperismo en Puerto Rico, Ventajas e inconvenientes del lujo); Ensayos cortos y artículos, 1963; Fuga de ideas, 1942; Lecturas puertorriqueñas, 1919–1950; Obras completas, 1963; Una oración en Montebello, 1963; Retablo puertoriqueño, 1944–1960; Retazos, 1905; Sobre esto y aquello, 1963; Yuyo, 1913–1988. See also #1764.

2046. *Méndez Ballester, Manuel,* 1909– (novelist, playwright, short story writer). El clamor de los surcos, 1940–1970; Cuatro cuentos de humor, 1986 (Los pobres ricos, Los animales, Los parientes, Los papeles); Hilarión, 1943; Isla cerrera, 1937–1990; Teatro de Manuel Méndez Ballester, 1991 (Vol. 1. Tiempo muerto [1940], Encrucijada [1958], Bienvenido, don Goyito [1967], La invasión, La polilla; vol. 2. El circo, El milagro, La feria, Arriba las mujeres, Los cocorocos [1977], Tambores en el Caribe); Las turbias aguas del pasado, 1994.

2047. *Miranda-Archilla, Graciany,* 1910– (poet). Camino de la sed, 1993; Himno a la caballa, 1971; Matria and Monody With Roses in Ash November, 1978; El oro en la espiga, 1941; Si de mi tierra, 1941.

2048. *Montero, Mayra,* 1952– (novelist, short story writer). Del rojo de su sombra, 1992; La trenza de la hermosa luna, 1987; Tú, la oscuridad, 1995; La última noche que pasé contigo, 1991–1994; Veintitrés y una tortuga, 1981.

2049. *Morales Cabrera, Pablo,* 1866–1933 (short story writer). Cuentos, 1966 (Cuentos populares [1939], Cuentos criollos [1925]; Esther Melón de Díaz, ed).

2050. *Morales, Jorge Luis,* 1930– (poet). Antología poética, 1968; Discurso a los pájaros, 1965; Elegías, 1994; Jornada precisa, 1962–1963; Metal y piedra, 1952; Nueva antología poética, 1975; Obelisco, 1990; Orbe, 1993; Ouranos, cinabrio verbo María, 1991; Los ríos redimidos, 1969; Salvado margen, 1983; Sartoria labor, 1991; La ventana y yo, 1960–1973.

2051. *Moreira Velardo, Sixto* (novelist). Almas rotas, 1972; Añoranzas en mi huerto, 1984; El caballero del mar, 1946; Fugitivo de a bordo, 1975; Mi novia de ojos verdes, 1975; Una mujer en mi vida, 1972; El vía crucis de una familia, 1990.

2052. *Muñoz Igartúa, Angel,* 1905– (poet). Por el sendero, 1954; Savia íntima, 1927; Versos de ayer y de hoy, 1946; Vibraciones, 1960.

2053. *Murillo, Antonio Esteban,* 1864–1931 (poet). Sonetinos, madrigales y sonetos, 1928–1963.

2054. *Nieves Albert, Dalia,* 1948– (poet). La calle, 1977; En el diario asombro de lo humano, 1989; Poemas por encargo y otras recetas de amor, 1995; Vamos a subir la voz para morir mariposas, 1989.

2055. *Nolla, Olga,* 1938– (novelist, poet, short story writer). Clave de sol, 1976; Dafne en el mes de marzo, 1989; De lo familiar, 1973; Dulce hombre prohibido, 1994; El ojo de la tormenta, 1976; Porque nos queremos tanto, 1989; La segunda hija, 1992; El sombrero de plata, 1976.

2056. *Noriega, Carlos,* 1932– (poet). Búsqueda y encuentro, 1968; Musgos de soledad y silencio, 1990; Presencia en el tiempo, 1964; El tiempo y las raíces, 1976.

2057. *Ochart, Yvonne,* 1951– (novelist, poet, short story writer). Este es nuestro paraíso, 1981; El fuego de las cosas, 1990; Obra poética, 1989 (Rantamplán [1975], El salto domado, Poemas de Nueva York).

2058. *Oliver Frau, Antonio,* 1902–1945 (short story writer). Cuentos y leyendas del cafetal, 1938–1967.

2059. *Orsini Luiggi, Sadí,* 1938– (novelist, poet). El encubierto, 1973; Los integrados, 1964; Lamento negro, dios-hombre, hombre-miedo, 1964; El obispo, todas las noches, 1993; El renacido, 1967.

2060. *Palés Matos, Gustavo,* 1907–1963 (poet). Obras, 1986 (Alfredo Matilla Rivas, ed.); Romancero de Cofresí, 1942.

2061. *Palés Matos, Luis,* 1898–1959 (novelist, poet). Azaleas, 1915; Luis Palés Matos [poesía], 1959–1989; Obras (1914–1959), 1984 (Margot Arce de Vázquez, ed.); Poesía, 1975 (Raúl Hernández Novás, ed.); Poesía (1915–1956), 1957–1974 (Federico de Onís, ed.); Poesía completa y prosa selecta, 1978–1988 (Margot Arce de Vázquez, ed.); Tuntún de pasa y grifería, y otros poemas, 1937–1995 (Trinidad Barrera, ed. [1995]).

2062. Agrait, Gustavo. *Luis Palés Matos: un poeta puertorriqueño*. San Juan: Biblioteca de Autores Puertorriqueños, 1988. 78 pp. Reprint of the 1973 ed.

2063. Blanco, Tomás. *Sobre Palés Matos*. San Juan: Biblioteca de Autores Puertorriqueños, 1950. 62 pp.

2064. Clar, Raymond. *Lo antillano en la poesía de Luis Palés Matos*. San Juan: Oficina del Gobernador de Puerto Rico, 1982. 31 pp.

2065. Diego Padró, José Isaac de. *Luis Palés Matos y su trasmundo poético: estudio biográfico-crítico*. Río Piedras, P.R.: Ediciones Puerto, 1973. 121 pp.

2066. Enguídanos, Miguel. *La poesía de Luis Palés Matos*. 2a ed., aum. Río Piedras, P.R.: Editorial de la Universidad de Puerto Rico, 1976. 109 pp.

2067. Marzán, Julio. *The Numinous Site: The Poetry of Luis Palés Matos*. Madison, NJ: Fairleigh Dickinson University Press, 1995. 199 pp.

2068. Onís, Federico de. *Luis Palés Matos, 1898–1959: vida y obra, bibliografía, antología, poesías inéditas*. San Juan: Ediciones Ateneo Puertorriqueño, 1960. 90 pp.

2069. Puebla, Manuel de la, ed. *Homenaje a Luis Palés Matos*. Río Piedras, P.R.: Ediciones Mairena, 1979. 120 pp.

2070. Romero García, Luz Virginia. *El aldeanismo en la poesía de Luis Palés Matos*. Río Piedras, P.R.: Editorial Universitaria, Universidad de Puerto Rico, 1973. 119 pp.

See also #40, #1765.

2071. *Palés Matos, Vicente,* 1903–1963 (poet, short story writer). La fuente de Juan Ponce de León y otros poemas, 1967; Viento y espuma, 1945–1981.

2072. López Román, Juan Edgardo. *La obra literaria de Vicente Palés Matos*. Río Piedras, P.R.: Editorial de la Universidad de Puerto Rico, 1984. 293 pp.

2073. *Palma, Marigloria,* 1920– (novelist, poet, short story writer). Agua
suelta, 1942; Aire habitado, 1981; Amy Kootsky, 1973; Arboles
míos, 1965; Bolitas de mármol, 1989; Canto de los olvidos, 1965;
Los cuarenta silencios, 1973; Cuentos de la abeja encinta, 1975;
Cuentos de Mamita Chepa, 1984; Entre Francia y Suiza, 1968; La
herencia, 1968; Mamita Chepa y su perro Sopa, 1984; La noche y
otras flores eléctricas, 1976; Palomas frente al eco, 1968; La razón
del cuadrante, 1968; Saludando la noche, 1968; San Juan entre dos
azules, 1965; El señor Don Güí-Güí, y otros cuentos, 1979; Teatro
infantil, 1970–1985; Teatro para niños, 1968; Versos de cada día,
1980; Viento salado, 1981; Voz de lo transparente, 1965.

2074. *Paralitici Rivera, José M.* (poet, short story writer). Cantera de
amor, 1993; La cotorra, el coquí y el higüero, 1989; Huela encendida, 1984; Rastreando, 1984; Tierra adentro/ Cuentos y estampas
puertorriqueñas, 1983.

2075. *Passalacqua, Carlos M.* (poet). Al decir de las estrellas, 1968; Antología poética, 1984 (Francisco Lluch Mora, ed.); Confluencia en
la luz, 1987; La fe de la estrella, 1985; El fondo y la ola, 1972;
Fuente, 1981 (María Teresa Babín, ed.); El llanto de la nada,
1967–1988; Luz y vida, 1990; Noche, 1981 (María Teresa Babín,
ed.); Los pergaminos del abismo, 1986.

2076. *Passalacqua, José Rafael* (poet). Breviario lírico, 1991; Horizontes, 1984.

2077. *Pedreira, Antonio Salvador,* 1899–1939 (poet). Obras completas,
1969.

2078. *Pérez Pierret, Antonio,* 1885–1937 (poet). Antología, 1959 (Félix
Franco Oppenheimer, ed.); Bronces y otros poemas, 1914–1968.

2079. *Puebla, Manuel de la* (poet). Anillos del amor y de la muerte,
1991; Espejitos de luna, 1988 (with Alicia Fernández Gill); No es
desamor tu viaje, 1986; Romances para decir en las calles de Río
Piedras, 1978; Unos apuntes líricos, 1972.

2080. *Quiñones, Magaly,* 1945– (poet). Cantándole a la noche misma,
1978; Cosas de poetas, cosas nuestras, 1977; En la pequeña Antilla, 1982; Entre mi voz y el tiempo, 1969; Nombrar, 1985; Razón
de lucha, razón de amor, 1989.

2081. *Ramírez Brau, Enrique,* 1894– (poet). El arquero soy yo, 1944;
Bajo tu cielo azul, 1928; Canciones en la sombra, 1954; Esplín,

1950; Frisos inmortales, 1964; Lira rebelde, 1925; Memoria de un periodista, 1968.

2082. *Ramírez de Arellano, Haydée,* 1912– (poet). Poemas, 1951–1992; Versos de ella, 1985.

2083. *Ramírez de Arellano de Nolla, Olga,* 1911– (poet, short story writer). A la luz del flamboyán, 1962; Amor que es como un rezo, 1972; Antología poética, 1972; Cada ola, 1966; Cauce hondo, 1947; Clave de sol, 1977 (Clave de sol—La princesa y el juglar); Cundeamor, 1967; Diario de la montaña, 1967; Dos veces retoño, 1965; En mis ojos verás todos los mundos, 1968; Escucha mi alma un canto, 1966; Mar de poesía, 1963; Orbe, 1966; El rosal fecundo, 1962; Te entrego, amor, 1962; La tierra de la diafanidad, 1962; Traigo un ramillete, 1972.

2084. *Ramos Albelo, Rafael,* 1935– (poet, short story writer). Cantos de mi aldea, 1986–1991; Los C.R.A. en el callejón, 1993; Greenfires, 1994; Poetical Trilogy/Trilogía poética/Trilogie poétique, 1990.

2085. *Ramos Escobar, José Luis* (playwright, short story writer). En la otra orilla, 1992; Indocumentados, 1991–1993; Mano dura, 1994; Sintigo, 1985.

2086. *Ramos Hernández, Mariano,* 1929– (poet). Desde la distancia, 1991; Intimidades y versos, 1992.

2087. *Ramos, Juan Antonio,* 1948– (short story writer). Démosle luz verde a la nostalgia, 1978; En casa de Guillermo Tell, 1991; Hilando mortajas, 1983; El manual del buen modal y otras ocurrencias "lite", 1993; Pactos de silencio y algunas erratas de fé, 1980; Papo Impala está quitao, 1983–1991; Vive y vacila, 1986.

2088. *Ramos Llompart, Arturo* (poet). Dos temas taínos, 1990; Gris en oro, 1948; San Juan heróico en tres siglos, 1984.

2089. *Ramos-Perea, Roberto,* 1959– (playwright). Censurado, el lado oscuro de las arañas, 1988; Cueva de ladrones/Revolución en el paraíso, 1992; Malasangre, 1990; Melodía salvaje, 1992; Módulo 104, revolución en el purgatorio, 1986; Revolución en el infierno, 1983; Teatro de luna, 1989 (Llanto de luna, Obsesión); Teatro secreto, 1993 (Las amantes pasan el año nuevo solas, A puro bolero, Motel, Miénteme más, Melodía salvaje, Tuya siempre, Julita, Mistiblú, Morir de noche).

2090. *Rechani Agrait, Luis,* 1902– (playwright, poet). Teatro de Luis Rechani Agrait, 1991 (Vol. 1. Mi señoría [1940], Todos los ruiseñores cantan [1966], ¿Cómo se llama esta flor? [1966], Tres piraguas en un día de calor. Vol. 2. Llora en el atardecer la fuente [1971], Oh, dorada ilusión de alas abiertas, Oblomós).

2091. *Rentas Lucas, Eugenio,* 1910– (poet). Campo de mieses, 1982; Decir la luz amanecida, 1990; Mañana en el alba, 1949; Poemas, 1976; Salmos en la aurora, 1963.

2092. *Reyes, Edwin,* 1944– (poet). Balada del hombre huérfano, 1990; Crónica del vértigo, 1977; Son cimarrón por Adolfina Villanueva, 1987.

2093. *Ribera Chevremont, Evaristo,* 1896–1976 (novelist, poet, short story writer). Anclas de oro, 1945; Antología poética (1924–1950), 1954–1957; Antología poética (1929–1965), 1967; Barro, 1945; Canto de mi tierra, 1971; El caos de los sueños, 1974; Color, 1938; Creación, 1951; Elegías de San Juan, 1980; Evaristo Ribera Chevremont [poesías], 1960–1990; El hondero lanzó la piedra, 1975; Inefable orilla, 1961; Jinetes de la inmortalidad, 1977; El libro de las apologías, 1976; La llama pensativa, 1955; Memorial de arena, 1962; El niño de Arcilla, 1950–1989; Nueva antología, 1966; Obra poética, 1980; Principio de canto, 1965; Punto final, 1963; Río volcado, 1968; El semblante, 1964; El templo de los alabastros, 1919; Tonos y formas, 1943; Tú, mar, y yo y ella, 1946; Verbo, 1947.

2094. Gallego, Laura. *Las ideas literarias de Evaristo Ribera Chevremont.* San Juan: Instituto de Cultura Puertorriqueña, 1983. 142 pp.

2095. Marxuach, Carmen Irene. *Evaristo Ribera Chevremont: voz de vanguardia.* San Juan: Centro de Estudios Avanzados de Puerto Rico y el Caribe, 1987. 323 pp.

2096. Meléndez, Concha. *La inquietud sosegada: poética de Evaristo Ribera Chevremont.* 3a ed. San Juan: Editorial Cordillera, 1970. 144 pp.

2097. *Ribera Chevremont, José Joaquín,* 1897– (poet). Barandales del mundo, 1944; Brevario de vanguardia, 1930; Elegías románticas, 1918; La lámpara azul, 1933; Poemas, 1934.

2098. *Rivera, Etnairis,* 1949– (poet). El día del polen, 1980; Entre ciudades y casi paraísos, 1989; Lírica colérica, 1977 (with Vicente

Rodríguez Nietzche, Andrés Castro Ríos, and Angelamaría Dávila Malavé); María mar moriviví, 1976; Pachamamapa takin, 1976; Wydondequiera, 1974.

2099. *Rivera Landrón, Francisco,* 1907– (novelist, poet). El alma de la huerta, 1945–1962; Cifra y signo, 1963; Flor de cinco pétalos, 1951; Humo de incenso, 1964; Mi terruño en el surco, 1962; El refugio, 1963; Remansos plácidos, 1961; Sementeras de lumbre, 1956; Tierras de Dios, 1962.

2100. *Rivera, María Zoraida* (poet). Mis versos . . . tienen alas, 1991; Mis versos vuelan a tí, 1995.

2101. *Rivera Robles, Carlos,* 1915– (poet). Albiumbras, 1991; Ruta de ensueños y pesadillas, 1984.

2102. *Rodríguez, Guillermo* (poet, short story writer). Misericordia, 1984; Mística, 1993; El río que quería ser mar, 1988; Somos peregrinos, 1990; El verso y la sabanera, 1993.

2103. *Rodríguez Juliá, Edgardo,* 1946– (novelist). El camino de Yyaloide, 1994; Campeche/Los diablos de la melancolía, 1986; El cruce de la Bahía de Guánica, 1989; Una noche con Iris Chacón, 1986; La noche oscura del Niño Avilés, 1984–1991; Puertorriqueños, 1988; La renuncia del héroe Baltasar, 1974–1986; Las tribulaciones de Jonás, 1981–1984.

 2104. González, Rubén. *La historia puertorriqueña de Rodríguez Juliá.* San Juan: Editorial de la Universidad de Puerto Rico, 1996.

2105. *Rodríguez Nietzsche, Vicente,* 1942– (poet). Amor como una flauta, 1978; Del dulce pie tu caminar tranquilo, 1983; Estos poemas, 1967 (with Andrés Castro Ríos); Lírica colérica, 1977 (with Etnairis Rivera, Andrés Castro Ríos, and Angelamaría Dávila Malavé); No supe enamorarme de azucenas, 1994; Vuelvo a enhebrar la musical costura, 1989.

2106. *Rodríguez Torres, Carmelo,* 1941– (novelist, poet, short story writer). La casa y la llama fiera, 1982; Cinco cuentos negros, 1976; Este pueblo no es un manto de sonrisas, 1991–1993; Veinte siglos después del homicidio, 1971–1980. See also #85, #1770.

2107. *Roque, Ana,* 1853–1933 (novelist, short story writer). Luz y sombra, 1903–1991.

2108. *Rosa Soberal, Guillermo* (poet). Del planetoide a los paramos floridos, 1994; La patria, el amor y la filosofía, 1989.

2109. *Rosa-Nieves, Cesáreo,* 1901–1974 (novelist, playwright, poet). Calambreñas, 1964; La canción de los luceros, 1972; Diapason negro, 1960; Los espejos de sal bajo la luna, 1972; Estrellas y caramelos, 1972; La feria de las burbujas, 1930; Girasol, 1960–1969; Mañana será la esperanza, 1964; El mar bajo de la montaña, 1963; Mi vocación por el véspero, 1965; Los nísperos del alba maduraron, 1959; El plenamar de las garzas de ámbar, 1964; Román Baldorioty de Castro, 1948–1978; Siete caminos en la luna de sueños, 1957; El sol pintó de oro los bohíos, 1965; Teatro escolar, 1932 (with Marina L. Molina); Undumbre, 1953.

2110. Figueroa de Cifredo, Patria. *Apuntes biográficos en torno a la vida y obra de Cesáreo Rosa-Nieves.* San Juan: Editorial Cordillera, 1965. 319 pp.

2111. ————. *Nuevo encuentro con la estética de Rosa-Nieves: varios ensayos y una breve antología poética.* San Juan: [s.n.], 1969. 106 pp.

See also #1764.

2112. *Sanabria Santaliz, Edgardo,* 1951– (short story writer). Cierta inevitable muerte, 1988 (Cierta inevitable muerte, Edi en la urna, Marcolina debajo del húcar, Borinquen Restaurant, Carmina y la noche, El libro); Delfia cada tarde, 1978; El día que el hombre pisó la luna, 1984; Las horas púrpuras, 1994.

2113. *Sánchez, Luis Rafael,* 1936– (novelist, playwright, short story writer). Casi el alma, 1966–1993; En cuerpo de camisa, 1966–1990; La guagua aérea, 1994; La importancia de llamarse Daniel Santos, 1989; Macho Camacho's Beat, 1980–1982 (Translation of La guaracha del macho Camacho [1976–1993]; Gregory Rabassa, tr.); La pasión según Antígona Pérez, 1968–1993; Quíntuples, 1985–1992; Sol 13, interior/Teatro de Luis Rafael Sánchez, 1976–1987 (Farsa del amor compradrito [1960], La hiel nuestra de cada día [1962], Los ángeles se han fatigado [1960]).

2114. Colón Zayas, Eliseo. *El teatro de Luis Rafael Sánchez: códigos, ideología y lenguaje.* Madrid: Playor, 1985. 116 pp.

2115. Hernández Vargas, Nélida, and Daisy Caraballo Abréu, eds. *Luis Rafael Sánchez: crítica y bibliografía.* Río Piedras, P.R.: Editorial de la Universidad de Puerto Rico, 1985. 292 pp.

2116. Vázquez Arce, Carmen. *Por la vereda tropical: notas sobre la cuentística de Luis Rafael Sánchez*. Buenos Aires: Ediciones de la Flor, 1994. 244 pp.

2117. Waldman, Gloria F. *Luis Rafael Sánchez: pasión teatral*. San Juan: Instituto de Cultura Puertorriqueña, 1988. 386 pp.

2118. *Santaliz Avila, Pedro,* 1938– (playwright). Teatro, 1992 (Olla, El castillo interior de Medea Camuñas, Las sombras del chisme/La historia de Evaristo y Matera, El teatro personal de Meaíto Laracuente).

2119. *Santaliz, Coqui* (playwright, poet, short story writer). Canto al espacio mujer, 1985; Con el pecho metido en el tiempo, 1984; Cuentos del sí y del no, 1992; Juanita lagartija, 1989; El nacimiento de Laranih, 1991; Poemas para mis vecinos, 1987; Poemas para un esposo encarcelado, 1986; La tierra diaria, 1985 (La tierra diaria, Huyo de los dioses de todos, Caminantes diarios, De nuevo a nacer en tu voz, En este minuto).

2120. *Santos Febres, Mayra,* 1966– (poet). Anamú y manigua, 1991; El orden escapado, 1991; Pez de vidrio, 1995.

2121. *Santos Silva, Loreina,* 1933– (poet). Amor, amor una veleta, 1990; Como puñales, 1993; Del onto, 1978; Este ojo que me mira, 1995 (Autobiographical); Incertidumbre primera, 1973; Mi ria, 1981; Motor mutable, 1984; Poemas para la madre ausente, 1995; Rikelme, 1974; Umbral de soledad, 1987; Vocero del mar, 1982.

2122. *Sedeño, Livia* (novelist). En tiempo de marzo, en tiempo de abril, 1981; Los gnomos no tienen bibliotecas, 1973–1988; Matar la muerte, 1988; Pie del labio ausente, 1986.

2123. *Serra Deliz, Wenceslao* (poet, short story writer). Abra palabra, 1992; Adiós falcón, 1985; En las cavernas de Camuy, 1995; Memoria, 1970; Terón, una aventura bajo tierra, 1995; El trabajo diario, 1986.

2124. *Sierra Berdecía, Fernando,* 1903–1962 (novelist, playwright). Aguafuerte, 1963; La escuela del buen amor, 1963 (Emilio M. Colón, ed.); Esta noche juega el jóker, 1939–1976.

2125. *Silén, Iván,* 1944– (novelist, poet). La biografía, 1984; La casa de Ulimar, 1988; Después del suicidio, 1970; Edipo rey/La caperucita, 1974; El miedo del pantócrata, 1987; Las muñecas de la calle del Cristo, 1989; Nietzsche/La dama de las ratas, 1986; El pájaro loco, 1972; Los poemas de filí-melé, 1976–1987; La poesía como libertá, 1992; The Wail of the Nymphomaniacs/El llanto de las ninfómanas, 1980.

2126. *Silén, Juan Angel* (novelist, short story writer). Carpeta 20671, 1993; La guerra de los mil años, 1992; Las memorias de José Joaquín Henríquez, 1986; Las montoneras de Henríquez, 1991; Tierra firme, 1989; Yo el otro, 1995.

2127. *Soto, Pedro Juan,* 1928– (novelist, playwright, short story writer). Un decir, 1976; El francotirador, 1969–1978; Hot Land, Cold Season, 1973 (Translation of Ardiente suelo, fría estación [1961–1993]; Helen R. Lane, tr.); El huésped, 1955–1974; Las máscaras y otros disfraces, 1958–1973; Memoria de mi amnesia, 1991; Un oscuro pueblo sonriente, 1982–1984; Palabras al vuelo, 1990; Spiks, 1973 (Translation of Spiks [1956–1989]; Victioria Ortiz, tr.); Temporada de duendes, 1970; Usmaíl, 1959–1988.

2128. Soto, Pedro Juan. *A solas con Pedro Juan Soto: autoentrevista.* Río Piedras, P.R.: Ediciones Puerto, 1973. 110 pp.

See also #1800, #1806.

2129. *Soto Ramos, Julio,* 1903– (poet, short story writer). Cumbre y remanso, 1963; Don Julio Soto Ramos: [selecciones], 1966; Una pica en Flandes, 1959; Soledades en sol, 1952; Trapecio, cumarisotismo, 1955; Yo soy yo y mi verdad, 1955–1973.

2130. *Sotomayor, Aurea María* (poet). Aquelarre de una bobina tartamuda, 1973; La gula de la tinta, 1994; Sitios de la memoria, 1983; Velando mi sueño de madera, 1980.

2131. *Tío, Elsa,* 1951– (poet). Detrás de los espejos empañados, 1977–1979; Inventario de la soledad, 1987; Poesía, 1958–1978.

2132. *Toro Soler, Ricardo del* (novelist, poet). Huracán, 1897–1936; Livia, 1925.

2133. *Torres Alonso, Juan* (playwright, poet). Epica de un niño rico, 1978; Universo de sangre, 1990; La ventana, 1973.

2134. *Torres, Angel Luis* (poet, short story writer). En el Bosque Seco de Guánica, 1994; Ira lira, 1989 (Porque se levanta la ira, Hijos de la muerte, Itinerario, S.D., La ciudad asedia [1977], Oración por la elipse de un planeta, Cajón de sastre); Parcelaciones, 1988; Parcelas magas, 1989.

2135. *Torres Rosado, Félix Juan,* 1913– (novelist, poet). Ciudadela rendida, 1967; Epoca, 1964; En tinte de rosicler, 1983; Golgotha, 1965 (Translation of Gólgota [1963]; Anna M. Torres. tr.); Pausa entre el deber y el haber, 1977; Poncio Pilatos, 1968; Sol de vida, 1940.

2136. *Torres Santiago, José Manuel,* 1940– (poet). En las manos del pueblo, 1972; Mi abecé, 1992; La paloma asesinada, 1967; Sobre casas de muertos va mi sombra, 1988.

2137. *Torres Vega, Armando* (poet). Antología poética, 1990; Ecos de la gesta heroica, 1969.

2138. *Umpierre, Luz María,* 1945– (poet, short story writer). And Other Misfortunes/Y otras desgracias, 1985; En el país de las maravillas, 1982–1990; Kempis puertorriqueño, 1982–1990; The Margarita Poems, 1987; Una puertorriqueña en Penna, 1979.

2139. *Valle, Carmen,* 1948– (poet, short story writer). De todo da la noche al que la tienta, 1987; Diarios robados, 1982; From Morocco I Write/Desde Marruecos te escribo, 1993 (Agueda Pizarro Rayo, tr.); Glenn Miller y varias vidas después, 1983; Un poco de lo no dicho, 1980.

2140. *Vega, Ana Lydia,* 1946– (playwright, short story writer). Cuentos calientes, 1992; Encancaranublado y otros cuentos de naufragio, 1982–1994; Esperando a Loló y otros delirios generacionales, 1994; Falsas crónicas del sur, 1991; Pasión de historia y otras historias de pasión, 1987–1994; True and False Romances, 1994 (Andrew Hurley, tr.); Vírgenes y mártires/ Scaldada y Cuervo, S.A., presentan . . . , 1981–1994 (with Carmen Lugo Filippi).

See also #85, #1733.

2141. *Venegas, Guillermo* (poet, short story writer). Así hablará Jesús, 1982; Las cien caras del amor, 1970; Flor de intermezzo, 1953; Marzo dos, una voz para los siglos (1955–1990), 1990–1991.

2142. *Villahermosa, Anselmo* (poet). Fe y poesía, 1992.

2143. *Villanueva Collado, Alfredo* (poet). Grimorio 1986, 1988; La guerrilla fantasma, 1989; El imperio de la papa frita/En el imperio de la papa frita, 1987; Pato salvaje, 1991; Las transformaciones del vidrio, 1984; La voz de la mujer que llevo dentro, 1990.

2144. *Villanueva, Salvador,* 1947– (poet). La comatosa noche, 1989; Expulsado del paraíso, 1981; Fin, 1987; Libro de los delirios, 1989.

2145. *Villaronga, Luis,* 1891–1964 (novelist). Alas victoriosas, 1925; Alma y paisaje, 1954; Banderas rojas, 1933; Carmencita, 1933; Contemplación, 1947; Los motivos eternos, 1945; El peregrino en la senda del sol, 1950; La república sentimental, 1933; La torre de marfil, 1952.

2146. *Vivas Maldonado, José Luis,* 1926– (novelist, playwright, short story writer). A vellón las esperanzas o Melania, 1971; Luces en sombra, 1955; Mis cuentos, 1986.

    2147. Ruscalleda Bercedóniz, Isabel María. *La cuentística de José Luis Vivas Maldonado.* San Juan: Instituto de Cultura Puertorriqueña, 1982. 145 pp.

    See also #1806.

2148. *Vizcarrondo, Carmelina,* 1906– (poet, short story writer). Minutero en sombras, 1941; Pregón en llamas, 1935.

    2149. Ramírez Mattei, Aida Elsa. *Carmelina Vizcarrondo: vida, obra y antología.* San Juan: Editorial Universitaria, Universidad de Puerto Rico, 1972. 261 pp.

2150. *Vizcarrondo, Fortunato,* 1896– (poet). Dinga y mandinga, 1942–1983.

2151. *Zavala, Iris M.,* 1936– (novelist, poet). Barro doliente, 1964; Chiliagony, 1985 (Translation of Kiliagonía [1980]; Susan Pensak, tr.); Escritura desatada, 1973; El libro de Apolonia o de las islas, 1993; Nocturna más no funesta, 1987; Poemas prescindibles, 1971; Que nadie muera sin amar el mar, 1982.

    2152. *Iris M. Zavala: una poética del imaginario social.* Barcelona: Editorial del Hombre, 1993. 95 pp. Special issue of *Anthropos* (no. 145, June 1993).

2153. *Zeno Gandía, Manuel,* 1855–1930 (novelist, poet, short story writer). Abismos, 1885; La charca, 1983 (Translation of La charca

[1894–1992]; Kai Wagenheim, tr.); Cuentos, 1958; Obras completas, 1955–1973 (La charca [1894], El negocio [1922], Garduña [1890], Redentores [1925]); Poesías, 1969 (Margarita Gardón Franceschi, ed.).

2154. Alvarez, Ernesto. *Manuel Zeno Gandía: estética y sociedad.* Río Piedras, P.R.: Editorial de la Universidad de Puerto Rico, 1987. 253 pp.

2155. Casanova Sánchez, Olga. *"La Charca" de Manuel Zeno Gandía: temas y estilo.* Río Piedras, P.R.: Editorial Plaza Mayor, 1992. 152 pp.

2156. Darbouze, Gilbert. *Dégénerescence et régénerescence dans l'oeuvre d'Emile Zola et celle de Manuel Zeno Gandía.* New York: P. Lang, 1995.

2157. Gardón Franceschi, Margarita. *Manuel Zeno Gandía: vida y poesía.* San Juan: Editorial Coquí, 1969. 175 pp.

2158. Palmer de Dueño, Rosa M. *Sentido, forma y estilo de "Redentores" de Manuel Zeno Gandía.* Río Piedras, P.R.: Editorial Universitaria, Universidad de Puerto Rico, 1974. 119 pp.

2159. Quiñones, Samuel R. *Manuel Zeno Gandía y la novela en Puerto Rico.* Mexico City: Editorial Orion, 1955. 36 pp.

See also #1797, #1800.

2160. *Zorilla de San Martín, Enrique,* 1880–1929 (poet). Trovas de amor y gesta, 1951–1990.

III
THE ENGLISH-SPEAKING CARIBBEAN

GENERAL

A. BIBLIOGRAPHIES AND BIO-BIBLIOGRAPHIES

2161. Carnegie, Jeniphier R. *Critics on West Indian Literature: A Selected Bibliography*. Mona, Jamaica: Research and Publications Committee, University of the West Indies, 1979. 74 pp.

2162. Dance, Daryl Cumber. *Fifty Caribbean Writers: A Bio-Bibliographical-Critical Sourcebook*. Westport, CT: Greenwood Press, 1986. 530 pp.

2163. Hughes, Michael. *A Companion to West Indian Literature*. London: Collins, 1979. 135 pp.

2164. Merriman, Stella E., and Joan Christiani, eds. *Commonwealth Caribbean Writers: A Bibliography*. Georgetown: Guyana Public Library, 1970. 98 pp.

2165. University of the West Indies (Mona, Jamaica), Library. *West Indian Literature: A Select Bibliography*. Mona, Jamaica: [s.n.], 1964. 32 pp.

Twentieth Century

2166. Allis, Jeannette B. *West Indian Literature: An Index to Criticism, 1930–1975*. Boston: G. K. Hall, 1981. 353 pp.

2167. Hughes, Roger, ed. *Caribbean Writing: A Checklist*. London: Commonwealth Institute, 1986. 49 pp.

2168. Nasta, Susheila. *African, Caribbean and South Asian Fiction in English: A Select Bibliography*. London: British Council, 1992. 37 pp.

2169. Poynting, Jeremy. *East Indians in the Caribbean: A Bibliography of Imaginative Literature in English, 1894–1984*. St. Augustine, Trinidad/Tobago: Library, University of the West Indies, 1984. 59 pp.

B. DICTIONARIES AND ENCYCLOPEDIAS

2170. Banham, Martin, Errol Hill and George William Woodyard, eds. *The Cambridge Guide to African and Caribbean Theatre*. New York: Cambridge University Press, 1994. 259 pp.

2171. Lindfors, Bernth, and Reinhard Sander, eds. *Twentieth-Century Caribbean and Black African Writers*. Third series. Detroit, MI: Gale Research, 1996. 461 pp.

C. ANTHOLOGIES

General

2172. Donnell, Alison, and Sarah Lawson Welsh, eds. *The Routledge Reader in Caribbean Literature*. New York: Routledge, 1996.

2173. Jones, Esmor, and Wenty Bowen, eds. *Heritage: A Caribbean Anthology*. London: Cassell, 1981. 224 pp.

2174. Pollard, Velma, ed. *Anansesem: A Collection of Caribbean Folk Tales, Legends, and Poems*. Kingston: Longman Jamaica, 1985. 88 pp.

2175. Thieme, John, Annette Warren and George Cave, eds. *Anthology of West Indian Literature*. Georgetown: University of Guyana, 1970. 124 pp.

2176. Walmsley, Anne, ed. *The Sun's Eye: West Indian Writing for Young Readers*. New rev. ed. Harlow, Eng.: Longman, 1989. 160 pp.

General: Twentieth Century

2177. Bensen, Robert, ed. *One People's Grief: Recent Writings from the Caribbean*. Hamilton, N.Z.: Outrigger Publishers, 1983. 144 pp.

2178. Birbalsingh, Frank, ed. *Jahaji Bhai: An Anthology of Indo-Caribbean Literature*. Toronto: TSAR, 1988. 151 pp.

2179. Brown, Stewart, ed. *Caribbean New Voices*. Harlow, Eng.: Longman Caribbean, 1995– [vol. 1–].

2180. Butcher, Maggie, ed. *Tibisiri: Caribbean Writers and Critics*. Sydney, N.S.W.: Dangaroo Press, 1989. 138 pp.

2181. Livingston, James T., ed. *Caribbean Rhythms: The Emerging English Literature of the West Indies.* New York: Washington Square Press, 1974. 379 pp.

2182. Saakana, Amon Saba, ed. *New Planet: Anthology of Modern Caribbean Writing.* London: Caribbean Culture International, 1978. 93 pp.

2183. Walmsley, Anne, and Nick Caistor, eds. *Facing the Sea: A New Anthology from the Caribbean Region.* London: Heinemann, 1986. 151 pp.

Poetry

Poetry: General

2184. Dathorne, Oscar Ronald, ed. *Caribbean Verse: An Anthology.* London: Heinemann, 1979. 131 pp. Reprint of the 1967 ed.

2185. Figueroa, John J., ed. *Caribbean Voices: An Anthology of West Indian Poetry.* 2d ed. London: Evans, 1982– [vol. 1–].

2186. Forde, Alfred Nathaniel, ed. *Talk of the Tamarinds: An Anthology of Poetry.* London: E. Arnold, 1971. 104 pp.

2187. Giuseppe, Neville, and Undine Giuseppe, eds. *Out For Stars: An Anthology of Poetry.* London: Macmillan, 1975–1976. 2 vols.

2188. Seymour, Arthur J., ed. *Anthology of West Indian Poetry.* Rev. ed. Georgetown: [s.n.], 1957. 99 pp.

2189. Wilson, Donald G., ed. *New Ships: An Anthology of West Indian Poems.* London: Oxford University Press, 1975. 96 pp.

Poetry: Twentieth Century

2190. Agard, John, and Grace Nichols, eds. *A Caribbean Dozen: Poems from Caribbean Poets.* Cambridge, MA: Candlewick Press, 1994. 93 pp.

2191. Berry, James, ed. *Bluefoot Traveller: Poetry by Westindians in Britain.* Rev. ed. London: Harrap, 1985. 64 pp. Reprint of the 1981 ed. First ed. (1976) has title *Bluefoot Traveller: An Anthology of Westindian Poets in Britain.*

2192. ———. *News for Babylon: The Chatto Book of Westindian-British Poetry*. London: Chatto and Windus, 1984. 212 pp.

2193. Brown, Stewart, ed. *Caribbean Poetry Now*. 2d ed. New York: E. Arnold, 1992. 212 pp.

2194. Brown, Stewart, and Ian McDonald, eds. *The Heinemann Book of Caribbean Poetry*. Portsmouth, NH: Heinemann, 1992. 236 pp.

2195. Brown, Stewart, Mervyn Morris and Gordon Rohlehr, eds. *Voiceprint: An Anthology of Oral and Related Poetry from the Caribbean*. Harlow, Eng.: Longman Caribbean, 1989. 276 pp.

2196. Burnett, Paula, ed. *The Penguin Book of Caribbean Verse in English*. New York: Penguin, 1986. 447 pp.

2197. Dawes, Neville, and Anthony McNeill, eds. *The Caribbean Poem: An Anthology of Fifty Caribbean Voices*. [s.l.]: Carifesta 76, 1976. 112 pp.

2198. Espinet, Ramabai, ed. *Creation Fire: A CAFRA Anthology of Caribbean Women's Poetry*. Toronto: Sister Vision, 1990. 371 pp.

2199. Hippolyte, Kendel, ed. *So Much Poetry in We People: An Anthology of Performance Poetry*. [s.l.]: Eastern Caribbean Popular Theatre Organisation, 1990. 76 pp.

2200. Jekyll, Walter, and Neil Philip, eds. *I Have News: Rhymes from the Caribbean*. New York: Lothrop, Lee and Shepard, 1994. 1 vol. (unpaged).

2201. Jones-Hendrickson, Simon B., ed. *Of Masks and Mysteries: Poems*. Frederiksted, VI: Eastern Caribbean Institute, 1993. 61 pp. Poems by Michael H. Lythoe, Vincent O. Cooper, Earthla Arthur, Simon B. Jones-Hendrickson, Lillian Sutherland, and Regina Joseph.

2202. Kellman, Tony, ed. *Crossing Water: Contemporary Poetry of the English-Speaking Caribbean*. Greenfield Center, NY: Greenfield Review Press, 1992. 219 pp.

2203. Markham, Edward Archibald, ed. *Hinterland: Caribbean Poetry from the West Indies and Britain*. Newcastle upon Tyne, Eng.: Bloodaxe, 1989. 335 pp.

2204. Mordecai, Pamela, and Grace Walker Gordon, eds. *Sunsong Tide Rising: Anthology*. San Juan, Trinidad: Longman Caribbean, 1994. 184 pp.

2205. Pollard, Velma, ed. *Nine West Indian Poets: An Anthology*. London: Collins, 1980. 95 pp.

2206. Ramchand, Kenneth, and Cecil Gray, eds. *West Indian Poetry: An Anthology*. 2d rev. ed. Harlow, Eng.: Longman Caribbean, 1989. 238 pp.

2207. Salkey, Andrew, ed. *Breaklight: The Poetry of the Caribbean*. Garden City, NY: Doubleday, 1972. 265 pp. British ed. has title *Breaklight: An Anthology of Caribbean Poetry*.

Fiction

Fiction: General

2208. Dathorne, Oscar Ronald, ed. *Caribbean Narrative: An Anthology of West Indian Writing*. London: Heinemann, 1979. 247 pp. Reprint of the 1966 ed.

2209. D'Costa, Jean, and Velma Pollard, eds. *Over Our Way*. 2d ed., rev. and enl. Port of Spain: Longman Caribbean, 1994. 254 pp.

2210. Giuseppe, Neville, and Undine Giuseppe, eds. *Backfire: A Collection of Short Stories from the Caribbean*. London: Macmillan Caribbean, 1976. 114 pp. Reprint of the 1973 ed.

2211. Mouttet, Leslie et al. *Love and the Hardware Store and Other Stories*. Port of Spain: Imprint Publications, 1977. 128 pp.

2212. Ramchand, Kenneth, ed. *West Indian Narrative: An Introductory Anthology*. Walton-on-Thames, Eng.: Nelson Caribbean, 1988. 214 pp. Reprint of the 1980 (2d. rev.) ed.

2213. Salkey, Andrew, ed. *Caribbean Essays: An Anthology*. London: Evans, 1973. 131 pp.

2214. ———. *Caribbean Prose: An Anthology*. London: Evans, 1967. 127 pp.

2215. ———. *Stories from the Caribbean: An Anthology.* 2d ed. London: Elek, 1972. 257 pp. First ed. has title *Island Voices.*

2216. ———. *West Indian Stories.* London: Faber, 1968. 224 pp. Reprint of the 1960 ed.

Fiction: Twentieth Century

2217. Acosta, Blanca, Samuel Goldberg and Ileana Sanz, eds. *Caribbean Stories: Barbados, Guyana, Jamaica, Trinidad-Tobago/Cuentos del Caribe.* Havana: Casa de las Américas, 1977. 274 pp.

2218. Brown, Stewart, ed. *Caribbean New Wave: Contemporary Short Stories.* Portsmouth, NH: Heinemann, 1990. 181 pp.

2219. Carr, Ernest A. et al., eds. *Caribbean Anthology of Short Stories.* Kingston: Pioneer Press, 1953. 146 pp.

2220. Fraser, Robert ed. *This Island Place: Short Stories.* London: Harrap, 1981. 115 pp.

2221. Marland, Michael ed. *Caribbean Stories: Fifteen Short Stories by Writers from the Caribbean.* London: Longman, 1978. 152 pp.

2222. Morris, Mervyn, ed. *The Faber Book of Contemporary Caribbean Short Stories.* Boston, MA: Faber and Faber, 1990. 275 pp.

2223. Ramchand, Kenneth, ed. *Best West Indian Stories.* Kingston: Nelson Caribbean, 1982. 186 pp.

2224. Waters, Erika J., ed. *New Writing from the Caribbean: Selections from the Caribbean Writer.* London: Macmillan Caribbean, 1994. 120 pp.

2225. Wickham, John, ed. *West Indian Stories.* London: Ward Lock Educational, 1981. 136 pp.

Drama

Drama: Twentieth Century

2226. Corsbie, Ken. *Theatre in the Caribbean.* London: Hodder and Stoughton, 1984. 58 pp.

2227. Hill, Errol, ed. *Three Caribbean Plays*. Port of Spain: Longman Caribbean, 1979. 116 pp. During Lunch-Time They Had the Revolution (C. Tipling), Dance Bongo (E. Hill), The Master of Carnival (E. Jarvis, R. Amoroso).

2228. ———. *Plays for Today*. London: Longman, 1985. 233 pp. Ti-Jean and His Brothers (Derek Walcott), An Echo in the Bone (Dennis Scott), Man Better Man (Errol Hill).

2229. Noel, Keith, ed. *Caribbean Plays for Playing*. Portsmouth, NH: Heinemann, 1985. 163 pp.

2230. Waite-Smith, Cicely, et al. *Five West Indian Plays*. Mona, Jamaica: Extra-Mural Dept., University College of the West Indies, 1958. 147 pp. Africa Sling-shot (C. Waite-Smith), The Sea at Dauphin (D. Walcott), Junction Village (D. Archibald), The Harrowing of Benjy (R. Walcott), Wey-wey (E. Hill).

2231. Wilson, Jeanne, ed. *West Indian Plays For Schools*. Kingston: Jamaica Publishing House, 1979. 2 vols.

D. HISTORY AND CRITICISM

General

2232. Baugh, Edward, ed. *Critics on Caribbean Literature: Readings in Literary Criticism*. New York: St. Martin's Press, 1978. 164 pp.

2233. ———. *Language and Literature in the Commonwealth Caribbean*. Kingston: West Indian Association for Commonwealth Literature and Language Studies, 1979. 84 pp.

2234. Brathwaite, Kamau. *Roots*. Ann Arbor, MI: University of Michigan Press, 1993. 304 pp. Reprint of the 1986 ed.

2235. Conference on Critical Approaches to West Indian Literature (1981, St. Thomas, USVI); Knowles, Roberta, and Erika Smilowitz, eds. *Critical Approaches to West Indian Literature*. Charlotte Amalie: Humanities Division, College of the Virgin Islands, 1981. 281 pp.

2236. Conference on West Indian Literature (Ninth, 1989, St. Lucia); Roydon Salick, ed. *The Comic Vision in West Indian Literature*. Marabella, Trinidad: [s.n.], 1993. 207 pp.

2237. Dabydeen, David, ed. *A Handbook for Teaching Caribbean Literature*. London: Heinemann Educational, 1988. 144 pp.

2238. Dabydeen, David, and Nana Wilson-Tagoe, eds. *A Reader's Guide to West Indian and Black British Literature*. London: Hansib, 1988. 182 pp.

2239. Ferguson, Moira. *Colonialism and Gender Relations from Mary Wollstonecraft to Jamaica Kincaid: East Caribbean Connections*. New York: Columbia University Press, 1993. 175 pp.

2240. James, Louis, ed. *The Islands In Between: Essays on West Indian Literature*. London: Oxford University Press, 1968. 166 pp.

2241. Jones, Joseph Jay, and Johanna Jones. *Authors and Areas of the West Indies*. Austin, TX: Steck-Vaughn, 1970. 82 pp.

2242. Juneja, Renu. *Caribbean Transactions: West Indian Culture in Literature*. London: Macmillan Caribbean, 1996. 240 pp.

2243. King, Bruce Alvin, ed. *West Indian Literature*. Hamden, CT: Archon Books, 1979. 247 pp.

2244. Mackey, Nathaniel. *Discrepant Engagement: Dissonance, Cross-Culturality, and Experimental Writing*. New York: Cambridge University Press, 1993. 313 pp.

2245. Moore, Gerald. *The Chosen Tongue: English Writing in the Tropical World*. New York: Harper and Row, 1970. 222 pp.

2246. Ngugi, James. *Homecoming: Essays on African and Caribbean Literature, Culture and Politics*. Westport, CT: L. Hill, 1983. 155 pp. Reprint of the 1972 ed.

2247. Ramchand, Kenneth. *An Introduction to the Study of West Indian Literature*. Kingston: Nelson Caribbean, 1976. 183 pp.

2248. Rohlehr, Gordon. *My Strangled City and Other Essays*. Port of Spain: Longman Trinidad, 1992. 341 pp.

2249. ———. *The Shape of That Hurt and Other Essays*. Port of Spain: Longman Trinidad, 1992. 371 pp.

2250. Smilowitz, Erika, and Roberta Knowles, eds. *Critical Issues in West Indian Literature: Selected Papers from West Indian Litera-*

ture Conferences, 1981–1983. Parkersburg, IA: Caribbean Books, 1984. 136 pp.

2251. Smith, Rowland, ed. *Exile and Tradition: Studies in African and Caribbean Literature*. London: Longman, 1976. 190 pp.

2252. Van Sertima, Ivan. *Caribbean Writers: Critical Essays*. London: New Beacon Press, 1968. 67 pp.

General: Twentieth Century

2253. Acosta, Blanca, ed. *The Literature of the English-Speaking Caribbean*. Havana: Editorial Pueblo y Educación, 1988. 395 pp.

2254. Birbalsingh, Frank. *Passion and Exile: Essays in Caribbean Literature*. London: Hansib, 1988. 186 pp.

2255. ———, ed. *Frontiers of Caribbean Literature in English*. New York: St. Martin's Press, 1996. 206 pp.

2256. Brathwaite, Kamau. *The Love Axe: Developing a Caribbean Aesthetic*. Leeds, Eng.: Peepal Tree Press, 1994. 200 pp.

2257. CARIFESTA Symposium (Fifth, 1992, Port of Spain); Pearl Eintou Springer, ed. *The New Aesthetic and the Meaning of Culture in the Caribbean: The Dream Coming in with the Rain—Proceedings*. Port of Spain: National Carnival Committee, CARIFESTA Secretariat, 1995. 211 pp.

2258. Conference on West Indian Literature (Fourth, 1984, University of the West Indies); Mark A. McWatt, ed. *West Indian Literature and Its Social Context*. Cave Hill, Barbados: Dept. of English, University of the West Indies, 1985. 163 pp.

2259. Conference on West Indian Literature (Second, 1982, University of the West Indies); Edward Baugh, Mervyn Morris, eds. *Progressions: West Indian Literature in the 1970's*. Mona, Jamaica: Dept. of English, University of the West Indies, 1990. 263 pp.

2260. Conference on West Indian Literature (Seventh, 1987, University of Puerto Rico); Lowell Fiet and Faculty of Humanities, University of Puerto Rico, eds. *West Indian Literature and Its Political Context*. Río Piedras, P.R.: University of Puerto Rico, 1988. 223 pp.

2261. Dance, Daryl Cumber. *New World Adams: Conversations with Contemporary West Indian Writers.* 2d ed. Leeds, Eng.: Peepal Tree Press, 1996. 288 pp.

2262. Griffiths, Gareth. *A Double Exile: African and West Indian Writing Between Two Cultures.* London: Boyars, 1978. 205 pp.

2263. International Conference on the Women Writers of the English-Speaking Caribbean (First, 1988, Wellesley College); Selwyn Reginald Cudjoe, ed. *Caribbean Women Writers: Essays.* Wellesley, MA: Cataloux Publications, 1990. 382 pp.

2264. James, Louis. *Writers from the Caribbean.* London: Book Trust, 1990. 38 pp.

2265. Marsh-Lockett, Carol P., ed. *Decolonising Caribbean Literature.* Atlanta, GA: Georgia State University, 1993. 110 pp.

2266. Maximin, Colette. *La parole aux masques: littérature, oralité et culture populaire dans la Caraïbe anglophone au XXe siècle.* Paris: Editions caribéennes, 1991. 287 pp.

2267. Munro, Ian, and Reinhard W. Sander, eds. *Kas-Kas: Interviews with Three Caribbean Writers in Texas—George Lamming, C.L.R. James, Wilson Harris.* Austin, TX: African and Afro-American Research Institute, University of Texas, 1972. 56 pp.

2268. Raiskin, Judith L. *Snow on the Cane Fields: Women's Writing and Creole Subjectivity.* Minneapolis, MN: University of Minnesota Press, 1996. 305 pp.

Poetry

Poetry: General

2269. Baugh, Edward, ed. *The Caribbean Poem.* Kingston: West Indian Association for Commonwealth Literature and Language Studies, 1989. 92 pp.

2270. Chamberlin, J. Edward. *Come Back To Me My Language: Poetry and the West Indies.* Urbana, IL: University of Illinois Press, 1993. 325 pp.

2271. Pearn, Julie. *Poetry in the Caribbean.* London: Hodder and Stoughton, 1985. 60 pp.

Poetry: Twentieth Century

2272. Brathwaite, Kamau. *History of the Voice: The Development of Nation Language in Anglophone Caribbean Poetry*. London: New Beacon Books, 1984. 87 pp.

2273. Brown, Lloyd Wellesley. *West Indian Poetry*. 2d ed. Exeter, NH: Heinemann, 1984. 202 pp.

2274. Chang, Victor L., ed. *Three Caribbean Poets on Their Work: E. Kamau Brathwaite, Mervyn Morris, Lorna Goodison*. Mona, Jamaica: University of the West Indies, Institute of Caribbean Studies, 1993. 68 pp.

2275. Habekost, Christian. *Verbal Riddim: The Politics and Aesthetics of African-Caribbean Dub Poetry*. Atlanta, GA: Rodopi, 1993. 262 pp.

2276. Seymour, Arthur J. *West Indian Poetry: Five Essays*. Georgetown: [s.n.], 1981. 64 pp. Cover title *Studies in West Indian Poetry*.

Fiction

Fiction: General

2277. Broek, Aart G. *Something Rich Like Chocolate: Introduction to Caribbean Prose Writing in English*. Willemstad: Editorial Kooperativo Antiyano "Kolibri," 1985. 317 pp.

2278. Conference of Hispanists (Ninth, 1984, University of the West Indies); Ena V. Thomas, ed. *The Caribbean Novel in Comparison*. St. Augustine, Trinidad/Tobago: Dept. of French and Spanish Literature, University of the West Indies, 1986. 140 pp.

2279. Gilkes, Michael. *The West Indian Novel*. Boston, MA: Twayne, 1981. 168 pp.

2280. Griffith, Glyne A. *Reconstruction, Imperialism and the West Indian Novel*. Kingston: University of the West Indies, 1996. 147 pp.

2281. Kirpal, Viney. *The Third World Novel of Expatriation: A Study of Emigre Fiction by Indian, West African, and Caribbean Writers*. New Delhi: Sterling Publishers, 1989. 174 pp.

2282. O'Callaghan, Evelyn. *Woman Version: Theoretical Approaches to West Indian Fiction by Women*. New York: St. Martin's Press, 1993. 126 pp.

Fiction: Twentieth Century

2283. Cartey, Wilfred G. *Whispers from the Caribbean: I Going Away, I Going Home*. Los Angeles, CA: Center for Afro-American Studies, University of California, 1991. 503 pp.

2284. Jonas, Joyce. *Anancy in the Great House: Ways of Reading West Indian Fiction*. New York: Greenwood Press, 1990. 149 pp.

2285. Joseph, Margaret Paul. *Caliban in Exile: The Outsider in Caribbean Fiction*. New York: Greenwood Press, 1992. 147 pp.

2286. Ramchand, Kenneth. *The West Indian Novel and Its Background*. 2d ed. London: Heinemann, 1983. 310 pp.

Drama

Drama: General

2287. Baugh, Edward, and Mervyn Morris, eds. *Caribbean Theatre*. Kingston: West Indian Association for Commmonwealth Literature and Language Studies, 1986. 79 pp.

2288. Omotoso, Kole. *The Theatrical into Theatre: A Study of the Drama and Theatre of the English-Speaking Caribbean*. London: New Beacon, 1982. 173 pp.

2289. Stone, Judy S. J. *Theatre*. London: Macmillan Caribbean, 1994. 268 pp.

ANTIGUA AND BARBUDA

A. ANTHOLOGIES

2290. Antigua and Barbuda, Ministry of Education and Culture. *Young Antiguans Write: Prize-Winning Selections in Poetry and Prose.* St. John's, Antigua: The Ministry, 1979. 168 pp.

B. HISTORY AND CRITICISM

Sixteenth to Nineteenth Centuries

2291. Ferguson, Moira, ed. *The Hart Sisters: Early African Caribbean Writers, Evangelicals, and Radicals.* Lincoln, NE: University of Nebraska Press, 1993. 214 pp.

C. INDIVIDUAL AUTHORS

2292. *Bernard, Veronica E.* (poet). Pineapple Rhymes, 1989.

2293. *Butler, Lorinda T.* (poet). Antigua Me Come From, 1994.

2294. *Faulkner-Lashley, Jacqueline* (poet). The Highest Joy, 1974.

2295. *Hewlett, Agnes Cecilia,* 1948– (poet). 'Allo et au'voir, 1972.

2296. *Kincaid, Jamaica,* 1949– (novelist, poet, short story writer). Annie, Gwen, Lilly, Pam, and Tulip, 1986–1989; Annie John, 1985–1995; At the Bottom of the River, 1984–1994 (Girl, In the Night, At Last, Wingless Holidays, The Letter From Home, What I have Been Doing Lately, Blackness, My Mother, At the Bottom of the River); Autobiography of My Mother, 1995; Lucy, 1990–1994; A Small Place, 1988–1989.

2297. Ferguson, Moira. *Jamaica Kincaid: Where the Land Meets the Body.* Charlottesville, VA: University Press of Virginia, 1994. 206 pp.

2298. Simmons, Diane. *Jamaica Kincaid*. New York: Twayne, 1994. 155 pp.

2299. *McDonald, Donald* (poet). Songs of an Islander, 1918.

2300. *McDonald, Hilda,* 1917– (poet). Sunflakes and Stardust, 1956.

2301. *Prince, Althea,* 1945– (short story writer). Ladies of the Night and Other Stories, 1993.

2302. *Prince, Ralph,* 1923– (poet, short story writer). Jewels of the Sun, 1979.

2303. *Richards, Novelle Hamilton,* 1917– (novelist, poet). Tropic Gems, 1971; The Twilight Hour, 1971; Vines of Freedom, 1982.

2304. *Westcott, Lee H. C.,* 1920– (poet). The Garden of Life, 1950–1982.

BAHAMAS

A. ANTHOLOGIES

General

2305. College of the Bahamas, ed. *Bahamian Anthology*. London: Macmillan Caribbean, 1984. 172 pp.

2306. Nassau Poetry Conference (First, 1985, College of the Bahamas); Eunice Bethel Humblestone, ed. *Junction: An Anthology of Writing by Participants in the First Nassau Poetry Conference, May 1985*. London: Macmillan Caribbean, 1987. 120 pp. Poems and short stories.

2307. Sanz Cabrera, Ileana, ed. *From the Shallow Seas: Bahamian Creative Writing Today*. Havana: Casa de las Américas, 1993. 143 pp. Prose, poetry, and a play.

2308. Turner, Telcine, ed. *Climbing Clouds: Stories and Poems from the Bahamas*. London: Macmillan Caribbean, 1988. 96 pp.

Poetry

2309. Culmer, Jack, ed. *A Book of Bahamian Verse*. [2d ed.]. London: J. Culmer, 1948. 41 pp.

2310. Sawyer, Tyrone G., ed. *Bahamian Odyssey: A Book of Island Poetry and Illustrations*. Decatur, GA: National Graphics, 1989. 93 pp.

Fiction

2311. Turner, Telcine, ed. *Once Below a Time: Bahamian Stories*. London: Macmillan Caribbean, 1988. 80 pp.

B. HISTORY AND CRITICISM

2312. Dahl, Anthony George. *Literature of the Bahamas, 1724–1992: The March Towards National Identity.* Lanham, MD: University Press of America, 1995. 219 pp.

C. INDIVIDUAL AUTHORS

2313. *Brown, Barbara L.* (poet). Poems Soothe the Soul, 1988.

2314. *Brown, Raymond Waldin* (poet, short story writer). The Bahamas in Poetry and Prose, 1960–1978.

2315. *Brusch, Clayton Alexander* (poet). Of Human Condition, 1986; Sharing the Caring, 1985.

2316. *Catalyn, James J.* (playwright, poet, short story writer). An A Don' Mean Cola, 1986; Expressing Myself, 1979–1986; Laughin' At Wesef, 1986; 'Nough Said, 1987; Readings Roast and Other Writings, 1986.

2317. *Christie, Henry Christopher* (poet, short story writer). The Man With the Wart, 1928.

2318. *Christie, Huntley P.* (short story writer). Intrigue and Mystery in the Bahamas, 1988.

2319. *Dahl, Tony* (poet). Grouper Jump an' Pop duh Line, 1986.

2320. *Dupuch, Eugene,* 1912–1981 (short story writer). Smoky Joe Says, 1936.

2321. *Eneas, Cleveland W.,* 1915– (novelist, short story writer). Bain Town, 1976–1988; Tuskgegee, Ra! Ra!, 1986 (Autobiographical).

2322. *Gardiner, Beatrice I.* (poet). The Other Footprint, 1992.

2323. *Gilcud, Turpie* (poet). Treasures from My heart, 1986; The Winds of Fresh Creek, 1985.

2324. *Johnson, Robert Elliott,* 1948– (poet). The Road, 1972.

2325. *Johnson, William R.* (short story writer). Seapath and Other Stories, 1980.

2326. *Jordan, Portia Brown* (novelist). The Crack of Dawn, 1991.

2327. *Knowles, Dennis J.,* 1948–1980 (poet). Refracted Thought, 1976.

2328. *Miller, Percival A.* (poet). At Summer's End, 1980.

2329. *Missick, Rupert,* 1940– (poet, short story writer). Naked Moon, 1970; No Cure For Sure, 1975.

2330. *Pinder, Wilfred Hannah,* 1936– (poet). Poetry for All Occasions, 1973; Who Am I?, 1980.

2331. *Pintard, Michael C.* (poet). Still Standing, 1995.

2332. *Rahming, Patrick,* 1944– (poet). Reflections, 1976; Thoughts in Black and White, 1986.

2333. *Riley, Sandra* (novelist, short story writer). Bloody Bay/ The Captain's Ladies, 1980; The Lucayans, 1991; Sometimes Towards Eden, 1986.

2334. *Roberts, Freda* (poet). Bahama Bounty, 1980.

2335. *Robinson, Reynold* (poet). Andrumeda, 1990.

2336. *Russell, Keith A.* (short story writer). Passage of a Native Son, 1988.

2337. *Saunders, Ashley B.,* 1945– (poet). The Night of the Lionhead, 1979; Searching for Atlantis, 1980; The Sun Makes it Red, 1977; Voyage into the Sunset, 1976.

2338. *Smith, Obediah Michael* (poet). Acts, 1983; Bicentennial Blues, 1977; Forty-three Poems, 1979; Fruits from Africa, 1987; Ice Cubes, 1982.

2339. *Tatem, Colin,* 1942– (short story writer). Ordeal At Sea, 1975 (Ordeal At Sea, The Homecoming, The Bombara Incident, Russell's Point).

2340. *Tertullien, Mizpah C.,* 1929– (short story writer). Old Stories and Riddles, 1977.

2341. *Tree, Iris,* 1897–1968 (poet). The Marsh Picnic, 1966; Poems, 1919–1920; The Traveller and Other Poems, 1927.

2342. *Turner, Telcine* (playwright, poet). Song of the Surreys, 1977; Woman Take Two, 1987–1994.

2343. *Wallace, Susan J.,* 1935– (playwright, poet, short story writer). Back Home, 1975–1992; Bahamian Scene, 1970–1972; Island Echoes, 1973.

2344. *Williams, Mackey* (playwright, poet). Four Native Plays for Stage and Radio, 1984; A Toast to You, 1982.

BARBADOS

A. BIBLIOGRAPHIES AND BIO-BIBLIOGRAPHIES

2345. Brathwaite, Kamau. *Barbados Poetry, 1661–1979: A Checklist— Books, Pamphlets, Broadsheets.* Mona, Jamaica: Savacou Publications, 1979. 16 pp.

B. ANTHOLOGIES

2346. Creative Writers Association (Cave Hill, Barbados). *My Slice of the Pie: An Anthology of Verse and Prose.* Cave Hill, Barbados: CREWA, 1988. 30 pp.

C. INDIVIDUAL AUTHORS

Sixteenth to Nineteenth Centuries

2347. Chapman, Matthew James, 1796–1865 (poet). Barbados and Other Poems, 1833.

Twentieth Century

2348. *Beadon, Colin Leslie,* 1935– (short story writer). Escapades and Islands, 1995.

2349. *Blackman, Peter* (poet). My Song Is for All Men, 1952–1970.

2350. *Brathwaite, Kamau,* 1930– (novelist, poet). The Arrivants, 1973–1981; Barabajan Poems, 1994; Black and Blues, 1976–1995; Days and Nights, 1975; DreamStories, 1994; French Town Rock, 1994; JAH Music, 1986; Masks, 1968; Middle Passages, 1992–1993; Mother Poem, 1977; Odale's Choice, 1967; Other Exiles, 1975; The Poet and His Place in Barbadian Culture, 1994; Rights of Passage, 1967; Roots, 1986–1993; Sappho Sakyi's Meditations, 1989; Shar/Hurricane Poem, 1990; Sun

Poem, 1982; Third World Poems, 1983; Trench Town Rock, 1994; X/Self, 1987; The Zea Mexican Diary, 1993 (Autobiographical).

2351. Brathwaite, Doris Monica. *EKB: His Published Prose and Poetry, 1948–1986—A Checklist.* Mona, Jamaica: Savacou, 1986. 139 pp.

2352. Brown, Stewart, ed. *The Art of Kamau Brathwaite.* Bridgend, Wales: Seren, 1995. 275 pp.

2353. Fraser, Robert, and Yolande Cantu, ed. *Edward Brathwaite's "Masks" : A Critical View.* London: Collins, 1981. 40 pp. Cover title *A Critical View on Edward Brathwaite's "Masks."*

2354. Lewis, Maureen Warner. *E. Kamau Brathwaite's "Masks": Essays and Annotations.* Rev. ed. Mona, Jamaica: Institute of Caribbean Studies, University of the West Indies, 1992. 98 pp. First ed. (1977) has title *Notes to "Masks."*

2355. Rohlehr, Gordon. *Pathfinder: Black Awakening in "The Arrivants" of Edward Kamau Brathwaite.* Tunapuna, Trinidad: G. Rohlehr, 1981. 344 pp.

See also #2274.

2356. *Callender, Timothy,* 1936– (novelist, playwright, short story writer). How Music Came to the Ainchan People, 1979; Independence and Freedom, 1987 (Grandfather Willia and Mr. Hitler, Independence and Freedom, Independence); It So Happen, 1975–1991; Schoolboys, 1984; The Timothy Callender Collected Christmas Stories, 1994 (Tatanka Yotanka, ed.).

2357. *Clarke, Austin,* 1934– (novelist, poet, short story writer). Among Thistles and Thorns, 1965–1984; The Bigger Light, 1975; Growing Up Stupid under the Union Jack, 1980; In This City, 1992; The Meeting Point, 1967–1972; Nine Men Who Laughed, 1986; The Prime Minister, 1977–1994; Proud Empires, 1986–1989; Storm of Fortune, 1973; The Survivors of the Crossing, 1964; There Are No Elders, 1993; When He Was Free and Young and He Used to Wear Silks, 1971–1973; When Women Rule, 1985.

2358. Algoo-Baksh, Stella. *Austin C. Clarke: A Biography.* Toronto: ECW Press, 1994. 234 pp.

2359. Brown, Lloyd Wellesley. *El Dorado and Paradise: Canada and the Caribbean in Austin Clarke's Fiction.* London, Ont.: University of Western Ontario, Centre for Social and Humanistic Studies, 1989. 207 pp.

2360. *Collymore, Frank A.,* 1893–1980 (poet, short story writer). Beneath the Casaurinas, 1945; Collected Poems, 1959; Flotsam, 1948; The Man Who Loved Attending Funerals and Other Stories, 1993 (Harold Barratt, Reinhard Sander, eds.); Rhymed Ruminations on the Fauna of Barbados, 1968; Selected Poems, 1971; Thirty Poems, 1944.

2361. *Drayton, Geoffrey,* 1924– (novelist, poet, short story writer). Christopher, 1959–1979; Three Meridians, 1950; Zohara, 1961.

2362. *Forde, Alfred Nathaniel,* 1923– (playwright, poet, short story writer). Canes by the Roadside, 1951; The Passing Cloud, 1966.

2363. *Greenidge, Gracelyn* (poet). The Children's Voices, 1985; Echoes, 1993.

2364. *Hamilton, Bruce,* 1900–1975 (novelist, poet). The Brighton Murder Trial, 1937; Dead Reckoning/Middle Class Murder, 1936–1938; Hanging Judge, 1948; So Sad, So Fresh, 1952; To be Hanged, 1930; Too Much of Water, 1958–1983; Traitor's Way, 1938.

2365. *Henfrey, June,* 1939–1992 (short story writer). Coming Home and Other Stories, 1994.

2366. *Kellman, Tony,* 1955– (poet, short story writer). The Broken Sun, 1984; The Coral Rooms, 1994; In Depths of Burning Light, 1982; The Long Gap, 1996; Watercourse, 1990.

2367. *Kwamdela, Odimumba,* 1943– (poet). Bitter Soul, 1970; A Black British Soldier, 1969–1986 (Autobiographical); Blood-boiling Black Blues, 1983–1989; The Grassroots Philosopher, 1977–1992; Niggers . . . This Is Canada, 1971–1986; The Prophet Next Door, 1981–1992; Raining Ruins and Rockstones, 1992; The Righteous Blackman, 1972; Soul in the Wilderness, 1970–1993.

2368. *Lamming, George,* 1927– (novelist, poet, short story writer). The Emigrants, 1954–1994; In the Castle of My Skin, 1953–1991; Natives of My Person, 1971–1992; Of Age and Innocence,

1958–1981; The Pleasures of Exile, 1960–1992 (Autobiographical); Season of Adventure, 1960–1979; Water with Berries, 1971–1973.

2369. Gikandi, Simon. *George Lamming's "In the Castle of My Skin."* Nairobi: Heinemann Kenya, 1984. 67 pp.

2370. Lamming, George, Richard Drayton and Andaiye, eds. *Conversations with George Lamming: Essays, Addresses and Interviews, 1953–1990.* London: Karia Press, 1992. 300 pp.

2371. Nair, Supriya. *Caliban's Curse: George Lamming and the Revisioning of History.* Ann Arbor, MI: University of Michigan Press, 1996.

2372. Paquet, Sandra Pouchet. *The Novels of George Lamming.* Exeter, NH: Heinemann, 1982. 130 pp.

See also #2267.

2373. *Layne-Clark, Jeannette* (poet, short story writer). Bajan Badinage, 1993.

2374. *Savory, Elaine* (poet). Flame Tree Time, 1993.

2375. *St. John, Bruce,* 1923– (poet). At Kairi House, 1975; Bumbatuk One, 1982; Celebrating Lovers, Family, Community, 1981; Joyce and Eros and Varia, 1976.

2376. *Vaughan, Hilton A.,* 1901– (poet). Sandy Lane and Other Poems, 1985.

2377. *Ward, Arnold Francis* (poet, short story writer). Bajan Love, 1992; Knock! and Wait, 1991; Sandbox, 1985.

2378. *Wickham, John,* 1923– (short story writer). Casuarina Row, 1974; Discoveries, 1993; World Without End, 1982 (Autobiographical).

2379. *Worrell, Vernon,* 1952– (poet). A Rumpunch Sunset, 1994; Under the Flambo, 1986.

BELIZE

A. ANTHOLOGIES

2380. Belize, Ministry of Education. *Voices of Belizean Children*. Belmopan, Belize: UNICEF, 1990. 93 pp.

2381. Belize, Ministry of Education, Sports, and Culture. *Belizean Poets*. Belmopan, Belize: The Ministry, 1980– [vol. 1–].

2382. Musa, Yasser, Kiren Shoman and Simone Waight. *Shots from the Heart: Three Young Belizean Poets*. Benque Viejo del Carmen: Cubola Productions, 1991. 81 pp. Just-Things (Y. Musa), Moments (K. Shoman), Courage (S. Waight).

B. INDIVIDUAL AUTHORS

2383. *Arana, Milton E.* (short story writer). Cry Wolf, 1993.

2384. *Auxillou, Ray* (novelist). Belize Secret Service Sarin Project, 1992; The Belize Vortex, 1989; The Blue Hole, 1990; Mafia Double Cross/The Belize Connection, 1988.

2385. *Bradley, Leo,* 1926– (poet, short story writer). Belizean Flavour, 1991 (The Way of the Bridge, My Morning Prayer, Mango Melody, This Land I Love, The Drama of Life, The Road, His Trouble, Santapi, The Case of the Ruined Temple, Sum Umbra, His Christmas Animal, Belizean Lullaby, The Black Boat, Marimba Tunes, The Tank and the Tiger, My Maya Land, Two Boys and One Christmas, Tropical Hurricane).

2386. *Burgess, Karl Luther* (poet). Poems, 1991.

2387. *Cano, Luis E.,* 1927– (poet). The Middle Way, 1981.

2388. *Delsoin, Theresa* (poet). Perceptions of the Human Condition, 1993.

2389. *Edgell, Zee* (novelist, short story writer). Beka Lamb, 1982–1986; In Times Like These, 1991.

2390. *Ellis, Zoila, 1957–* (short story writer). On Heroes, Lizards and Passion, 1988.

2391. *Esquivel, Kathleen Levy* (novelist). Under the Shade, 1993.

2392. *Gann, Mary* (short story writer). Caribbean Adventures and Other Stories, 1937.

2393. *Godfrey, Glenn D., 1949–* (novelist, poet). The Sinners' Bossanova, 1987.

2394. *Hernández, Felica* (short story writer). Those Ridiculous Years and Other Garifuna Stories, 1988.

2395. *Hyde, Evan X.* (playwright, poet). Feelings, 1975; North Amerikkan Blues, 1971.

2396. *King, Emory* (novelist). Belize 1798, the Road to Glory, 1991.

2397. *Lemus, Veronica* (short story writer). The Old Woman and the Animals, 1992.

2398. *Muhammad, Sakinah Carol* (poet). Rain Lover, 1990.

2399. *Ramirez, Luke E.* (poet). The Poems I Write, 1990.

2400. *Ruiz Puga, David Nicolás* (short story writer). Old Benque, 1990.

2401. *Usher, Edd P.* (poet). Just As It Is, 1992.

2402. *Young, Colville N.* (poet, short story writer). Caribbean Corner Calling, 1988; From One Caribbean Corner, 1983; Pataki Full, 1991–1993.

BERMUDA

A. ANTHOLOGIES

Poetry

2403. Griffith, William ed. *Bermuda Troubadours: An Anthology of Verse*. New York: C. Kendall and W. Sharp, 1935. 91 pp.

2404. Lightbourne, Ronald, ed. *This Is My Country: Prize Winning Poetry from Bermuda*. Southampton, Bermuda: Bermuda for Bermudians, 1978. 50 pp.

2405. Seymour, Stanley, ed. *Bermuda Folklore and Calypso Poems*. London: Avon, 1995. 119 pp.

Fiction

2406. Barry, Angela et al., eds. *An Isle So Long Unknown: Short Stories*. Devonshire, Bermuda: Bermuda Writers' Collective, 1993. 212 pp.

2407. Bermuda Writers' Collective. *Palmetto Wine: Short Stories*. Devonshire, Bermuda: The Collective, 1990. 149 pp. Waiting Room (Frances Drewery), Hot Sauce. Sunday Mornings (Meredith Ebbin), Saturday Night Out, Tea at Fayes's (Cheryl Peck-Ball), Brothers, You're the Nicest . . . Nicest (Margaret Carter), Tora. Consummation (Nelda L. Simons), Room for Excitement (T. James Hogan), Marc (Louise Lamphier), Layers (Rawle Frederick), Song for Man. A Cherry for Christmas (Angela Berry).

B. INDIVIDUAL AUTHORS

Sixteenth to Nineteenth Centuries

2408. *Tucker, Nathaniel,* 1750–1807 (poet). The Anchoret, 1776–1846; The Bermudian, 1774–1982; The Complete Published Poems of Nathaniel Tucker, 1973 (Lewis Leary, ed.).

Twentieth Century

2409. *Bean, Judyann* (poet). Life's Changes, 1980.

2410. *Blackburne, Robin* (poet). Vintage versage, 1984.

2411. *Darrell, Dorian* (poet). Words Add New Meaning to Life, 1976.

2412. *Morse-Brown, Sam* (short story writer). A Dog Called Bethlehem, 1978.

2413. *Rouja, Sandra Taylor* (short story writer). The St. Georges Dream, 1988.

2414. *Tucker, Terry* (playwright, short story writer). Hang the Witch High/The False Ebony Tree, 1977; Rendezvous with Destiny, 1958; The Unravished Bride, 1970–1973.

CAYMAN ISLANDS

A. INDIVIDUAL AUTHORS

2415. *Barnett, Curtis L. E.* (poet). Something About Us, 1978.

2416. *Fuller, Robert Sevier* (short story writer). Duppies Is, 1967–1981.

2417. *McField, Frank Swarres* (playwright). Time Longer Dan Rope, 1979.

2418. *Turen, Teppo,* 1919– (novelist, short story writer). The Invulnerable Rulers of Banner Reef, 1966.

DOMINICA

A. ANTHOLOGIES

Poetry

2419. Casimir, Joseph Raphael Ralph, ed. *Poesy: An Anthology of Dominica Verse*. Bridgetown: Advocate, 1948. 4 vols.

2420. Jolly, Clement S., ed. *A Rainbow of Delight: Poems*. Roseau, Dominica: [s.n.], 1993. 78 pp.

2421. Kwashi, Nii, ed. *Rampart II: As We Ponder—Poems*. Roseau, Dominica: Frontline Co-operative, 1988. 35 pp.

Fiction

2422. Lazare, Alick, ed. *Dominican Short Stories*. Roseau: Arts Council of Dominica, 1974– [vol. 1–]. Vol. 1. The Case of the Dead Chicken (Eleanor Roberts), Where Vultures Gather (Joan Bernard), The Bamboo Flute (Lennox Honeychurch), Toubac (Useline T. Pascal), Dog Trap (C. Seraphine), The Morning After (Anna Burnette), The Jêre (Mark Sylvester).

B. INDIVIDUAL AUTHORS

2423. *Allfrey, Phyllis Shand,* 1915–1986 (novelist, poet, short story writer). In Circles, 1940; The Orchid House, 1953–1992; Palm and Oak, 1950–1974.

    2424. Paravisini-Gebert, Lizabeth. *Phyllis Shand Allfrey: A Caribbean Life*. New Brunswick, NJ: Rutgers University Press, 1996. 325 pp.

2425. *Baptiste, Judith V.* (poet). Antillean Viewpoint from a Caribbean Perspective in Support of (O.E.C.S.) Unity and Tourism/Caribbean Viewpoint, 1992.

2426. *Bully, Alwin,* 1935– (playwright). J.D., D-J., 1984.

2427. *Casimir, Joseph Raphael Ralph,* 1898– (poet). Africa Arise and Other Poems, 1967; Dominica (and Other Poems), 1968; Farewell (and Other Poems), 1971; Freedom Poems, 1987; A Little Kiss and Other Poems, 1968; Pater Noster and Other Poems, 1967.

2428. *Daway, Dawen* (poet). We Are Fighting, 1983.

2429. *Douglas, Ian,* 1970– (poet). Inspiring Poems, 1987 (with Mervin Paul).

2430. *Grell, Jane* (poet). Doctor Knickerbocker and Other Poems, 1994.

2431. *Hawys, Stephen,* 1878–1968 (poet). Dominican Lyrics, 1963; Egyptian Love, 1924.

2432. *Jolly, Clement S.* (novelist). Rainbow Man, 1993.

2433. *Lockhart, Anthony* (short story writer). Man in the Hills, 1987 (Man in the Hills, Burning an Illusion Tonight, Sic Semper Tyrannis, A Letter to a Friend).

2434. *Paul, Mervin,* 1969– (poet). Inspiring Poems, 1987 (with Ian Douglas).

2435. *Polydore, Kay* (poet). Pause to Ponder, 1992; Reflect and Chuckle, 1985; The Sublime and the Facetious, 1991.

2436. *Rabess, Gregory,* 1953– (poet). Eruptions, 1983.

2437. *Rhys, Jean,* 1890–1979 (novelist, poet, short story writer). After Leaving Mr. MacKenzie, 1931–1990; Jean Rhys: The Collected Short Stories, 1976–1992; Jean Rhys: The Complete Novels, 1985 (Voyage in the Dark [1934], Postures/Quartet [1929], After Leaving Mr. MacKenzie, Good Morning, Midnight [1939], Wide Sargasso Sea [1966]); The Left Bank and Other Stories, 1927–1984; Let Them Call It Jazz and Other Stories, 1995; The Lonely Ones, 1956; My Day, 1975; Quartet/Postures, 1928–1994; Sleep It Off Lady, 1976–1981; Smile Please: An Unfinished Autobiography, 1979–1983; Tales of the Wide Caribbean, 1985 (Kenneth Ramchand, ed.); Tigers Are Better-Looking, 1968–1981; Wide Sargasso Sea, 1966–1994.

2438. Augier, Carole. *Jean Rhys: Life and Work*. Boston, MA: Little, Brown, 1991. 762 pp.

2439. ———. *Jean Rhys*. New York: Viking, 1985. 125 pp.

2440. Carr, Helen. *Jean Rhys*. London: British Council, 1996. 112 pp.

2441. Davidson, Arnold E. *Jean Rhys*. New York: Ungar Pub. Co., 1985. 165 pp.

2442. Emery, Mary Lou. *Jean Rhys at World's End: Novels of Colonial and Sexual Exile*. Austin, TX: University of Texas Press, 1990. 219 pp.

2443. Frickey, Pierrette M., ed. *Critical Perspectives on Jean Rhys*. Washington, DC: Three Continents Press, 1990. 235 pp.

2444. Harrison, Nancy R. *Jean Rhys and the Novel as Women's Text*. Chapel Hill, NC: University of North Carolina Press, 1988. 289 pp.

2445. Hemmerechts, Kristien. *A Plausible Story and a Plausible Way of Telling It: A Structuralist Analysis of Jean Rhys's Novels*. New York: P. Lang, 1987. 460 pp.

2446. Howells, Coral Ann. *Jean Rhys*. New York: St. Martin's Press, 1991. 171 pp.

2447. James, Louis. *Jean Rhys*. London: Longman, 1978. 74 pp.

2448. James, Selma. *The Ladies and the Mammies: Jane Austen and Jean Rhys*. Bristol, Eng.: Falling Wall Press, 1983. 96 pp.

2449. Jordis, Christine. *Jean Rhys: qui êtes-vous?* Paris: La Manufacture, 1990. 222 pp. Includes an interview by David Plante.

2450. Kloepfer, Deborah Kelly. *The Unspeakable Mother: Forbidden Discourse in Jean Rhys and H. D.* Ithaca, NY: Cornell University Press, 1989. 191 pp. Comparison with Hilda Doolittle.

2451. Le Gallez, Paula. *The Rhys Woman*. New York: St. Martin's Press, 1990. 183 pp.

2452. Malcolm, Cheryl Alexander, and David Malcolm. *Jean Rhys: A Study of the Short Fiction*. New York: Twayne, 1996. 144 pp.

2453. Mellown, Elgin W. *Jean Rhys: A Descriptive and Annotated Bibliography of Works and Criticism*. New York: Garland, 1984. 218 pp.

2454. Nebeker, Helen. *Jean Rhys, Woman in Passage: A Critical Study of the Novels of Jean Rhys*. St. Albans, VT: Eden Press Women's Publications, 1981. 223 pp.

2455. O'Connor, Teresa F. *Jean Rhys: The West Indian Novels*. New York: New York University Press, 1986. 247 pp.

2456. Rhys, Jean, Francis Wyndham and Diana Melly, eds. *Letters 1931–1966*. Harmondsworth [Eng.]: Penguin, 1985. 313 pp. Reprint of the 1964 ed.

2457. Staley, Thomas F. *Jean Rhys: A Critical Study*. Austin, TX: University of Texas Press, 1979. 140 pp.

2458. Wolfe, Peter. *Jean Rhys*. Boston, MA: Twayne, 1980. 186 pp.

2459. *Williams, Albert,* 1962– (poet). One Dominica, 1985.

2460. *Williams, Augustus* (poet). Today I Rise, 1991.

GRENADA

A. ANTHOLOGIES

General

General: Twentieth Century

2461. Ross, Jacob et al. *Callaloo: A Grenada Anthology*. London: Young World Books, 1984. 108 pp.

Poetry

Poetry: Twentieth Century

2462. Searle, Chris. *Words Unchained: Language and Revolution in Grenada*. Totowa, NJ: Zed Books, 1984. 260 pp.

B. INDIVIDUAL AUTHORS

Twentieth Century

2463. *Buffong, Jean* (novelist, short story writer). Jump-Up-and-Kiss Me, 1990 (with Nellie Payne); Snowflakes in the Sun, 1995; Under the Silk Cotton Tree, 1992–1993.

2464. *Charles, Bernadette M.* (poet). Slave Spirit Speaks, 1993.

2465. *Collins, Merle* (novelist, poet, short story writer). Angel, 1987–1988; Because the Dawn Breaks, 1985; The Colour of Forgetting, 1995; Rain Darling, 1990; Rotten Pomerack, 1992.

2466. *Franklyn, Omowale David* (poet). Tongue of Another Drum, 1994.

2467. *Humfrey, Michael,* 1936– (novelist). A Kind of Armour, 1985; No Tears for Massa's Day, 1987; Portrait of a Sea Urchin, 1979 (Autobiographical); A Shadow in the Weave, 1986–1987.

2468. *Paterson, Maurice* (novelist, short story writer). Big Sky/Little Bullet, 1992; So Far So Mad, 1994.

2469. *Payne, Nellie* (short story writer). Jump-Up-and-Kiss-Me, 1990 (with Jean Buffong).

GUYANA

A. BIBLIOGRAPHIES AND BIO-BIBLIOGRAPHIES

2470. McDowell, Robert Eugene. *Bibliography of Literature from Guyana*. Arlington, TX: Sable, 1975. 117 pp.

B. ANTHOLOGIES

General

2471. Searwar, Lloyd et al, eds. *They Came in Ships: An Anthology of Indo-Guyanese Imaginative Writing*. Leeds, Eng.: Peepal Tree Press, 1996.

General: Twentieth Century

2472. Michael, Ras, ed. *Survival: New Writing from Guyana*. Georgetown: Demerara Publishers, 1988. 64 pp.

2473. National History and Arts Council (Guyana). *Independence Ten: Guyanese Writing, 1966–1976*. Georgetown: The Council, 1976. 222 pp.

Poetry

Poetry: General

2474. Seymour, Elma, ed. *Sun Is a Shapely Fire: Fifty Guyanese Poems*. Georgetown: Labour Advocate, 1973. 80 pp.

Poetry: Sixteenth to Nineteenth Centuries

2475. Cameron, Norman Eustace, ed. *Guianese Poetry: Covering the Hundred Years' Period 1831–1931*. Nendeln, Liechtenstein: Kraus Reprint, 1970. 186 pp. Reprint of the 1931 ed.

Poetry: Twentieth Century

2476. Seymour, Arthur J., ed. *A Treasury of Guyanese Poetry*. Georgetown: Guyana National Lithographic, 1980. 233 pp.

Fiction

Fiction: Twentieth Century

2477. Cromwell, Liz, ed. *The River Between: Short Stories*. Linden, Guyana: Cultural Development Unit, 1979. 193 pp.

2478. Munroe, Andrew Adrian, ed. *Caribbean Stories: Supernatural Tales of Guyana*. Linden, NJ: Golden Grove, 1994. 144 pp.

2479. National History and Arts Council (Guyana). *Discoveries: An Anthology of Guyanese Short Stories*. Georgetown: The Council, 1976. 63 pp.

C. HISTORY AND CRITICISM

General

2480. Seymour, Arthur J. *The Making of Guyanese Literature*. Georgetown: Guyana National Lithographic, 1980. 108 pp.

Poetry

2481. ———. *Studies of Ten Guyanese Poems*. Georgetown: Ministry of Education, Social Development and Culture, 1982. 52 pp.

D. INDIVIDUAL AUTHORS

Sixteenth to Nineteenth Centuries

2482. *Martin, Egbert,* 1859–1887 (poet, short story writer). Poetical Works, 1883.

Twentieth Century

2483. *Agard, John,* 1949– (novelist, poet, short story writer). Border Country, 1991; The Calypso Alphabet, 1989–1993; Dig Away

Two-Hole Tim, 1981–1990; Grandfather's Old Bruk-A-Down Car, 1994; The Great Snakeskin, 1993; I Din Do Nuttin and Other Poems, 1983–1993; Laughter Is an Egg, 1990–1991; Lend Me Your Wings, 1987; Letters for Lettie and Other Stories, 1979; Life Doesn't Frighten Me at All, 1989–1990; Limbo Dancer in Dark Glasses, 1983; Lovelines for a Goat-Born Lady, 1990; Man to Pan, 1982; Mangoes and Bullets, 1985–1990; No Hickory, No Dickory, No Dock, 1991–1995 (with Grace Nichols); Oriki and the Monster Who Hated Balloons, 1994; Poems in My Earphone, 1995; Say It Again, Granny, 1986–1990; Shoot Me with Flowers, 1974.

2484. *Bissundyal, Churaumanie* (novelist, playwright, poet). Cleavage, 1986; The Jaguar and the Flute, 1990; Labaria puraan, 1995; Whom the Kiskadees Call, 1994.

2485. *Braithwaite, Edward Ricardo,* 1922– (novelist). Choice of Straws, 1965–1972; Islands, 1969; A Kind of Homecoming, 1962; Paid Servant, 1962–1968; Reluctant Neighbors (Autobiographical), 1972–1978; To Sir With Love, 1959–1994.

2486. *Budhos, Marina* (novelist, short story writer). Father's Tale, 1989; House of Waiting, 1995.

2487. *Cameron, Norman Eustace,* 1903– (playwright, poet). Balthasar, 1931; Interlude, 1944; Jamaica Joe, 1962; Kayssa/ Hear the Other Side, 1959; Three Immortals, 1953 (Adoniya, Ebedmelech, Sabaco); The Trumpet, 1969; The Price of Vistory, 1965.

    2488. Cameron, Norman Eustace. *Guide to the Published Works of a Guyanese Author and Playwright.* Georgetown: [s.n.], 1966. 47 pp.

    2489. Loncke, Joycelynne. *Norman E. Cameron: The Man and His Works.* Georgetown: Ministry of Education, Social Development and Culture, 1981. 68 pp.

2490. *Carew, Jan R.,* 1925– (novelist, playwright, poet, short story writer). The Cat People, 1979; Children of the Sun, 1980; Computer Killer, 1985; Dark Night, Deep Water, 1981; Dead Man's Creek, 1981; Don't Go Near the Water, 1982; Green Winter/Moscow Is Not My Mecca, 1964; House of Fear, 1981; The Last Barbarian, 1961; The Lost Love and Other Stories, 1978; The Man Who Came Back, 1979; No Entry, 1985–1991 (No Entry—Bed and Breakfast); Save the Last Dance For Me and Other

Stories, 1976; Sea Drums in My Blood, 1981; Stranger Than Tomorrow, 1976; The Third Gift, 1974; Time Loop, 1983; A Touch
of Midas/Black Midas, 1958–1980; The Wild Coast, 1958–1983.

2491. *Carter, Martin Wylde,* 1927– (poet). The Hill of Fire Glows Red,
1951; Poems of Affinity, 1980; Poems of Resistance/Poems of Resistance from British Guiana/Poems of Resistance from Guyana,
1954–1979; Poems of Succession, 1977; Selected Poems, 1989.

    2492. Rohlehr, Gordon. *The Poet and Citizen in a Degraded
    Community: Martin Carter's "Poems of Affinity."* [St.
    George's, Grenada: s.n.], 1982. 29 pp.

    2493. Roopnaraine, Rupert. *Web of October: Rereading Martin
    Carter.* Leeds, Eng.: Peepal Tree Press, 1988. 73 pp.

2494. *Chan, Brian,* 1942– (poet). Fabula rasa, 1994; Thief With Leaf,
1988.

2495. *Dabydeen, Cyril,* 1942– (novelist, poet, short story writer).
Berbice Crossing, 1996; Coastland, 1989; Dark Swirl, 1989; Dis-
cussing Columbus, 1996; Distances, 1977; Elephants Make Good
Stepladders, 1982; Goatsong, 1977; Heart's Frame, 1979; Islands
Lovelier Than a Vision, 1986–1990; Jogging in Havana, 1992; Poems in Recession, 1972; Still Close to the Island, 1980; Stoning
the Wind, 1994; This Planet Earth, 1979; To Monkey Jungle,
1988; The Wizard Swami, 1985–1989.

2496. *Dabydeen, David,* 1957– (novelist, poet, short story writer).
Coolie Odyssey, 1988; Disappearance, 1993; The Intended, 1992;
Rented Rooms, 1988; Slave Song, 1984; Turner, 1994.

2497. *D'Aguiar, Fred,* 1960– (novelist, playwright, poet). Airy Hall,
1989; British Subjects, 1993; Dear Future, 1996; Explainer, 1988;
The Longest Memory, 1994–1996; Mama Dot, 1985.

2498. *Das, Mahadai* (poet). Bones, 1988; A Collection of Poems, 1977;
I Want to Be a Poetess of My People, 1977; My Finer Steel Will
Grow, 1982.

2499. *Dathorne, Oscar Ronald,* 1934– (novelist, poet, short story
writer). Dele's Child, 1986; Dumplings in the Soup, 1963; The
Scholar-Man, 1964; Songs for a New World, 1988.

2500. *Farrier, Francis Quamina,* 1938– (playwright). Manaka, 1978;
The Plight of the Wright, 1969; The Slave and the Scroll, 1969.

2501. *Fenty, Alan A.* (short story writer). Cumfa Drums Are Calling, 1973; Stories of Protest, 1978; Those Dark Days of the Past, 1980 (with Henry W. Josiah).

2502. *Gilroy, Beryl* (novelist, poet, short story writer). Boy-Sandwich, 1989; Echoes and Voices, 1991; Frangipani House, 1986–1989; Gather the Faces, 1996; In for a Penny, 1980–1982; In Praise of Love and Children, 1996; Inkle and Yarico, 1996; Stedman and Joanna, 1991; Sunlight on Sweet Water, 1994.

2503. *Harris, Denise* (novelist). Web of Secrets, 1996.

2504. *Harris, Wilson,* 1921– (novelist, poet, short story writer). The Age of the Rainmakers, 1971; The Angel at the Gate, 1982; Ascent to Omai, 1970; Black Marsden, 1972; The Carnival Trilogy, 1993 (Carnival [1985], The Infinite Rehearsal [1987], The Four Banks of the River of Space [1990]); Companions of the Day and Night, 1975; Da Silva da Silva's Cultivated Wilderness, 1977; Eternity To Season, 1954–1978; Explorations, 1981; The Eye of the Scarecrow, 1965–1974; Fossil and Psyche, 1974; Genesis of the Clowns, 1977; The Guyana Quartet, 1985 (Palace of the Peacock [1960–1989], The Far Journey of Oudin [1961], The Whole Armour [1962], The Secret Ladder [1963]); Heartland, 1964; The Radical Imagination, 1992 (Alan Riach, Mark Williams, eds.); Resurrection at Sorrow Hill, 1993; The Sleepers of Roraima, 1970; Tradition, the Writer and Society, 1967; The Tree of the Sun, 1978; Tumatumari, 1968; The Waiting Room, 1967.

2505. Drake, Sandra E. *Wilson Harris and the Modern Tradition: A New Architecture of the World.* Westport, CT: Greenwood Press, 1986. 213 pp.

2506. Gilkes, Michael. *Wilson Harris and the Caribbean Novel.* London: Longman Caribbean, 1975. 159 pp.

2507. ———, ed. *The Literate Imagination: Essays on the Novels of Wilson Harris.* London: Macmillan Caribbean, 1989. 208 pp.

2508. Maes-Jelinek, Hena. *The Naked Design: A Reading of "Palace of the Peacock."* Arhus, Denmark: Dangaroo Press, 1976. 68 pp.

2509. ———. *Wilson Harris.* Boston, MA: Twayne, 1982. 191 pp.

2510. ———, ed. *Wilson Harris: The Uncompromising Imagination.* Sydney, N.S.W.: Dangaroo Press, 1991. 277 pp.

See also #45, #2267.

2511. *Heath, Roy Aubrey Kelvin,* 1926– (novelist, playwright, short story writer). The Armstrong Trilogy, 1994 (From the Heat of the Day [1979], One Generation [1981], Genetha [1981]); Kwaku/The Man Who Could Not Keep His Mouth Shut, 1982–1985; A Man Come Home, 1974; The Murderer, 1978–1992; Orealla, 1984–1986; The Shadow Bride, 1988–1996; Shadows Round the Moon, 1990 (Autobiographical).

2512. *Heydorn, Bernard,* 1945– (poet). Song of the West Indies, 1986; Walk Good Guyana Boy, 1994.

2513. *Hopkinson, Abdur-Rahman Slade,* 1934– (playwright, poet). The Four and Other Poems, 1954; The Friend, 1976; The Madwoman of Papine, 1976; The Onliest Fisherman, 1967; Snowscape With Signature, 1993.

2514. *Jeffrey, Derrick John* (short story writer). Demerara, 1992; Under the Essequibo Clouds, 1970.

2515. *Josiah, Henry W.* (novelist, poet, short story writer). Makonaima Returns, 1966; Tales of Makonaima's Children, 1994; Those Dark Days of the Past, 1980 (with Alan A. Fenty).

2516. *Kempadoo, Manghanita* (novelist). Letters of Thanks, 1969–1986.

2517. *Khalideen, Rosetta* (poet). Leguan, 1979; Portrait in Poetry, 1989.

2518. *Matthews, Marc,* 1937– (poet, short story writer). Guyana My Altar, 1987; A Season of Sometimes, 1992.

2519. *McAndrew, Wordsworth Albert,* 1936– (playwright, poet, short story writer). Blue Gaulding, 1950–1973; Meditations on a Theme, 1963; More Poems, 1970–1973; Poems to St. Agnes, 1962; Selected Poems, 1966.

2520. *McWatt, Mark A.* (poet). Interiors, 1988; The Language of Eldorado, 1994.

2521. *Mittelhölzer, Edgar Austin,* 1909–1965 (novelist, playwright, poet, short story writer). The Adding Machine, 1954; The Aloneness of Mrs. Chatham, 1965; Children of Kaywana/Savage Destiny, 1952–1986; Corentyne Thunder, 1941–1977; Eltonsbrody, 1960; The Harrowing of Hubertus/Hubertus/Kaywana Stock,

1954–1986; The Jilkington Drama, 1965; Kaywana Blood/The Old Blood, 1958–1986; Kaywana Heritage, 1952–1986; Latticed Echoes, 1960; The Life and Death of Sylvia/Sylvia, 1953–1976; The Mad Macmullochs, 1959–1963; A Morning at the Office/A Morning in Trinidad, 1950–1974; My Bones and My Flute, 1955–1986; Of Trees and the Sea, 1956; The Piling of Clouds, 1961–1964; Shadows Move Among Them, 1951; A Swarthy Boy, 1963 (Autobiographical); A Tale of Three Places, 1957; Thunder Returning, 1961; A Tinkling in the Twilight, 1959; Uncle Paul, 1963; The Weather Family, 1958; The Weather in Middenshot, 1952; The Wounded and the Worried, 1962.

2522. Gilkes, Michael. *Racial Identity and Individual Consciousness in the Caribbean Novel.* Georgetown: Ministry of Information and Culture, National History and Arts Council, 1975. 52 pp.

2523. Seymour, Arthur J. *Edgar Mittelhölzer: The Man and His Work.* Georgetown: [s.n.], 1968. 53 pp.

2524. *Monar, M. R.,* 1944– (novelist, poet, short story writer). Backdam People, 1985–1987; Estate People, 1994; High House and Radio, 1992; Janjhat, 1989; Koker, 1987; Meanings, 1972; Poems from Annandale, 1973 (with Brahmdeo Persaud and Randall Butisingh).

2525. *Nichols, Grace,* 1950– (novelist, poet). Come On Into My Tropical Garden, 1988–1993; The Discovery, 1986; The Fat Black Woman's Poems, 1984; Give Yourself a Hug, 1994–1996; I is a Long-Memoried Woman, 1983–1990; Lazy Thoughts of a Lazy Woman and Other Poems, 1989; Leslyn in London, 1978–1984; No Hickory, No Dickory, No Dock, 1991–1995 (with John Agard); Poetry Jump Up, 1989; Whole of a Morning Sky, 1986.

2526. *Nicole, Christopher,* 1930– (novelist). The Amyot Crime, 1965–1974; Amyot's Cay, 1964–1974; The Anderson Line, 1988 (Vol. 1. The Seas of Fortune [1983]); Appointment in Kiltone, 1972; Black Dawn, 1977–1978; Black Majesty, 1984–1987 (The Seeds of Rebellion, The Wild Harvest); Blood Amyot, 1964–1974; Bloody Sunrise, 1993; Bloody Sunset, 1994; Brothers and Enemies, 1982–1984; The Captain's Woman, 1977; The Captivator, 1973–1976; Caribee, 1974–1990; The Combination, 1983–1987; The Command, 1989; The Co-ordinator, 1967–1968; The Crimson Pagoda, 1983–1986; Dark Noon, 1963; Dark Passage, 1975–1976; Dark Sun, 1990; The Daughter, 1992; Days of Wine and Roses?, 1991; Death of the Devil, 1994; December Passion/Brumaire,

1977–1979; The Deviator, 1969–1971; The Devil's Emissary, 1968; The Devil's Own, 1975–1976; The Dominator, 1969–1971; The Doom Fisherman, 1969; Dragon's Blood, 1989–1991; The Eliminator, 1966–1967; The Expurgator, 1972–1985; The Face of Evil, 1971–1972; The Fascinator, 1975–1977; The Fear Dealers, 1974; First Class, 1984–1986; The Friday Spy, 1981–1989; Golden Girl, 1992; The Golden Goddess, 1973; Guillotine, 1976; Haggard, 1980–1981; Haggard's Inheritance, 1981–1982; The Happy Valley, 1989–1991; Heroes, 1973–1988; The High Country, 1988–1992; Hotel De Luxe, 1985–1986; The Infiltrator, 1971–1972; The Inheritors, 1981; Iron Ships, Iron Men, 1987–1989; King Creole, 1966; The Last Battle, 1993; The Longest Pleasure, 1970–1971; Lord of Sin/The Secret Memoirs of Lord Byron, 1978–1980; Lord of the Golden Fan, 1973–1975; Manhunt for a General, 1970; The Masters, 1995; Mistress of Darkness, 1976–1977; Off White, 1959; Old Glory, 1986–1988; Operation Destruct, 1969–1974; Operation Manhunt, 1970–1980; Operation Neptune, 1972–1973; The Passion and the Glory, 1989–1991; Pearl of the Orient, 1988; The Power and the Passion, 1977–1983; The Predator, 1968–1977; The Queen of Paris, 1979–1985; Raging Sea, Searing Sky, 1988–1991; Ratoon, 1962–1978; Red Dawn, 1985–1989; The Regiment, 1988–1990; Resumption, 1992–1993; The Rivals, 1985–1988; The Savage Sands, 1978–1983; The Scarlet Princess, 1984–1988; The Sea and the Sand, 1986–1989; The Self Lovers, 1968–1969; The Seeds of Power, 1994; The Shadow of Death, 1989; Shadows in the Jungle, 1961; The Ship With No Name, 1987–1990; Singapura, 1990; Spares, 1993; Spawn of the Devil, 1993–1994; The Sun and the Dragon, 1986–1990; The Sun On Fire, 1986–1987; The Sun Rises, 1984–1988; Sunset, 1978–1979; Sword of Empire, 1991; Sword of Fortune, 1990; Sword of the Devil, 1994; Tallant for Disaster, 1978–1979; Tallant for Trouble, 1977–1978; The Third Life, 1988–1989; The Thunder and the Shouting, 1969–1980; Titans, 1991–1992; The Triumph, 1989; The Tumult At the Gate, 1970; Victoria's Walk, 1986–1989; When the Cavern Ends, 1970–1971; White Boy, 1966; White Rani, 1986–1987; Wind of Destiny, 1988–1990; A Woman of Her Time, 1995.

2527. *Persaud, Sasenarine* (novelist, poet, short story writer). Between the Dash and the Comma, 1989; Dear Death, 1989; Demerary Telepathy, 1988; The Ghost of Bellow's Man, 1992; The Wintering Kundalini, 1996.

2528. *Richmond, Angus* (novelist). A Kind of Living, 1978; The Open Prison, 1988.

2529. *Sadeek, Sheik M.,* 1921– (novelist, playwright, poet, short story writer). Across the Green Fields, 1974 (Across the Green Fields, The Sissy, The Magnificent Customer, The Sugar Strike, No Slip-up, Wet and Wild); Black Bush, 1974; Bundarie Boy, 1969–1976; The Diamond Thieves and Four More Stories, 1974 (The Diamond Thieves, The Only Man, Sheena's Two Loves, The Caller, Circumstances); Dreams and Reflections, 1969; Fish Koker, 1967; Goodbye Corentyne, 1974; He, 1967; The Malali Makers, 1979; Namaste, 1965; No Greater Day, 1965; Porkknockers, 1974; Reflections and Dreams and More Poems, 1974; Savannah's Edge, 1968; Song of the Sugarcanes, 1975; Two Stage Sketches, 1976 (The Gap, The Gift); Windswept and Other Stories, 1968–1980.

2530. *Seymour, Arthur J.,* 1914–1989 (poet, short story writer). Autobiography, 1976 (Growing Up in Guyana, Pilgrim Memories, The Years in Puerto Rico and MacKenzie); A Bethlehem Alleluia, 1974; Black Song, 1971; Coronation Ode, 1937; The Guiana Book, 1948; I, Anancy, 1971; I Live in Georgetown, 1974 (Autobiographical); Images of Majority, 1978; Italic, 1974; Leaves from the Tree, 1951; Love Song, 1975; Mirror, 1975; Monologue, 1968; My Lovely Native Land, 1971 (with Elma Seymour); Over Guiana Clouds, 1944; Passport, 1972; Religious Poems, 1980; Selected Poems, 1965–1983; Sun's In My Blood, 1945; Ten Poems, 1953; Three Voluntaries, 1953; Verse, 1937; Water and Blood, 1952.

    2531. Christiani, Joan. *A. J. Seymour: A Bibliography.* Georgetown: National Library, 1974. 110 pp.

    2532. McDonald, Ian, ed. *AJS at 70: A Celebration on His 70th Birthday of the Life, Work, and Art of A. J. Seymour.* Georgetown: Autoprint, 1984. 122 pp.

2533. *Shewcharan, Narmala,* 1958– (novelist, poet). Beauty Lies Within and Other Poems, 1980; The Dream of Every Heart, 1979; Tomorrow Is Another Day, 1994.

2534. *Shinebourne, Janice,* 1947– (novelist, short story writer). The Last English Plantation, 1988; Timepiece, 1986.

2535. *Singh, Doodnauth* (poet). Hunted!, 1990; Showers of Betrayal, 1991.

2536. *Singh, Rajkumari* (playwright, poet, short story writer). Days of the Sahib, 1971; A Garland of Stories, 1960.

2537. *Singh, Roopnandan* (novelist, poet). Dimensions of Life, 1993; Eve, 1995; Introspection, 1994; Talking With Myself, 1993; Thorn in the Rose, 1994; Wild Maami, 1995.

2538. *Taharally, Kenneth,* 1934– (poet). Anthrophanies, 1972–1983.

2539. *Valz, Ian* (playwright). Masquerade, 1988.

2540. *Walrond, Eric,* 1898–1966 (novelist, poet, short story writer). Tropic Death, 1926–1972 (Drought, Panama Gold, The Yellow One, The Wharf Rats, The Palm Porch, Subjection, The Beach Pin, The White Snake, The Vampire Bat, Tropic Death).

2541. *Williams, Denis,* 1923– (novelist, short story writer). Other Leopards, 1963–1983; The Third Temptation, 1968.

2542. *Williams, Milton Vishnu,* 1936– (poet). Sources of Agony, 1979; Years of Fighting Exile, 1986.

2543. *Williams, Noel Desmond,* 1921– (novelist, poet, short story writer). The Crying of Rainbirds, 1992; Ikael Torass, 1976; The Silence of Islands, 1994.

JAMAICA

A. BIBLIOGRAPHIES AND BIO-BIBLIOGRAPHIES

2544. Brathwaite, Kamau. *Jamaica Poetry: A Checklist—Books, Pamphlets, Broadsheets, 1686–1978.* Kingston: Jamaica Library Service, 1979. 36 pp.

B. ANTHOLOGIES

General

General: Sixteenth to Nineteenth Centuries

2545. D'Costa, Jean, and Barbara Lalla, eds. *Voices in Exile: Jamaican Texts of the 18th and 19th Centuries.* Tuscaloosa, AL: University of Alabama Press, 1989. 157 pp.

General: Twentieth Century

2546. Hendriks, Arthur Lemiere, and Cedric Lindo, eds. *The Independence Anthology of Jamaican Literature.* Kingston: Ministry of Development and Welfare, Arts Celebration Committee, 1962. 227 pp.

2547. Manley, Edna, ed. *Focus: An Anthology of Contemporary Jamaican Writing.* Millwood, NY: Kraus Reprint, 1976. 2 vols. Reprint of the 1943–1960 eds. of the periodical.

2548. Morris, Mervyn, ed. *Focus 1983: An Anthology of Contemporary Jamaican Writing.* Kingston: Caribbean Authors, 1983. 294 pp.

Poetry

Poetry: General

2549. McFarlane, John Ebenezer Clare, ed. *A Treasury of Jamaican Poetry.* London: University of London Press, 1949. 159 pp.

2550. Mordecai, Pamela, and Mervyn Morris, eds. *Jamaica Woman: An Anthology of Poems.* Kingston: Heinemann, 1985. 110 pp. Reprint of the 1980 ed.

Poetry: Twentieth Century

2551. Brathwaite, Kamau ed. *New Poets from Jamaica: An Anthology.* Kingston: Savacou Publications, 1979. 134 pp.

2552. McFarlane, John Ebenezer Clare, ed. *Voices from Summerland: An Anthology of Jamaican Poetry.* London: Fowler Wright, 1929. 307 pp.

2553. Mordecai, Pamela, ed. *From Our Yard: Jamaican Poetry Since Independence—the First Twenty-five Years.* Rev. ed. Kingston: Institute of Jamaica, 1994. 251 pp.

2554. Morris, Mervyn, ed. *Seven Jamaican Poets: An Anthology of Recent Poetry.* Kingston: Bolivar Press, 1971. 58 pp. E. Baugh, A. L. Hendriks, B. McFarlane, R. L. C. McFarlane, A. McNeill, M. Morris, D. Scott.

Fiction

Fiction: General

2555. Tanna, Laura, ed. *Jamaican Folk Tales and Oral Histories.* Kingston: Institute of Jamaica, 1984. 143 pp.

Fiction: Twentieth Century

2556. Reid, Victor Stafford et al. *Fourteen Jamaican Short Stories.* Kingston: Pioneer Press, 1950. 135 pp.

2557. Scott, Dennis C. et al. *Jamaican Short Stories: A Selection of Prize-Winning Stories.* Kingston: Kingston Publishers, 1992. 196 pp.

2558. *Twenty-two Jamaican Short Stories: A Selection of Prize-winning Short Stories.* 2d ed. Kingston: Kingston Publishers, 1992. 196 pp. Originally published as *Festival Literary Anthology* in 1987.

C. HISTORY AND CRITICISM

2559. McFarlane, John Ebenezer Clare. *A Literature in the Making.* Kingston: Pioneer Press, 1956. 117 pp.

Poetry

Poetry: Twentieth Century

2560. Pollard, Velma. *Dread Talk: The Language of the Rastafari.* Kingston: Canoe Press, 1994. 84 pp.

Fiction

Fiction: General

2561. Lalla, Barbara. *Defining Jamaican Fiction: Marronage and the Discourse of Survival.* Tuscaloosa, AL: University of Alabama Press, 1996. 224 pp.

D. INDIVIDUAL AUTHORS

Twentieth Century

2562. *Abrahams, Peter,* 1919– (novelist, poet, short story writer). Dark Testament, 1942–1970; The Fan, 1995–1996; The Fury of Rachel Monette, 1980–1982; Hard Rain, 1988–1989; Lights Out, 1994; Mine Boy, 1946–1992; A Night of Their Own, 1965; The Path of Thunder, 1948–1987; Pressure Drop, 1989–1991; Red message, 1986; Return to Goli, 1953; Revolution #9, 1992–1993; Tell Freedom, 1954–1982; Song of the City, 1943; This Island Now, 1966–1985; Tongues of Fire, 1982–1985; The View from Coyaba, 1985; The Voice of the Island, 1966; Wild Conquest, 1950–1982; A Wreath for Udomo, 1956–1971.

2563. Ensor, Robert. *The Novels of Peter Abrahams and the Rise of Nationalism in Africa.* Essen: Verlag Die Blaue Eule, 1992. 333 pp.

2564. Nesbitt, Rodney. *Notes on Peter Abrahams' "Mine Boy."* Nairobi: Heinemann Educational Books, 1975. 52 pp.

2565. Ogungbesan, Kolawole. *The Writing of Peter Abrahams*. New York: Africana Publishing, 1979. 156 pp.

2566. *Adisa, Opal Palmer,* 1954– (poet, short story writer). Bake-Face and Other Guava Stories, 1986–1989; Piña, the Many-Eyed Fruit, 1985; Tamarind and Mango Women, 1992; Traveling Women, 1989 (with Devorah Major).

2567. *Allen, Lillian,* 1951– (playwright, poet, short story writer). If You See Truth, 1990; Rhythm an' Hardtimes, 1982; Why Me?, 1991; Women Do This Every Day, 1993.

2568. *Ashe, Rosalind* (novelist). Dark Runner, 1985; The Hurricane Wake, 1977–1979; The Laying of the Noone Walker, 1988; Moths, 1976–1989; Starcrossed, 1979; Take Over, 1982.

2569. *Babatunji, Ayotunde Amtac,* 1951– (poet, short story writer). Dread Thoughts, 1978; Echoes of Mount Portland, 1977; The Farmers' Songs, 1975; In Portland's Valley of Beauty, 1973; In the Valley of Love, 1977; Prophet on Reggae Mountain, 1994; Vision of Apartheid's Death, 1994.

2570. *Barrett, Lindsay,* 1941– (novelist, playwright, poet, short story writer). The Conflicting Eye, 1973; Lipskybound, 1977; A Quality of Pain and Other Poems, 1986; Song for Mumu, 1967–1974; The State of Black Desire, 1966–1974; Veils of Vengeance Falling, 1985.

2571. *Baugh, Edward,* 1936– (poet). A Tale from the Rainforest, 1988. See also #2554.

2572. *Bennett, Louise,* 1919– (poet, short story writer). Anancy and Miss Lou, 1979; Anancy Stories and Dialect Verse, 1950–1973; Anancy Stories and Poems in Dialect, 1944; Aunty Roachy Seh, 1992–1993 (Mervyn Morris, ed,); Jamaica Labrish, 1966–1983 (Rex M. Nettleford, ed.); Jamaica Maddah Goose, 1981; Jamaican Dialect Poems/Mis' Lulu Sez, 1950; Laugh with Louise, 1961; Selected Poems, 1982–1983.

2573. *Berry, James,* 1924– (playwright, poet, short story writer). Ajeemah and His Son, 1991–1994; Celebration Song, 1994; Chain of Days, 1985; Cut-Way Feelins, 1981–1983; Don't Leave an Elephant to Go and Chase a Bird, 1996; Fractured Circles, 1979; The Future-Telling Lady and Other Stories, 1991–1995; The Girls and

Yanga Marshall, 1987; Hot Earth Cold Earth, 1995; Isn't My Name Magical?, 1991; Loving, 1981–1983; Lucy's Letters, 1981–1983; Playing a Dazzler, 1996; Rough Sketch Beginning, 1996; Spiderman Anancy/Anancy-Spiderman, 1988–1991; A Thief in the Village and Other Stories, 1987–1990; When I Dance, 1988–1991.

2574. *Bland, Anthony* (novelist, poet). The Song and the City, 1965; Statements, 1988.

2575. *Bloom, Valerie,* 1956– (poet). Duppy Jamboree and Other Jamaican Poems, 1992; Touch Mi, Tell Mi, 1983–1990.

2576. *Breeze, Jean Binta* (poet). Answers, 1983; Riddym Ravings and Other Poems, 1988; Spring Cleaning, 1992.

2577. *Brodber, Erna,* 1940– (novelist, short story writer). Jane and Louisa Will Soon Come Home, 1980; Louisiana, 1994; Myal, 1988–1995.

2578. *Brown, Lloyd Wellesley,* 1938– (poet). Duppies, 1996.

2579. *Campbell, George,* 1902– (playwright, poet). Cry for Happy, 1958; Earth Testament, 1983; First Poems, 1945–1970.

2580. *Campbell, Hazel Dorothy,* 1940– (short story writer). Juice Box and Scandal, 1992; The Rag Doll and Other Stories, 1978 (The Carrion Eaters, The Rag Doll, First Love, See Me in Me Benz an T'ing, A District Called Fellowship); Singerman, 1992; Tilly Bummie and Other Stories, 1993 (Life in Country, Brenton Park, The Ark, Tillie Bummie, Mathilda's Day, Life in Town, Sylvie in Town, Best Friends, Champion, Hurricane Charlie); Walk Good, 1988; Woman's Tongue, 1985–1988.

2581. *Carberry, Hugh Doston,* 1921–1989 (poet). It Takes a Mighty Fire, 1995.

2582. *Carnegie, James,* 1938– (novelist). Wages Paid, 1976.

2583. *Cliff, Michelle,* 1946– (novelist, poet, short story writer). Abeng, 1984–1995; Bodies of Water, 1990–1991; Claiming an Identity They Taught Me to Despise, 1980; Free Enterprise, 1993–1994; The Land of Look Behind, 1985; No Telephone to Heaven, 1987–1996.

2584. *Cooper, Afua Pam* (poet). Breaking Chains, 1983; Memories Have Tongue, 1992; The Red Caterpillar On College Street, 1989.

2585. *Craig, Christine,* 1943– (poet, short story writer). Mint Tea and Other Stories, 1993 (Sister Mary, Case Study, The More You Look, Night Thoughts, The Bower, Roots, The Virgin, Burnt Hill, The Colony, In the Hills, Mint Tea, Nellie, Through A Glass Darkly, The Cousin, Riding the Bus); Quadrille For Tigers, 1984.

2586. *Dawes, Kwame Senu Neville,* 1962– (poet). Progeny of Air, 1994; Prophets, 1995; Resisting the Anomie, 1995.

2587. *Dawes, Neville,* 1926–1984 (novelist, poet). Interim, 1978; The Last Enchantment, 1960–1970.

2588. *D'Costa, Jean,* 1937– (novelist, poet, short story writer). Escape to Last Man Peak, 1975–1980; Sprat Morrison, 1972–1990; Voice in the Wind, 1978–1980.

2589. *De Lisser, Herbert George,* 1878–1944 (novelist, short story writer). The Arawak Girl, 1958–1968; The Cup and the Lip, 1956; Jane: A Story of Jamaica/Jane's Career, 1913–1972; Morgan's Daughter, 1953–1980; Psyche, 1952–1980; Susan Proudleigh, 1915; Under the Sun, 1937; The White Witch of Rosehall, 1929–1982.

2590. *Escoffery, Gloria,* 1923– (poet). Landscape in the Making, 1976; Loggerhead, 1988.

2591. *Farki, Neville* (novelist). Countryman Karl Black, 1981; The Death of Tarzana Clayton, 1985; The Unexpected Visitor, 1991; A Week in Blue Hole, 1977.

2592. *Figueroa, John J.,* 1920– (poet, short story writer). The Chase, 1992 (The Chase, Utopia, Ars longa, Vita brevis); Ignoring Hurts, 1976; Love Leaps Here, 1962–1970.

2593. *Goodison, Lorna,* 1947– (poet, short story writer). Baby Mother and the King of Swords, 1990; Heartease, 1988; I Am Becoming My Mother, 1986; Selected Poems, 1992; Tamarind Season, 1980; To Us, All Flowers Are Roses, 1995. See also #2274.

2594. *Goulbourne, Jean,* 1948– (poet). Actors in the Arena, 1977; Under the Sun, 1992.

2595. *Hamilton, Judith,* 1952– (poet). Rain Carvers, 1992.

2596. *Hearne, John,* 1925– (novelist, short story writer). The Autumn Equinox, 1959–1961; The Candywine Development, 1970 (with Morris Cargill); The Eye of the Storm/The Faces of Love, 1957; Fever Grass, 1969 (with Morris Cargill); Land of the Living, 1951–1962; Stranger at the Gate, 1956; The Sure Salvation, 1981–1985; Voices Under the Window, 1955–1985.

2597. *Hendriks, Arthur Lemiere,* 1922– (poet, short story writer). Check, 1988 (with Alan Edward Harris); The Islanders and Other Poems, 1983; Madonna of the Unknown Nation, 1974; Muet, 1971; The Naked Ghost and Other Poems, 1984; On This Mountain and Other Poems, 1965; These Green Islands and Other Poems, 1971; To Speak Simply, 1988. See also #2554.

2598. *Johnson, Linton Kwesi,* 1952– (poet). Dread Beat and Blood, 1975; Five Nights of Bleeding, 1974; Inglan Is a Bitch, 1980–1981; Tings and Times, 1991; Voices of the Living and the Dead, 1974; Youths of Hope, 1974.

2599. *Jones, Evan,* 1927– (playwright, poet). Tales of the Caribbean, 1986–1992 (Anansi Stories, Stories from History, The Beginning of Things, Witches and Duppies); Skylarking, 1994; Stone Haven, 1993; Understandings, 1967.

2600. *Kent, Lena A.* (poet). Dew on the Branch, 1933; Hills of St. Andrew and Other Poems, 1931.

2601. *King, Washington,* 1936– (playwright, poet, short story writer). Collected Poems of Our Times, 1972; David and the Mountain City, 1975; The Factory People (A Little Child Shall Lead Them), 1976; The Fire, 1977; King David and King Saul, 1973; New Modern Poems, 1968; Our Times, 1977; The Racing Time, 1978; Seven at a Blow, 1974; Some Poems, 1974; The Task, 1978; Verses of the Time, 1975.

2602. *Knight, Clyde* (novelist). We Shall Not Die, 1983; Woman, Hold Your Head and Cry, 1992.

2603. *Levi, Makeda* (short story writer). Joseph, a Rasta Reggae Fable, 1985–1991.

2604. *Lopez, Basil* (playwright, poet, short story writer). Easy Street, 1981; In Another's House, 1973; The New Jamaica, 1967; On Top of Blue Mountain, 1976; Only as the Wind Blows, 1987.

2605. *MacDermot, Thomas Henry,* 1870–1933 (novelist, poet). Brown's Town Ballads and Other Poems, 1958; One Brown Girl and . . . , 1909; Orange Valley and Other Poems, 1951.

2606. *Mais, Roger,* 1905–1955 (novelist, playwright, poet, short story writer). And Most of All Man, 1940; Black Lightning, 1955–1983; Brother Man, 1954–1974; Come Love, Come Death, 1951; Face and Other stories, 1942; The Hills Were Joyful Together, 1953–1981; Listen, the Wind, 1986 (Kenneth Ramchand, ed.); The Three Novels of Roger Mais, 1966–1970 (The Hills Were Joyful Together, Brother Man, Black Lightning).

    2607. D'Costa, Jean. *Roger Mais: "The Hills Were Joyful Together" and "Brother Man."* London: Longman, 1978. 74 pp.

    2608. Hawthorne, Evelyn J. *The Writer in Transition: Roger Mais and the Decolonization of Caribbean Culture.* New York: P. Lang, 1989. 191 pp.

    2609. Thorpe, Marjorie. *Roger Mais, "Brother Man."* Harlow [Eng.]: Longman, 1979. 50 pp.

2610. *Manley, Rachel,* 1947– (poet). A Light Left On, 1992; Poems Two, 1978; Prisms, 1972.

2611. *Marson, Una* (playwright, poet). The Moth and the Star, 1937; Pocomania, 1938; Towards the Stars, 1945; Tropic Reveries, 1930.

2612. *Maxwell, Marina Ama Omowale* (novelist). Chopstix in Mauby, 1996.

2613. *McFarlane, Basil,* 1922– (playwright, poet). Jacob and the Angel and Other Poems, 1952–1970. See also #2554.

2614. *McFarlane, John Ebenezer Clare,* 1894–1962 (poet). Daphne, a Tale of the Hills of St. Andrew, 1931; The Magdalen, 1957; Selected Shorter Poems, 1954.

2615. *McFarlane, Roy L. C.,* 1925– (poet). Buttercups in a Dry Time, 1982; Hunting the Bright Stream, 1960; In Search of Gold, 1986;

Poems in Three Phases, 1976; Selected and New Poems, 1988; Selected Poems, 1952–1970; Suddenly, the Lignum Vitae, 1978. See also #2554.

2616. *McKay, Claude,* 1890–1948 (novelist, poet). Banana Bottom, 1933–1986; Banjo, 1920–1970; Constab Ballads, 1912; The Dialect Poetry of Claude McKay, 1972–1987 (Wayne F. Cooper, ed.); Gingertown, 1932–1991; Harlem, Negro Metropolis, 1940–1978; Harlem Glory, 1990; Harlem Shadows, 1922–1985; Home to Harlem, 1928–1987; A Long Way From Home, 1937–1985; My Green Hills of Jamaica and Five Jamaican Short Stories, 1946–1979; The Passion of Claude McKay, 1973 (Wayne F. Cooper, ed.); Selected Poems, 1953–1981 (John Dewey, Max Eastman, eds.); Songs of Jamaica, 1912–1969; Sping in New Hampshire and Other Poems, 1920; This Is the life, 1961 (Autobiographical).

2617. Cooper, Wayne F. *Claude McKay: Rebel Sojourner in the Harlem Renaissance—A Biography.* Baton Rouge, LA: Louisiana State University Press, 1996. 441 pp. Reprint of the 1987 ed.

2618. Gayle, Addison. *Claude McKay: The Black Poet At War.* Detroit, MI: Broadside Press, 1972. 46 pp.

2619. Giles, James Richard. *Claude McKay.* Boston, MA: Twayne, 1976. 170 pp.

2620. McLeod, Alan L., ed. *Claude McKay: Centennial Studies.* New Delhi: Sterling Publishers, 1992. 181 pp.

2621. Tillery, Tyrone. *Claude McKay: A Black Poet's Struggle for Identity.* Amherst, MA: University of Massachusetts Press, 1992. 235 pp.

See also #40.

2622. *McKenzie, Alecia,* 1960– (poet, short story writer). Poems and Other Crimes, 1983; Satellite City and Other Short Stories, 1992; When the Rain Stopped in Natland, 1995.

2623. *McKenzie, Earl,* 1943– (poet, short story writer). Against Linearity, 1992; A Boy Named Ossie, 1991; Two Roads to Mount Joyful and Other Stories, 1992.

2624. *McNeill, Anthony,* 1941– (poet). Credences at the Altar of Cloud, 1979; Reel from "The Life Movie," 1972–1975. See also #2554.

2625. *Mordecai, Pamela,* 1942– (poet, short story writer). Don't Ever Wake a Snake, 1991; From Our Yard, 1988; Journey Poem, 1989.

2626. *Morris, Mervyn,* 1937– (poet). Examination Centre, 1992; On Holy Week, 1976–1993; The Pond, 1973; Shadowboxing, 1979. See also #2554, #2274.

2627. *Mutabaruka,* 1952– (poet). First Poems, 1980–1987; Outcry, 1973; Sun and Moon, 1976 (with Faybiene).

2628. *Palmer, C. Everard,* 1930– (novelist). Baba and Mr. Big, 1972–1992; Big Doc Bitteroot, 1968–1992; A Broken Vessel, 1960–1982; The Cloud with the Silver Lining, 1966–1987; A Cow Called Boy, 1972–1985; Crab Hunt and Other Stories, 1980 (Crab Hunt, The Rescue, Ordeal At Sea, The Fife-man); The Hummingbird People, 1971–1979; The Sun Salutes You, 1970–1984; The Wooing of Beppo Tate, 1972–1979.

2629. *Patterson, Orlando,* 1940– (novelist, short story writer). An Absence of Ruins, 1967; The Children of Sisyphus/Dinah, 1964–1986; Die the Long Day, 1972.

2630. *Philp, Geoffrey* (poet). Exodus and Other Poems, 1990; Florida Bound, 1995.

2631. *Pollard, Velma,* 1937– (poet, short story writer). Considering Woman, 1989; Crown Point and Other Poems, 1988; Homestretch, 1994; Karl and Other Stories, 1994; Shame Trees Don't Grow Here . . . But Poincianas Bloom, 1992.

2632. *Powell, Patricia,* 1966– (novelist, short story writer). Me Dying Trial, 1993; A Small Gathering of Bones, 1994.

2633. *Reid, Victor Stafford,* 1913– (novelist, short story writer). The Jamaicans, 1978; The Leopard, 1958–1980; Nanny-Town, 1983; New Day, 1949–1973; Peter of Mount Ephraim, 1971; Sixty-Five, 1960–1980; The Young Warriors, 1967–1979.

2634. *Riley, Joan,* 1950– (novelist, short story writer). A Kindness to the Children, 1992; Leave to Stay, 1906 (with Briar Wood); Romance, 1988; The Unbelonging, 1985; Waiting in the Twilight, 1987.

2635. *Roberts, Walter Adolphe,* 1886–1962 (novelist, poet). Brave Mardi Gras, 1946; Creole Dusk, 1948; The Haunting Hand,

1926; Medallions, 1950; The Mind Reader, 1929–1974; The Moralist, 1931–1974; Pan and Peacocks, 1928; Pierrot Wounded and Other Poems, 1919; The Pomegranate, 1941; Royal Street, 1944–1974; The Single Star, 1949–1956; The Strange Career of Bishop Sterling, 1932–1974; The Top Floor Killer, 1935–1976.

2636. *Rogers, Joel Augustus,* 1883–1965 (novelist). From Superman to Man, 1917–1993; She Walks in Beauty, 1963.

2637. *Roy, Namba,* 1910–1961 (novelist). Black Albino, 1961–1986; No Black Sparrows, 1989 (Jacqueline Roy, ed.).

2638. *Salkey, Andrew,* 1928– (novelist, poet, short story writer). The Adventures of Catullus Kelly, 1969; Anancy Traveller, 1992; Anancy's Score, 1973–1992; Away, 1980; Brother Anancy and Other Stories, 1993; Come Home Malcolm Heartland, 1976; Danny Jones, 1980; Drought, 1966–1973; Earthquake, 1965–1985; Escape to an Autumn Pavement, 1960–1970; Georgetown Journal, 1972; Havana Journal, 1971; Hurricane, 1964–1983; In the Hills Where Her Dreams Live, 1979–1981; Jamaica, 1973–1983; Joey Tyson, 1974–1991; Jonah Simpson, 1970; The Late Emancipation of Jerry Stover, 1968–1982; The One: The Story of How the People of Guyana Avenge the Murder of Their Pasero With Help from Brother Anancy and Sister Buxton, 1985; A Quality of Violence, 1959–1978; Riot, 1967–1980; The River That Disappeared, 1979; The Shark Hunters, 1966–1981.

2639. Nazareth, Peter. *In the Trickster Tradition: The Novels of Andrew Salkey, Francis Ebejer and Ishmael Reed.* London: Bogle-L'Ouverture Press, 1994. 262 pp.

2640. *Scott, Dennis C.,* 1939– (playwright, poet). Dreadwalk, 1982; An Echo in the Bone, 1974–1985; The Fantasy of Sir Gawain and the Green Knight, 1978; Strategies, 1989; Terminus, 1966; Uncle Time, 1973. See also #2228, #2554.

2641. *Senior, Olive,* 1938– (playwright, poet, short story writer). Arrival of the Snake-Woman and Other Stories, 1989; Discerner of Hearts and Other Stories, 1995; Gardening in the Tropics, 1994; Summer Lightning and Other Stories, 1986; Talking of Trees, 1985.

2642. *Sherlock, Philip Manderson,* 1902– (playwright, poet, short story writer). Anansi, the Spider Man, 1954–1983; From Tiger to Anansi, 1975–1988; The Iguana's Tail, 1969–1979; The Illustrated Anansi, 1995; The Man in the Web and Other Folktales,

1959–1973; Shout for Freedom, 1976; Ten Poems, 1953; Three Finger Jack's Treasure, 1961–1969.

2643. *Simpson, Louis Aston Marantz,* 1923– (poet). Adventures of the Letter, 1971; The Arrivistes, 1949; At the End of the Open Road, 1963; The Best Hour of the Night, 1983; Caviare at the Funeral, 1980–1981; The Character of the Poet, 1986; Collected Poems, 1988–1990; A Company of Poets, 1981; A Dream of Governors, 1959–1967; In the Room We Share, 1990; The Invasion of Italy, 1976; Jamaica Poems, 1993; The King My Father's Wreck, 1995; North of Jamaica, 1972; Out of Season, 1979; People Live Here, 1983; Poems, 1989; Riverside Drive, 1962–1972; Searching for the Ox, 1976; Selected Poems, 1965; Selected Prose, 1989; Ships Going Into the Blue, 1994; There You Are, 1995.

2644. Moran, Ronald. *Louis Simpson.* New York: Twayne, 1972. 187 pp.

2645. Robertson, William H. *Louis Simpson: A Reference Guide.* Boston, MA: G. K. Hall, 1980. 172 pp.

2646. *Smalling, Milton* (poet). The Battlefield, 1986; Community Brigade, 1992; Fighting Spirit, 1983; Lyrics and Illustration, 1982.

2647. *Smith, Malachi D. Sankey* (poet). Black Boy Blue, 1992.

2648. *Spence, Vanessa* (novelist). The Roads Are Down, 1993.

2649. *Stewart, Bob* (poet). Cane Cut, 1988.

2650. *Taylor, Mervyn* (poet). An Island of His Own, 1992.

2651. *Thomas, Elean* (poet). Before They Can Speak of Flowers, 1988; The Last Room, 1992; Word Rhythms From the Life of a Woman, 1986.

2652. *Thompson, Ralph* (poet). The Denting of a Wave, 1992.

2653. *Virtue, Vivian L.,* 1911– (poet). Wings of the Morning, 1938.

2654. *Whitfield, Dorothy* (poet). Carib Breeze, 1993.

2655. *Winkler, Anthony C.* (novelist). The Great Yacht Race, 1992; The Lunatic, 1985–1987; The Painted Canoe, 1983–1989.

2656. *Wynter, Sylvia,* 1928– (novelist, playwright, poet). The Hills of Hebron, 1962–1984.

MONTSERRAT

A. ANTHOLOGIES

General

2657. Fergus, Howard A., ed. *Dreams of Alliougana: An Anthology of Montserrat Prose and Poetry*. Plymouth, Montserrat: University Centre, University of the West Indies, 1974. 45 pp.

2658. Fergus, Howard A., and Larry Rowdon, eds. *Dark Against the Sky: An Anthology of Poems and Short Stories from Montserrat*. Montserrat: School of Continuing Studies, University of the West Indies, 1990. 96 pp.

Poetry

Poetry: Twentieth Century

2659. Fergus, Howard A., ed. *Flowers Blooming Late: Poems From Montserrat*. Plymouth, Montserrat: University Centre, University of the West Indies, 1984. 72 pp.

2660. ———. *Horrors of a Hurricane: Poems*. Plymouth, Montserrat: School of Continuing Studies, University of the West Indies, 1990. 104 pp. Running title *From Hugo with Love*.

Fiction

Fiction: Twentieth Century

2661. Fergus, Howard A., and V. Jane Grell, eds. *The Sea Gull and Other Stories*. Plymouth, Montserrat: Alliouagana Commune, 1976. 95 pp.

B. INDIVIDUAL AUTHORS

Twentieth Century

2662. *Edgecombe, David* (playwright, poet, short story writer). Coming Home to Roost, 1988; Heaven and Other Plays, 1993; Sonuvabitch, 1975.

2663. *Fergus, Howard A.,* 1937– (poet, short story writer). Calabash of Gold, 1993; Cotton Rhymes, 1976; Eruption, 1995; Gran' Stan' and Elections Ninety-one, 1991 (with V. Jane Grell); Green Innocence, 1978; Politics for Sport, 1987; Stop the Carnival, 1980.

2664. *Irish, J. A. George* (poet, short story writer). Alliouagana Folk, 1985; A Song for Alliouagana, 1988.

2665. *Lewis, Lowell L.* (poet). Hugo and Us, 1990; Montserrat, I Love You, 1990; Old and Relaxed in Montserrat, 1990.

2666. *Markham, Edward Archibald,* 1939– (poet, short story writer). Cross-Fire, 1972; Family Matters, 1984; Games and Penalties, 1980; Human Rites, 1984; Lambchops, 1976; Lambchops in Disguise, 1976; Lambchops in Papua New Guinea, 1986; Letter From Ulster and the Hugo Poems, 1993; Living In Disguise, 1986; Love, Politics and Food, 1982; Love Poems, 1978; Mad and Other Poems, 1973; Maze, 1978; Philpot in the City, 1976; Pierrot, 1979; Something Unusual, 1986; Ten Stories, 1994; Towards the End of a Century, 1989.

2667. *Osborne, Sonja* (playwright). Mermaids and Curses, 1984.

2668. *White, Edgar,* 1947– (novelist, playwright). Children of Night, 1974; The Crucificado, 1973; Lament for Rastafari and Other Plays, 1983 (Lament for Rastafari, Like Them That Dream [Children of Ogun], The Long and Cheerful Road to Slavery, The Case of Dr. Kola); The Life and Times of J. Walter Smintheus, 1973; The Nine Night, 1984; Omar at Christmas, 1973; The Rising, 1988; Ritual by Water, 1984; Sati, the Rastafarian, 1973; Three Plays, 1985 (Redemption Song, The Boot Dance, Les femmes noires); Underground, 1970 (The Burghers of Calais, Fun in Lethe [or The Feast of Misrule], The Mummer's Play, The Wonderfull Yeare).

ST. CHRISTOPHER, NEVIS, AND ANGUILLA

A. ANTHOLOGIES

2669. Brown, John, ed. *Poems and Stories of St. Christopher, Nevis and Anguilla*. [s.l.]: Extra Mural Dept., University of the West Indies, 1960. 27 pp.

B. INDIVIDUAL AUTHORS

Twentieth Century

2670. *Bakari, Ishaq Imruh* (playwright, poet). Secret Lives, 1986; Sounds and Echoes, 1980.

2671. *Bowry, Andrea Barbara* (poet). Independence, 1983.

2672. *Fahie, Fabian* (poet). To Be Somebody, 1986.

2673. *Gilchrist, Rupert,* 1940– (novelist). Dragonard, 1975–1984; Dragonard Blood, 1977; Dragonard Rising, 1978–1979; A Girl Called Friday Night, 1983; The Guns of Dragonard, 1982; The House At Three O'Clock, 1982; The Master of Dragonard Hill, 1976; The Siege of Dragonard Hill, 1979–1982; The Wrong Side of Town, 1985.

2674. *Gumbs, Lena* (poet). The Experience, 1986.

2675. *Gumbs, Marvin* (poet). A Tribute to the Anguilla Revolution, 1992.

2676. *Hecox, Don A.* (poet). Portraits from the Virgins, 1991; Portraits of Nevis and Leeward Islands, 1984; Portraits of the U.S. Virgin Islands, 1986; Seeing Nevis, 1990.

2677. *Hodge, George* (playwright). Bless Britain, 1986.

2678. *Jones-Hendrickson, Simon B.* (novelist, poet). Death on the Pasture, 1994; Hugo and Friends, 1990; Reflections Through Time,

1989; Sonny Jim of Sandy Point, 1991; A Virgin Islands Sojourn, 1990.

2679. *Killikelly, Kathleen* (novelist). The Fig Tree, 1974; The Power of the Dog, 1974.

2680. *Phillips, Caryl,* 1958– (novelist, playwright). Cambridge, 1991–1993; Crossing the River, 1991–1995; The European Tribe, 1987–1993; The Final Passage, 1985–1995; Higher Ground, 1989–1995; Playing Away, 1987; The Shelter, 1984; A State of Independence, 1986–1995; Strange Fruit, 1981; Where There Is Darkness, 1982.

2681. *Wrensford, Agatha James* (poet). The Emotion It Evokes, 1988.

ST. LUCIA

A. ANTHOLOGIES

General

2682. Brathwaite, Kamau, ed. *Iounaloa: Recent Writing from St. Lucia.* Castries: Dept. of Extra Mural Studies, University of the West Indies, 1963. 86 pp.

2683. Hippolyte, Kendel and Melchoir Henry, eds. *Pulse: A Collection of Essays by St. Lucian Writers.* Castries, St. Lucia: The Source, 1980. 43 pp.

Poetry

Poetry: Twentieth Century

2684. Hippolyte, Kendel, ed. *Confluence: Nine St. Lucian Poets.* Castries, St. Lucia: The Source, 1988. 64 pp.

2685. Odlum, Yasmin and Melania Daniel, eds. *Walking Iyanola on Pious Feet: An Anthology of Poems on the Environment in St. Lucia.* Castries: St. Lucia National Trust, 1989. 28 pp.

Fiction

Fiction: General

2686. Folk Research Centre (St. Lucia). *Oral Literature of Saint Lucia.* Castries: The Centre, 1992. 26 pp.

B. INDIVIDUAL AUTHORS

Twentieth Century

2687. *Dalphinis, Morgan* (poet). For Those Who Will Come After!, 1985.

2688. *Daniel, Melania* (poet). Mindfield, 1994.

2689. *Dixon, McDonald,* 1945– (poet). Pebbles, 1973; The Poet Speaks and Other Poems, 1980–1993.

2690. *Dorville, Laureen* (poet). Déjà vu, 1993.

2691. *Gustave, Christine* (poet). Against the Tides, 1990.

2692. *Henry, Melchoir* (poet). Dead Country, 1981.

2693. *Hippolyte, Kendel,* 1952– (poet). Bearings, 1986; Island in the Sun, 1980; The Labyrinth, 1993.

2694. *King, Jane* (poet). Fellow Traveller, 1994; In to the Centre, 1993.

2695. *Lee, John Robert,* 1948– (playwright, poet, short story writer). Translations, 1993 (Vocation and Other Poems [1975], Dread Season [1978], The Prodigal [1983], Possessions [1984], Saint Lucian [1988], Clearing Ground [1991]).

2696. *Long, Earl G.* (novelist, short story writer). Consolation, 1994; Voices from a Drum, 1996.

2697. *Mondesir, Jones E.,* 1915– (poet). Annou di-i an Kwéyòl, 1985?; Pas mon Dieu qui faire?, 1980–1984.

2698. *St. Clair, Gandolph,* 1951– (poet). The Moon in Daylight, 1987.

2699. *St. Omer, Garth,* 1931– (novelist, short story writer). J— , Black Bam and the Masqueraders, 1972; The Lights On the Hill, 1986; Nor Any Country, 1969; A Room On the Hill, 1968; Shades of Grey, 1968; Syrop, 1964.

2700. *Walcott, Derek,* 1930– (playwright, poet). Another Life, 1973–1982; The Arkansas Testament, 1987; The Caribbean Poetry of Derek Walcott, 1983; The Castaway and Other Poems, 1965–1969; Collected Poems (1948–1984), 1986–1992; Derek Walcott in Caribbean Quarterly (Selections), 1992; Dream on Monkey Mountain and Other Plays, 1970–1991 (The Sea at Dauphin [1958], Ti-Jean and His Brothers [1970], Malcauchon/The Six in the Rain [1966], Dream on Monkey Mountain [1967]); Drums and Colours, 1961; Epitaph for the Young, 1949; The Fortunate Traveller, 1981; The Gulf and Other Poems, 1969–1974; Henri Christophe, 1950; In a Green Night,

1962–1969; Ione, 1957; The Joker of Seville, 1978; Midsummer, 1984–1989; O Babylon, 1978; The Odyssey, 1993; Omeros, 1990–1992; Pantomine, 1980; Poems (1965–1980), 1992–1993; Remembrance, 1980; Sea Grapes, 1976; Selected Poems, 1964; Selected Poetry, 1981–1993 (Wayne Brown, ed.); The Star-Apple Kingdom, 1979; Three Plays, 1986 (The Last Carnival, Beef No Chicken, A Branch At the Blue Nile).

2701. Baugh, Edward. *Derek Walcott: Memory As Vision—Another Life*. London: Longman, 1978. 85 pp.

2702. Brown, Stewart, ed. *The Art of Derek Walcott*. Chester Springs, PA: Dufour Editions, 1991. 231 pp.

2703. Goldstraw, Irma E. *Derek Walcott: An Annotated Bibliography of His Works*. New York: Garland, 1984. 238 pp.

2704. ———. *Derek Walcott: A Bibliography of Published Poems—With Dates of Publication and Variant Versions, 1944–1979*. St. Augustine, Trinidad: Research and Publications Committee, University of the West Indies, 1979. 43 pp.

2705. Hamner, Robert D., ed. *Critical Perspectives on Derek Walcott*. Washington, DC: Three Continents Press, 1993. 482 pp.

2706. Hamner, Robert D. *Derek Walcott. Updated ed.* Boston, MA: Twayne, 1993. 199 pp.

2707. Terada, Rei. *Derek Walcott's Poetry: American Mimicry*. Boston, MA: Northeastern University Press, 1992. 260 pp.

2708. Todd, Loreto. *Derek Walcott: Selected Poems*. Harlow: Longman, 1993. 94 pp.

2709. Walcott, Derek, and William Baer, ed. *Conversations with Derek Walcott*. Jackson, MS: University Press of Mississippi, 1996. 211 pp.

See also #2228, #2230, #2732.

2710. *Walcott, Roderick,* 1930– (playwright). The Banjo Man, 1972; A Flight of Sparrows, 1966; The Harrowing of Benjy, 1958–1979; Malfinis/The Heart of a Child, 1967–1981; Shrove Tuesday March, 1966; The Trouble With Albino Joe, 1966. See also #2230.

ST. VINCENT AND THE GRENADINES
(INCLUDING BEQUIA)

A. ANTHOLOGIES

Poetry

Poetry: Twentieth Century

2711. Joyette, Anthony, ed. *Vincentian Poets, 1950–1980*. St. Laurent, Que.: AFO Enterprises, 1990. 128 pp.

Fiction

Fiction: Twentieth Century

2712. Thomsen, Thomas Carl, ed. *Tales of Bequia*. Cross River, NY: Cross River Press, 1988.

B. INDIVIDUAL AUTHORS

Twentieth Century

2713. *Carr, Peggy* (poet). Echoes From a Lonely Nightwatch, 1989.

2714. *Daisy, Al T.,* 1939– (poet). Dedications on Turning Thirty, 1971.

2715. *Dey, Richard Morris* (poet). The Bequia Poems, 1979–1988.

2716. *Keane, Shake* (poet). One A Week With Water, 1979; The Volcano Suite, 1979.

2717. *King, Camm G. O.* (poet). Aibel in Pain, 1983; Too Deep for Tears, 1980; Vision, 1973; Voice of the Poet, 1984?

2718. *Nanton, Philip,* 1947– (playwright). Anancy's Magic, 1987 (with Veronica Nanton); Gypsy Fortunes, 1987 (with Veronica Nanton).

2719. *Phillips, Travers* (poet). The Phoenix and Other Poems, 1975?; Quiet Days Near the Ocean, 1985; Sunrise, 1984.

2720. *Robinson, Nelcia* (poet). Pictures Remain, 1987; Poetry As Feeling, 1988.

2721. *Thomas, H. Nigel,* 1947– (novelist, short story writer). How Loud Can the Village Cock Crow and Other Stories, 1994; Spirits in the Dark, 1993–1994.

TRINIDAD AND TOBAGO

A. BIBLIOGRAPHIES AND BIO-BIBLIOGRAPHIES

2722. Pantin, Maritza, and Diane Hunte. *Creative Writers in Trinidad and Tobago: A Bibliography.* St. Augustine, Trinidad/Tobago: Library, University of the West Indies, 1970. 34 pp.

2723. Wharton-Lake, Beverly D. *Creative Literature of Trinidad and Tobago: A Bibliography.* Washington, DC: Columbus Memorial Library, Organization of American States, 1988. 102 pp.

B. ANTHOLOGIES

General

General: Sixteenth to Nineteenth Centuries

2724. Sander, Reinhard W., and Peter K. Ayers, eds. *From Trinidad: An Anthology of Early West Indian Writing.* New York: Africana, 1978. 310 pp.

General: Twentieth Century

2725. Gonzalez, Anson, and Kenneth Vidia Parmasad, eds. *Arising: W[riters] U[nion of] T[rinidad] & T[obago] Fifth Anniversary Anthology.* St. James, Trinidad/Tobago: Writers Union of Trinidad and Tobago, 1985. 72 pp.

Poetry

Poetry: General

2726. Lewis, Maureen Warner, ed. *Yoruba Songs of Trinidad with Translations.* London: Karnak House, 1994. 158 pp.

Poetry: Twentieth Century

2727. Watts, Margaret, ed. *Washer Woman Hangs Her Poems in the Sun: Poems by Women of Trinidad and Tobago.* Tunapuna, Trinidad: G. V. Ferguson, 1990. 152 pp.

C. HISTORY AND CRITICISM

General

General: Twentieth Century

2728. Gonzalez, Anson. *Self-Discovery Through Literature: Creative Writing in Trinidad and Tobago.* Diego Martin, Trinidad/Tobago: A. Gonzalez, 1972. 55 pp.

2729. ———, ed. *Trinidad and Tobago Literature: On Air.* Port of Spain: National Cultural Council of Trinidad and Tobago, 1974. 120 pp.

2730. Harney, Stefano. *Nationalism and Identity: Culture and the Imagination in a Caribbean Diaspora.* Atlantic Highlands, NJ: Zed Books, 1996. 216 pp.

2731. Sander, Reinhard W. *The Trinidad Awakening: West Indian Literature of the Nineteen-thirties.* New York: Greenwood Press, 1988. 168 pp.

Drama

Drama: Twentieth Century

2732. King, Bruce Alvin. *Derek Walcott and West Indian Drama: Not Only a Playwright But a Company—the Trinidad Theatre Workshop 1953–1993.* New York: Oxford University, Press, 1995. 410 pp.

D. INDIVIDUAL AUTHORS

Twentieth Century

2733. *Abdul Malik* (poet). De Homeplace, 1990; The Whirlwind, 1990.

2734. *Alexander, Francine,* 1968– (poet). The Aftermath, 1988 (with Candyce Kelshall and Laila Haidarali).

2735. *Allen, Oswald,* 1927– (poet). Moment of Eternal Years, 1987; Moment of Time, 1964; Thoughts and Visions of Christopher Columbus, 1992.

2736. *Alleyne-Forte, Learie* (short story writer). Jokers on the Abyss' Edge, 1994.

2737. *Als, Michael R.,* 1946– (novelist, poet). Bill of Rights, 1985; Detention, 1970?–1985; Love on the River Stone and Other Stories, 1992; No Half a Loaf, 1992; Pickers and Flowers, 1970?–1985; Poems on Life and Soul, 1973?; Speaking of My Country, 1975.

2738. *Anthony, Michael,* 1932– (novelist, poet, short story writer). All That Glitters, 1983; Bright Road to El Dorado, 1982; The Chieftain's Carnival and Other Stories, 1993 (The Chieftain's Carnival, The Blue Skies of Danger, Duel in the Sun (for Columbus), Soledad, They Better Don't Stop the Carnival, Rebels in the Night, Bay of Song, Run Eva Run, Little Winston, Butler on the Road, Victory Ever More, Red Is the Noonday Soil); Cricket in the Road, 1973; Folk Tales and Fantasies, 1976; The Games Were Coming, 1963–1977; Green Days By the River, 1967–1989; King of the Masquerade, 1974; Sandra Street and Other Stories, 1973; Streets of Conflict, 1976; The Year in San Fernando, 1965–1978.

2739. *Archibald, Douglas N.,* 1919– (novelist, playwright, poet, short story writer). Annie-Marie, 1967; The Bamboo Clump, 1967; Defeat with Honor, 1977; Isidore and the Turtle, 1977; Island Tide, 1972; Junction Village, 1958–1967; Old Maid's Tale, 1966; The Rose Slip, 1967. See also #2230.

2740. *Belgrave, Valerie* (novelist). Sun Valley Romance, 1993; Ti Marie, 1988.

2741. *Bhajan, Selwyn,* 1945– (poet). Another Shore, 1992; Quest, 1975; Season of Songs, 1973; Voyage, 1981; Whispers of Dawn, 1978.

2742. *Bissoondath, Neil,* 1955– (novelist, short story writer). A Casual Brutality, 1988–1990; Digging Up the Mountains, 1986; The Innocence of Age, 1992–1993; On the Eve of Uncertain Tomorrows, 1990–1991.

2743. *Boodhoo, Isaiah James,* 1932– (novelist). Between Two Seasons, 1994.

2744. *Brand, Dionne,* 1953– (poet, short story writer). Bread out of Stone, 1994 (Autobiographical); Chronicles of the Hostile Sun, 1984; Earth Magic, 1979–1993; Epigrams to Ernesto Cardenal in Defense of Claudia, 1983; 'Fore Day Morning, 1978; Grammar of Dissent: Poetry and Prose, 1994 (Carol Morrell, ed.); No Language Is Neutral, 1990; Primitive Offensive, 1982; Sans Souci and Other Stories, 1988–1994; Winter Epigrams, 1983.

2745. *Brown, Wayne Vincent,* 1944– (poet, short story writer). The Child of the Sea, 1989; On the Coast, 1972; Voyages, 1989.

2746. *Cambridge, E. M.,* 1904– (novelist). Feet of Clay, 1944–1979.

2747. *Cartey, Wilfred G.,* 1931– (novelist, poet). Black Velvet Time, 1984; Children of Lalibela, 1985?; Choreographers of the Dawn, 1989; Fires in the Wind, 1980; The House of Blue Lightning, 1973; Kundya, 1982; Potentialities, 1987; Red Rain, 1977; Suns and Shadows, 1978; Waters of My Soul, 1975.

2748. *Charles, Faustin,* 1944– (novelist, poet, short story writer). The Black Magic Man of Brixton, 1985; Crab Track, 1973; Days and Nights in the Magic Forest, 1986; The Expatriate, 1969; Signposts of the Jumbie, 1981; Tales from the West Indies, 1985.

2749. *Clarke, Alfred McDonald,* 1912– (novelist, poet, short story writer). Ballads of Selassie and the Rastafarians and Other Verse, 1983; Black and White Lovers By Ritual, 1991; The Black Madonna and Other Stories of Our Heritage, 1985; Caribbean Coup, 1979; Little Flames of Freedom, 1990; Revolution at Grass Roots and Other Stories, 1970; Verses for Emancipation, 1986; Wheels Within Wheels, 1975.

2750. *Clarke, Leroy* (poet). Douens, 1981; Taste of Endless Fruit, 1974–1992.

2751. *Cruickshank, Alfred M.,* 1880–1940 (poet). Poems in All Moods, 1937.

2752. *Cummings, Joseph* (poet, short story writer). Dedicated (To You With Love) and Other Poems, 1985; Heart Beat, 1974?; In Journey Now and Other Poems, 1987; Uphill Downhill, 1981.

2753. *Darklight, Senya,* –1987 (poet). Companion to Senya, 1989 (Marty Campbell, ed.); Rise in Love, 1986; Senya, 1988.

2754. *De Boissiere, Ralph,* 1907– (novelist, short story writer). Crown Jewel, 1952–1981; No Saddles for Kangaroos, 1964; Rum and Coca-Cola, 1956–1984.

2755. *De Lima, Arthur,* 1915– (novelist, poet, short story writer). Bits and Pieces, 1976; Chinabound, 1984; The Community, 1979; Don José, 1993; Echoes of Oritumbe, 1985; The Great Quake, 1982; The House of Jacob, 1981–1982; A Mixed Grill, 1982; Oritumbe, 1982; Who Killed Amandela Delapina, 1987.

2756. *De Lima, Clara Rosa,* 1921– (novelist, poet). Countdown to Carnival, 1978; Currents of the Yuna, 1978; Dreams Non-Stop, 1974; Kilometre Nineteen, 1980; Not Bad, Just a Little Mad, 1975; Reminiscing, 1975; Thoughts and Dreams, 1973; Tomorrow Will Always Come, 1965.

2757. *Doodnath, Samuel,* 1911– (novelist). From India to Trinidad, 1987; Indian Prince and Chinese Princess in Love, 1995; Santiago and Kumar, 1980.

2758. *Dorant, St. Clair Wesley* (playwright). Born to Live, 1973; The Burning Question?, 1978; Feelings, 1978; Hannah, the Domestic, 1977; A Moment with Fear, 1973; No Crocodile Tears, 1983; Panyard, 1974; The Reckless Lovers, 1973.

2759. *Espinet, Ramabai,* 1948– (poet, short story writer). Ninja's Carnival, 1993; Nuclear Seasons, 1991; The Princess of Spadina, 1992.

2760. *Frederick, Rawle,* 1945– (poet, short story writer). Trans Atlantic Cargo, 1973; The Vendor of Dreams and Other Stories, 1992.

2761. *Gibbings, Wesley A.* (poet). Cold Bricks and Warm Nights, 1988; Lost in the City, 1993; On Life, 1977; The Poetry of the Ages, 1980; Simon and the Prophet, 1980.

2762. *Gonzalez, Anson,* 1934– (playwright, poet). Collected Poems, 1979; The Love Song of Boysie B. and Other Poems, 1974; Merry-Go-Round and Other Poems, 1992; Moksha, 1988; Score, 1972 (with Victor David Questel).

2763. *Gonzalez, Maria,* 1963– (poet). Feelings, 1977; Step by Step, 1974; A Young Girl's Poems, 1992.

2764. *Gosine, Vishnu Ramsamooj* (novelist, short story writer). The Coming of Lights, 1992; My Grandfather's Story, 1985.

2765. *Gray, Cecil Roderick,* 1923– (poet). The Woolgatherer, 1994.

2766. *Gray, Christopher Randolph,* 1968– (poet). Along the Sea Shore, 1995; Cry of My Soul, 1989; Towards a State of Being, 1992; Voices of the Silent, 1991.

2767. *Guy, Rosa,* 1925– (novelist). And I Heard a Bird Sing, 1987–1994; Bird at My Window, 1966–1989; The Disappearance, 1979–1992; Edith Jackson, 1976–1992; The Friends, 1973–1992; A Measure of Time, 1983–1986; Mirror of Her Own, 1981; The Music of Summer, 1992; My Love, My Love, or the Peasant Girl, 1985–1991; New Guys Around the Block, 1982–1992; Paris, Pee Wee, and Big Dog, 1984–1988; Ruby, 1976–1992; The Sun, the Sea, a Touch of Wind, 1995 (Autobiographical); The Ups and Downs of Carl Davis III, 1989–1994.

2768. *Haidarali, Laila,* 1969– (poet). The Aftermath, 1988 (with Francine Alexander and Candyce Kelshall).

2769. *Hallworth, Grace,* 1935– (short story writer). Cric Crac, 1990–1994; Listen to This Story, 1977–1992.

2770. *Haynes, Martin De Coursey,* 1939– (poet). Charybdis, 1986; A Doc in the Making, 1992; The Moving Finger, 1985; The Quintessential College Boy, 1990; Windows, 1993.

2771. *Herbert, Cecil L.,* 1926– (poet). The Poems of Cecil Herbert, 1979 (Danielle Gianetti, ed.).

2772. *Hercules, Frank,* 1920– (novelist). I Want a Black Doll, 1967–1969; On Leaving Paradise, 1980; Where the Hummingbird Flies, 1961–1969.

2773. *Hill, Errol,* 1921– (playwright, poet). Caribbean Plays, 1958–1978 (Broken Melody, Dance Bongo, Dilemma, Oily Portraits/Brittle and the City Fathers, The Ping-Pong, Square Peg, Strictly Matrimony, Wey-wey); Man Better Man, 1985. See also #2227, #2228, #2230.

2774. *Hill, Sonné* (playwright, short story writer). Jack's Dilemma and Other Local Plays, 1995; Phantom of the Cemetery Wall and Other Stories, 1984.

2775. *Hodge, Merle,* 1944– (novelist). Crick Crack, Monkey, 1970–1981; For the Life of Laetitia, 1993–1994.

2776. *Horsham, Maurice M.* (poet, short story writer). Blood That Thickens, 1995.

2777. *James, Cynthia* (poet, short story writer). Iere, My Love, 1990; Smoothe Me, Music, Soothe Me, 1990; La Vega and Other Poems, 1995; Vigil, 1995.

2778. *James, Cyril Lionel Robert,* 1901–1989 (novelist, playwright, short story writer). At the Rendezvous of Victory, 1984; C.L.R. James (Selections), 1970; The C.L.R. James Reader, 1992 (Anna Grimshaw, ed.); The Future in the Present, 1977; Mariners, Renegades and Castaways, 1953–1985; Minty Alley, 1936–1981; Spheres of Existence, 1980.

    2779. Buhle, Paul. *C.L.R. James: The Artist as Revolutionary.* New York, NY: Verso, 1988. 197 pp.

    2780. ———, ed. *C.L.R. James: His Life and Works.* London: Alison and Busby, 1986. 256 pp.

    2781. Cudjoe, Selwyn Reginald, and William E. Cain, eds. *C.L.R. James: His Intellectal Legacies.* Amherst, MA: University of Massachussetts Press, 1995. 476 pp.

    2782. Farred, Grant, ed. *Rethinking C.L.R. James.* Cambridge, MA: Blackwell, 1996. 225 pp.

    2783. Grimshaw, Anna. *The C.L.R. James Archive: A Reader's Guide.* New York, NY: C.L.R. James Institute, 1991. 108 pp.

    2784. ———. *Popular Democracy and the Creative Imagination: The Writings of C.L.R. James, 1950–1963.* New York: C.L.R. James Institute, 1991. 48 pp.

    2785. Grimshaw, Anna, and Keith Hart. *C.L.R. James: The Struggle for Happiness.* New York: C.L.R. James Institute, 1991. 57 pp.

    2786. Henry, Paget, and Paul Buhle, eds. *C.L.R. James's Caribbean.* Durham, NC: Duke University Press, 1992. 287 pp.

    2787. James, Cyril Lionel Robert, and Anna Grimshaw, ed. *Special Delivery: The Letters of C.L.R. James to Constance Webb, 1939–1948.* Cambridge, MA: Blackwell, 1996. 393 pp.

    2788. McLemee, Scott, and Paul Le Blanc, eds. *C.L.R. James and Revolutionary Marxism: Selected Writings of C.L.R.*

James, 1939–1949. Atlantic Highlands, NJ: Humanities Press, 1994. 252 pp.

2789. Ragoonath, Bishnu, ed. *Tribute to a Scholar: Appreciating C.L.R. James.* Kingston: Consortium Graduate School of Social Sciences, 1990. 114 pp.

2790. Sancho, T. Anson. *CLR, the Man and His Work: A Study of Cyril Lionel Robinson James—the Father of Modern West Indian Life and Literature.* 2d ed. Georgetown: Guyana Printers, 1976. 86 pp.

2791. Worcester, Kent. *C.L.R. James: A Political Biography.* Albany, NY: State University of New York Press, 1996. 311 pp.

See also #2267.

2792. *James, LeRoy Martin,* 1945– (novelist, poet). Cannibal Island, 1983; Drysdale's Estate, 1975; The Fisherman, 1991; The Lawless Bunch, 1994; A Quiet Resort, 1975; Rhythm of Coger Street, 1966; A Short Peaceful Walk, 1975.

2793. *John, Errol,* 1918– (playwright). Moon on a Rainbow Shawl, 1958–1985; The Tout, 1966.

2794. *John, Frank,* 1941– (playwright, poet). The Beat Within, 1985; Before the Thunder Rolls, 1980; Black Songs, 1969; Black Waves, 1973; Boogoo Boogoo, 1973; Dreadness, 1978; Light a Fire, 1973; Love in Black Soul, 1977; Naked Image, 1974; Orange Lady, 1973; Street Beat Blues, 1982; The Tenderness of Life's Emotions, 1979; Time Ah Soon Come, 1976; We Will Meet Again, 1978.

2795. *Johnson, Amryl,* 1944– (poet, short story writer). Gorgons, 1992; Long Road to Nowhere, 1982–1985; Sequins for a Ragged Hem, 1988; Tread Carefully in Paradise, 1991.

2796. *Keens-Douglas, Paul,* 1942– (playwright, poet, short story writer). Is Town Say So, 1981; Lal Shop, 1984; Tanti at de Oval, 1992; Tell Me Again, 1979; Tim Tim, 1976; Twice Upon a Time, 1989; When Moon Shine, 1975–1979.

2797. *Kelshall, Candyce* (poet). The Aftermath, 1988 (with Francine Alexander and Laila Haidarali); Voices On the Sea, 1990 (with Naomi Laird and Alan Tang).

2798. *Khan, Ismith,* 1925– (novelist, short story writer). The Crucifixion, 1986; A Day in the Country and Other Stories, 1994; The Jumbie Bird, 1961–1985; The Obeah Man, 1964–1995.

2799. *Kissoon, Freddie* (playwright). Calabash Alley, 1973; Common Entrance, 1970; Do Your Home-Lesons, Daddy, 1970; Mamaguy, 1961–1978; One Hundred Exercises in Creative Drama, 1970; We Crucify Him, 1967; Zingay, 1966–1978.

2800. *La Rose, John,* 1927– (poet). Eyelets of Truth Within Me, 1992; Foundations, 1966.

    2801. John La Rose Tribute Committee. *Foundations of a Movement: A Tribute to John La Rose on the Occasion of the Tenth International Book Fair of Radical Black and Third World Books.* London: The Committee, 1991. 195 pp.

    2802. La Rose, John et al. *The New Cross Massacre Story: Interviews with John La Rose.* London: Alliance of the Black Parents Movement, 1984. 38 pp.

2803. *Ladoo, Harold Sonny,* 1942–1973 (novelist, short story writer). No Pain Like This Body, 1972–1987; Yesterdays, 1974.

2804. *Laird, Naomi* (poet). Voices on the Sea, 1990 (with Candyce Kelshall and Alan Tang).

2805. *Lovelace, Earl,* 1935– (novelist, playwright, poet, short story writer). A Brief Conversation and Other Stories, 1988; The Dragon Can't Dance, 1979–1986; Jestina's Calypso and Other Plays, 1984 (Jestina's Calypso, The New Hardware Store, My Name Is Village); The Schoolmaster, 1968–1979; While Gods Are Falling, 1965–1984; The Wine of Astonishment, 1982–1986.

2806. *Lyons, John,* 1953– (poet). Behind the Carnival, 1994; Lure of the Cascadura, 1989.

2807. *Maharaj, Rabindranath* (short story writer). The Interloper, 1995; The Writer and His Wife and Other Stories, 1996.

2808. *Matura, Mustapha,* 1939– (playwright, poet, short story writer). Black Pieces, 1972; The Coup, 1991; Moon Jump, 1988–1990; Playboy of the West Indies, 1988–1989; Rum an' Coca Cola, 1976–1980; Six Plays, 1991–1992 (As Time Goes By [1972],

Nice [1980], Play Mas [1974], Independence [1979], Welcome Home Jacko [1980], Meetings [1982]).

2809. *Maynard, Olga Comma* (poet, short story writer). Carib Echoes, 1934–1972; My Yesterdays, 1992.

2810. *McDonald, Ian,* 1933– (novelist, playwright, poet, short story writer). Essequibo, 1992; The Humming-Bird Tree, 1969–1992; Jaffo the Calypsonian, 1994; Mercy Ward, 1988; Poems, 1971; Selected Poems, 1983.

2811. *Mendes, Alfred H.,* 1897– (novelist, poet, short story writer). Black Fauns, 1935–1984; Pitch Lake, 1934–1980; The Wages of Sin and Other Poems, 1925.

2812. *Naipaul, Seepersad,* 1906– (short story writer). The Adventures of Gurudeva and Other Stories, 1976–1995.

2813. *Naipaul, Shiva,* 1945–1985 (novelist, short story writer). Beyond the Dragon's Mouth, 1985; The Chip-Chip Gatherers, 1973–1983; Fireflies, 1970–1983; Love and Death in a Hot Country/A Hot Country, 1985); A Man of Mystery and Other Stories, 1995; An Unfinished Journey, 1986–1988.

2814. *Naipaul, V. S.,* 1932– (novelist, poet, short story writer). A Bend in the River, 1979–1989; A Congo Diary, 1980; The Enigma of Arrival, 1987–1988; Finding the Center, 1984–1986; A Flag on the Island, 1967–1981 (My Aunt Gold Teeth, The Raffle, A Christmas Story, The Mourners, The Night Watchman's Occurrence Book, The Enemy, Greenie and Yellow, The Perfect Tenants, The Heart, The Baker's Story, A Flag on the Island); Guerrillas, 1975–1990; A House for Mr. Biswas, 1961–1992; In a Free State, 1971–1984; The Killings in Trinidad, 1960–1981; Miguel Street, 1959–1993; The Mimic Men, 1967–1992; Mr Stone and the Knights Companion, 1963–1985; The Overcrowded Barracoon, 1958–1984; The Return of Eva Perón, 1981; Three Novels, 1982 (The Mystic Masseur [1957], The Suffrage of Elvira [1958], Miguel Street [1959]); A Way in the World, 1994–1995.

2815. Boxill, Anthony. *V.S. Naipaul's Fiction: In Quest of The Enemy.* Fredericton, NB: York Press, 1983. 88 pp.

2816. Cudjoe, Selwyn Reginald. *V.S. Naipaul: A Materialist Reading.* Amherst, MA: University of Massachusetts Press, 1988. 287 pp.

2817. Dissanayake, Wimal, and Carmen Wickramagamage. *Self and Colonial Desire: Travel Writings of V.S. Naipaul.* New York: P. Lang, 1993. 160 pp.

2818. Hamner, Robert D. *V.S. Naipaul.* Boston, MA: Twayne, 1973. 181 pp.

2819. Hamner, Robert D., ed. *Critical Perspectives on V.S. Naipaul.* London: Heinemann Educational, 1987. 300 pp. Reprint of the 1977 ed.

2820. Hassan, Dolly Zulakha. *V.S. Naipaul and the West Indies.* New York: P. Lang, 1989. 376 pp.

2821. Hughes, Peter. *V.S. Naipaul.* New York: Routledge, 1988. 114 pp.

2822. Jarvis, Kelvin. *V.S. Naipaul: A Selective Bibliography with Annotations, 1957–1987.* Metuchen, NJ: Scarecrow Press, 1989. 205 pp.

2823. Joshi, Chandra B. *V.S. Naipaul: The Voice of Exile.* New Delhi: Sterling, 1994. 238 pp.

2824. Kamra, Shashi. *The Novels of V.S. Naipaul: A Study in Theme and Form.* New Delhi: Prestige Books, 1990. 174 pp.

2825. Kelly, Richard Michael. *V.S. Naipaul.* New York: Continuum, 1989. 182 pp.

2826. King, Bruce Alvin. *V.S. Naipaul.* New York: St. Martin's Press, 1993. 170 pp.

2827. Levy, Judith. *V.S. Naipaul: Displacement and Autobiography.* New York: Garland, 1995. 151 pp.

2828. Madhusudana Rao, K. I. *Contrary Awareness: A Critical Study of the Novels of V.S. Naipaul.* Madras, India: Centre for Research on the New International Economic Order, 1982. 232 pp.

2829. Mason, Nondita. *The Fiction of V. S. Naipaul.* Calcutta: World Press, 1986. 131 pp.

2830. Morris, Robert K. *Paradoxes of Order: Some Perspectives on the Fiction of V.S. Naipaul.* Columbia, MO: University of Missouri Press, 1975. 105 pp.

2831. Mustafa, Fawzia. *V.S. Naipaul*. New York: Cambridge University Press, 1995. 255 pp.

2832. Nightingale, Peggy. *Journey Through Darkness: The Writing of V.S. Naipaul*. St. Lucia, Australia: University of Queensland Press, 1987. 255 pp.

2833. Nixon, Rob. *London Calling: V.S. Naipaul, Postcolonial Mandarin*. New York: Oxford University Press, 1992. 229 pp.

2834. Rai, Sudha. *V.S. Naipaul: A Study in Expatriate Sensibility*. Atlantic Highlands, NJ: Humanities Press, 1982. 136 pp.

2835. Theroux, Paul. *V.S. Naipaul: An Introduction to His Work*. New York: Africana, 1972. 144 pp.

2836. Thieme, John. *The Web of Tradition: Uses of Allusion in V.S. Naipaul's Fiction*. London: Dangaroo Press, 1987. 224 pp.

2837. Thieme, John, and Yolande Cantù, ed. *V.S. Naipaul: The Mimic Man—A Critical View*. London: Collins, 1985. 42 pp.

2838. Thorpe, Michael. *V.S. Naipaul*. Harlow, Eng.: Longman, 1976. 47 pp.

2839. Thorpe, Michael, and Yolande Cantù, ed. *V.S. Naipaul: "A House for Mr. Biswas"—a Critical View*. London: Collins, 1985. 144 pp.

2840. Walsh, William. *V.S. Naipaul*. New York: Barnes and Noble, 1973. 94 pp.

2841. Weiss, Timothy. *On the Margins: The Art of Exile in V. S. Naipaul*. Amherst, MA: University of Massachusetts Press, 1992. 276 pp.

2842. White, Landeg. *V.S. Naipaul: A Critical Introduction*. New York: Barnes and Noble, 1975. 217 pp.

2843. *O'Callaghan, Marion,* 1934– (novelist). J'Ouvert Morning, 1976; Pan Beat, 1973.

2844. *Persaud, Lakshmi* (novelist). Butterfly in the Wind, 1990–1996; Sastra, 1993.

2845. *Philip, Marlene Nourbese,* 1947– (novelist, poet, short story writer). Grammar of Dissent: Poetry and Prose, 1994 (Carol Morrell, ed.); Harriet's Daughter, 1987–1988; In Search of Livingston, 1991; Salmon Courage, 1983; She Tries Her Tongue, Her Silence Softly Breaks, 1989–1993; Thorns, 1980.

2846. *Phillips, Nathan,* 1923– (poet, short story writer). The Caribbean Alive, 1989; Chukwuma Nwankwo, 1993; A Voice from the Bush, 1989.

2847. *Questel, Victor David,* 1948– (playwright, poet, short story writer). Hard Stares, 1982; Near Mourning Ground, 1979; Score, 1972 (with Anson Gonzalez).

2848. *Rahim, Jennifer Ann* (poet). Mothers Are Not the Only Linguists, and Other Poems, 1992.

2849. *Ramkeesoon, Peter,* –1988 (novelist). Sunday Morning Coming Down, 1975–1991.

2850. *Ramon-Fortuné, Barnabas J.,* 1905– (novelist, poet, short story writer). Black Aphrodite and Poems of Love and Passion, 1976; The Kite, 1976; The Undertones of Victory, 1990.

2851. *Roach, Eric Merton,* 1915–1974 (novelist, playwright, poet). Belle Fanto, 1967–1984; A Calabash of Blood, 1971; The Flowering Rock, 1992; Letter from Leonora, 1966–1978.

2852. *Saakana, Amon Saba,* 1948– (novelist, poet). Blues Dance, 1985; Sun Song, 1973; Tones and Colours, 1985.

2853. *Sanowar, Wilmot* (novelist, poet). The Changing World, 1988; The Pendulum Swings, 1987; Under the Boughs, 1991; Within the Storm, 1991.

2854. *Scott, Lawrence* (novelist, short story writer). Ballad for the New World and Other Stories, 1994 (Malgrétoute, King Sailor One J'ouvert Morning, The Fitful Muse, Rabbits, Chameleon, The Watchman, Ballad for the New World, The Question of the Keskidee, The Pond, I Want to Follow My Friend, Sylvia's Room, The House of Funerals); Witchbroom, 1993.

2855. *Sealy, Clifford,* 1927– (playwright, poet, short story writer). The Professor, 1966–1991.

2856. *Seetahal, Bhadase* (poet). Arrivals and Departures, 1986; Paramparaa, Unbroken Tradition, 1992.

2857. *Selvon, Samuel,* 1923– (novelist, playwright, poet, short story writer). A Brighter Sun, 1952–1985; A Drink of Water, 1968–1979; Eldorado West One, 1988; Foreday Morning, 1989; Highway in the Sun and Other Plays, 1967–1991 (Home Sweet India, Turn Again Tiger [1958], The Harvest in Wilderness); The Housing Lark, 1965–1990; I Hear Thunder, 1963; An Island Is a World, 1955–1993; The Lonely Londoners/The Lonely Ones, 1956–1991; Moses Ascending, 1975–1984; Moses Migrating, 1983–1992; The Plains of Caroni, 1970–1985; Those Who Eat the Cascadura, 1972–1990; Turn Again Tiger, 1958–1979; Ways of Sunlight, 1957–1987.

2858. Clarke, Austin. *A Passage Back Home: A Personal Reminiscence of Samuel Selvon.* Toronto: Exile Editions, 1994. 143 pp.

2859. Looker, Mark. *Atlantic Passages: History, Community, and Language in the Fiction of Sam Selvon.* New York: P. Lang, 1996. 243 pp.

2860. Nasta, Susheila, ed. *Critical Perspectives on Sam Selvon.* Washington, DC: Three Continents Press, 1988. 285 pp.

2861. Nasta, Susheila, and Anna Rutherford, eds. *Tiger's Triumph: Celebrating Sam Selvon.* Armidale, N.S.W.: Dangaroo Press, 1995. 150 pp.

2862. Wyke, Clement H. *Sam Selvon's Dialectical Style and Fictional Strategy.* Vancouver, B.C.: University of British Columbia Press, 1991. 144 pp.

2863. *Sharlowe* (novelist). Apartheid Love, 1982; The Elect, 1992; The Promise/After All We've Done For You, 1995; Requiem For a Village, 1982; When Gods Were Slaves/A Search for Truth, 1993.

2864. *Tang, Alan* (poet). Voices on the Sea, 1990 (with Candyce Kelshall and Naomi Laird).

2865. *Taylor, Daphne* (short story writer). The Pompous Parrot and Other West Indian Tales, 1947; Star O'er the Valley, 1983.

2866. *Telemaque, Harold Minton,* 1909– (poet). Burnt Bush, 1947–1973; Scarlet, 1953–1973.

2867. *Thomas, Paula Obe* (poet). Passages, 1995.

2868. *Ward, Keith Mervyn,* 1961– (poet). Moments of Indecision, 1993; Reflections, 1986.

2869. *Warner, Keith Quinley,* 1943– (poet). And I'll Tell You No Lies, 1993.

2870. *Webber, Albert Raymond Forbes,* 1880–1932 (novelist). Those That Be in Bondage, 1917–1988.

VIRGIN ISLANDS

A. ANTHOLOGIES

General

General: Twentieth Century

2871. Moll, Verna Penn, ed. *Reminiscences: Award Winning Stories and Poems, Creative Arts Festival, 1981.* Road Town, Tortola, BVI: Public Library, 1981. 94 pp.

Poetry

Poetry: General

2872. Allis, Jeanette B., and Latifah Lois Chinnery, eds. *Proud of Our Land and People: A Virgin Islands Poetry Collection.* Charlotte Amalie, USVI: Bureau of Libraries, Museums and Archeological Services, 1984. 56 pp.

2873. Gimenez, Joseph Patrick, ed. *Virgin Islands Folklore and Other Poems.* New York: F. Harding, 1933. 103 pp.

2874. Hill, Valdemar A., ed. *Sun Island Jewels: An Anthology of Virgin Islands Poetry.* Charlotte Amalie, USVI: Val Hill Enterprises, 1975. 64 pp.

Poetry: Twentieth Century

2875. Campbell, Marty, ed. *Collage Two: Poems by Poets of St. Croix.* Christiansted, St. Croix, USVI: Antilles Press, 1991. 64 pp.

2876. Figueredo, Alfredo E., ed. *Collage Three: Poets of St. Croix.* Christiansted, St. Croix, USVI: Antilles Press, 1993. 154 pp.

2877. Highfield, Arnold R., ed. *Collage One: Poems by Poets of St. Croix.* Christiansted, St. Croix, USVI: Antilles Press, 1990. 78 pp.

Fiction

Fiction: General

2878. Schrader, Richard A., ed. *Kallaloo: A Collection of Crucian Stories.* St. Croix, USVI: R. A. Schrader, 1991. 124 pp.

2879. ———. *Fungi: More Crucian Stories.* Saint Croix, USVI: Antilles Graphic Arts, 1993. 114 pp.

Fiction: Twentieth Century

2880. Moll, Verna Penn, ed. *Tales of Virgin Treasure: Literary Award Winners.* Road Town, Tortola, BVI: Public Library, 1985. 26 pp.

B. HISTORY AND CRITICISM

Poetry

Poetry: Twentieth Century

2881. Simmonds, Ruby. *The Words Beneath the Sand: An Examination of the Works of Three Virgin Islands Poets—Cyril Creque, J. P. Gimenez and J. Antonio Jarvis.* Ann Arbor, MI: University Microfilms International, 1995. 160 pp.

C. INDIVIDUAL AUTHORS

Twentieth Century

2882. *Anduze, Alfred L.* (short story writer). A West Indian Fish Tale and Other Stories, 1993.

2883. *Anduze, Aubrey A.,* 1917– (poet). Reminiscence I–II, 1940–1984.

2884. *Augustin, Fermin J.* (poet). The Moon On My Patio/La luna en mi patio, 1987; Rapsodia hispano Caribe, 1979.

2885. *Brown, Paula* (poet). Out of an Island, 1974; Songs for My Children, 1968; A Woman Singing, 1958.

2886. *Campbell, Marty* (poet). Saint Sea, 1986 (with Joe Blondo).

2887. *Combs, Tram,* 1924– (poet). As God Made the World, 1956; Briefs, 1966; But Never Mind, 1961; Ceremonies in Mind, 1959; Pilgrim's Terrace, 1957; Saint Thomas, 1965; Saints Thomas and Francis, 1958; Zen Man, 1953.

2888. *Cooper, Vincent O.* (poet). Three Islands, 1987 (with Trevor Parris and Joseph Lisowski); Tremors, 1989 (with Joseph Lisowski).

2889. *Creque, Cyril Felix William,* 1899– (poet). Panorama, 1947; Trade Winds, 1934. See also #2881.

2890. *Gershator, David,* 1937– (poet). Bread Is for Eating, 1995 (with Phyllis Gershator); Elegy for Val, 1975; Elijah's Child, 1992; Kanji, 1977; Play Mas', 1981.

2891. *Gershator, Phyllis,* 1942– (poet). Bang Bang Lulu, 1977; Bread Is for Eating, 1995 (with David Gershator); The Iroko-Man, 1994; Rata-Pata-Scata-Fata, 1993–1994; Sambalena Show-off, 1995; Sweet Sweet Fig Banana, 1996.

2892. *Gimenez, Joseph Patrick* (poet). Caribbean Echoes, 1934; Deep Waters, 1939; Voice of the Virgin Islands, 1952. See also #2881.

2893. *Gumbs, Wycherley* (poet). Inner Hunger, 1993.

2894. *Hatchette, Wilfred Irwin,* 1918– (poet). Blood, Sweat and Tears, 1947; Youth's Flight, 1938.

2895. *Heyn, Jean* (novelist). The Governor-General's Lady, 1988; The Tessie C. Price, 1979.

2896. *Highfield, Arnold R.* (poet). An Archaeology of Names, 1993.

2897. *Hyndman, Sheila* (poet). Reflections, 1989.

2898. *Jarvis, Jose Antonio,* 1902–1963 (playwright, poet). Bamboula Dance and Other Poems, 1935–1970; Fruits in Passing, 1932; The King's Mandate, 1960. See also #2881.

2899. *Jenai* (poet). Musings, 1982; Rays of Sunshine, 1983.

2900. *Lettsome, Quincy F. V.,* 1913– (poet). Sunlit Voices of Our Destiny, 1984; Virgin Verses, 1969–1976.

2901. *Lisowski, Joseph* (poet, short story writer). Near the Narcotic Sea, 1992; Three Islands, 1987 (with Vincent O. Cooper and Trevor Parris); Tremors, 1989 (with Vincent O. Cooper).

2902. *Liss, Miles* (poet). Sneezeweed and Polemonium, 1994.

2903. *Lythgoe, Michael Hugh* (poet). Visions, Revisions, 1994. See also #2201.

2904. *Moll, Verna Penn,* 1946– (playwright, poet). The Essence of Life, 1976; Johny-Cake Country, 1990.

2905. *Moorhead, Mario C.* (novelist, short story writer). Black Star, 1983 (What a Plot, The Inner Circle, The Boss' End); Special Delivery, 1981; Who Feels It Knows It, 1994.

2906. *Morris, J. F.* (poet). Paradise Blues, 1995.

2907. *Paiewonsky, Isidor,* 1903– (poet). Poems for My Son Paul, 1985.

2908. *Parris, Trevor* (poet). Three Islands, 1987 (with Vincent O. Cooper and Joseph Lisowski).

2909. *Petersen, Arona* (short story writer). Kreole Ketch n' Keep, 1975–1987.

2910. *Schjang, Aster Coff* (short story writer). Grandma's Island, 1991.

2911. *Schrader, Richard A.* (poet, short story writer). Home Sweet Home, 1986; Maufé, Quelbé, and T'ing: A Calabash of Stories, 1994; A Sharing of My Thoughts, 1984; Walking Through Kasha and Roses (Autobiographical), 1988.

2912. *Sylvester, Mark,* 1948– (poet). The Road I Walk, 1986.

2913. *Teytaud, Anton C.* (playwright, poet, short story writer). A Glance Astern, 1980; Sarah and Addie, 1974–1978.

2914. *Thomas, Ruth E.* (poet). Sounding Off, 1995; When I Was a Child, 1993.

2915. *Tiwoni, Habib,* 1939– (poet). Attacking the Moncada of the Mind, 1970; Islands of My Mind, 1975; Wet Poems and Dry Dreams, 1981.

2916. *Turnbull, Patricia* (poet). Rugged Vessels, 1992.

2917. *Wheatley, Jennie N.* (poet, short story writer). Pass It On!, 1991.

2918. *Williams, Marvin E.* (poet). Dialogue at the Hearth, 1993.

IV
THE FRENCH-SPEAKING CARIBBEAN

GENERAL

A. ANTHOLOGIES

General

2919. Confiant, Raphaël, and Marcel Lebielle, eds. *Les maîtres de la parole créole*. Paris: Gallimard, 1995. 201 pp.

2920. Corzani, Jack, ed. *Littérature antillaise*. Fort-de-France: Désormeaux, 1971–1972. 2 vols.

General: Twentieth Century

2921. Armet, Auguste et al., eds . *Cri et société: littérature antillaise de combat*. Fort-de-France: Société d'impr. martiniquaise, 1978. 309 pp.

2922. Kesteloot, Lilyan, ed. *Anthologie négro-africaine: panorama critique des prosateurs, poètes, et dramaturges noirs du XXe siècle*. Nouv. éd. Vanves, France: EDICEF, 1992. 555 pp.

2923. Ludwig, Ralph, ed. *Ecrire la parole de nuit: la nouvelle littérature antillaise—nouvelles, poèmes et réflexions poétiques*. Paris: Gallimard, 1994. 190 pp.

Poetry

2924. Condé, Maryse, and Bernard Lecherbonnier, eds. *La poésie antillaise*. Paris: F. Nathan, 1977. 96 pp.

2925. Lebielle, Marcel, ed. *Fléri-nowél: des fleurs du temps de l'Avent*. Fort-de-France: Presses universitaires créoles, 1988. 85 pp. Collection of French creole poetry.

2926. Shapiro, Norman R., ed. and tr. *Negritude: Black Poetry from Africa and the Caribbean*. New York: October House, 1970. 247 pp.

Fiction

2927. Bocaly, Gisèle, ed. *Contes des îles caraïbes.* [s.l.]: Fondation Clément, 1990. 384 pp.

2928. Cholakian, Rouben Charles, ed. *Complete Narratives of Francophone Caribbean Tales.* Lewistown, NY: E. Mellen Press, 1996. 175 pp. Text in French, with an introd. in English.

2929. Condé, Maryse, and Bernard Lecherbonnier, eds. *Le roman antillais.* Paris: F. Nathan, 1977. 2 vols.

B. HISTORY AND CRITICISM

General

2930. André, Jacques. *Caraïbales: études sur la littérature antillaise.* Paris: Editions caribéennes, 1981. 169 pp.

2931. Antoine, Régis. *La littérature franco-antillaise.* 2e éd. augm. et mise à jour. Paris: Karthala, 1995. 381 pp.

2932. Chamoiseau, Patrick, and Raphaël Confiant. *Lettres créoles: tracées antillaises et continentales de la littérature—Haïti, Guadeloupe, Martinique, Guyane (1635–1975).* Paris: Hatier, 1991. 225 pp.

2933. Condé, Maryse, and Madeleine Cottenet-Hage, eds. *Penser la créolité.* Paris: Editions Karthala, 1995. 320 pp. Papers from a conference held in 1993 at the University of Maryland.

2934. Corzani, Jack. *La littérature des Antilles-Guyane françaises.* Fort-de-France: Désormeaux, 1978. 6 vols. Vols. 1–2. *Exotisme et régionalisme.*—Vols. 3–4. *La négritude.*—Vols. 5–6. *Les choix contemporains.*

2935. Hawkins, Peter, and Annette Lavers, eds. *Protée noir: essais sur la littérature francophone de l'Afrique noire et des Antilles.* Paris: L'Harmattan, 1992. 299 pp. English and French.

2936. Lara, Oruno. *La littérature antillaise.* Paris: F. Drubay, 1913. 206 pp. Vol. 1. *Poésie.*—Vol. 2. *Prose.*

2937. Ménil, René. *Tracées: identité, négritude, esthétique aux Antilles.* Paris: R. Laffont, 1981. 233 pp.

2938. Rosello, Mireille. *Littérature et identité créole aux Antilles*. Paris: Editions Karthala, 1992. 202 pp.

2939. Toumson, Roger. *La transgression des couleurs: littérature et langage des Antilles, XVIIIe, XIXe, XXe siècles*. Paris: Editions caribéennes, 1990. 2 vols.

General: Twentieth Century

2940. Anderson, Debra L. *Decolonizing the Text: Glissantian Readings in Caribbean and African-American Literatures*. New York: P. Lang, 1995. 118 pp.

2941. Bouygues, Claude, ed. *Texte africain et voies/voix critiques: essais sur les littératures africaines et antillaises de graphie française/African Text and Critical Voices/Approaches: Essays on African and West Indian Literatures of French Expression*. Paris: L'Harmattan, 1992. 295 pp.

2942. Condé, Maryse, ed. *L'héritage de Caliban*. Paris: Editions Jasor, 1992. 287 pp. Traces Aimé Césaire's influence on 20th century French Caribean literature.

2943. Richardson, Michael, ed. *Refusal of the Shadow: Surrealism and the Caribbean*. Krzysztof Fijalkowski, Michael Richardson, trs. New York: Verso, 1996. 287 pp.

Fiction

2944. Case, Frederick Ivor. *The Crisis of Identity: Studies in the Guadeloupean and Martiniquan Novel*. Sherbrooke, Que.: Naaman, 1985. 190 pp.

2945. Condé, Maryse. *La parole des femmes: essai sur des romancières des Antilles de langue française*. Paris: L'Harmattan, 1993. 136 pp. Reprint, with an updated bibliography, of the 1979 ed.

2946. Kyiiripuo Kyoore, Paschal B. *The African and Caribbean Historical Novel in French*. New York: P. Lang, 1996.

2947. Ntonfo, André. *L'homme et l'identité dans le roman des Antilles et Guyane françaises*. Sherbrooke, Que.: Naaman, 1982. 254 pp.

2948. Ormerod, Beverley. *An Introduction to the French Caribbean Novel*. Portsmouth, NH: Heinemann, 1985. 152 pp.

GUADELOUPE

A. BIBLIOGRAPHIES AND BIO-BIBLIOGRAPHIES

2949. Dupland, Edmond, ed. *Les poètes de la Guadeloupe: anthologie bio-bibliographique et critique.* Paris: J. Grassin, 1978. 317 pp.

B. ANTHOLOGIES

Poetry

Poetry: Twentieth Century

2950. Association guadeloupéenne des amis de la poésie. *Karukéra anthologie: poèmes.* Pointe-à-Pitre: AGAP, 1983. 254 pp.

2951. ———. *Vingt poèmes pour Saint-Domingue.* Pointe-à-Pitre: AGAP, 1980. 91 pp.

Fiction

Fiction: General

2952. Lucain, Pierre Clotaire, ed. *Veillées guadeloupéennes: recueil de treize contes créoles.* Paris: Nouvelles Editions Debresse, 1967. 186 pp.

Fiction: Sixteenth to Nineteenth Centuries

2953. Schont, Mme, ed. *Quelques contes créoles.* Basse-Terre: Impr. catholique, 1935. 110 pp.

Fiction: Twentieth Century

2954. Centre d'action culturelle de la Guadeloupe. *Paroles de terre en larmes: nouvelles.* Paris: Hatier, 1988. 159 pp. Gisèle Pineau, Louis

Zou, Maguy Bibrac, Marius Franck, Franciane Galou, Marie-Laure Marcimain-Verton, Alain Rinaldo, Joseph Tramis, Emmanuel Venet.

2955. Rice-Maximin, Micheline P., ed. *Karukéra: présence littéraire de la Guadeloupe*. New York: P. Lang, 1996.

C. INDIVIDUAL AUTHORS

Twentieth Century

2956. *Alante-Lima, Willy,* 1942– (novelist, poet). Clin-din-dins des îles, 1982; Mémoires d'un bananier, 1991; Plaquettes de défoliants, 1976; Poèmes à dépression, 1977; Requiem de minuit, 1988.

2957. *Baghio'o, Jean-Louis,* 1910– (novelist, poet). The Blue Flame-Tree, 1984 (Translation of Le flamboyant à fleurs bleues [1973–1981]; Stephen Romer, tr.); Choutoumounou, 1995; Le colibri blanc, 1980; Issandre le mulâtre, 1949; Les jeux du soleil, 1960.

2958. *Bazile, Corneille,* 1895– (novelist). La terreur noire à la Guadeloupe, 1925–1976.

2959. *Bloncourt-Herselin, Jacqueline,* 1917– (poet). Mirages des vertes îles, 1957; Nouveaux mirages des vertes îles, 1981.

2960. *Chambertrand, Gilbert de,* 1890–1973 (novelist, playwright, poet, short story writer). L'Album de famille, 1969; Coeurs créoles, 1958; D'azur et de sable, 1961; Dix bel conte avant cyclone, 1970?; Femme, qu'y a-t-il entre moi et toi?, 1976; Images guadeloupéennes, 1939; Mi io!, 1926–1963; Théatre, 1976 (L'honneur des Monvoisin [1917], Les méfaits d'Athénaïse [1918], Le prix du sacrifice [1918]); Titine Grosbonda, 1947.

2961. Lara, Bettino, and Roger Fortuné. *Un héraut du régionalisme antillais: Gilbert de Chambertrand.* Basse-Terre: Impr. officielle, 1948. 124 pp.

2962. *Condé, Maryse,* 1936– (novelist, playwright, short story writer). An tan revolisyon, 1989; The Children of Segu, 1989 (Translation of Ségou II [1985]; Linda Coverdale, tr.); La colonie du nouveau monde, 1993; Crossing the Mangrove, 1995 (Translation of Traversée de la mangrove [1989–1992]; Richard Philcox, tr.); Les

derniers rois mages, 1992; Dieu nous l'a donné, 1972; Here-
makhonon, 1982 (Translation of Hérémakhonon/En attendant le
bonheur [1976–1988]; Richard Philcox, tr.); Hugo le terrible,
1991; I Tituba, Black Witch of Salem, 1992–1994 (Translation of
Moi Tituba, sorcière noire de Salem [1986–1988]; Richard
Philcox, tr.); Mort d'Oluwémi d'Ajumako, 1973; Nanna-ya, 1985;
Pays mêlé, 1985; Pension les Alizés, 1988; A Season in Rihata,
1988 (Translation of Une saison à Rihata [1981]; Richard Philcox,
tr.); Ségou, 1984–1985 (Les murailles de terre, La terre en mi-
ettes); Segu, 1988 (Translation of Ségou I [1984]; Barbara Bray,
tr.); Tree of Life, 1992 (Translation of La vie scélérate [1987];
Victoria Reiter, tr.).

2963. Condé, Maryse, and Françoise Pfaff, ed. *Conversations
with Maryse Condé*. Lincoln, NE: University of Nebraska
Press, 1996. 178 pp. Translation of *Entretiens avec Maryse
Condé* (1993).

2964. Fendler, Ute. *Interkulturalität in der frankophonen Literatur der Karibik: der europäisch-afrikanisch-amerikanis-
che Intertext im Romanwerk von Maryse Condé*. Frankfurt
am Main: IKO, 1994. 444 pp.

2965. *Corbin, Henri,* 1932– (playwright, poet, short story writer). Le
Baron-Samedi, 1962–1986; La lampe captive, 1979; Le privilège
de l'histoire, 1984; Le sud rebelle, 1990.

2966. *Juliá, Lucie* (novelist). Les gens de Bonne-Espérance, 1982;
Mélody des faubourgs, 1989; Tim tim, bwa sek!, 1992.

2967. *Lacrosil, Michèle,* 1915 (novelist, short story writer). Cajou, 1961;
Demain Jab-Herma, 1967; Sapotille et le serin d'argile, 1960.

2968. *Lara, Sully,* 1867–1950 (novelist, playwright). Moeurs créoles
sous l'esclavage, 1935–1966.

2969. *Léopold, Emmanuel Flavia,* 1896–1962 (poet). Adieu foulards,
adieu madras, 1948; Le chateau du Tauzia, 1963; La clarté des
jours, 1924; Poèmes, 1949; Soleils caraïbes, 1953.

2970. *Maximin, Daniel,* 1947– (novelist). L'île et une nuit, 1995; Lone
Sun, 1989 (Translation of L'isolé soleil [1981–1987]; Clarisse
Zimra, tr.); Soufrières, 1987–1995.

2971. *Morand, Florette,* 1926– (poet, short story writer). Biguines, 1956–1970; Chanson pour ma savane, 1958–1970; Feu de brousse, 1967; Mon coeur est un oiseau des îles, 1954.

2972. *Moutoussamy, Ernest,* 1941– (novelist, poet). Chacha et Sosso, 1994; Des champs de canne à sucre à l'Assemblée nationale, 1993.

2973. *Niger, Paul,* 1915–1962 (novelist, poet). Les grenouilles du mont Kimbo, 1964; Initiation, 1954; Les puissants, 1956.

2974. *Pépin, Ernest* (novelist, poet). Au verso du silence, 1984; Boucan de mots libres, 1991; Coulée d'or, 1995; L'homme-au-bâton, 1992; Salve et salive, 1986.

2975. *Pineau, Gisèle* (novelist, short story writer). La grande drive des esprits, 1993; Un papillon dans la cité, 1992.

2976. *Saint-John Perse,* 1887–1975 (poet). Amitié du prince, 1924–1979; Anabasis, 1930–1985 (Translation of Anabase [1924–1994]) T. S. Eliot, tr. [1924]; Birds, 1967 (Translation of L'ordre des oiseaux [1962–1992]; J. Roger Little, tr.); Chant pour un équinoxe, 1975–1992; Chanté par celle qui fut là, 1970; Chronique, 1960–1992; Collected Poems, 1971–1983 (W. H. Auden [et al.], trs.); Eloges and Other Poems, 1944–1965 (Translation of Eloges [1911–1994]; Louise Varèse, tr. [1944, 1965]; Exile and Other Poems, 1949–1962 (Translation of Exil [1942–1995]; Dennis Devlin, tr. [1949, 1962]; La gloire des rois, 1967–1994; Nocturne, 1985 (Albert Henry, ed.); Oeuvre poétique, 1953–1974; Oeuvres complètes, 1972–1989; Poésie, 1957–1992; Rains, 1945 (Translation of Pluies [1944]; Denis Devlin, tr.); Saint-John Perse [Selections], 1953–1971 (Alain Bosquet, ed.); Seamarks, 1958–1964 (Translation of Amers [1953–1992]; Wallace Fowlie, tr. [1958, 1964]); Selected Poems, 1982 (Mary Ann Caws, ed.); Winds, 1953–1961 (Translation of Vents [1946–1992]; Hugh Chisholm, tr. [1953, 1961]).

2977. Aigrisse, Gilberte. *Saint-John Perse et ses mythologies.* Paris: Imago, 1992. 196 pp.

2978. Aquien, Michèle. *Saint-John Perse: l'être et le nom.* Paris: Presses universitaires de France, 1985. 190 pp.

2979. Arland, Marcel et al. *Hommage à Saint-John Perse, 1887–1975.* Paris: La Nouvelle revue française, 1991. 170

pp. First published in 1976 as no. 278 of the *La Nouvelle revue française.*

2980. Assoun, Paul Laurent et al. *Analyses et reflexions sur Saint-John Perse, "Eloges": la nostalgie.* Paris: Elipses, 1986. 286 pp.

2981. Bosquet, Alain. *Saint-John Perse.* Nouv. éd., rev. et augm. Paris: Seghers, 1990. 194 pp.

2982. Caduc, Eveline. *Index de l'oeuvre poétique de Saint-John Perse.* Paris: H. Champion, 1993. 269 pp.

2983. ———. *Saint-John Perse: connaissance et création.* Paris: J. Corti, 1977. 158 pp.

2984. Caillois, Roger. *Poétique de St.-John Perse.* Nouv. éd., rev. et augm. Paris: Gallimard, 1986. 224 pp. Reprint of the 1981 ed.

2985. Centre Saint-John Perse. *Saint-John Perse et les Etats-Unis: colloque 1980.* Aix-en-Provence [France]: Le Centre, 1981. 357 pp.

2986. Charpier, Jacques. *Saint-John Perse.* Paris: Gallimard, 1962. 299 pp.

2987. Clerc, Gabrielle. *Saint-John Perse; ou, De la poésie comme acte sacré.* Neuchâtel [Switzerland]: A la Baconnière, 1990. 221 pp.

2988. Clergue, Lucien, and Christiane Baroche. *Saint-John Perse: poète devant la mer.* Biarritz [France]: J & D Editions, 1996. 99 pp.

2989. Colloque de Bordeaux (1994); Jack Corzani, ed. *Saint-John Perse: les années de formation—actes du colloque de Bordeaux (17, 18 et 19 mars 1994).* Paris: L'Harmattan, 1996. 299 pp.

2990. Coss, Elisabeth. *Saint-John Perse: poésie, science de l'être—une lecture ontologique de l'oeuvre de Saint-John Perse.* Nancy [France]: Presses universitaires de Nancy, 1993. 553 pp.

2991. Crouy-Chanel, Etienne de. *Alexis Léger; ou, L'autre visage de Saint-John Perse.* Paris: Picollec, 1989. 296 pp.

2992. Elbaz, Shlomo. *Lectures d' "Anabase" de Saint-John Perse: le désert, le désir.* Lausanne: Editions l'Age d'homme, 1977. 293 pp.

2993. Emmanuel, Pierre. *Saint-John Perse: Praise and Presence.* Washington, DC: GPO, 1971. 82 pp.

2994. Eudeville, Jean d'. *Saint-John Perse; ou, La poésie pour mieux vivre.* Paris: Asiathèque, 1984. 235 pp.

2995. Favre, Yves Alain. *Saint-John Perse: le langage et le sacré.* Paris: J. Corti, 1977. 120 pp.

2996. Frédéric, Madeleine. *La répétition et ses structures dans l'oeuvre poétique de Saint-John Perse.* Paris: Gallimard, 1984. 251 pp.

2997. Galand, René. *Saint-John Perse.* New York: Twayne, 1972. 172 pp.

2998. Guerre, Pierre, and Roger Little, ed. *Portrait de Saint-John Perse.* Marseille: Sud, 1989. 378 pp.

2999. Henry, Albert. *"Amers" de Saint-John Perse: une poésie du mouvement.* Ed. rev. Paris: Gallimard, 1981. 201 pp.

3000. *Honneur à Saint-John Perse: hommages et témoignages littéraires suivis d'une documentation sur Alexis Léger.* Paris: Gallimard, 1965. 817 pp.

3001. Knodel, Arthur J. *Saint-John Perse: A Study of His Poetry.* Edinburgh: Edinburgh University Press, 1966. 214 pp.

3002. Le Guen, Jean Michel. *L'ordre exploratoire: l' "Anabase".* Paris: Sedea, 1985. 267 pp.

3003. Levillain, Henriette. *Sur deux versants: la création chez Saint-John Perse—d'après les versions anglaises de son oeuvre poétique.* Paris: J. Corti, 1987. 358 pp.

3004. Levillain, Henriette, and Mireille Sacotte, eds. *Saint-John Perse: antillanité et universalité—colloque, Pointe-à-*

Pitre, 30 mai-1er juin 1987. Paris: Editions caribéennes, 1988. 202 pp.

3005. Little, Roger. *Etudes sur Saint-John Perse*. Paris: Klinck-sieck, 1984. 224 pp.

3006. ———. *Saint-John Perse*. London: Athlone Press, 1973. 139 pp.

3007. ———. *Saint-John Perse: A Bibliography for Students of His Poetry*. London: Grant and Cutler, 1971. 76 pp. (+ two supplements issued in 1976 [88 pp.] and 1982 [58 pp.] respectively).

3008. ———. *Word Index of the Complete Poetry and Prose of Saint-John Perse*. Durham, Eng.: Durham University, 1965. 290 pp.

3009. Loranquin, Albert. *Saint-John Perse*. Paris: Gallimard, 1963. 221 pp.

3010. Lucrèce, André. *Saint-John Perse: une lecture*. Paris: Editions Caractères, 1987. 131 pp.

3011. Mayaux, Catherine. *Les lettres d'Asie de Saint-John Perse: les récrits d'un poète*. Paris: Gallimard, 1994. 297 pp.

3012. Murciaux, Christian. *Saint-John Perse*. Paris: Editions universitaires, 1965. 128 pp. Reprint of the 1960 ed.

3013. Nasta, Dan Ion. *Saint John-Perse et la découverte de l'être*. Paris: Presses universitaires de France, 1980. 200 pp.

3014. Ostrovsky, Erika. *Under the Sign of Ambiguity: Saint-John Perse/Alexis Léger*. New York: New York University Press, 1985. 280 pp.

3015. Parent, Monique. *Saint-John Perse et quelques devanciers: études sur le poème en prose*. Paris: C. Klincksieck, 1960. 258 pp.

3016. Pinalie, Pierre, ed. *Pour Saint-John Perse: études et essais pour le centenaire de Saint-John Perse, 1887–1987*. Paris: L'Harmattan, 1988. 220 pp.

3017. Pruner, Francis. *L'ésotérisme de Saint-John Perse: dans "Anabase."* Paris: Klincksieck, 1977. 93 pp.

3018. Racine, Daniel L., ed. *L'obscure naissance du langage.* Paris: Lettres modernes, 1987. 230 pp.

3019. ————. *Saint-John Perse: antillais universel—actes du colloque tenu à Pointe-à-Pitre du 31 mai au 2 juin 1987, pour la commémoration du centième anniversaire de la naissance de Saint-John Perse.* Paris: Libr. Minard, 1991. 396 pp.

3020. Robichez, Jacques. *Sur Saint-John Perse: "Eloges," "La gloire des rois," "Anabase."* 2e éd. rev. et corr. Paris: Société d'édition d'enseignement supérieur, 1982. 215 pp.

3021. Rutten, Pierre van. *Le langage poétique de Saint-John Perse.* The Hague: Mouton, 1975. 248 pp.

3022. Sacotte, Mireille. *Saint-John Perse.* Paris: P. Belfond, 1991. 340 pp.

3023. Saillet, Maurice. *Saint-John Perse: poète de gloire.* Paris: Mercure de France, 1952. 190 pp.

3024. Saint-John Perse, and Albert Henry, ed. *Lettres d'Alexis Léger à Gabriel Frizeau, 1906–1912.* Brussels: Académie royale de Belgique, 1993. 192 pp.

3025. Saint-John Perse, and Arthur J. Knodel, ed. and tr. *Letters.* Princeton, NJ: Princeton University Press, 1979. 719 pp.

3026. Saint-John Perse, and Mauricette Berne, ed. *Lettres à l'étrangère.* Paris: Gallimard, 1987. 150 pp.

3027. Saint-John Perse, Dag Hammarskjöld and Marie Noëlle, ed. *Correspondance 1955–1961.* Paris: Gallimard, 1993. 270 pp. Cover title *Correspondance avec Dag Hammarskjöld.*

3028. Saint-John Perse, Jean Paulhan and Joëlle Tamine-Gardes, ed. *Correspondance 1925–1966.* Paris: Gallimard, 1991. 378 pp.

3029. Saint-John Perse, Roger Caillois and Joëlle Tamine-Gardes, ed. *Correspondence 1942–1975.* Paris: Gallimard,

1996. 212 pp. Running title *Correspondence avec Roger Caillois.*

3030. Sterling, Richard L. *The Prose Works of Saint-John Perse: Towards an Understanding of His Poetry.* New York: P. Lang, 1994. 160 pp.

3031. Taconet, Noël. *Lectures d' "Eloges" de Saint-John Perse.* Paris: Belin, 1986. 127 pp.

3032. Torrens, Martine. *La imaginación poética de Saint-John Perse: temas y símbolos.* Salamamca, Spain: Ediciones Universidad de Salamanca, 1983. 329 pp.

3033. Ventresque, Renée. *Les Antilles de Saint-John Perse: itinéraire intellectuel d'un poète.* Paris: L'Harmattan, 1993. 255 pp.

3034. ———. *Le songe antillais de Saint-John Perse.* Paris: L'Harmattan, 1995. 239 pp.

3035. Winspur, Steven. *Saint-John Perse and the Imaginary Reader.* Geneva: Droz, 1988. 192 pp.

3036. *Schwarz-Bart, André,* 1928– (novelist). The Last of the Just, 1960–1992 (Translation of Le dernier des justes [1959–1980]; Stephen Becker, tr.); Un plat de porc aux bananes vertes, 1967 (with Simone Schwarz-Bart); A Woman Named Solitude, 1973–1985 (Translation of La mulâtresse Solitude [1967–1983]; Ralph Manheim, tr.).

3037. *Schwarz-Bart, Simone,* 1938– (novelist, playwright). Between Two Worlds, 1981–1992 (Translation of Ti Jean l'Horizon [1979]; Barbara Bray, tr.); The Bridge of Beyond, 1974–1982 (Translation of Pluie et vent sur Télumée Miracle [1972–1995]; Barbara Bray, tr.); Un plat de porc aux bananes verts, 1967 (with André Scharz-Bart); Your Handsome Captain, 1989 (Translation of Ton beau capitaine [1987]; Jessica Harris, Catherine Temerson, trs.).

3038. *Tirolien, Guy,* 1917– (poet). Balles d'or, 1960–1982; Feuilles vivantes au matin, 1977.

3039. Alante-Lima, Willy. *Guy Tirolien: l'homme et l'oeuvre.* Paris: Présence africaine, 1991. 318 pp.

3040. Condé, Maryse, and Alain Rutil, eds. *Bouquet de voix pour Guy Tirolien*. Pointe-à-Pitre: Editions Jasor, 1990. 222 pp.

3041. Tirolien, Guy, Michel Tétu and Glenn Davin, eds. *De Marie-Galante à une poétique afro-antillaise: entretiens*. Paris: Editions caribéennes, 1990. 200 pp.

3042. *Vélayoudon-Faithful, Francesca,* 1951– (novelist, poet). Peau de banane, 1986; Poèmes aux quatre vents, 1984.

3043. *Warner-Vieyra, Myriam* (novelist, short story writer). As the Sorcerer Said—, 1982 (Translation of Le quimboiseur l'avait dit [1980]; Dorothy S. Blair, tr.); Femmes échouées, 1988; Juletane, 1988 (Translation of Juletane [1982–1995]; Betty Wilson, tr.).

GUYANE

A. ANTHOLOGIES

Poetry

3044. Rollé, Christian, ed. *Littérature guyanaise: poésie*. Fort-de-France: Désormeaux, 1985. 193 pp.

B. INDIVIDUAL AUTHORS

Sixteenth to Nineteenth Centuries

3045. *Parépou, Alfred* (novelist). Atipa, 1885–1987.

    3046. Fauquenoy, Marguerite, ed. *Atipa revisité; ou, Les itinéraires de Parépou*. Fort-de-France: Presses universitaires créoles, 1989. 324 pp.

Twentieth Century

3047. *Bonneton, André,* 1925– (poet). Aquilon, 1953; Echo, 1966; Etoiles amères, 1951; La lèpre, 1976; Mage, 1973; Takari, 1968.

3048. *Brugerie, Tessa* (poet). Guyanariane, 1990.

3049. *Damas, Léon-Gontran,* 1912–1978 (poet, short story writer). African Songs of Love, War, Grief, and Abuse, 1961 (Miriam Koshland, Ulli Beier, trs.); Black-Label, 1956–1988; Graffiti, 1952; Névralgies, 1965–1972; Pigments, 1937–1972; Poèmes nègres sur des airs africains, 1948; Retour de Guyane, 1938; Veillées noires, 1943–1972.

    3050. Colloque Léon-Gontran Damas (1988, Paris); Michel Tétu, ed. *Léon-Gontran Damas: actes du Colloque Léon-*

324

Gontran Damas, Paris, décembre 1988. Paris: Agence de cooperation culturelle et technique, 1990. 316 pp.

3051. *Hommage posthume à Léon-Gontran Damas (1912–1978)*. Paris: Présence africaine, 1979. 430 pp. French or English.

3052. Piquion, René. *Léon-Gontran Damas: un poète de la négritude*. Port-au-Prince: Centre audio visuel, Education nationale, 1964. 34 pp.

3053. Racine, Daniel L. *Léon-Gontran Damas: l'homme et l'oeuvre*. Paris: Présence africaine, 1983. 238 pp.

3054. ————, ed. *Léon-Gontran Damas, 1912–1978: Founder of Negritude—a Memorial Casebook*. Washington, DC: University Press of America, 1979. 298 pp.

3055. Warner, Keith Quinley, ed. *Critical Perspectives on Léon-Gontran Damas*. Washington, DC: Three Continents Press, 1988. 178 pp.

3056. *Galmot, Jean,* 1879–1928 (novelist). Un mort vivait parmi nous, 1922–1994; Quelle étrange histoire, 1918–1990.

3057. *Jadfard, René,* 1901–1947 (novelist, playwright, poet). L'assassin joue et perd, 1941–1988; Deux hommes et l'aventure, 1946–1988; Drôle d'assassin, 1939–1988; Nuits de Cachiri, 1946–1988; La télegramme de minuit, 1941–1988.

3058. Othily, Georges. *René Jadfard; ou, L'éclair d'une vie*. Paris: Editions caribéennes, 1989. 139 pp.

3059. *Juminer, Bertène,* 1927– (novelist). Au seuil d'un nouveau cri, 1963–1978; The Bastards, 1989 (Translation of Les bâtards [1961–1977]; Keith Q. Warner, tr.); Bozambo's Revenge/ Colonialism Inside Out, 1976–1980 (Translation of La revanche de Bozambo [1968]; Alexandra Bonfante Warren, tr.); La fraction de seconde, 1990; Les héritiers de la presqu'île, 1979.

3060. *Patient, Serge,* 1934– (playwright, poet, short story writer). Guyane pour tout dire, 1980; Le mal du pays, 1967–1980; Le nègre du gouverneur, 1972–1978.

3061. *Stephenson, Elie,* 1944– (playwright, poet). Catacombes de soleil, 1979; Comme des gouttes de sang, 1988; Les Délinters, 1978; Une flèche pour le pays à l'encan, 1975; O Mayouri, 1988; Poèmes négro-indiens aux enfants de Guyane, 1978; Terres mêlées, 1984.

3062. Ndagano, Biringanine. *La Guyane entre mots et maux: une lecture de l'oeuvre d'Elie Stephenson.* Paris: L'Harmattan, 1994. 191 pp.

3063. *Verderosa, Constantin,* 1889–1970 (playwright, poet). Scènes créoles, 1994 (Biringanine Ndagano, Monique Blérald-Ndagano, Daniel Schlupp, eds.); Les chaines du passé, 1961.

HAITI

A. BIBLIOGRAPHIES AND BIO-BIBLIOGRAPHIES

3064. Daniel, Neptune. *Dissertations de littérature haïtienne.* 3e éd. augm. Port-au-Prince: [s.n.], 1984. 277 pp.

3065. Hoffmann, Léon Francois. *Bibliographie des études littéraires haïtiennes, 1804–1984.* Vanves [France]: EDICEF, 1992. 240 pp.

B. ANTHOLOGIES

General

3066. Bellegarde, Dantès. *Ecrivains haïtiens: notices biographiques et pages choisis.* 2e éd. Port-au-Prince: Deschamps, 1950– [vol. 1–].

3067. Fardin, Dieudonné, and Eddy Benoît Pierre, eds. *Anthologie des poètes et écrivains du Nord-Ouest d'Haïti.* Port-de-Paix, Haiti: Atelier Capois-la-Mort, 1962– [vol. 1–].

3068. Gouraige, Ghislain. *Les meilleurs poètes et romanciers haïtiens: pages choisies.* [Port-au-Prince]: Phalange, 1963. 414 pp.

3069. Pompilus, Pradel. *Pages de littérature haïtienne: accompagnés de notices biographiques et d'études critiques.* 2e éd., rev. et augm. Port-au-Prince: Impr. Théodore, 1955. 307 pp.

3070. Van Zeebroeck, Maurice A., ed. *Anthologie de la littérature française d'Haïti.* Port-au-Prince: Editions du Soleil, 1985. 392 pp.

General: Sixteenth to Nineteenth Centuries

3071. Menos, Solon et al., eds. *Auteurs haïtiens: morceaux choisis.* Port-au-Prince: F. Smith, 1904. 2 vols. Running title *Oeuvre des écrivains haïtiens.*

General: Twentieth Century

3072. Charles, Christophe, ed. *Autobiographie des écrivains d'Haïti.* Port-au-Prince: Editions Choucoune, 1994– [vol. 1–].

Poetry

Poetry: General

3073. Charles, Christophe, ed. *Anthologie de la poésie haïtienne d'expression créole.* 2e éd. augm. de notices bio-bibliographiques. Port-au-Prince: Editions Choucoune, 1980– [vol. 1–].

3074. ———. *Rêves d'or: cinquante poèmes-naïfs de 27 poètesécoliers.* 2e éd. Port-au-Prince: Revue des Ecoliers, 1977. 48 pp.

3075. Lubin, Maurice Alcibiade. *L'Afrique dans la poésie haïtienne.* Port-au-Prince: Editions Panorama, 1965. 99 pp.

3076. Morand, Paul, ed. *Anthologie de la poésie haïtienne "indigène."* Port-au-Prince: Impr. Modèle, 1928. 82 pp. Running title *Anthologie des indigènes.*

3077. Saint-Louis, Carlos, and Maurice Alcibiade Lubin, eds. *Panorama de la poésie haïtienne.* Nendeln, Liechtenstein: Kraus Reprint, 1970. 635 pp. Reprint of the 1950 ed.

3078. Underwood, Edna Worthley, ed. and tr. *The Poets of Haiti, 1782–1934.* Portland, ME: Mosher Press, 1934. 159 pp.

Poetry: Sixteenth to Nineteenth Centuries

3079. Morpeau, Louis. *Anthologie d'un siècle de poésie haïtienne, 1817–1925: avec une étude sur la muse haïtienne d'expression française et une étude sur la muse haïtienne d'expression créole.* Nendeln, Liechtenstein: Kraus Reprint, 1970. 382 pp. Reprint of the 1925 ed.

Poetry: Twentieth Century

3080. Baridon, Silvio F., and Raymond Philoctète, eds. *Poésie vivante d'Haïti.* Paris: M. Nadeau, 1986. 292 pp. Reprint of the 1978 ed.

3081. Charles, Christophe, ed. *Anthologie de la nouvelle poésie d'expression francaise: 60 poètes des années 70–80–le paysage politique et poétique sous la dictadure.* Port-au-Prince: Centre de recherches littéraires et sociales, 1991. 348 pp.

3082. Gousse, Edgard, and St. John Kauss, eds. *Poésie haïtienne de l'exil, 1946–1991.* Montreal: Guernica, 1992. 297 pp.

3083. Lubin, Maurice Alcibiade. *Anthologie de la jeune poésie d'Haïti.* [Honolulu]: Mele, 1967. 1 vol. (unpaged).

3084. Morpeau, Louis. *Anthologie haïtienne des poètes contemporains, 1904–1920.* Port-au-Prince: Imor. A. A. Heraux, 1920. 237 pp.

Fiction

3085. Centre de recherches littéraires et sociales (Port-au-Prince). *Contes et légendes d'Haïti.* Port-au-Prince: Editions Choucoune, 1993. 149 pp.

3086. Confiant, Raphaël, ed. *Contes créoles des Amériques.* Paris: Stock, 1995. 406 pp.

3087. Rey, Ghislaine, ed. *Anthologie du roman haïtien.* 2e éd. Sherbrooke, Que. : Naaman, 1982– [vol. 1–]. Vol. 1. De 1859 à 1946.—Vol. 2. De 1946 à 1967.

C. HISTORY AND CRITICISM

General

3088. Berrou, Raphaël, and Pradel Pompilus. *Histoire de la littérature haïtienne: illustrée par les textes.* Port-au-Prince: Editions Caraïbes, 1975–1977. 3 vols.

3089. Dash, J. Michael. *Haiti and the United States: National Stereotypes and the Literary Imagination.* New York: St. Martin's Press, 1988. 152 pp.

3090. Dominique, Max. *L'arme de la critique littéraire: littérature et idéologie en Haïti.* Montreal: CIDIHCA, 1988. 238 pp.

3091. Fleischmann, Ulrich. *Ideologie und Wirklichkeit in der Literatur Haitis.* Berlin: Colloquium-Verlag, 1969. 308 pp.

3092. Fouchard, Jacques. *Regards sur la littérature et —*. Port-au-Prince: H. Deschamps, 1988. 163 pp.

3093. Fouché, Franck. *Guide pour l'étude de la littérature haïtienne.* Port-au-Prince: Editions Panorama, 1964. 158 pp.

3094. Gardiner, Madeleine. *Visages de femmes: portraits d'écrivains — étude.* Port-au-Prince: H. Deschamps, 1981. 199 pp.

3095. Gouraige, Ghislain. *Histoire de la littérature haïtienne: de l'indépendance à nos jours.* Port-au-Prince: Editions de l'action sociale, 1982. 507 pp. Reprint of the 1961 ed.

3096. Hoffmann, Léon François. *Essays on Haitian Literature.* Washington, DC: Three Continents Press, 1984. 184 pp.

3097. ———. *Haïti: lettres et l'être.* Toronto: Editions du GREF, 1992. 371 pp.

3098. ———. *Littérature d'Haïti.* Vanves [France]: EDICEF, 1995. 288 pp.

3099. Jadotte, Hérard, and Dieudonné Fardin. *Cours d'histoire de la littérature haïtienne.* 3e éd., rev. et corr. Port-de-Paix, Haiti: Atelier Capois-la-Mort, 1967–1969. 4 vols. in 5. First ed. by Hérard Jadotte and Dieudonné Fardin; 2d ed. by Hérard Jadotte.

3100. Jean, Eddy Arnold, and Justin O. Fièvre. *Histoire de la littérature haïtienne.* Port-au-Prince: Impr. des Antilles, 1986– [vol. 1–].

3101. ———. *Pour une littérature haïtienne nationale et militante.* Port-au-Prince: J. Soleil, 1975. 181 pp.

3102. Laroche, Maximilien. *L'avènement de la littérature haïtienne.* Sainte-Foy, Que.: GRELCA, 1987. 219 pp.

3103. ———. *Contribution à l'étude du réalisme merveilleux.* Sainte-Foy, Que.: GRELCA, 1987. 154 pp.

3104. ———. *La double scène de la représentation: oraliture et littérature dans la Caraïbe.* Sainte-Foy, Que.: GRELCA, 1991. 234 pp.

3105. ———. *Haïti et sa littérature.* Montreal: A.G.E.U.M., 1963. 93 pp.

3106. ———. *L'image comme écho: essais sur la littérature et la culture haïtiennes.* Montreal: Editions Nouvelle Optique, 1978. 240 pp.

3107. ———. *La littérature haïtienne: identité, langue, réalité.* Montreal: Leméac, 1981. 127 pp.

3108. Lhérisson, Justin. *Manuel de littérature haïtienne et textes expliqués.* Port-au-Prince: Impr. du Collège Vertières, 1945. 409 pp.

3109. Marc, Jules André. *Regard sur la littérature haïtienne.* [Port-au-Prince: s.n.], 1973– [vol. 1–].

3110. Souffrant, Claude et al. *Littérature et société en Haïti.* 2. éd. Port-au-Prince: H. Deschamps, 1991. 286 pp.

3111. Trouillot, Hénock. *Les origines sociales de la littérature haïtienne.* Port-au-Prince: Editions Fardin, 1986. 376 pp. Reprint of the 1962 ed.

3112. Vallès, Max. *Ecriture libérée.* [Port-au-Prince]: Presses Port-au-Princiennes, 1986. 256 pp.

3113. Vaval, Duraciné. *Histoire de la littérature haïtienne; ou, "L'âme noir."* Port-au-Prince: Editions Fardin, 1986. 2 vols. Reprint of the 1933 ed.

General: Sixteenth to Nineteenth Centuries

3114. Dolcé, Jacquelin, Gérald Dorval and Jean Miotel Casthely. *Le romanticisme en Haïti: la vie intellectuelle, 1804–1915.* Port-au-Prince: Editions Fardin, 1983. 269 pp.

3115. Marcelin, Emile. *Médaillons littéraires: poètes et prosateurs haïtiens.* Port-au-Prince: Impr. de l'abeille, 1906. 158 pp.

3116. La Selve, Edgar. *Histoire de la littérature haïtienne: depuis ses origines jusqu'a nos jours—suivi d'une anthologie haïtienne.* Versailles: Impr. Cerf, 1875. 239 pp.

3117. Vaval, Duraciné. *La littérature haïtienne: essais critiques.* Paris: E. Sansot, 1911. 330 pp.

General: Twentieth Century

3118. Charles, Christophe. *Dix nouveaux poètes et écrivains haïtiens.* Port-au-Prince: Union nationale haïtienne des travailleurs intellectuels, 1974. 116 pp.

3119. Dash, J. Michael. *Literature and Ideology in Haiti, 1915–1961.* Totowa, NJ: Barnes and Noble, 1981. 213 pp.

3120. Dumas, Pierre Raymond, and Josaphat-Robert Large. *Panorama de la littérature haïtienne de la diaspora.* Port-au-Prince: L'Imprimeur II, 1996. 126 pp.

3121. Gouraige, Ghislain et al. *Littérature et société en Haïti: Davertige, Philoctète, Phelps.* Montreal: Centre international de documentation et d'information haïtienne, caribéenne et afro-canadienne, 1987. 88 pp.

3122. Jean, Eddy Arnold. *L'échec d'une élite: indigénisme, négritude, noirisme.* Port-au-Prince: Editions Haïti-demain, 1992. 176 pp.

3123. Jean, Eddy Arnold, and Jacquelin Dolcé. *Paroles en liberté.* Port-au-Prince: Editions Haïti-Demain, 1992. 380 pp.

3124. Jean, Eddy Arnold, and Justin O. Fièvre. *L'immense cri des damnés de la terre: étude sur Jacques Roumain, Jean F. Brierre, Roussan Camille, Jacques S. Alexis.* Port-au-Prince: Edition "Courrier d'Haïti", 1975. 69 pp.

3125. Lahens, Yanick. *L'exil: entre l'ancrage et la fuite—l'écrivain haïtien.* Port-au-Prince: H. Deschamps, 1990. 79 pp.

3126. Laroche, Maximilien. *Sémiologie des apparences.* Sainte-Foy, Que.: GRELCA, 1994. 210 pp.

Poetry

Poetry: General

3127. Charles, Christophe. *La poésie féminine haïtienne: histoire et anthologie de Virginie Sampeur à nos jours.* Port-au-Prince: Editions Choucoune, 1980. 218 pp.

3128. Desrosiers, Toussaint. *Amour à l'haïtienne et société idéale: un plaidoyer pour une civilisation de l'amour.* [Port-au-Prince]: Editions Beaux-Arts, 1986. 241 pp.

3129. Florvil, Hugues. *La poésie du départ: essai.* Port-au-Prince: Editions Fardin, 1986. 99 pp. Text in French and Creole.

3130. Valmy-Baysse, Jean. *La poésie française chez les noirs d'Haïti.* Paris: Nouvelle revue moderne, 1903. 46 pp.

Poetry: Twentieth Century

3131. Charles, Christophe. *La poésie au corps: études et entretiens sur la poésie et la littérature haïtienne contemporaines.* Port-au-Prince: Editions Choucoune, 1986. 223 pp.

3132. Garrett, Naomi Mills. *The Renaissance of Haitian Poetry.* Paris: Présence africaine, 1963. 257 pp.

Fiction

Fiction: General

3133. Babin, Céline, Marcia Brown and Pedro A. Sandin-Fremaint. *Le roman féminin d'Haïti: forme et structure.* Quebec: GRELCA, 1985. 89 pp.

3134. Hoffmann, Léon François. *Le roman haïtien: idéologie et structure.* Sherbrooke, Que.: Editions Naaman, 1982. 329 pp.

3135. Laroche, Maximilien. *Le patriarche, le marron et la dossa: essai sur les figures de la gémellité dans le roman haïtien.* Sainte-Foy, Que.: GRELCA, 1988. 279 pp.

3136. Shelton, Marie-Denise. *Image de la société dans le roman haïtien.* Paris: L'Harmattan, 1993. 186 pp.

3137. Vilaire, Maurice, ed. *Prosateurs protestants haïtiens.* Port-au-Prince: Impr. des Antilles, 1964. 124 pp.

Fiction: Twentieth Century

3138. Chancy, Myriam J. A. *Framing Silence: Revolutionary Novels by Haitian Women.* New Brunswick, N.J.: Rutgers University Press, 1996. 224 pp.

3139. Jean, Eddy Arnold, and Jacquelin Dolcé. *Lectures: Jacques Roumain, Edris St.-Amand, Jacques S. Alexis, Anthony Lespès.* Port-au-Prince: Editions Haïti-demain, 1985. 59 pp.

3140. Jonassaint, Jean. *Le pouvoir des mots, les maux du pouvoir: des romanciers haïtiens de l'exil.* Montreal: Presses de l'Université de Montréal, 1986. 271 pp.

Drama

3141. Cornevin, Robert. *Le théatre haïtien des origines à nos jours.* Montréal: Leméac, 1973. 301 pp.

D. INDIVIDUAL AUTHORS

Sixteenth to Nineteenth Centuries

3142. *Ardouin, Coriolan,* 1812–1835 (poet). Poésies, 1881; Poésies complètes, 1916; Reliques d'un poète haïtien, 1837.

3143. *Battier, Alcibiade Fleury,* 1841–1881 (poet). Le génie de la patrie, 1877–1930; Luména/Le génie de la liberté, 1869; Sous les bambous, 1881.

3144. *Bergeaud, Eméric,* 1818–1858 (novelist). Stella, 1859–1887.

3145. *Chauvet, Henri,* 1863–1928 (playwright, poet). La fille du Kacik, 1894–1976; La fleur d'or, 1892–1899; Fleurs et peurs, 1900?; Une nuit de noces, 1901 (with Fleury Féquière); Toréador pour amour, 1892.

3146. *Coicou, Massillon,* 1867–1908 (playwright, poet). L'empereur Dessalines, 1907–1988; Impressions, 1903; L'oracle, 1893–1901; Passions, 1903; Poésies nationales, 1892–1970.

3147. *Durand, Oswald,* 1840–1906 (poet). Poésies choisies, 1964–1992; Quatre nouveaux poèmes, 1900; Rires et pleurs, 1896–1970.

3148. Fignolé, Jean Claude. *Oswald Durand: essai critique.* Port-au-Prince: Presses Port-au-Princiennes, 1968. 76 pp.

3149. *Faubert, Pierre,* 1806–1868 (playwright). Ogé/Le préjugé de couleur, 1856–1979.

3150. *Guilbaud, Tertullien,* 1856–1939 (playwright, poet). Feuilles au vent, 1888; Higuenamota, 1876; Moeurs électorales, 1890?; Patrie, espérances et souvenirs, 1885.

3151. *Héraux, Edmond,* 1858–1920 (poet). Fleurs des mornes, 1894; Mélanges politiques et littéraires, 1896; Les préludes, 1883.

3152. *Lhérisson, Justin,* 1873–1907 (novelist, poet). Les chants de l'aurore, 1893; Myrtha, 1892; Oeuvres romanesques, 1978–1992 (La famille des Petite-Caille [1905], Zoune chez sa ninnaine [1906]); Passe-temps, 1895; Portraitins, 1894.

3153. Joassaint, Erick. *Haïti, Golimin et les autres: une lecture de Justin Lhérisson.* Port-au-Prince: Presses de l'Impr. Nouvelle, 1986. 165 pp.

3154. *Lochard, Paul,* 1835–1919 (poet). Les chants du soir, 1878; Les feuilles de chène, 1901.

3155. *Vieux, Isnardin,* 1865–1941 (playwright, poet). La chanson du desert, 1900; Les chants d'automne, 1911; Chants et rêves, 1896; Le drame du 6 décembre 1897, 1903; Mackendal, 1925–1974; Les vibrations, 1895.

Twentieth Century

3156. *Alcindor, Joscelyn,* 1961– (novelist). Cravache/Le nègre soubarou, 1995.

3157. *Alexandre, Antoine C.,* 1917– (poet). Chansons nègres, 1946; Rythmes indigènes, 1943.

3158. *Alexis, Jacques Stéphen,* 1922–1961 (novelist, playwright, short story writer). Les arbres musiciens, 1957–1992; Compère Général Soleil, 1955–1988; L'espace d'un cillement, 1959–1986; Romancero aux étoiles, 1960–1988.

3159. Antoine, Yves. *Sémiologie et personnage romanesque chez Jacques Stéphen Alexis.* Montreal: Editions Balzac, 1993. 256 pp.

3160. Boadas, Aura Marina. *Lo barroco en la obra de Jacques Stéphen Alexis.* Caracas: Fundación CELARG, 1992. 101 pp.

3161. Jean-Charles, Georges. *Jacques Stéphen Alexis: combattant et romancier d'avant-garde—ou, L'humanisme de Jacques Stéphen Alexis.* West Palm Beach, FL: LQ Editions, 1993. 253 pp.

3162. Laroche, Maximilien, and Michel Tétu. *Le romancero aux étoiles et l'oeuvre romanesque de Jacques-Stéphen Alexis.* Paris: F. Nathan, 1978. 77 pp.

3163. Mudimbe-boyi, M. Elisabeth. *L'oeuvre romanesque de Jacques-Stéphen Alexis: une écriture poétique, un engagement politique.* Montreal: Humanitas nouvelle optique, 1992. 136 pp.

3164. Pierre-Charles, Gérard et al. *Présence de Jacques Stéphen Alexis.* Port-au-Prince: Centre de recherche et formation économiques et sociales pour le développement, CRESPED, 1980. 141 pp.

3165. Ponte, Haydée-Cecilia. *Le réalisme merveilleux dans "Les arbres musiciens" de Jacques-Stéphen Alexis.* Sainte-Foy, Que.: GRELCA, 1987. 121 pp.

3166. Séonnet, Michel. *Jacques Stéphen Alexis; ou, Le voyage vers la lune de la belle amour.* Toulouse, France: Atelier de Création populaire, 1983. 175 pp.

See also #1605, #3000, #3124, #3139, #3273.

3167. *Alexis, Stéphen,* 1889–1962 (novelist, playwright). Le nègre masqué, 1933–1980.

3168. *Apollon, Georges* (novelist, poet). Anita Petithomme, 1995; Floraison d'or, raisins amers, raison de croire, 1987.

3169. *Assali, Nicholas Donald,* 1945– (poet). Chanson boula et autres poèmes, 1978; Prière caraïbe solaire, 1983; Symphonamour en nous majeur, 1990.

3170. *Beaugé-Rosier, Jacqueline,* 1932– (poet). A vol d'ombre, 1966; Les cahiers de la mouette, 1983; Climats en marche, 1962; D'or vif et de pain, 1992.

3171. *Bélance, René,* 1915– (poet). Epaule d'ombre, 1945; Luminaires, 1941; Nul ailleurs, 1978–1984; Pour célébrer l'absence, 1943–1947; Rythme de mon coeur, 1940; Survivances, 1944.

3172. *Bernard, Regnor Charles,* 1915– (poet). Nègre, 1945; Pêche d'é-
toiles, 1943; Le souvenir demeure, 1940; Sur les routes qui mon-
tent, 1954.

3173. *Brierre, Jean Fernand,* 1909– (novelist, playwright, poet). Les
Aïeules, 1950–1973; Au milieu des flammes, 1953 (with Clovis
Bonhomme); Aux champs pour Occide, 1960; Belle, 1948–1973;
Black Soul, 1947–1973; Cantique à trois voix pour une poupée
d'ébène, 1960; Chansons secrètes, 1933–1973; Découvertes, 1966;
Dessalines nous parle, 1953–1973; Le drapeau de demain, 1931;
Gerbe pour deux amis, 1945 (with Roussan Camille and Félix
Morisseau-Leroy); Les horizons sans ciel/ Province, 1935–1970;
Images d'argile et d'or, 1977; Un Noël pour Gorée, 1980; Nous
garderons le dieu, 1945–1973; La nuit, 1957–1973; Or, uranium,
cuivre, radium, 1961–1973; Pétion et Bolivar/L'adieu à la Mar-
seillaise, 1955–1973; Le petit soldat, 1934; Sculptures de proue,
1983; La source, 1956–1973. See also #3124.

3174. *Brouard, Carl,* 1902–1965 (poet). Ecrit sur du ruban rose,
1938–1965; Pages retrouvées, 1963.

3175. Gaillard, Roger. *La destinée de Carl Brouard: essai ac-
compagné de documents photographiques, d'un choix de
textes et d'une suite chronologique établis par l'auteur.*
Port-au-Prince: H. Deschamps, 1966. 89 pp.

3176. Jean, Eddy Arnold, and Justin O. Fièvre. *Carl Brouard cet
immortel.* Port-au-Prince: Presses Port-au-Princiennes,
1973. 67 pp.

3177. *Burr-Reynaud, Frédéric,* 1884–1946 (playwright, poet). Anacaona,
1941 (with Dominique Hippolyte); Anathèmes, 1930; Ascensions,
1924; Au fil de l'heure tendre, 1929; C'est la guerre, 1944?; La Corbeille, 1943 (with Edgar Nérée Numa, Dominique Hippolyte, Lys
Ambroise, and Luc Grimard); Illusion et autres nouvelles, 1989
(Pierre-Raymond Dumas, ed.); Poèmes quisqueyens, 1926; Visages
d'arbres et de fruits haïtiens, 1940–1986.

3178. *Cadet, Maurice* (poet). Chalè piman, 1990; Haute dissidence,
1991; Itinéraires du enchantement, 1992; Réjouissances, 1994.

3179. *Camille, Roussan,* 1915–1961 (poet). Assaut à la nuit, 1940;
Gerbe pour deux amis, 1945 (with Jean Fernand Brièrre and Félix
Morisseau-Leroy); La multiple présence, 1978. See also #3124.

3180. Posy, Bonnard. *Roussan Camille: le poète d' "Assaut à la nuit."* Port-au-Prince: Impr. des Antilles, 1963. 39 pp.

3181. *Castera, Georges,* 1936– (poet). A wòdpòte, 1993; Bidsuit léta, 1978; Gate priyè, 1990; Konbèlann, 1976; Quasi parlando, 1993; Ratures d'un miroir, 1992; Le retour à l'arbre, 1974.

3182. *Célestin-Mégie, Emile,* 1922– (novelist, poet). Bouquets de glanures, 1974; Byin viv, 1973; Coeur de silex, 1963; Feuilles d'ortie, 1958; Lanmou pa gin baryè, 1975–1984; Lettre à une poétesse, 1985; Trayizon/Trahisons, 1956; Vers la nouvelle saison, 1968; Vouayaj, 1968.

3183. *Charles, Carmin,* 1916– (poet, short story writer). Contes des tropiques, 1962–1975; Les sentiers du soleil, 1990.

3184. *Charles, Christophe,* 1951– (poet). L'aventure humaine, 1971; Cicatrices, 1979; Le cycle de la parole, 1973–1981; Désastre, 1975; Obsessions, 1985; Poèmes pour la paix et la libération, 1986; La terre promise, 1989.

3185. *Chauvet, Marie,* 1917–1975 (novelist, playwright). Amour, colère et folie, 1968; Dance on the Volcano, 1959 (Translation of La danse sur le volcan [1957–1980]; Salvator Attanasio, tr.); Fille d'Haïti, 1954; Fonds des nègres, 1961; La légende des fleurs, 1947; Moments, 1974; Les rapaces, 1986.

3186. Laroche, Maximilien. *Trois études sur "Folie" de Marie Chauvet.* Sainte-Foy, Que.: GRELCA, 1984. 70 pp.

3187. Sandin-Fremaint, Pedro A. *A Theological Reading of Four Novels by Marie Chauvet: In Search of Christic Voices.* San Francisco, CA: Mellen Research University Press, 1992. 365 pp.

3188. *Chevallier, André Fontanges,* 1881–1953 (novelist). L'amiral Killick, 1943 (with Charles Moravia); Mon petit Kodak, 1916–1930.

3189. *Chevry, Arsène,* 1867–1915 (poet). Les areytos, 1892; Voix du centenaire, 1904; Voix perdues, 1896; Voix de l'exil, 1908.

3190. *Cinéas, Jean Baptiste,* 1895–1958 (novelist, poet). Le choc en retour, 1948–1980; La dernière flamme, 1989 (Pierre-Raymond Dumas, ed.); Le drame de la terre, 1933–1981; L'héritage sacré,

1945–1981; La morte, 1989 (Pierre-Raymond Dumas, ed.); La vengeance de la terre, 1933.

3191. *Clitandre, Pierre* (novelist). Cathedral of the August Heat, 1987 (Translation of Cathédrale du mois d'août [1980–1982]; Bridget Jones, tr.).

3192. *Colimon Hall, Marie Thérèse,* 1918– (novelist, playwright, poet, short story writer). Bernadette Soubirous, 1955; Le chant des sirènes, 1979; Le chant du musicien, 1960; La fille de l'esclave, 1949; Fils de misère, 1974; Marie-Claire Heureuse, 1955; Le message des aïeules, 1974; Mon cahier d'écritures, 1973; La source, 1973; Vision d'Anacoana, 1955 (with Elodie de Wend).

3193. *Dalembert, Louis Philippe* (poet, short story writer). Et le soleil se souvient, 1989; Pages cendres et palmes d'aube, 1989; Le songe d'une photo d'enfance, 1993.

3194. *Dambreville, Claude,* 1934– (novelist). L'Amérique saigne/Gun Blesse America, 1995 (with Frankétienne); Un goût de fiel, 1983.

3195. *Dauphin, Marcel,* 1910– (playwright, poet, short story writer). Boisrond Tonnerre, 1954; Cantilènes tropicales, 1940; Le chant de l'esclave, 1950; Coeurs en écharpe, 1979 (Pointe Rouge, Ti Loulou, Marianne, Ti Pierre, Claudette, Explications de quelques termes et expressions); Le culte du drapeau, 1943; Flammèches, 1976; Haiti mon pays, 1963; Pierre Sully, 1960; Reflet des heures, 1961; La sérénade des opprimés, 1946.

3196. *Davertige,* 1940 (poet). Idem, 1962–1983; Idem et autres poèmes, 1964; Le passage et les voyageurs, 1978. See also #3121.

3197. *Dépestre, René,* 1926– (novelist, poet, short story writer). Alléluia pour une femme-jardin, 1973–1988; Anthologie personelle, 1993; Cantate d'octubre à la vie et à la mort du commandant Ernesto Che Guevara, 1969; En état de poésie, 1980; Eros dans un train chinois, 1990–1993; Etincelles, 1945–1970; The Festival of the Greasy Pole, 1990 (Translation of Le Mât de cocagne [1979]; Carrol F. Coates, tr.); Gerbe de sang, 1946–1970; Hadriana dans tous mes rêves, 1988–1990; Journal d'un animal marin, 1964–1990; Minerai noir, 1956; Poète à Cuba, 1976; A Rainbow for the Christian West, 1972–1977 (Translation of Un arc-en-ciel pour l'occident chrétien [1967]; Joan Dayan, tr.); Traduit du grand large, 1952; Vegetations of

Splendor, 1980 (Translation of Végétations de clarité [1951];
Jack Hirschman, tr.).

3198. Carré Crosley, Bernadette. *Haïtianité et mythe de la femme
dans "Hadriana dans tous mes rêves" de René Dépestre.*
Montreal: CIDHICA, 1993. 54 pp.

3199. ————. *René Dépestre et la défense et l'illustration de la
créolité/haitianité dans "Bonjour et adieu a la Négritude"
(1980) et "Hadriana dans tous mes rêves" (1988).* Port-au-
Prince: H. Deschamps, 1993. 167 pp.

3200. Couffon, Claude. *René Dépestre.* Paris: Seghers, 1986.
201 pp.

3201. Dépestre, René, and Etzer Dépestre, ed. *Entretiens avec
René Dépestre.* Port-au-Prince: E. Dépestre, 1989. 45 pp.

3202. *Doret, Michel R.,* 1938– (playwright, poet). Antipalinodie, 1983;
Cinq dialogues, 1980; Dégré zéro, 1988; Divagations, 1990; En
Berne/Une journée plutôt spéciale, 1989; Esquisses, 1981; Hier et
demain, 1989; Isolement, 1979; Les mamelles de Lutèce, 1989;
Poèmes en marge, 1982; Situation poésie 83, 1984; Topologie,
1982; L'univers de Marie, 1991; Volutes, 1988.

3203. *Dorsinville, Roger,* 1911– (novelist, playwright, poet, short story
writer). Accords perdus, 1987; L'Afrique des rois, 1975–1990;
Barrières, 1946; Les contes de la forêt atlantique, 1986; De Fratas
Bâton à Toussaint Louverture, 1983; Etincelles, 1945–1970; Gens
de Dakar, 1978–1990 (Charles de Fadiouth, Maître Moussa et le
sexe des anges, Les cinq prières de M.F., La grande fille et le petit garçon, Le mariage de Soukeyna, Dieynaba et l'amour); Le
grand devoir, 1962; Une haïtienne à New York, 1991; Un homme
en trois morceaux, 1975–1990; Ils ont tué le vieux blanc, 1988;
Kimby/La loi de Niang, 1973–1990; Le mâle de l'espèce, 1990;
Mourir pour Haïti/Les croisés d'Esther, 1990; Pour célébrer la
terre, 1955; Pour saluer l'écrivain Roger Dorsinville [sélections],
1990; Renaître à Dendé, 1980–1990; Les vèvès du Créateur, 1989.

3204. Dorsinville, Roger, and Jean Coradin. *Marche arrière: entretiens.* Port-au-Prince: Editions des Antilles, 1986–1990.
2 vols.

3205. *Etienne, Gérard Vergniaud,* 1936– (novelist, poet). Un ambas-
sadeur macoute à Montréal, 1979; Au milieu des larmes, 1960; La

charte des crépuscules, 1993; Cri pour ne pas crever de honte, 1982; Dialogue avec mon ombre, 1972; Une femme muette, 1983; Gladys, 1963; Lettre à Montréal, 1966; Le nègre crucifié, 1974–1994; La pacotille, 1991; Plus large qu'un rêve, 1960; La raison et mon amour, 1961; La reine soleil levée, 1987–1989.

3206. *Exavier, Marc* (poet). Les sept couleurs du sang, 1983; Soleil, 1994.

3207. *Fardin, Dieudonné,* 1936– (poet). Aux saisons de moi-même, 1973; Collier la rosée, 1964; Déblozailles, 1961; Futur simple, 1964 (with Cauvin L. Paul and Hérard Jadotte); Les grandes orgues, 1973; Isabelle, 1958; K . . . k . . . chate, 1960; Letilia, 1966; Lyre déclassée, 1962; Mélancolie des heures vécues, 1958; Mon poème de chair, 1972; Port-de-Paix multicolore, 1965; Pour toi et pour elle, 1962; Sept fleurs soleil, 1963; Souvenirs d'un autre âge, 1960.

3208. *Faubert, Ida,* 1882–1969 (poet, short story writer). Coeur des îles, 1939; Sous le ciel caraïbe, 1959.

3209. Gardiner, Madeleine. *Sonate pour Ida.* Port-au-Prince: H. Deschamps, 1984. 124 pp.

3210. *Féthière, Sténio,* 1908– (poet). Archipels, 1945; Clartés, 1988.

3211. *Figaro, Georges Jacques,* 1918– (poet, short story writer). Les ailes au vent, 1942; L'angoisse, 1942; Le coffret de cedre, 1972; Dialogue avec une ombre, 1946; L'écrin de mes rêves, 1941; Fusées, 1943; Le Papillon noir, 1953; Stèle à Jean Remy, 1948.

3212. *Figaro, Morille P.,* 1922– (novelist, poet). Cadidja, la noire négresse, 1947; Du soleil sur les sables, 1958–1959; Le duc de Tabara révolutionnaire, 1948; Feuilles à la brise, 1937; La fleur qui s'ouvre, 1958.

3213. *Fignolé, Jean Claude,* 1942– (novelist, poet). Aube tranquille, 1990; Hofuku, 1993; Les possédés de la pleine lune, 1987; Voeu de voyage et intention romanesque, 1978.

3214. *Fouché, Franck,* 1915–1978 (playwright, poet). Général Baron-La-Croix/Le silence masqué, 1974; Message, 1946; Symphonie en noir majeur, 1962; Trou de dieu, 1970.

3215. *Frankétienne,* 1936– (novelist, playwright, poet). Adjanoumelezo, 1987; Les affres d'un défi, 1979; L'Amérique saigne/Gun Blesse America, 1995 (with Claude Dambreville); Au fil du temps, 1964; Bobomasouri, 1984; Chevaux de l'avant-jour, 1967; Dézafi, 1975; Fleurs d'insomnie, 1986; La marche, 1964; Mon côté gauche, 1965; Mûr à crever, 1968–1995; L'oiseau schizophone, 1993; Pèlin-tèt, 1978; Troufoban, 1978; Ultravocal, 1972–1995; Vigie de verre, 1965.

3216. *Geaniton, Roger* (poet). Cris du silence, 1971; Premiers cris, 1960; Saisons d'exil, 1988; Vox sanguini, 1966.

3217. *Gousse, Edgar,* 1950– (poet). Jeux de sang pour une corvée noire, 1970?; Mémoires du vent, 1993; Le monde à la lisière de l'opium, 1970?.

3218. *Grimard, Luc,* 1886–1954 (poet). Bakoulou, 1950; La Corbeille, 1943 (with Frédéric Burr-Reynaud, Edgar Nérée Numa, Dominique Hippolyte, and Lys Ambroise); Du sable entre les doigts, 1941; L'offrandre du laurier, 1950; Ritournelles, 1927; Sur ma flûte de bambou, 1926.

3219. *Guérin, Mona,* 1934– (playwright, poet, short story writer). Chambre vint-six, 1973; Les cinq chéris, 1973; Mi-figue mi-raisin, 1980–1989; L'oiseau de ces dames, 1973; La pension Vacher, 1977; La pieuvre, 1973; Sur les vieux thèmes, 1958; Sylvia, 1977.

3220. *Hibbert, Fernand,* 1873–1928 (novelist, playwright, short story writer). Une affaire d'honneur, 1916; L'aventure de M. Héllénus Caton, 1923; Le manuscrit de mon ami, 1923–1988; Masques et visages, 1910–1988; Scènes de la vie haïtienne, 1907–1974; Romulus, 1908–1988; Séna, 1907–1988; Les simulacres, 1923–1988; Les Thazar, 1907–1988; Théatre, 1988 (Pauléus Sanon, ed.).

3221. *Hippolyte, Dominique,* 1889–1967 (playwright, poet, short story writer). Anacaona, 1941 (with Frédéric Burr-Reynaud); Le baiser de l'aïeul, 1924–1970; La Corbeille, 1943 (with Edgar Nérée Numa, Frédéric Burr-Reynaud, Lys Ambroise, and Luc Grimard); Le forçat, 1933–1970; Quand elle aime, 1918–1962; La route ensoleillée, 1927; Le torrent, 1940–1965.

3222. *Innocent, Antoine,* 1874–1960 (novelist). Mimola/L'histoire d'une cassette, 1906–1981.

3223. *Jolicoeur, Marie Ange*, 1947–1976 (poet). Guitare de vers, 1967; Oiseaux de mémoire, 1972; Transparence en bleu d'oubli, 1978; Violon d'espoir, 1970.

3224. *Juste-Constant, Voegeli*, 1946– (novelist). Quand tonnent les canins, 1994; Symphonie en do "bourriqwue", 1988.

3225. *Kauss, St John* (poet). Au filin des coeurs, 1981; Autopsie du jour, 1979; Chants d'homme pour les nuits d'ombre, 1979; La danseuse exotique, 1987; Ombres du Quercy, 1981; Pages fragiles, 1991; Protocole ignifuge, 1987; Tel quel, 1986; Territoires, 1995; Testamentaire, 1993; Twa degout: pwezi kreyòl, 1983.

3226. *Klang, Gary* (novelist). Les fleurs ont la saveur de l'aube, 1993; Haiti! Haiti!, 1985 (with Anthony Phelps); Je veux chanter la mer, 1993.

3227. *Laforest, Edmond*, 1876–1915 (poet). Cendres et flammes, 1912; La dernière fée, 1909; L'évolution, 1901; Poèmes mélancoliques, 1901; Sonnets-médaillons du dix-neuvième siècle, 1909.

3228. *Laleau, Léon*, 1892– (playwright, poet). Amitiés impossibles, 1916 (with Georges Nicolas Léger); Apothéoses, 1952; Une cause sans effet, 1916 (with Georges Nicolas Léger); Le choc, 1932–1975; La danse des vagues, 1919; Divagations, 1980; Jusqu'a bord—, 1916; Oeuvre poétique, 1978 (A voix basse [1919], La flêche au coeur [1926], Le rayon des jupes [1926], Abréviations [1929], Musique nègre [1931], De bronze et d'ivoir); Ondes courtes, 1933; Orchestre, 1937.

3229. *Laraque, Paul*, 1920– (poet). Les armes quotidiennes, 1979; Camourade, 1988 (Rosemary Manno, tr.); Ce qui demeure, 1973; Liberty Drum, 1995 (French/French Creole/English ed.); Poésie quotidienne, 1979; Slingshot/Fistibal, 1989 (Jack Hirschman, tr.; orig, French Creole ed. [1974]); Soldat marron/Sòlda mawon, 1987 (Jean F. Bière, tr.); Le vieux nègre et l'exil, 1988.

3230. *Large, Josaphat*, 1942– (poet). Nerfs du vent, 1975; Pè sèt!, 1994.

3231. *Leconte, Vergniaud*, 1866–1932 (playwright). Théatre, 1930 (Le roi Christophe [1901], Coulou [1916], Une princesse aborigène [1926]).

3232. *Lemaire, Emmeline Carriès* (poet). Chant pour toi, 1944; Coeur de héros, coeur d'amant, 1950; Hommage à Simon Bolívar, 1953;

Mon âme vous parle, 1941; Poèmes à Bolívar, 1948; Songs of Love, 1973.

3233. *Lemoine, Lucien,* 1923– (poet). Onze et un poème d'amour, 1966; Le veilleur de jour, 1980.

3234. *Lespès, Anthony,* 1907–1978 (poet). Les clefs de la lumière, 1955; Les semences de la colère, 1949–1983. See also #3139.

3235. *Libose, Jean,* 1911– (poet). Bouquet à la naïade, 1941; Les cendres du passé, 1948; Cinq sonnets à la mère, 1955; Confidences, 1951; La Corbeille, 1943 (with Frédéric Burr-Reynaud, Edgar Nérée Numa, Dominique Hippolyte, and Luc Grimard); Grappes de souvenir, 1940; L'île paradisiaque, 1955; L'île songeuse, 1947; Une palme et des roses, 1941; Valparaiso, 1951.

3236. *Lotu, Denize* (poet, short story writer). Boula pou yon metamòfoz zèklè nan peyi a, 1988; Father and Son, 1992–1996; Running the Road to ABC, 1996; When the Denizen Weeps, 1988.

3237. *Magloire-Saint-Aude, Clément,* 1912– (novelist, poet, short story writer). Déchu, 1956–1970; Dialogue de mes lampes, 1941–1970; Dimanche, 1973; Parias, 1949; Tabou, 1941–1970; Veillée, 1956.

3238. Charles, Christophe. *Magloire Saint-Aude: griot et surréaliste—essai critique.* Port-au-Prince: Editions Choucoune, 1982. 114 pp.

3239. Saint-Amand, Edris. *Essai d'explication de "Dialogue de mes lampes."* 2e. éd. Port-au-Prince: Ateliers Fardin, 1975. 51 pp.

3240. *Marcelin, Frédéric,* 1848–1917 (novelist). Au gré du souvenir, 1913–1975; La confession de Bazoutte, 1909; Marilisse, 1903–1976; Propos d'un haïtien, 1915; Thémistocle-Epaminondas Labasterre, 1901–1982; La vengeance de Mama, 1902–1974.

3241. *Métellus, Jean,* 1937– (novelist, playwright, poet). Anacaona, 1986; L'année Dessalines, 1986; Au pipirite chantant, 1978; Les cacos, 1989; Charles-Honoré Bonnefoy, 1990; Colomb, 1992; Une eau-forte, 1983; Hommes de plein vent, 1981–1992; Jacmel au crépuscule, 1981; Louis Vortex, 1992; La parole prisonnière, 1986; Le pont rouge, 1991; Voix nègres, 1992; The Vortex Family, 1993 (Translation of La famille Vortex [1982]; Michael Richardson, tr,).

3242. *Moïse, Rodolphe,* 1914–1977 (poet). Aux armes guérilleros, 1975; Gueles de feu, 1947.

3243. *Moravia, Charles,* 1875–1938 (playwright, poet). L'amiral Killick, 1943–1988 (with André Fontanges Chevalier); La Crête-à-Pierrot, 1908; Le fils du tapissier, 1923.

3244. *Morisseau, Roland,* 1933– (poet). Cinq poèmes de reconnaisance, 1961; Clef du soleil, 1963; Germination d'espoir, 1962; Poésie, 1993 (Chanson de Roland, Raison ensanglantée, La promeneuse au jasmin).

3245. *Morisseau-Leroy, Félix,* 1912– (novelist, playwright, poet, short story writer). Antigone en créole, 1954–1970; Degi, 1988; Dyakout/Diacoute (1–4), 1953–1990; Gerbe pour deux amis, 1945 (with Roussan Camille and Jean Fernand Brièrre); Haitiad and Oddities, 1991 (Jeffrey Knapp [et al], trs.); Kasamansa, 1977; Natif-natal, 1948–1970; Pep-la, 1978; Plénitudes, 1940–1973; Ravinodyab/La ravine aux diables, 1982; Récolte, 1946–1970; Roua kréon, 1978; Ten Selected Poems, 1980 (Jean Small, Daphne Moriss, Raymond Mair, trs.); Vilbone, 1982.

3246. *Numa, Edgar Nérée,* 1881–1979 (novelist, poet). Clercina destinée, 1975; La Corbeille, 1943 (with Frédéric Burr-Reynaud, Dominique Hippolyte, Lys Ambroise, and Luc Grimard).

3247. *Numa, Saint Arnaud* (playwright, poet, short story writer). Anacaona reine martyre, 1981; Boukmann towokòn, 1990; Les échos du silence, 1962; Jénéral Rodrig, 1975; Les roses noires, 1973.

3248. *Ollivier, Emile,* 1940– (novelist). La discorde aux cent voix, 1986; Mother Solitude, 1989 (Translation of Mère Solitude [1983–1994]; David Lobdell, tr.); Passages, 1991–1994; Paysage de l'aveugle, 1977.

3249. *Papillon, Margaret,* 1958– (novelist). La marginale, 1987; Martin Toma, 1991.

3250. *Papillon, Pierre,* 1927– (novelist). L'âme qui meurt, 1950–1984; L'exil du ciel, 1949.

3251. *Paret, Timothée L. J.,* 1887–1942 (novelist, poet). L'âme vibrante, 1913–1929; Dans la mêlée, 1932; Fleurs détachées, 1917; Jeanine, 1907; Lueurs sereines, 1908; Nouvelle floraison, 1927.

3252. *Paul, Cauvin L.*, 1938– (poet). Bourgeon de soleil, 1965; Cantilènes d'un naufragé, 1962; Futur simple, 1964 (with Hérard Jadotte and Dieudonné Fardin); Laetitia, 1970; Nuit sans fond, 1976.

3253. *Péan, Stanley*, 1966– (novelist, short story writer). L'emprise de la nuit, 1993; La mémoire ensanglantée, 1994; La plage des songes et autres récits d'exil, 1988; Sombres allées et autres endroits peu hospitaliers, 1992; La tumulte de mon sang, 1992.

3254. *Perrier, Rose Marie*, 1944– (novelist, poet, short story writer). Cantilène à Zouki, 1965; Dans les embarras de New York, 1981; La nuit de mon exil, 1963; Retour à minuit, 1969; Sacrilège et jugement, 1970.

3255. *Phelps, Anthony*, 1928– (novelist, playwright, poet). La bélière caraïbe, 1980; Le conditionnel, 1970; Les dits du fou-aux-cailloux, 1968; Eclats de silence, 1962; Et moi je suis un île, 1973; Eté, 1960; Haiti! Haiti!, 1985 (with Gary Klang); Même le soleil est nu, 1983; Mémoire en colin-maillard, 1976; Moins l'infini, 1973; Mon pays que voici/Este es mi país, 1967–1987 (Mónica Mansour, tr.); Motifs pour le temps saisonnier, 1976; Orchidée nègre, 1985–1987; Points cardinaux, 1966. See also #3121.

3256. *Philoctète, René*, 1932– (novelist, playwright, poet, short story writer). Caraibe, 1995; Ces îles qui marchent, 1969–1974; Et coetera, 1967; Le huitième jour, 1973; Il faut des fois que les dieux meurent, 1992; Margha, 1961; Les tambours du soleil, 1962; Le peuple des terres mêlées, 1989; Une saison de cigales, 1993; Saison des hommes, 1960; Les tambours du solel, 1962. See also #3121.

3257. Fignolé, Jean Claude. *Pour une poésie de l'authentique et du solidaire: "Ces iles qui marchent" de René Philoctète*. Port-au-Prince: Editions Fardin, 1974. 57 pp.

3258. *Posy, Bonnard*, 1931– (novelist, poet). Les chants du silence, 1962; Jusqu'au bout du chemin, 1966; Les matins sur la colline, 1978; Le relais des étoiles, 1993.

3259. *Poujol Oriol, Paulette*, 1926– (novelist, short story writer). Le creuset, 1980–1985; La fleur rouge, 1992.

3260. *Pressoir, Charles Fernand*, 1910–1973 (poet). Au rythme des coumbites, 1933; Sè-t poèm ki sò-t nan mò-n, 1954.

3261. *Rigaud, Milo,* 1904– (poet). Jésus ou Legba?/Les dieux se battent, 1933; Rhythmes et rites/Rites et rhythmes, 1932; Tassos, 1933.

3262. *Romeus, Wilhem,* 1947– (novelist, poet). Email, 1990; Grande Yaya, 1988; Leftover (manjé dòmi), 1984; Terre cassée, 1984.

3263. *Roumain, Jacques,* 1907–1944 (novelist, poet, short story writer). Ebony Wood/Bois d'ébène [1945], 1972 (Sidney Shapiro, tr.); Les fantoches, 1931–1977; Jacques Roumain [poèmes], 1993; Masters of the Dew, 1947–1988 (Translation of Gouverneurs de la rosée [1944–1992]; Langston Hughes, Mercer Cook, trs.); La montagne ensorcelée, 1931–1987; Oeuvres choisis, 1964; Poèmes, 1993; La proie et l'ombre, 1930–1977; When the Tom-Tom Beats, 1995 (Joanne Fungaroli, Ronald Sauer, trs.).

3264. Conturie, Christiane. *Comprendre "Gouverneurs de la rosée" de Jacques Roumain.* Issy-les-Moulineaux [France]: Clasiques africains, 1980. 96 pp.

3265. Dorsinville, Roger. *Jacques Roumain.* Paris: Présence africaine, 1981. 123 pp.

3266. Fowler, Carolyn. *A Knot in the Thread: The Life and Work of Jacques Roumain.* Washington, DC: Howard University Press, 1980. 383 pp.

3267. Gaillard, Roger. *L'univers romanesque de Jacques Roumain.* Port-au-Prince: H. Deschamps, 1965. 23 pp.

3268. Jean, Eddy Arnold. *"Gouverneurs de la rosée": le texte et ses lectures.* New York: Editions J. Soleil, 1975. 40 pp.

3269. ———. *Pour une relecture de "Gouverneurs de la rosée."* Port-au-Prince: Edition Haïti-demain, 1990. 72 pp.

3270. Magloire, Hébert. *Actualité de Jacques Roumain: le Christ noir.* Montreal: [s.n.], 1975. 32 pp.

3271. Paul, Cauvin L. *Manuel . . . !: un dieu tombé—essai sur "Gouverneurs de la rosée."* Port-au-Prince: [s.n.], 1975. 41 pp.

3272. Prat, Michel. *"Gouverneurs de la rosée": Jacques Roumain—analyse critique.* Paris: Hatier, 1986. 78 pp.

3273. Souffrant, Claude. *Une négritude socialiste: religion et développement chez J. Roumain, J.-S. Alexis, L. Hughes.* Paris: L'Harmattan, 1978. 238 pp.

3274. Trouillot, Hénock. *Dimension et limites de Jacques Roumain.* Port-au-Prince: Editions Fardin, 1981. 206 pp. Reprint of the 1975 ed.

See also #36, #3124, #3139.

3275. *Roumer, Emile,* 1903– (poet). Le caïman étoile, 1963; Couronne sonnets, 1964; Poèmes d'Haïti et de France, 1925–1972; Rosaire, 1964.

3276. Roumer, Emile, and Christophe Charles. *Dialogue avec Emile Roumer, 1903–1988.* Port-au-Prince: Editions Christophe, 1992. 35 pp.

3277. *Saint Eloi, Rodney,* 1963– (poet). Graffitis pour l'aurore, 1989; Pierres anonymes, 1994; Voyelles adultes, 1994.

3278. *Saint-Amand, Edris,* 1918– (novelist). Bon Dieu rit, 1952–1989; Le vent de janvier, 1985. See also #3139.

3279. *Soukar, Michel,* 1955– (playwright, poet). La cour de miracles, 1995; L'homme aux sept noms de poussière, 1983; L'île de braise et de pluie, 1984–1995; La maison de Claire, 1995; Le pain se fait la nuit, 1982; Requiem pour un empire païen, 1988.

3280. *Sylvain, Georges,* 1866–1925 (poet). Confidences et mélancolies, 1901–1979; Cric? Crac!, 1901–1980; Trois noëls, 1891.

3281. *Tavernier, Janine,* 1935– (poet). Ombre ensoleillée, 1961; Splendeur, 1962.

3282. *Thoby-Marcelin, Philippe,* 1904–1975 (novelist, poet, short story writer). A fonds perdu, 1953; All Men Are Mad, 1970 (with Pierre Marcelin; translation of Tous les hommes sont fous [1970– 1980]; Eva Thoby-Marcelin, tr.); The Beast of the Haitian Hills, 1946–1986 (with Pierre Marcelin; translation of La bête de Musseau [1946]; Peter C. Rhodes, tr.); Canapé-Vert, 1944 (with Pierre Marcelin; translation of Canapé-Vert [1944]; Edward Larocque Tinker, tr.); Dialogue avec la femme endormie, 1941; Lago-Lago, 1943; La négresse adolescente, 1932; The Pencil of

God, 1951 (with Pierre Marcelin; translation of Le crayon de Dieu [1952]; Leonard Thomas, tr.); The Singing Turtle and Other Tales from Haiti, 1971 (with Pierre Marcelin; translation of Contes et légendes d'Haïti [1967]; Eva Thoby-Marcelin, tr.).

3283. Fowler, Carolyn. *Philippe Thoby-Marcelin, écrivain haïtien, et Pierre Marcelin, romancier haïtien.* Sherbrooke, Que.: Naaman, 1985. 131 pp.

3284. *Thoby-Marcelin, Pierre,* 1907– (novelist, short story writer). All Men Are Mad, 1970 (with Philippe Thoby-Marcelin; translation of Tous les hommes sont fous [1970–1980]; Eva Thoby-Marcelin, tr.); The Beast of the Haitian Hills, 1946–1986 (with Philippe Thoby-Marcelin; translation of La bête de Musseau [1946]; Peter C. Rhodes, tr.); Canapé vert, 1944 (with Philippe Thoby-Marcelin; translation of Canapé vert [1944]; Edward Larocque Tinker, tr.); The Pencil of God, 1951 (with Philippe Thoby-Marcelin; translation of Le crayon de Dieu [1952]; Leonard Thomas, tr.); The Singing Turtle, and Other Tales from Haiti, 1971 (with Philippe Thoby-Marcelin; translation of Contes et légendes d'Haïti [1967]; Eva Thoby-Marcelin, tr.). See also #3283.

3285. *Trouillot, Lyonel,* 1956– (novelist, poet). Dé-palé, 1979 (with Pierre-Richard Narcisse); Les fous de Saint-Antoine, 1989; Le livre de Marie, 1993; La petite fille au régard d'île, 1994.

3286. *Valcin, Virgile,* Mme (novelist, poet). La blanche négresse, 1934; Cruelle destinée, 1929–1989; Deux héroïnes, 1989 (Pierre-Raymond Dumas, ed.); Fleurset peurs, 1924.

3287. *Vallès, Max,* 1939– (playwright, poet, short story writer). Confidences du tambour, 1969; Coumbite des chansons quisqueyennes, 1972; Le milicien des mornes, 1985; Pages choisies de Max Vallès, 1974; La récolte sera belle, 1973; Le rêve de Joaérus, 1984; Roi Angole, 1971–1985; Yanvalou des premières fleurs, 1970.

3288. *Vaval, Duraciné,* 1879–1952 (poet). Stances haïtiennes, 1912.

3289. *Victor, Gary,* 1958– (novelist, poet, short story writer). Albert Buron/Profil d'une "élite", 1988–1989; Clair de Manbo, 1990; Nouvelles interdites/Recueil de nouvelles, 1989; Un octobre d'Elyaniz, 1992; Sonson Pipirit, 1988; Le sorcier qui n'aimait pas la neige, 1995; Symphonie pour demain, 1981.

3290. *Vieux, Damoclès,* 1876–1936 (poet, short story writer). L'aile captive, 1913; Amour de libellule, 1989 (Pierre-Raymond Dumas, ed.); Dernière épreuve, 1989 (Pierre-Raymond Dumas, ed.); Dernières floraisons, 1947; Jacques Breffort, 1989 (Pierre-Raymond Dumas, ed.).

3291. *Vilaire, Etzer,*1872–1951 (novelist, poet). Les dix hommes noirs, 1901–1994; Le filibustier, 1902; Homo, vision de l'enfer, 1902; Nouveaux poèmes, 1910 (Les voix, Terre et ciel, Au delà, Fantasies poétiques); Pages d'amour, 1901–1991; Poèmes a mon âme, 1905; Poésies complètes, 1914–1919 (Vol. 1. Les années tendres [1907], Vol. 2. Poèmes de la mort [1907], Vol. 3. Nouveaux poèmes [1912]); La vie solitaire pendant l'occupation américaine, 1937–1977.

   3292. Fignolé, Jean Claude. *Etzer Vilaire: ce méconnu.* Port-au-Prince: Impr. centrale, 1970. 217 pp.

   3293. Gaillard, Roger. *Etzer Vilaire: témoin de nos malheurs.* Port-au-Prince: Presses nationales, 1972. 162 pp.

   3294. Laforest, Edmond. *L'oeuvre poétique de M. Etzer Vilaire.* Jèrémie [Haiti]: Impr. du Centenaire, 1907. 40 pp.

   3295. Pompilus, Pradel. *Etzer Vilaire: études critiques et textes choisis.* Port-au-Prince: [s.n.], 1968. 132 pp.

3296. *Vilaire, Jean-Joseph,* 1881–1967 (poet, short story writer). Au crépuscule du coeur, 1930; Aube, 1914; Entre maîtres et esclaves, 1943–1970; Le fond du tiroir, 1965–1979; Gens du peuple et gens de la campagne, 1954–1970; Une histoire d'amour de notre histoire d'Haïti, 1985?; Ode à Raymond Vilaire Cabèche, 1965–1979; Paysages et paysans, 1930; Sonnets héroiques sur la mort de Gérin, 1925.

3297. *Werleigh, Christian,* 1895–1947 (poet). Défilée-la-folle, 1927; Ma ville, mon pays, 1947?; Le palmiste dans la lumière, 1938; Le palmiste dans l'ouragan, 1943.

MARTINIQUE

A. ANTHOLOGIES

General: Sixteenth to Nineteenth Centuries

3298. Joyau, Auguste, ed. *Panorama de la littérature à la Martinique.* Fort-de-France: Editions des Horizons Caraïbes, 1974–1977. 2 vols. Vol. 1. XVIIe et XVIIIe siècles.—Vol. 2. XIXe siècle.

Poetry

3299. Joyau, Auguste. *Anthologie des poètes martiniquais.* Fort-de-France: Editions des Horizons Caraïbes, 1959. 147 pp.

B. HISTORY AND CRITICISM

3300. Relouzat, Raymond. *Le référent ethno-culturel dans le conte créole.* Paris: L'Harmattan, 1989. 163 pp.

C. INDIVIDUAL AUTHORS

Sixteenth to Nineteenth Centuries

3301. *Agricole, Eugène,* 1834–1901 (poet). Les soupirs et les rêves, 1936.

3302. *Bentzon, Thérèse,* 1840–1907 (novelist). Yette, histoire d'une jeune créole, 1880–1977.

3303. *Bonneville, René,* 1870–1902 (novelist, poet). Le fruit défendu, 1899; Le mal d'amour, 1902–1977; Les soeurs ennemies, 1901–1977; Le triomphe d'Eglantine, 1899–1977; La vierge cubaine, 1897–1977.

3304. *Eyma, Louis Xavier,* 1816–1876 (novelist, short story writer). Aventuriers et corsaires, 1861; Emmanuel, 1841–1977; Les peaux noires, 1857; Le roi des tropiques, 1860–1890; Le trône d'argent, 1857.

3305. *Levilloux, J.* (novelist). Les créoles/La vie aux Antilles, 1835–1977.

3306. *Prévost de Sansac, Auguste,* 1754–? (novelist). Les amours de Zémédare et Carina, 1806–1977.

3307. *Salavina,* 1866–1920 (novelist, playwright, poet). Amours tropicales/Martinique aux siècles des rois, 1912; Madellina, 1895–1896; Saint-Pierre, la Venise tropicale/Trente ans de Saint-Pierre, 1909–1986 (Autobiographical); Les Tropicales, 1921; Les Volcaniques, 1921.

Twentieth Century

3308. *Adréa, Albert,* 1901– (novelist, poet). Bluets d'Avril, 1944; Le chant des sources, 1967; Dans l'oasis du coeur, 1947; Des scabieuses et des violettes, 1980; Fleurs du soir, 1957; Roses d'automne, 1967; Sommets, 1960.

3309. *André, Marcel,* 1932– (novelist, playwright, poet). Les fortes nourritures, 1968; Poèmes d'or et d'argent, 1983; La révolution, 1962–1981; Le temps des dieux, 1989.

3310. *Armet, Auguste,* 1939– (playwright, poet). Boutou grand soir, 1978; Le cri antillais, 1964; Eïa! Man-maille là, 1968–1981.

3311. *Audiberti, Marie Louise* (novelist). La cadette, 1995; La dent d'Adèle, 1978; La peau et le sucre, 1993; Viens, il y aura des hommes, 1977; Volcan sur l'île, 1986.

3312. *Bémont, Frédy* (novelist). La métisse blanche, 1982–1995; Panique chez les humains, 1985; Question de peau, 1979.

3313. *Boukman, Daniel,* 1936– (playwright, poet). Anba fèy, 1985?; Chants pour hâter la mort, 1987–1993; Délivrans, 1995; Et jusqu'à la dernière pulsation de nos veines, 1976–1993; Les négriers, 1971–1978; Ventres pleins, ventres creux, 1971–1980.

3314. *Calixte, Charles,* 1923– (poet). Antilles à main armée, 1952–1970.

3315. *Capécia, Mayotte,* 1928–1953 (novelist). Je suis martiniquaise, 1948 (Autobiographical); La négresse blanche, 1950.

3316. *Carbet, Claude* (poet, short story writer). Braves gens de la Martinique, 1957 (with Marie Magdeleine Carbet); Ça et là dans la Caraïbe, 1939 (with Marie Magdeleine Carbet); Chansonelles, l'île aux oiseaux, 1938–1956 (with Marie Magdeleine Carbet); Chansons des îles, 1937–1955 (with Marie Magdeleine Carbet); Et Lazare sortit du tombeau, 1939–1967; Féfé et Doudou, 1936 (with Marie Magdeleine Carbet); Piment rouge, 1938 (with Marie Magdeleine Carbet).

3317. *Carbet, Marie Magdeleine,* 1906– (novelist, poet, short story writer). Au péril de ta joie, 1972; Au sommet la sérénité, 1980; Au village en temps longtemps, 1977; Braves gens de la Martinique, 1957 (with Claude Carbet); Ça et là dans la Caraïbe, 1939 (with Claude Carbet); Chansonelles, l'île aux oiseaux, 1938–1956 (with Claude Carbet); Chansons des îles, 1937–1955 (with Claude Carbet); Comptines et chansons antillaises, 1975; Contes de Tantana, 1980; D'une rive à l'autre, 1975; Ecoute Soleil-Dieu, 1961–1974; Et merveille de vivre, 1973; Féfé et Doudou, 1936 (with Claude Carbet); Mini-poèmes sur trois méridiens, 1977; Musique noire, 1958; Piment rouge, 1938 (with Claude Carbet); Point d'orgue, 1958–1974; Rose de ta grâce, 1970–1979; Suppliques et chansons, 1965–1974; Viens voir ma ville, 1963–1974.

3318. *Césaire, Aimé,* 1913– (playwright, poet). Aimé Césaire, 1962–1989 (Lilyan Kesteloot, ed.); Aimé Césaire, 1967 (Simon Battestini, ed.); Aimé Césaire, 1983 (Clayton Eshleman, Annette Smith, eds. and trs.); Aimé Césaire, 1995 (Guy Ossito Midiohouan, ed.); Les armes miraculeuses, 1946–1970; Cadastre, 1973 (Translation of Cadastre [1961]; Emile Snyder, Sanford Upson, trs.); Et les chiens se taisaient, 1956–1989; Ferrements, 1960; Lost Body, 1986 (Translation of Corps perdu [1950]; Clayton Eshleman, Annette Smith, trs.); Lyric and Dramatic Poetry (1946–1982), 1990 (Clayton Eshleman, Annette Smith, trs.); Moi, laminaire, 1982–1991; Non-Vicious Circle, 1984 (Gregson Davis, ed. and tr.); Oeuvres complètes, 1976; La poésie, 1994 (Daniel Maximin, Gilles Carpentier, eds.); Return to My Native Land/Cahier d'un retour au pays natal [1939–1994], 1968–1971 (Emil Snyders, tr.); A Season in the Congo, 1969 (Translation of Une saison au Congo [1967–1990]; Ralph Manheim, tr.); Soleil cou-coupé, 1948–1970; State of the Union (Selections), 1966 (Clayton Eshleman, Denis Kelly, trs.); A Tempest, 1986–1992

(Translation of *Une tempête* [1969–1980]; Richard Miller, tr.); The Tragedy of King Christophe, 1970 (Translation of *La tragédie du roi Christophe* [1963–1988]; Ralph Manheim, tr.).

3319. Antoine, Régis. *"La tragédie du roi Cristophe" de Aimé Césaire*. Paris: Pédagogie moderne, 1984. 127 pp.

3320. Armet, Auguste et al. *Aimé Césaire: textes*. Quebec: Presses de l'Université Laval, 1973. 141 pp.

3321. Arnold, Albert James. *Modernism and Negritude: The Poetry and Poetics of Aimé Césaire*. Cambridge, MA: Harvard University Press, 1981. 318 pp.

3322. Arnold, Albert James, Mbwil a Mpaang Ngal and Martin Steins. *Césaire 70 [Césaire soixante-dix]*. Paris: Silex, 1985. 308 pp.

3323. Bailey, Marianne Wichmann. *The Ritual Theater of Aimé Césaire: Mythic Structures of the Dramatic Imagination*. Tübingen: G. Narr, 1992. 255 pp.

3324. Bouelet, Rémy Sylvestre. *Espaces et dialectique du héros césairien*. Paris: L'Harmattan, 1987. 219 pp.

3325. Brichaux-Houyoux, Suzanne. *Quand Césaire écrit, Lumumba parle: édition commentée de "Une saison au Congo"*. Paris: L'Harmattan, 1993. 335 pp.

3326. Cailler, Bernadette. *Proposition poétique: une lecture de l'oeuvre d'Aimé Césaire*. Sherbooke, Que.: Naaman, 1976. 244 pp.

3327. Carpentier, Gilles. *Scandale de bronze: lettre à Aimé Césaire*. Paris: Editions du Seuil, 1994. 76 pp.

3328. Case, Frederick Ivor, and Carol A. Thomas. *Aimé Césaire: bibliographie*. Toronto: Manna, 1973. 57 pp.

3329. Colloque international de Fort-de-France (1993); Roger Toumson and Jacqueline Leiner, eds. *Aimé Césaire: du singulier à l'universal—actes du colloque international de Fort-de-France, 28–30 juin 1993*. Tübingen: G. Narr, 1994. 424 pp.

3330. Colloque international sur l'oeuvre littéraire d'Aimé Césaire (First, 1985, Paris). *Aimé Césaire; ou, L'athanor d'un alchimiste—actes du premier Colloque international sur l'oeuvre littéraire d'Aimé Césaire, Paris 21–22–23 novembre 1985.* Paris: Editions caribéennes, 1987. 381 pp.

3331. Combe, Dominique. *Aimé Césaire: "Cahier d'un retour au pays natal."* Paris: Presses universitaires de France, 1993. 126 pp.

3332. Condé, Maryse. *"Cahier d'un retour au pays natal": Césaire—analyse critique.* Paris: Hatier, 1978. 79 pp.

3333. Confiant, Raphaël. *Aimé Césaire: une traversée paradoxale du siècle.* Paris: Stock, 1993. 354 pp.

3334. Delas, Daniel. *Aimé Césaire.* Paris: Hachette, 1991. 223 pp.

3335. Frutkin, Susan. *Aimé Césaire: Black Between Worlds.* Coral Gables, FL: Center for Advanced International Studies, University of Miami, 1973. 66 pp.

3336. Harris, Rodney E. *L'humanisme dans le théâtre d'Aimé Césaire: étude de trois tragédies.* Sherbrooke, Que.: Naaman, 1973. 170 pp.

3337. Hountondji, Victor. *Le "Cahier" d'Aimé Césaire: événement littéraire et facteur de révolution—essai.* Paris: L'Harmattan, 1993. 135 pp.

3338. Jouanny, Robert A. *"Cahier d'un retour au pays natal" [et] "Discours sur le colonialism" [de] Césaire: résumé, personnages, thèmes.* Paris: Hatier, 1994. 79 pp.

3339. Juin, Hubert. *Aimé Césaire: poète noir.* Paris: Présence africaine, 1995. 105 pp.

3340. Kesteloot, Lilyan. *Comprendre le "Cahier d'un retour au pays natal" d'Aimé Césaire.* Bar-le-Duc [France]: Classiques africains, 1992. 127 pp. Reprint of the 1982 ed.

3341. Kesteloot, Lilyan, and Barthélémy Kotchy. *Aimé Césaire: l'homme et l'oeuvre.* Nouv. éd. Paris: Présence africaine, 1993. 223 pp.

3342. Lebrun, Annie. *Pour Aimé Césaire*. Paris: J.-M. Place, 1994. 66 pp.

3343. Leiner, Jacqueline. *Aimé Césaire: le terreau primordial*. Tübingen, Ger.: G. Narr, 1993. 172 pp.

3344. ———, ed. *Soleil éclaté: mélanges offerts à Aimé Césaire à l'occasion de son soixante-dixième anniversaire*. Tübingen, Ger.: G. Narr, 1984. 439 pp.

3345. Mbom, Clément. *Le théâtre d'Aimé Césaire; ou, La primauté de l'universalité humaine*. Paris: F. Nathan, 1979. 175 pp.

3346. Ngal, Mbwil a Mpaang. *Aimé Césaire: un homme à la recherche d'une patrie*. 2. éd. rev., corr. et augm. Paris: Présence africaine, 1994. 328 pp.

3347. Nisbet, Anne Marie, and Beverley Ormerod. *Négritude et antillanité: étude d' "Une tempête" d'Aimé Césaire*. Kensington, NSW, Australia: University of New South Wales Press, 1982. 88 pp.

3348. Nne Onyeoziri, Gloria. *La parole poétique d'Aimé Césaire: essai de sémantique littéraire*. Paris: L'Harmattan, 1992. 239 pp.

3349. Owusu-Sarpong, Albert. *Le temps historique dans l'oeuvre théâtrale d'Aimé Césaire*. Sherbrooke, Que.: Editions Naaman, 1986. 270 pp.

3350. Pallister, Janis L. *Aimé Césaire*. New York: Twayne, 1991. 149 pp.

3351. Ruhe, Ernstpeter. *Aimé Césaire et Janheinz Jahn: les débuts du théâtre césairien—la nouvelle version de "Et les chiens se taisaient."* Würzburg, Ger.: Königshausen und Neumann, 1990. 168 pp.

3352. Scharfman, Ronnie Leah. *Engagement and the Language of the Subject in the Poetry of Aimé Césaire*. Gainesville, FL: University Presses of Florida, 1987. 133 pp.

3353. Toumson, Roger. *Trois calibans: essai*. Havana: Casa de las Américas, 1981. 638 pp. Comparison of Aimé Césaire and William Shakespeare.

3354. Toumson, Roger, and Simonne Henry Valmore. *Aimé Césaire: le nègre inconsolé.* Paris: Syros, 1993. 239 pp.

3355. Trouillot, Hénock. *L'itinéraire d'Aimé Césaire.* Port-au-Prince: Impr. des Antilles, 1968. 178 pp.

3356. Walker, Keith Louis. *La cohésion poétique de l'oeuvre césairienne.* Tübingen, Ger.: G. Narr, 1979. 140 pp.

3357. Zadi Zaorou, Bernard. *Césaire entre deux cultures: problèmes théoriques de la littérature négro-africaine d'aujourd'hui.* Abidjan: Nouvelles Éditions africaines, 1978. 294 pp.

See also #40, #44, #970.

3358. *Césaire, Ina* (novelist, playwright, short story writer). Contes de mort et de vie aux Antilles, 1976 (with Joëlle Laurent); Contes de nuits et de jours aux Antilles, 1989; L'enfant des passages/La geste de Ti-Jean, 1987; Mémoires d'isles: Maman N. et Maman F., 1985; Zonzon Tête Carrée, 1994.

3359. *Chamoiseau, Patrick* (novelist, playwright, short story writer). Antan d'enfance, 1990–1993 (Autobiographical); Au temps de l'antan, 1988; Chemin-d'école, 1994; Chronique des sept misères, 1986–1988; Paroles de djobeurs, 1988; Manman Dlo contre la fée Carabosse, 1982; Solibo magnifique, 1988–1991; Texaco, 1992–1994.

3360. *Confiant, Raphaël,* 1951– (novelist, poet, short story writer). L'allée des soupirs, 1994; Bassin des ouragans, 1994; Bitako-a, 1985; Commandeur du sucre, 1994; Eau de café, 1991; Le gouverneur des dés, 1995 (Translation of Kòd yanm [1986]; Gerry L'Etang, tr.); Jik dèyè do bondyé, 1978; Jou baré, 1982; Mamzelle Libellule, 1994 (Translation of Marisosé [1987]); Le nègre et l'amiral, 1988; Ravines du devant-jour, 1993.

3361. *Delpech, Alice* (novelist). La dame de Balata, 1990; La dissidence, 1991.

3362. *Delsham, Tony* (novelist). L'ababa, 1987; Kout Fe, 1994; Lapo Farine, 1984; L'impuissant, 1986; Les larmes des autres, 1983; Ma justice, 1982; Panique aux Antilles, 1985; Le retour de Monsieur Coutcha, 1984; Tracée sans horizon, 1985; Xavier, 1981.

3363. *Desportes, Georges,* 1921– (novelist, poet, short story writer). L'amour m'aime, 1982; Cette île qui est la nôtre, 1973; Libre de tout engagement, 1993; Les marches souveraines, 1956; Soliloques pour mauvais rêves, 1958; Sous l'oeil fixe du soleil, 1961.

3364. *Duquesnay, Victor,* 1872–1920 (poet). La chanson des îles, 1926; Les martiniquaises, 1903.

3365. *Ega, Françoise,* 1924–1976 (novelist). Lettres à une noire, 1978; Le temps des madras, 1966–1989 (Autobiographical).

3366. *Glissant, Edouard,* 1928– (novelist, playwright, poet). La case du commandeur, 1981; Fastes, 1991; The Indies/Les Indes, 1992 (Dominique O'Neill, tr.; French ed. first published 1956); L'intention poétique, 1969; Mahagony, 1987; Malemort, 1975; Monsieur Toussaint, 1981 (Translation of Monsieur Toussaint [1961–1986]; Joseph G. Foster, Barbara A. Franklin, trs.); Poèmes complets, 1994 (Le sang rivé [1961], Un champ d'îles, [1953], La terre inquiète [1955], Les Indes [1956], Le sel noir [1960], Boises [1979], Pays rêvé, pays réel [1985], Pastes, Les grands chaos); Poétique de la relation, 1990; Le quatrième siècle, 1964–1990; The Ripening, 1959–1985 (Translation of La Lézarde [1958]; Michael Dash, tr.); Soleil de la conscience, 1956–1986; Tout-monde, 1993.

3367. Cailler, Bernadette. *Conquérants de la nuit nue: Edouard Glissant et l'histoire antillaise.* Tübingen, Ger.: G. Narr Verlag, 1988. 180 pp.

3368. Colloque de Pau (1990, Porto, Portugal); Yves Alain Favre and Antonio Ferreira de Brito, eds. *Horizons d'Edouard Glissant: actes.* Pau [France]: J & D Editions, 1992. 547 pp.

3369. Dash, J. Michael. *Edouard Glissant.* New York: Cambridge University Press, 1995. 202 pp.

3370. Madou, Jean Pol. *Edouard Glissant: de mémoire d'arbres.* Atlanta, GA: Rodopi, 1996. 114 pp.

3371. Radford, Daniel. *Edouard Glissant.* Paris: Seghers, 1982. 190 pp.

See also #45.

3372. *Gratiant, Gilbert,* 1895– (poet). An moué, 1950; Cinq poèmes martiniquais en créole, 1935; Credo des sang-mêlé, 1948–1961;

Fab' compè Zicaque, 1958–1976; Une fille majeure, 1961; Jeux et jouets de notre enfance, 1990; Poèmes en vers faux, 1931; Sel et sargasses, 1960–1964.

3373. *Joyau-Dormoy, Alice,* 1921– (novelist, poet). Chant des îles, 1953; Echo des océans, 1971; France à bientôt, 1943; Guiablesse Martinique, 1958; Mayouta au pays des flamboyants, 1977; La moisson du passé, 1971; La saison éternelle, 1957.

3374. *Kichenassamy, François,* 1943– (short story writer). Les aventures de Chabin, 1983; Les extravagances de Titine, 1995; La fugue, 1986; Les nouvelles aventures de Chabin, 1987.

3375. *Maran, René,* 1887–1960 (novelist, poet, short story writer). Asepsie noire, 1931; Bacouya, 1953; Batouala, 1922–1987 (Translation of Batouala [1921–1989]; Adèle Szold Seltzer, tr. [1922], Barbara Beck, Alexandre Mboukou, trs. [1972–1987]); Les belles images, 1935; Bêtes de la brousse, 1941–1965; Bokorro, 1937; Boum et dog, 1932; Le coeur serré, 1931; Deux amis, 1931; Djogoni, 1966; Djouma, 1927; Un homme pareil aux autres, 1947–1962; L'homme qui attend, 1936; Journal sans date/ Roman d'un noir, 1927; Le livre de la brousse, 1934–1956; Le livre du souvenir, 1958; La maison du bonheur, 1909; Mbala, l'éléphant, 1943–1947; Peines de coeur, 1944 (Peines de coeur, L'homme qui attend, Deux amis); Le petit roi de chimérie, 1924; René Maran: écrivain négro-africain—[textes choisis], 1977 (Femi Ojo-Ade, ed.); La vie intérieure, 1912; Le visage calme, 1922; Youmba, 1934.

3376. Cameron, Keith. *René Maran.* Boston, MA: Twayne, 1985. 176 pp.

3377. Hausser, Michel. *Les deux "Batouala" de René Maran.* Bordeaux: SOBODI, 1975. 105 pp.

3378. *Hommage à René Maran.* Paris: Présence africaine, 1965. 311 pp.

3379. Ojo-Ade, Femi. *René Maran: The Black Frenchman—A Bio-Critical Study.* Washington, DC: Three Continents Press, 1984. 277 pp.

3380. *Marbot, François Achille,* 1817–1866 (short story writer). Les bambous, 1846–1976.

3381. *Marie-Sainte, Kiki,* 1941– (novelist). L'Antillaise a l'amour double, 1966.

3382. *Melon-Degras, Alfred,* 1945– (poet). Avec des si, avec des mais, 1976; Battre le rappel, 1976; L'Habit d'arlequin, 1974; Le silence, 1975; Soleils de toute liberté, 1980. .

3383. *Monchoachi,* 1946 (poet). Bèl-bèl zobèl, 1985?; Dissidans, 1980; Konpè lawouzé, 1979; Nostrom, 1982; Nuit gagée, 1992.

  3384. Léotin, Georges-Henri. *Monchoachi.* Paris: L'Harmattan, 1994. 104 pp.

3385. *Monplaisir, Emma,* 1918– (novelist, short story writer). Christophe Colomb chez les indiens, 1969; Cric—crac—Martinique, 1957; La fille du Caraïbe, 1960.

3386. *Orville, Xavier* (novelist). Coeur à vie, 1993; Délice et le fromager, 1977; L'homme au sept noms et des poussières, 1981; Laissez brôler Laventurcia, 1989; Le marchand de larmes, 1985; La tapisserie du temps présent, 1979; La voie des cerfs-volants, 1994.

  3387. Centre régional de documentation pédagogique des Antilles-Guyane. *Rencontre avec Xavier Orville.* Fort-de-France: Le Centre, 1988. 174 pp.

3388. *Osenat, Pierre,* 1908– (poet). Cantate du paysan, 1993; Chant d'amour, 1973; Chants des Antilles, 1968; Les confidences de la mer, 1989; Elles et eux, 1987; Passage des vivants, 1962.

3389. *Parsemain, Roger,* 1944– (poet, short story writer). L'absence du destin, 1992; L'hidalgo des Campèches, 1987; Litanies pour un canal, 1982; Prières chaudes, 1982.

3390. *Pulvar, César,* 1927– (novelist). D'Jhébo, 1957; Liliane, 1989; La montagne pelée, 1985–1988; Terre-Sainte, 1975.

3391. *Rapon, Alain,* 1950– (short story writer). La présence de l'absent, 1982; Ti-Fène et la rivière qui chante, 1991.

3392. *Richer, Clément,* 1914–1968 (novelist, short story writer). La croisière de la Priscilla, 1947; Le dernier voyage du Pembroke, 1940–1947; Les femmes préfèrent les brutes, 1949; L'homme de la caravelle, 1952; Len Sly, 1949; Nouvelles aventures de Ti-Coyo et son requin, 1954; Les passagers du Perwyn, 1944; Son of Ti-Coyo, 1954–1956 (Translation of Le fils de Ti-Coyo [1954]; Gerard Hopkins, tr.); Ti-Coyo and His Shark, 1951–1956 (Translation of Ti-Coyo et son requin [1941–1954]; Gerard Hopkins, tr.).

3393. *Tally, Théodore* (novelist). Le colibri en deuil, 1995; Pluie d'étoiles sur Dallas, 1991.

3394. *Tardon, Raphaël,* 1911–1966 (novelist, short story writer). Bleu des îles, 1946; La Caldeira, 1949–1977; Christ au poing, 1950; Starkenfirst, 1947.

3395. *Thaly, Daniel,* 1880–1949 (poet). Chants de l'Atlantique, 1928; Héliotrope/Les amants inconnus, 1932; L'île et le voyage, 1923; Lucioles et Cantharides, 1900; Nostalgies francaises, 1913; Poèmes choisis, 1976; Sous le ciel des Antilles, 1928.

3396. *Thomarel, André,* 1893–1962 (novelist, poet, short story writer). Amours et esquisses, 1927; Coeurs meurtris, 1922; Contes et paysages de la Martinique, 1930; Les mille et un contes antillais, 1951; Naïma, fleur du Maghreb, 1950; Nuits tropicales, 1960; Parfums et saveurs des Antilles, 1935; Regrets et tendresses, 1936.

3397. *Villeronce, Guy* (poet). Contes de nuits et de jours aux Antilles, 1989; Le vent des mornes, 1986.

3398. *Zobel, Joseph,* 1915– (novelist, poet, short story writer). Black Shack Alley, 1980 (Translation of La rue Cases-Nègres [1948–1984]; Keith Q. Warner, tr.); Diab'lá, 1940–1989; Et si la mer n'était pas bleue, 1982; La fête à Paris, 1953–1970; Incantation pour un retour au pays natal, 1964; Les jours inmobiles, 1946–1970; Laghia de la mort, 1946–1978; Les mains pleines d'oiseuax, 1978; Mas Badara, 1983; Quand la neige aura fondu, 1979; Le soleil partagé, 1964–1984.

3399. César, Sylvie. *"La rue Cases-Nègres" : du roman au film—étude comparative.* Paris: L'Harmattan, 1994. 221 pp.

V
THE DUTCH-SPEAKING CARIBBEAN

GENERAL

A. ANTHOLOGIES

General

3400. Heuvel, Pim, and Freek J. van Wel. *Met eigen stem: herkenningspunten in de letterkunde van de Nederlandse Antillen en Aruba.* [With Their Own Voice: Points of Recognition in the Literature of the Netherlands Antilles and Aruba]. 2., herziende uitg. Assen: Van Gorcum, 1989. 245 pp. Rev. ed. of *Met eigen stem,* by Andries van der Wal en Freek J. van Wel [1980].

3401. Lauffer, Pierre A., ed. *Di nos: antologia di nos literatura.* [Ours: Anthology of Our Literature]. [Willemstad]: Boekhandel Salas, 1971. 241 pp.

3402. Lim, Hanny, ed. *Tussen cactus en agave: bloemlezing uit de literatuur in de Nederlandse Antillen en Suriname.* [Between Cactus and Aloe: An Anthology of Literature from the Netherlands Antilles and Suriname]. Oranjestad: De Wit, 1968. 92 pp.

Poetry

3403. Palm, Julius Philip de, and Hugo Pos, eds. *Kennismaking met de Antilliaanse en de Surinaamse poëzie.* [Getting Acquainted with Antillean and Surinamese Poetry]. Amsterdam: Stichting voor Culturele Samenwerking met Suriname en de Nederlandse Antillen [STICUSA], 1973. 32 pp.

Fiction

Fiction: Twentieth Century

3404. Instituto Lingwistiko Antiano, ed. *Mr. Chiclets en Binchi Five Guilders: en andere verhalen.* [Mr. Chiclets and Binchi Five Guilders: and Other Stories] . Willemstad: Departement van Onderwijs, 1992. 68 pp. Short stories in Dutch, English, Papiamento and Spanish by contemporary authors from the Netherlands Antilles.

B. HISTORY AND CRITICISM

General

3405. Debrot, Cola. *Literature of the Netherlands Antilles.* Willemstad: Departement van Cultuur en Opvoeding van de Nederlandse Antillen, 1964. 28 pp.

3406. Koeiman, Ruth. *Antilliaanse jeugdliteratuur.* [Antillean Juvenile Literature]. The Hague: Nederlands Bibliotheek en Lektuur Centrum, 1992. 88 pp.

3407. Korteweg, Anton et al., eds. *Schrijvers prentenboek van de Nederlandse Antillen.* [Illustrated Book of Authors from the Netherlands Antilles]. Amsterdam: Bezige Bij, 1980. 40 pp.

3408. Rutgers, Wim. *Beneden en boven de wind: literatuur van de Nederlandse Antillen en Aruba.* [Windward and Leaward: Literature of the Netherlands Antilles and Aruba]. Amsterdam: Bezige Bij, 1996. 468 pp.

3409. Smit, C. G. M., and W. F. Heuvel. *Autonoom: Nederlandstalige literatuur op de Antillen.* [Autonomous: Dutch-Language Literature in the Netherlands Antilles] 2. gewijzigde druk. Rotterdam: Flamboyant, 1976. 104 pp.

3410. Theirlynck, Harry. *Van Maria tot Rosy: over Antilliaanse literatuur.* [From Maria to Rosy: About Antillean Literature]. Leiden: Caraïbische Afdeling, Koninklijk Instituut voor Taal-, Land- en Volkenkunde, 1986. 107 pp.

3411. Verlooghen, Corly et al. *Letterkunde in Suriname en de Nederlandse Antillen.* [Literature in Suriname and the Netherlands Antilles]. The Hague: Kabinet van de Vice-Minister President, 1967. 28 pp.

General: Sixteenth to Nineteenth Centuries

3412. Rutgers, Wim. *Letterkundig leven rond de eeuwwisseling*. [Literary Life Around the Turn of the Century]. Oranjestad: Editorial Charuba, 1992. 100 pp.

General: Twentieth Century

3413. Debrot, Cola, and Henk Dennert. *Antilliaanse motieven*. [Antillean Motives]. Amsterdam: Holdert, 1959. 79 pp.

3414. Roo, Jos de. *Antilliaans literair logboek*. [Antillean Literary Diary]. Zutphen: Walburg Pers, 1980. 104 pp.

3415. Rutgers, Wim. *Dubbeltje lezen, stuivertje schrijven: over Nederlandstalige Caraïbische literatuur*. [A Dime to Read, a Nickel to Write: About Caribbean Literature in Dutch]. The Hague: Leopold, 1986. 248 pp.

ARUBA

A. ANTHOLOGIES

3416. Booi, Frank A. J. et al., eds. *Cosecha arubiano: un antologia dedicá na pueblo di Aruba.* [Aruban Harvest: An Anthology Dedicated to the People of Aruba]. Oranjestad, Aruba: Fundación Centro Cultural Aruba, 1983. 175 pp.

B. INDIVIDUAL AUTHORS

3417. *Changa, Ras,* 1957– (poet). Illegal Truth, 1991.

3418. *Ecury, Nydia,* 1926– (poet, short story writer). Bos di sanger, 1976–1984; Di kon anasa tin korona, 1981; Na mi kurason mará; 1978; Song for Mother Earth/Kantika pa mama tera, 1984; Tres rosea, 1970 (with Sonia Garmers and Mila Palm); Tres kuenta di ada, 1980.

3419. *Henriquez, Denis,* 1945– (novelist, playwright, poet). Delft Blues, 1995; Kas pabow, 1988; E soño di Alicia, 1988; Zuidstraat, 1992.

3420. *Wong, Philomena* (poet, short story writer). Crossing Borders/Crusando frontera, 1993 (Nydia Ecury, Madonna Sephens, Frank Williams, trs.); "Mi" ta biba den mi pensamento, 1987; Na kaminda pa independencia, 1986.

BONAIRE

A. INDIVIDUAL AUTHORS

3421. *Booi, Hubert,* 1919– (poet). Golgotha, 1967; Muchila, 1969.

3422. *Debrot, Cola,* 1902–1981 (novelist, playwright, poet, short story writer). De afwezigen, 1952; Bekentenis in Toledo, 1946; Bewolkt bestaan, 1948–1986; Bid voor Camille Willocq, 1946; Gedichten, 1985 (J. J. Oversteegen, ed.); Kanttekeningen, 1988; My Sister the Negress, 1958 (Translation of Mijn zuster de negerin [1935–1978]; Estelle Reed-Debrot, tr.); Navrante zomer, 1945; Pages from a Diary in Geneva, 1958 (Translation of Dagboekbladen uit Genève [1958–1989]; Estelle Reed Debrot, tr.); Toneel, 1989 (Pierre Hubert Dubois, ed.); Tussen de grijze lijnen en andere gedichten, 1976; Twee beschouwingen, 1938–1989; Van cuirassier tot clochard, 1936–1989; Verhalen, 1985 (Pierre Hubert Dubois, ed.); De vervolgden, 1982; Verzameld werk, 1985; Wie was Celine?, 1985–1989; Zon + zand + zee, 1983.

3423. Cola Debrot Symposium (1986, Willemstad, Curaçao); Alex Reinders and Frank Martinus, eds. *De eenheid van het kristal.* [The Unity of the Crystal]. Willemstad: Editorial Kooperativo Antiyano, 1988. 173 pp.

3424. Coomans-Eustatia, Maritza, and Alex Reinders. *Catalogus van werken van en over Cola Debrot, 1918–1985 [Catalogue of Works by and about Cola Debrot, 1918–1985].* Willemstad: Universiteit van de Nederlandse Antillen, 1986. 58 pp.

CURAÇAO

A. ANTHOLOGIES

Poetry

Poetry: Sixteenth to Nineteenth Centuries

3425. Rutgers, Wim. *Het nulde hoofdstuk van de Antilliaanse literatuur: koloniale poëzie in de Curaçaosche Courant.* [Chapter Zero in Antillean Literature: Colonial Poetry in the Curaçaosche Courant]. Oranjestad, Aruba: Editorial Charuba, 1988. 399 pp.

B. HISTORY AND CRITICISM

General

3426. Broek, Aart G. *The Rise of a Caribbean Island's Literature: The Case of Curaçao and Its Writing in Papiamento.* Alblasserdam: Haveka, 1990. 351 pp.

General: Twentieth Century

3427. Coomans-Eustatia, Maritza, Wim Rutgers and Henry E. Coomans, eds. *Drie Curaçaose schrijvers in veelvoud: Boeli van Leeuwen, Tip Marugg, Frank Martinus Arion.* [Three Curaçaoan Authors in Multiple: Boeli van Leeuwen, Tip Marugg, Frank Martinus Arion]. Zutphen: Walburg Pers, 1991. 544 pp.

Poetry

Poetry: Twentieth Century

3428. Palm, Julius Philip de, and Julian Coco. *Julio Perrenal: dichters van het Papiamentse lied.* [Julio Perrenal: Poets of the Papiamento Song]. Amsterdam: Bezige Bij, 1979. 141 pp. Julio Perrenal is the joint pseudonym for Jules Philip de Palm, Pierre A. Lauffer, and René de Rooy.

C. INDIVIDUAL AUTHORS

Twentieth Century

3429. *Beaujon, Alette,* 1927– (poet). Gedichten aan de baai en elders, 1957.

3430. *Blinder, Oda,* 1918–1969 (poet). Brieven van een Curaçaosche blinde en andere gedichten, 1968; Incognito, 1973; Vezamelde stilte, 1981.

3431. *Corsen, Charles,* 1927– (poet). Verzamelde gedichten (1948–1961), 1977.

3432. *Daal, Luis H.* (poet). Kosecha di maloa, 1963; Na ora orado/Te juister stonde, 1976 (Fred de Haas, tr.); Sinfonia de speransa, 1975.

3433. *Garmers, Sonia,* 1933– (novelist, poet, short story writer). Cuentanan pa mucha, 1956; Ieder diertje zijn pleziertje, 1983; Lieve Koningin, hierbij stuur ik U mijn dochter, 1976–1988; Un macutu jen di cuenta, 1960; Orkaan, 1977; Tres rosea, 1972 (with Nydia Ecury and Mila Palm); Wonen in een glimlach, 1985.

3434. *Haseth, Carel de,* 1950– (novelist, poet). Berceuse voor teleurgestelden, 1975; Bida na koló/Kleuren van leven, 1981; Drie dagen vóór Eva, 1969; Katibu di shon, 1988.

3435. *Henriquez, May,* 1915– (novelist, short story writer). Kuentí rei charada adivinansa, 1990; Loke a keda pa simia, 1991; E popchi de echèmber, 1987; Tres kuenta di wisiwas mantekabela, 1984; Vaya ta konta, 1986.

3436. *Jongh, Edward Arthur de,* 1923– (novelist, poet). Bon biaha, 1955; De boog, 1981; Capricho, 1955; E dia di mas histórico, 1970–1989; Dos plaka di palabra, 1971; Guillermo, 1953; Mi ta kòrda, 1978–1985; Morto di Enid Lacruz/Fata Morgana, 1969–1973; Na ora bon, 1987; Quietud, 1957; De steeg, 1976.

3437. *Juliana, Elis,* 1927– (poet, short story writer). Aventura di un kriki, 1960; Dama di anochi, 1959; Dede pikiña, 1964; Echa cuenta, 1970; Flor di anglo, 1961; Flor di datu, 1956; Gedichten, 1975; Kolokólo di mi wea, 1977; Maka taka, 1961; Nilo riku riku, 1978; OPI i e gran kamuflahe, 1989; Organisashon, planifikashon, independensia, 1979; Pina pa kaminda, 1991; Wazo riba rondu, 1967–1981.

3438. Coomans-Eustatia, Maritza, and Lucille Haseth, eds. *Catalogus van werken van en over Elis Juliana verschenen van 1956 tot 1989*. [Catalog of Works By and About Elis Juliana Published Between 1956 and 1989]. Willemstad: Universiteit van de Nederlandse Antillen, 1990. 72 pp.

3439. *Kleinmoedig, Nilo* (short story writer). Danki di mundu, 1989; Djina ku Riki, 1989; E ladron-maestro, 1989; Pachi Berná di Seru Chikí, 1991; Semper por tin un motibu, 1988; Shapo, 1993; Shon Sara, 1989; Shon To, 1980; Tres anekdota, 1989 (E emperador i boer Nelis, Un merikanu na Caracas, Shon Chas i Yeni).

3440. *Kroon, Willem Eligio,* 1886–1949 (novelist, poet). Algun poesia di Willem Eligio Kroon, 1966 (José M. P. Kroon, ed,); Dos novela, 1927 (E no por casa, Mester a deré prome el a drenta na casa); Giambo bieuw a bolbe na wea, 1956–1979; Su unico amor, 1940; Venganza di amor, 1930; Yiu di su mama o castigo di un abuso, 1947.

3441. *LaCroes, Eric* (poet). Carnival Tumba of Curaçao/Tumba di karnival, 1986; Sabidoría di nos bieunan, 1977; Sla habri i mi sere ku un sla será, 1976; Trinta di mèi mi ta konmemora bo/Dertig Mei ik herdenk je, 1979; Tutumba, 1986.

3442. *Lauffer, Pierre A.* (poet, short story writer). Un dia tabatin, 1975; Kantika pa bjentu, 1963; Kwenta pa caminda, 1964; Lagrima i sonrisa, 1973; Mangasina, 1974; Mangusá, 1975; Mi buki di bestia, 1981; Njapa, 1961; Ora sola baha, 1968; Patria, 1985; Un pulchi pa dia, 1970; Raspá, 1962; Sukuchi, 1974; Wiri-wiri, 1961; Zumbi, spiritu, almasola, 1975.

3443. Coomans-Eustatia, Maritza et al. *Catalogus van werken van en over Pierre Lauffer, 1942–1986*. [Catalogue of Works By and About Pierre Lauffer, 1942–1986]. Willemstad: Universiteit van de Nederlandse Antillen, 1986. 92 pp.

See also #3428.

3444. *Lebacs, Diana,* 1947– (novelist). Kompa datu ta konta, 1975; De langste maand, 1990?; Nancho, 1975–1982; Sherry, het begin van een begin, 1971; Suikerriet Rosy, 1983; Het witte licht, 1986; Yòmi-yòmi, 1982.

3445. Koeiman, Ruth. *Lezen over Diana Lebacs. [Reading About Diana Lebacs].* The Hague: Nederlands Bibliotheek en Lektuur Centrum, 1991. 21 pp.

3446. *Leeuwen, Boeli van,* 1922– (novelist). De eerste Adam, 1966–1979; Geniale anarchie, 1990; De rots der struikeling, 1959–1982; Schilden van leem, 1985; The Sign of Jonah, 1995; (Translation of Het teken van Jona [1988]; André Lefevere, tr.); Een vader, een zoon, 1978; Een vreemdeling op aarde, 1963–1977. See also #3427.

3447. *Martinus, Frank,* 1936– (novelist, playwright, poet). Afscheid van de koningin, 1975; Dubbelspel, 1973–1990; De eenheid van het kristal, 1988; De ibismensmuis/E ibis hende raton, 1993; Ilusion di un anochi, 1968; De laatste vrijheid, 1995; Nobele wilden, 1979; Ser Betris, 1968; Stemmen uit Afrika, 1957–1978. See also #3427.

3448. *Marugg, Tip,* 1923– (novelist, poet). Afschuw van licht, 1976; In de straten van Tepalka, 1967; De morgen loeit weer aan, 1988; Weekend Pilgrimage, 1960–1986 (Translation of Weekend pelgrimage [1957–1981]; Roy Edwards, tr.). See also #3427.

3449. *Miranda, Maria,* 1903–1988 (novelist). De costelijcke parel, 1977; De verwachting, 1959.

3450. *Palm, Julius Philip de,* 1922– (poet, short story writer). Antiya, 1981; Kinderen van de fraters, 1986 (Autobiographical); Lekker warm, lekker bruin, 1990 (Autobiographical). See also #3428.

3451. *Palm, Norman Ph. de* (playwright, poet). Desiree, 1984; Enzovoorts/Padilanti, 1979; Onderweg/Na kaminda, 1977.

3452. *Peters, Bernard R.* (poet). A Celebration, mi ta contentu, 1992.

3453. *Rosario, Guillermo E.,* 1917– (poet, short story writer). Amor i sakrifisio, 1974; E angel di San Kristòf, 1993; E angel pretu, 1975; Aventuranan di Geinchi, 1988–1991 (6 vols.); Dos bida, 1954–1989; E Korsow ku mi ta korda, 1970; Kwater "as", 1964 (E popchi di paña, Dos epoka, E bleki i e morokota, Bon aña); Kwater prenda, 1969; M'a bolbe, mi dushi, 1973; Máchu, 1980; Marina, e yu'i teduki, 1980; Mi nigrita papyamentu, 1972; The Most Precious Rose/E rosa di mas bunita, 1968; Orkaan, 1960; E raís ku no ke muri, 1969; Treinta di Mei di 1969, 1969.

WINDWARD ISLANDS
(SABA, ST. EUSTATIUS, ST. MAARTEN)

A. ANTHOLOGIES

Poetry

Poetry: Twentieth Century

3454. Smith, Wycliffe, and Linda Badejo-Richardson, eds. *Winds Above the Hills: A Collection of Poems from St. Maarten, Netherlands Antilles.* Philipsburg: St. Maarten Council on the Arts, 1982. 34 pp.

Fiction

3455. Johnson, Will, ed. *Tales from My Grandmother's Pipe: Saban Lore.* Leverock, Saba: Johnson, 1979. 104 pp.

B. HISTORY AND CRITICISM

Poetry

Poetry: Twentieth Century

3456. Smith, Wycliffe. *Windward Island Verse: A Survey of Poetry in the Dutch Windward Islands.* Philipsburg: St. Maarten Council on the Arts, 1982. 38 pp.

C. INDIVIDUAL AUTHORS

3457. *Bute, Ruby* (poet). Golden Voices of S'Maatin, 1989.

3458. *Johnson, David Jeffery* (poet). Rainbow Showers of Poetry, 1990.

3459. *Lopes, Ellis* (playwright). Three Plays, 1990 (Independence, Our Slow Death?, Forsaken Children, Dirty Hand).

3460. *Sekou, Lasana M.,* 1960– (poet, short story writer). Born Here, 1986; For the Mighty Gods an Offering, 1982; Images in the Yard, 1983; Love Songs Make You Cry, 1989; Maroon Lives for Grenadian Freedom Fighters, 1983; Moods for Isis, 1978; Mothernation, 1991; Nativity and Dramatic Monologues for Today, 1988; Quimbé, 1991.

3461. *Smith, Wycliffe,* 1948– (poet). Mind adrift, 1983; A Voice from W-Inward, 1976.

3462. *Zagers, Ingrid* (poet). Feelings, 1986; Images of Me, 1993.

SURINAME

A. DICTIONARIES AND ENCYCLOPEDIAS

3463. Kempen, Michiel van. *Surinaamse schrijvers en dichters: met honderd schrijversprofielen en een lijst van pseudoniemen.* [Surinamese Authors and Poets: With a Hundred Profiles and a List of Pseudonyms]. Amsterdam: Arbeiderspers, 1989. 191 pp.

B. ANTHOLOGIES

General

3464. Shrinivasi, and Thea Doelwijt, eds. *Rebirth in Words: Poetry and Prose from Suriname.* Paramaribo: Ministry of Culture, Youth and Sports, 1981. 85 pp. Poetry in English and Surinam languages on opposite pages; prose in English.

3465. Voorhoeve, Jan, and Ursy M. Lichtveld, eds. *Creole Drum: An Anthology of Creole Literature in Surinam.* Vernie A. February, tr. New Haven, CT: Yale University Press, 1975. 308 pp.

3466. ———. *Suriname: spiegel der vaderlandse kooplieden.* [Suriname: Mirror for the Patriotic Merchants]. 2e herz. druk. The Hague: Nijhoff, 1980. 323 pp.

General: Twentieth Century

3467. Ashruf, G. et al, eds . *Geluiden op een stem: een bloemlezing proza en poëzie van Surinaamse auteurs in Nederland.* [Voices: An Anthology of Prose and Poetry by Surinamese Authors in the Netherlands]. Nieuwegein, Netherlands: Stichting Landelijke Federatie van Welzijnsorganisaties voor Surinamers in Nederland, 1984.

Poetry

3468. Shrinivasi, ed. *Wortoe d'e tan abra: bloemlezing uit de Surinaamse poezie vanaf 1957.* [Anthology of Surinamese Poetry Since 1957] 4e uitgebreide druk. Paramaribo: Bureau Volkslektuur, 1979. 136 pp.

Fiction

Fiction: General

3469. Kempen, Michiel van, and Jan Bongers, eds. *Hoor di Tori!: Surinaamse vertellingen.* [Listen to the Story: Surinamese Tales]. Amsterdam: In de Knipscheer, 1990. 267 pp.

Fiction: Twentieth Century

3470. Doelwijt, Thea, ed. *Kri, kra!: proza van Suriname—bloemlezing.* [Kri, kra!: Prose from Suriname—Anthology]. Paramaribo: Bureau Volkslektuur, 1978. 187 pp. Reprint of the 1972 ed.

3471. Kempen, Michiel van, ed. *Verhalen van Surinaamse schrijvers.* [Short Stories by Surinamese authors]. Amsterdam: Arbeiderspers, 1989. 248 pp.

3472. ———. *Nieuwe Surinaamse verhalen.* [New Surinamese Short Stories]. Paramaribo: Volksboekwinkel, 1986. 202 pp.

C. HISTORY AND CRITICISM

3473. Borgers, Gerrit et al., eds. *Schrijvers prentenboek van Suriname.* [Illustrated Book of Surinamese Authors] . Amsterdam: Bezige Bij, 1979. 40 pp. With accompanying texts by Hugo Pos.

3474. Gangadin, Rabin. *De Surinaamse literatuur.* [Surinamese Literature]. Bergen op Zoom, Neth.: Heeffer, 1986. 66 pp.

3475. Kempen, Michiel van. *De knuppel in het doksenhok: leven in de Surinaamse letteren.* [The Bat in the Shed: Life in Surinamese Belle-Lettres]. Paramaribo: Volksboekwinkel, 1987. 54 pp.

Twentieth Century

3476. ———. *De Surinaamse literatuur, 1970–1985: een documentatie.* [Surinamese Literature, 1970–1985: A Record]. Paramaribo: Volksboekwinkel, 1987. 405 pp.

D. INDIVIDUAL AUTHORS

Twentieth Century

3477. *Breinburg, Petronella* (short story writer). Legends of Suriname, 1971.

3478. *Cairo, Edgar,* 1948– (novelist, playwright, poet). Adoebe-lobi/Alles tegen alles, 1977; Als je hoofd is geboord, 1981; Ba Kubu-ba-Buba/Het koninkrijk Ijmond, 1985; Dagrati! Dagrati!, 1984; Dante in motionaeii, 1989; Dat vuur der grote drama's, 1982; Djari/Erven, 1978; De doodboodschapsvogel, 1986; Famir man-sani/Kollektieve schuld, 1976; Hoogtezang, 1988; Ik ga dood om jullie hoofd, 1980; Jeje Disi, 1980; De Jezus Passion, 1989; Koewatra-djodjo/In de geest van mijn kultuur, 1979; Kra, 1970; Lelu! Lelu!, 1984; Mi boto doro/Droomboot havenloos, 1980–1983; A nowtoe foe mi ai/In de nood van het aangezicht, 1980; Obja sa tan a brewa/Er zal geen einde zijn aan brouwsels van magie, 1976; Powema di rutu/Gezangen van oorsprong en toekomst, 1982; Temekoe/Kopzorg, 1969–1988; Zij die liefhebben, 1989.

3479. *Choenni, Gharietje,* 1951– (novelist, poet, short story writer). Asa/Hoop, 1980; En dan . . . ineens zoeken ze een man voor je, 1982; Stroomopwaarts, 1991.

3480. *Emanuels, Orlando,* 1927– (poet). Getuige à decharge, 1991; Popki patu, 1986.

3481. *Ferrier, Leo Henri,* 1938– (novelist). Atman, 1968–1990; El Sisilobi of het basisonderzoek, 1969.

3482. *Gajadin, Chitra,* 1954– (novelist, poet, short story writer). Bari Dopahar/Het heetste uur van de dag, 1989; Kab ke yaad/Van wanneer een herinnering, 1984; Manai ka boli/Wat zullen de mensen wel zeggen, 1985; Padi voor Batavieren, 1979; Van erf tot skai, 1979; De zon vloeit weg uit mijn ogen, 1983.

3483. *Helman, Albert,* 1906–1996 (novelist, playwright, poet). Aansluiting gemist, 1936–1981; Adyos, 1994; Afdaling in de vulkaan, 1949–1986; Caraibisch passiespel, 1960; Celestina, 1954; De diepzee-duiker, 1945; De dierenriem, 1942; De dolle dictator, 1935; De eeuwige koppelaarster, 1949; Het einde van de kaart, 1980–1988; Het euvels Gods, 1928–1966; De G.G. van Tellus, 1994; De glorende dag, 1923; Hart zonder land, 1965; Hoofden van de Oayapok, 1984; De kostbare dood, 1936; Kroniek van El Dorado, 1995; De medeminnaars, 1953–1982; Mensen heen- en terugweg, 1937; Mijn aap lacht, 1953; Mijn aap schreit, 1928–1983; Miljoenenleed, 1940; Omnibus, 1947; Ontsporing, 1945; Orkaan bij nacht, 1934–1976; Overwintering, 1931; De put der zuchten, 1941; De Rancho der X mysteries, 1942–1985; Ratten, 1936; Rei van smeeckelingen, 1944; Sebastiaan, 1944; Semi-finale, 1977–1982; Serenitas, 1930–1980; Spokendans, 1934–1954; De stille plantage/De laaiende stilte, 1931–1958; Uit en thuis, 1984; Het vergeten gezicht, 1937–1939; Verhalend proza, 1981; Verzamelde gedichten, 1979; Voorjaarsmode, 1928; Waarom niet, 1933; Zomaar wat kinderen, 1995; Zuid-Zuid-West, 1926–1964; Zusters van liefde, 1988.

3484. Helman, Albert, and Tony van Verre. *Tony van Verre ontmoet Albert Helman: uit het leven van een dwarsliggende Indiaan.* [Tony van Verre Meets Albert Helman: From the Life of an Obstructionist Indian]. Bussum: Gooise Uitgeverij, 1980. 125 pp.

3485. Nord, Max. *Albert Helman: een inleiding tot zijn werk—met enkele teksten, handschriften, foto's, curiosa en een bibliographie.* [Albert Helman: An Introduction to His Works— with Some Texts, Manuscripts, Pictures, Curiosities and a Bibliography]. The Hague: Daamen, 1949. 168 pp.

3486. *Krishnadath, Ismene* (poet, short story writer). Bruine bonen met zoutvlees, 1992; De flaporen van Amar, 1989; Gevoelens, 1991; Lijnen van liefde, 1990; Mier-na de mier-in, 1990; Nieuwe streken van Koniman Anansi, 1989; De vangst van pake djasidin, 1992; Het zoo-syndroom, 1992.

3487. *Marlee, Paul,* 1938– (novelist, poet, short story writer). Guineapig, 1990 (Translation of Proefkonijn [1985]; PH-7, 1969.

3488. *McLeod, Cynthia,* 1936– (novelist). Hoe duur was de suiker?, 1987–1988; Lafu, het hondje van Sita, 1992.

3489. *Mungroo, Albert Walther,* 1931– (poet). Nayka, 1988; Sabana Bromki, 1991; Een zucht uit het hart, 1982.

3490. *Pos, Hugo,* 1913– (playwright, poet). Het doosje van Toeti, 1985; In triplo (Autobiographical), 1995; Het mausoleum van de innerlijke vrede, 1989; Oost en West in Nederland, 1986 (Autobiographical); Reizen en stilstaan, 1988; Van het een, 1992; Voordat ik afreis, 1993.

3491. *Ramdas, Anil* (novelist, short story writer). Het besluit van Mai, 1994; De papegaai, de stier en de klimmende bougainvillea, 1992.

3492. *Rappa,* 1954 (novelist, poet, short story writer). Friktie tories/Gevlochten verhalen, 1980; Silvie en Hexa, en andere verhalen, 1983; De vlek uit het verleden, 1982.

3493. *Roemer, Astrid,* 1947– (novelist, playwright, poet). De achtentwinstigste dag, 1988; De auditie, 1984; Alles wat gelukkig maakt, 1989; Dichter bij mij schreeuw ik, 1991; En wat dan nog?, 1985; Gewaagd leven, 1996; Levenslang gedicht/Een naam voor de liefde, 1987–1990; Lijf eigenen, 1984; Neem mij terug Suriname/Nergens ergens, 1975–1987; Niets wat pijn doet, 1993; Noordzee Blues, 1985; Oost west Holland best, 1989; De orde van de dag, 1988; Over de gekte van een vrouw, 1979–1985; Sasa, 1970; Het spoor van de jakhals, 1988; Een vrouw van een man, 1985; Waarom de rivier zo nat is, 1984; Waarom zou je huilen mijn lieve, lieve, 1977–1987; De wereld heeft gezicht verloren, 1975–1991; De zak van Santa Claus, 1983.

3494. *Shrinivasi,* 1926 (poet). Anjali, 1964–1971; Om de zon, 1972; Oog in oog, 1974; Sangam/Ontmoeting, 1991; Vrijgevig als altijd, 1977.

3495. *Slagveer, Jozef,* 1940– (poet, short story writer). Kankantri, 1968; Moord in Saramacca, 1980; De verpletterde droom, 1968; Een vrouw zoals ik, 1981.

3496. *Slory, Michaël,* 1935– (poet). Een andere weg, 1991; Brieven aan de guerrilla, 1968; Efu na Kodyo, 1985; Fresko, 1984; Sarka, 1961–1994.

3497. *Verlooghen, Corly,* 1932– (novelist, poet). Dans op de vuurgrens, 1961; De glinsterende revolutie, 1970; De held van Guyana, 1965; Jachtgebied, 1961; Juich maar niet te vroeg, 1979; Kans op onweer, 1960; De leba is gevangen, 1977; Oe, 1962.

3498. *Vianen, Bea,* 1935– (novelist, poet). Cautal, 1965; Geen onderdelen, 1979; Ik eet, ik eet, tot ik niet meer kan, 1972–1984; Liggend stilstaan bij blijvende momenten, 1974; Op het laatst krijgen wij met z'n allen donderop, 1989; Over de grens, 1986; Het paradijs van Oranje, 1973–1985; Sarnami hai, 1969–1988; Strafhok, 1971–1974.

3499. *Werners, Joanna,* 1953– (novelist, poet). Droomhuid, 1987; Zuigend moeras, 1990.

3500. *Wols, Frits* (poet). De bom van Saramacca, 1992; Surine cyclus, 1981; Verbroken cirkel, 1992; Zo anders—, 1991.

AUTHOR INDEX

References are to entry numbers, not page number.

Augier, Angel I. 163, 340, 363, 495,
519, 700, 960, 961, 962, 963, 1083
Augier, Carole. 2438, 2439
Augustin, Fermin J. 2884
Auxillou, Ray. 2384
Avellaneda y Arteaga, Gertrúdis
Gómez de. *See* Gómez de Avel-
laneda y Arteaga, Gertrudis.
Avila, Pedro Juan. 1657
Avila, Pedro Santaliz. *See* Santaliz
Avila, Pedro.
Avilés, Sotero Rivera-. *See* Rivera-
Avilés, Sotero.
Avilés Blonda, Máximo. 1468
Aybar, Néstor Contín. *See* Contín
Aybar, Néstor.
Aybar, Pedro René Contín. *See* Con-
tín Aybar, Pedro René.
Ayers, Peter K. 2724
Auguste-Macouba. *See* Armet, Au-
guste.
Azaret, Josefa de la Concepción
Hernández. *See* Hernández Azaret,
Josefa de la Concepción.
Azcuy Alón, Fanny. 590

Babatunji, Ayotunde Amtac. 2569
Babin, Céline. 3133
Babín, María Teresa. 1659, 1740,
1895, 1919
Bacardí Corporation (Puerto Rico).
1699
Bacardí Moreau, Emilio. 701
Badejo-Richardson, Linda. 3454
Baer, William. 2709
Báez, Yvette Jiménez de. *See*
Jiménez de Báez, Yvette.
Báez Díaz, Tomás. 1329
Báez Fumero, José Juan. 1696
Baeza Flores, Alberto. 117, 118, 137,
164, 304, 1339, 1419, 1420
Baeza Pérez, Francisco. 257
Baghio'o, Jean-Louis. 2957
Bailey, Marianne Wichmann. 3323
Bajeux, Jean-Claude. 40
Bakari, Ishaq Imruh. 2670
Baksh, Stella Algoo-. *See* Algoo-
Baksh, Stella.

Balaguer, Joaquín. 1387, 1388,
1389, 1399, 1463, 1469
Balboa, Silvestre de. 436
Baldran, Jacqueline. 779
Ballagas, Emilio. 702
Ballester, Ana Cairo. *See* Cairo
Ballester, Ana.
Ballester, Manuel Méndez. *See* Mén-
dez Ballester, Manuel.
Ballesteros, Mercedes. 479
Ballesteros Gaibrois, Manuel. 47
Balmaseda, Francisco Javier. 438
Balseiro, José Agustín. 1896
Bangou, Henri. 19
Banham, Martin. 2170
Baptista Gumucio, Mariano. 1112
Baptiste, Judith V. 2425
Baquero, Gastón. 481, 706, 707,
1069
Baragaño, José Alvarez. *See* Alvarez
Baragaño, José.
Baralt, Blanche Zacharie de. 520
Barba, Jaime. 708
Barca, Domingo Malpica de la. *See*
Malpica de la Barca, Domingo.
Barceló, Alejandro Querejeta. *See*
Querejeta Barceló, Alejandro.
Baridon, Silvio F. 3080
Barinas Coiscou, Sócrates. 1471
Barnet, Miguel. 709
Barnett, Curtis L. E. 2415
Baró, A. L. *See* Iglesia, Alvaro de la.
Baroche, Christiane. 2988
Barquet, Jesús J. 710
Barquín, Juan Nicolás Padrón. *See*
Padrón Barquín, Juan Nicolás.
Barradas, Efraín. 1670, 1697, 1725
Barreda, Pedro. 396
Barredo, Gloria. 317
Barreiro, Regino Eladio Boti y. *See*
Boti y Barreiro, Regino Eladio.
Barreras, Antonio. 994
Barreto, Lydia Zoraida. 1671
Barrett, Lindsay. 2570
Barroso, Carlos Augusto Alfonso.
See Alfonso Barroso, Carlos Au-
gusto.
Barroso, Juan. 780

Barry, Angela. 2406
Bart, André Schwarz-. *See* Schwarz-
  Bart, André.
Bart, Simone Schwarz-. *See*
  Schwarz-Bart, Simone.
Batista Reyes, Alberto. 235
Battier, Alcibiade Fleury. 3143
Baugh, Edward. 2232, 2233, 2259,
  2269, 2287, 2571, 2701
Bauzá, Guillermo. 1897
Bauzá, Obdulio. 1898
Baysse, Jean Valmy-. *See* Valmy-
  Baysse, Jean.
Bazil, Darío. 1353
Bazil, Osvaldo. 55, 1472
Bazile, Corneille. 2958
Beadon, Colin Leslie. 2348
Bean, Judyann. 2409
Beauchamp, José Juan. 1797
Beaugé-Rosier, Jacqueline. 3170
Beaujon, Alette. 3429
Bec, Marie. *See* Colimon Hall,
  Marie-Thérèse.
Becali, Ramón. 521
Bedacht, Rudy. *See* Verlooghen,
  Corly.
Beiro Alvarez, Luis. 1340
Béjar, Eduardo C. 681
Bejel, Emilio. 341, 1035, 1040
Bélance, René. 3171
Belaval, Emilio S. 1899
Belgrave, Valerie. 2740
Belize, Ministry of Education. 2380
Belize, Ministry of Education,
  Sports, and Culture. 2381
Bellegarde, Dantès. 3066
Bello, Antonio M. Martínez. *See*
  Martínez Bello, Antonio M.
Bello Valdés, Mayerín. 1036
Bémont, Frédy. 3312
Benet y Castellón, Eduardo. 711
Benítez, Francisco García. *See* Gar-
  cía Benítez, Francisco.
Benítez, José Gautier. *See* Gautier
  Benítez, José.
Benítez, María Bibiana. 1822
Benítez, Rafael Valera. *See* Valera
  Benítez, Rafael.

Benítez Rojo, Antonio. 34, 712
Bennett, Louise. 2572
Benoit, Louis Marie Pierre. *See*
  Fardin, Dieudonné.
Bensen, Robert. 2177
Bentzon, Thérèse. 3302
Beras, César Sánchez. *See* Sánchez
  Beras, César.
Beras Goico, Freddy. 1473
Bercedóniz, Isabel María Ruscalleda.
  See Ruscalleda Bercedóniz, Isabel
  María.
Bercedóniz, Jorge María Ruscalleda.
  See Ruscalleda Bercedóniz, Jorge
  María.
Berdecía, Fernando Sierra. *See* Sierra
  Berdecía, Fernando.
Berenguela. *See* Méndez Capote,
  Renée.
Bergeaud, Eméric. 3144
Bergh, Klaus Müller-. *See* Müller-
  Bergh, Klaus.
Bermuda Writers' Collective. 2407
Bermúdez, Federico Ramón. 1474
Bermúdez, Neyssa S. Palmer. *See*
  Palmer Bermúdez, Neyssa S.
Bermúdez, René del Risco. *See*
  Risco Bermúdez, René del.
Bernal, Emilia. 522, 713
Bernal, Mairym Cruz-. *See* Cruz-
  Bernal, Mairym.
Bernal, Sergio Valdés. *See* Valdés
  Bernal, Sergio.
Bernal Lumpuy, Luis. 715
Bernard, Jorge L. 408
Bernard, Regnor Charles. 3172
Bernard, Veronica E. 2292
Berne, Mauricette. 3026
Bernier, Félix Matos. *See* Matos
  Bernier, Félix.
Berrian, Brenda F. 1
Berrios, Edwin Figueroa. *See*
  Figueroa Berrios, Edwin.
Berrou, Raphaël. 3088
Berry, James. 2191, 2192, 2573
Bertot, Lillian. 342
Betances, Ramón Emeterio. 1825
Betancourt, José Victoriano. 439

De los Ríos, Tomás Alvarez, *See* Alvarez de los Ríos, Tomás.

De los Santos, Danilo. *See* Santos, Danilo de los.

De Marcos, Miguel. *See* Marcos, Miguel de.

De Montalver, Filián. *See* Póveda, José Manuel.

De Nolasco, Flérida. *See* Nolasco, Flérida de.

De Nolla, Olga Ramírez de Arellano de. *See* Ramírez de Arellano de Nolla, Olga.

De Nora, María Luz. *See* Torriente, Loló de la.

De Onís, Federico. *See* Onís, Federico de.

De Palm, Julius Philip. *See* Palm, Julius Philip de.

De Palm, Norman Ph. *See* Palm, Norman Ph. de.

De Rivera, Flor Piñeiro. *See* Piñeiro de Rivera, Flor.

De Rojas, Agustín. *See* Rojas, Agustín de.

De Roo, Jos. *See* Roo, Jos de.

De San Martín, Enrique Zorilla. *See* Zorilla de San Martín, Enrique.

De Solms, Marie Thérèse. *See* Bentzon, Thérèse.

De Victoria y Fernández, Magda López. *See* López de Victoria y Fernández, Magda.

Debrot, Cola. 3405, 3413, 3422

DeFilippis, Daisy Cocco-. *See* Cocco-DeFilippis, Daisy.

Dege, Lin. *See* Grimard, Luc.

Degras, Alfred Melon-. *See* Melon-Degras, Alfred.

Del Cabral, Manuel. *See* Cabral, Manuel del.

Del Casal, Julián. *See* Casal, Julián del.

Del Castillo, Amalia. *See* Castillo, Amalia del.

Del Monte, Domingo. 467, 469, 470

Del Monte, Filomena. *See* Zeno Gandía, Manuel.

Del Monte, Francisco Muñoz. *See* Muñoz del Monte, Francisco.

Del Páramo, Tristán. *See* Mendive y Daumy, Rafael María.

Del Pino, Amado. *See* Pino, Amado del.

Del Río, Amelia Agostini de. *See* Agostini de del Río, Amelia.

Del Risco Bermúdez, René. *See* Risco Bermúdez, René del.

Del Toro, Antonio García. *See* García del Toro, Antonio.

Del Toro Soler, Ricardo. *See* Toro Soler, Ricardo del.

Del Valle, Adrián. *See* Valle, Adrián del.

Del Valle, Gerardo. *See* Valle, Gerardo del.

Del Valle, José Zacarías González. *See* González del Valle, José Zacarías.

Del Valle, Luis. *See* Varona, Enrique José.

Del Valle Atiles, Francisco. *See* Valle Atiles, Francisco del.

Del Valle y Carvajal, Emilio Martín González. *See* González del Valle y Carvajal, Emilio Martín, marqués de la Vega de Anzó.

Del Vizo, Hortensia Ruiz. *See* Ruiz del Vizo, Hortensia.

Delas, Daniel. 3334

Delgado, Ana María. 1946

Delgado, Edna Licelott. *See* Licelott Delgado, Edna.

Delgado, Juan Manuel. 1932, 1947

Delgado, Luis Cabrera. *See* Cabrera Delgado, Luis.

Delgado, Martín Morúa. *See* Morúa Delgado, Martín.

Delgado, René Torres. *See* Torres Delgado, René.

Delgado Novoa, Mayra. 869

Delgado Pantaleón, Mélida. 1499

Delgado-Jenkins, Humberto. 870

Delgado-Sánchez, Joaquín. 871

Deligne, Gastón Fernando. 1443

Deligne, Rafael Alfredo. 1447

Sarmiento, Camilo. *See* Zeno
Gandía, Manuel.
Sarpong, Albert Owusu-. *See*
Owusu-Sarpong, Albert.
Sarramía, Tomás. 1796
Sarusky, Jaime. 1243
Saunders, Ashley B. 2337
Saunders, Rogelio. 1244
Savane, Virgile. *See* Salavina.
Savariego, Berta. 1245
Saviñón, Carlos Lebrón. *See* Lebrón
Saviñón, Carlos.
Saviñón, Mariano Lebrón. *See* Lebrón Saviñón, Mariano.
Savory, Elaine. 24, 2374
Sawyer, Tyrone G. 2310
Schäfer-Sackreuther, Dagmar. 823
Scharfman, Ronnie Leah. 3352
Scheker Hane, Luis. 1620
Schjang, Aster Coff. 2910
Schleifer, Harold B. 1645
Schont, Mme. 2953
Schrader, Richard A. 2878, 2879, 2911
Schulman, Iván A. 570, 571
Schwarz-Bart, André. 3036
Schwarz-Bart, Simone. 3037
Scott, Dennis C. 2557, 2640
Scott, Lawrence. 2854
Sealy, Clifford. 2855
Searle, Chris. 2462
Searwar, Lloyd. 2471
Seda, Olga Torres-. *See* Torres-Seda, Olga.
Seda de Laguna, Asela Rodríguez-. *See* Rodríguez-Seda de Laguna, Asela.
Sedeño, Livia. 2122
Seetahal, Bhadase. 2856
Segarra, Bonocio Tío. *See* Tío Segarra, Bonocio.
Sekou, Lasana M. 3460
Sellén, Antonio. 605
Sellén, Francisco. 150, 606
Selve, Edgar La. *See* La Selve, Edgar.
Selvon, Samuel. 2857
Seminar on the Acquisition of Latin

American Library Materials
(Thirty-ninth, 1994, Brigham
Young University). 39
Sención, Viriato. 1621
Senior, Edith Krenz-. *See* Miranda, Maria.
Senior, Olive. 2641
Séonnet, Michel. 3166
Serpa, Enrique. 1246
Serpa, Manuel Matías. *See* Matías, Manuel.
Serra Deliz, Wenceslao. 2123
Serrano, Manuel Mora. *See* Mora Serrano, Manuel.
Serret, Alberto. 1247
Sertima, Ivan Van. *See* Van Sertima, Ivan.
Serulle, Haffe. 1622
Seymour, Arthur J. 15, 2188, 2276, 2476, 2480, 2481, 2523, 2530
Seymour, Elma. 2474
Seymour, Stanley. 2405
Shapiro, Norman R. 2926
Sharlowe. 2863
Shaw, Donald Leslie. 824
Shelton, Marie-Denise. 3136
Sherlock, Philip Manderson. 2642
Shewcharan, Narmala. 2533
Shinebourne, Janice. 2534
Shoman, Kiren. 2382
Shrinivasi. 3464, 3468, 3494
Siaca Rivera, Manuel. 1984
Sicilia Martínez, Alberto. 1248
Sierra, Omar Felipe Mauri. *See*
Mauri Sierra, Omar Felipe.
Sierra Berdecía, Fernando. 2124
Silén, Iván. 1685, 1758, 1759, 1771, 2125
Silén, Juan Angel. 2126
Silva, Ana Margarita. 1760, 1819, 1847
Silva, Loreina Santos. *See* Santos Silva, Loreina.
Silva, Magaly. 325
Silva de Muñoz, Rosita. 1721
Silverio, Nicasio. 1249
Simmonds, Ruby. 2881
Simmons, Diane. 2298

TITLE INDEX

References are to entry numbers, not page numbers.

ABOUT THE AUTHOR

Marian Goslinga is the Latin American and Caribbean Librarian at Florida International University in Miami, Florida. She was born in Rotterdam, Netherlands, and had lived in Curaçao (Netherlands Antilles), Venezuela, and Mexico before coming to the USA. She has a B.A. in International Relations from the University of the Americas (Mexico), a M.A. in Latin American History and a M.L.S., both from the University of California (Berkeley). Ms. Goslinga has done extensive research on the Caribbean and was the bibliographer for the *Caribbean Review* from 1979 to 1988. Since 1988 she has been the bibliographer for *Hemisphere*. She was a regular contributor to the *Hispanic American Periodicals Index (HAPI)* from 1979 to 1995. She has also written several book reviews and articles for the *New West Indian Guide* and the *Interamerican Review of Bibliography*. Her *Women in the Caribbean* was published as Dialogue no. 134 in the Occasional Papers Series of the Latin American and Caribbean Center, Florida International University. In 1996, Scarecrow Press published her *A Bibliography of the Caribbean* as no. 8 in its Area Bibliographies series. Ms. Goslinga is an active member of SALALM (Seminar on the Acquisition of Latin American Library Materials).